Civil War Eyewitnesses

Annotated Bibliographies
by Garold L. Cole

American Travelers to Mexico, 1821–1972 (1978)
Travels in America: From the Voyages of Discovery to the Present (1984)
Civil War Eyewitnesses . . . 1955–1986 (1988)
Civil War Eyewitnesses . . . 1986–1996 (2000)

Civil War Eyewitnesses

An Annotated Bibliography
of Books and Articles,
1986–1996

Garold L. Cole

Foreword by James I. Robertson, Jr.

University of South Carolina Press

© 2000 University of South Carolina

Published in Columbia, South Carolina, by the
University of South Carolina Press

Manufactured in the United States of America

04 03 02 01 00   5 4 3 2 1

Library of Congress Cataloging-in-Publication Data

Cole, Garold.
    Civil War eyewitnesses : an annotated bibliography of books and
articles, 1986–1996 / Garold L. Cole ; foreword by James I. Robertson, Jr.
        p. cm.
    Includes index.
    ISBN 1-57003-327-7 (alk. paper)
    1. United States—History—Civil War, 1861–1865—Personal
narratives—Bibliography. I. Title.
Z1242 .C79 2000 [E601]
016.9737'8—dc21   99-050702

CONTENTS

v

FOREWORD

Civil War bibliographies provide the one printed tool for bringing a semblance of order to an atmosphere of publishing chaos.

Unlike practically every other period of American history, the era of the 1860s suffers from a glut of books rather than a sparseness. The reasons for this are twofold: studies on the Civil War that began appearing when the first shots were fired have never stopped, and for the past thirty years fascination with our American war has become in many quarters an obsession. As a result, somewhere around eighty thousand titles now exist—which averages out to more than one book or article per day since civil war began almost fourteen decades ago.

But it is not merely knowing what has been printed that is important for the serious student. Equally vital to an understanding of so vast a body of literature should be an awareness of the quality of each addition. One does not find balance in Civil War bibliographical listings. The North won the war; its soldiers were more numerous; a wealth of source material was at their disposal; and more outlets existed for them to get their stories in print. Hence, Confederate letters, diaries, reminiscences, and secondary studies are disproportionly fewer—and are likely to remain that way forevermore.

Throughout the evolution of this literary morass, precious few bibliographical guides have appeared to offer stable ground for research. Some of the earlier compilations—such as George M. Abbot, *Contributions Toward a Bibliography of the Civil War in the United States* (1886); U.S. War Dept., *Bibliography of State Participation in the Civil War, 1861–1865* (1913); and John P. Nicholson, *Catalogue of the Library of Brevet Lieutenant-Colonel John Page Nicholson* (1914)—were incomplete listings without descriptive commentary. The most thorough of the compilations, Charles E. Dornbusch, *Military Bibliography of the Civil War* (4 vols., 1961–1987), provides an exhaustive number of entries. Unfortunately, and like its predecessors, the Dornbusch bibliography does not include revealing annotations.

At the end of the one hundredth anniversary of the American conflict, the leaders of the U.S. Civil War Centennial Commission produced what they hoped would be an impetus for several bibliographical undertakings. Allan Nevins, Bell I. Wiley, and this writer were the compilers for *Civil War Books: A Critical Bibliography* (2 vols., 1967–1969). While this reference work supplied brief appraisals of some five thousand book and pamphlet titles, the editors were aware that much additional work remained to be done in the bibliographical field.

However, only a handful of such compilations have emerged. Pointing the way to the best book-length studies are E. Merton Coulter, *Travels in the Confederate States* (1948); Richard B. Harwell, *In Tall Cotton: The 200 Most Important Confederate Books for the Reader, Researcher, and Collector* (1978); Michael Mullins and Rowena Reed, *The Union Bookshelf: A Selected Civil War Bibliography* (1982); and David J. Eicher's indispensable eleven-hundred-title listing, *The Civil War in Books: An Analytical Bibliography* (1997).

But what about the writings of soldiers and civilians published in journals and periodicals? Certainly a collection of letters or a memoir brought into print in a historical society quarterly or respected monthly magazine has intrinsic quality far beyond the limited scope of the publication in which it appears. Yet for more than a century, only serious researchers have gone to the trouble to ferret out that semihidden material.

Garold Cole has long recognized the gaps inherent in Civil War bibliography. A professor of librarianship and history reference librarian at Illinois State University, Cole knew that a listing of personal accounts was needed. He felt strongly that such a listing should be fully annotated in order to give the user an overview of exactly what a book or article contained.

In 1988 Cole published his *Civil War Eyewitnesses: An Annotated Bibliography of Books and Articles, 1955–1986.* As the title states, he was interested in accounts by Civil War contemporaries. Cole amassed an incredible 1,395 entries. His detailed summaries made his bibliography the best ever done in the related areas of books, collections, and periodicals.

Fortunately for the Civil War field, Cole did not sit back and ride the waves of praise that greeted his efforts. Since then, he has remained abreast of subsequent eyewitness testimonies. The result is this second installment, which covers a recent ten-year period and contains an amazing 596 entries. The sheer volume of printed works reveals not only the continuing high interest in the Civil War, but also Cole's indefatigable labors for inclusiveness.

Cole's bibliography lists all the new accounts published during the past ten years, as well as century-old works reprinted for the first time. The earlier memoirs have been significantly enhanced by recent editorial additions. In all of the entries Cole has incorporated lengthy annotations for a better understanding of each account.

Bibliographies by nature are not exciting to read. Authors and titles too frequently become repetitious, if they leave any impression at all. Such is not the case with Cole's compilation. His annotations alert and inform, quote and explain; they take a vast forest of material and cast them into individual trees, each with its own particular attraction. Cole's two bibliographies are among the few such works that are actually enjoyable to read. The comprehensive index provides access to battles and units, all names, and many of the experiences of soldiers and civilians that render each personal narrative distinctive.

Not only is *Civil War Eyewitnesses II* bibliography in its best form, but it is also a new, needed, and surely welcome guide to writings by and about an embattled generation in America's most critical hour.

James I. Robertson, Jr.
Virginia Tech

Civil War Eyewitnesses

INTRODUCTION

Civil War Eyewitnesses II: An Annotated Bibliography of Books and Articles, 1986–1996 is a continuation of *Civil War Eyewitnesses: An Annotated Bibliography of Books and Articles, 1955–1986.* Like its predecessor, *Civil War Eyewitnesses II* is a compilation of personal narratives written by soldiers, civilians, and foreign travelers that were published as books or periodical articles in recent years. Diaries, journals, letters, and memoirs constitute the majority of the 596 items; however, scholarly studies that emphasize the importance of these personal writings as a historical resource are also included.

The first volume of *Civil War Eyewitnesses* documents the stimulus that the Civil War Centennial provided this genre of Civil War publishing during the 1950s and 1960s. But that earlier volume also demonstrates that the widespread interest in the writings of those who experienced the conflict continued throughout the 1970s and 1980s.

Civil War Eyewitnesses II indicates that Americans' interest in "our war," as described by rank-and-file soldiers and civilians on the home front, did not diminish between 1986 and 1996 but rather increased during this decade. Original accounts and reprint editions streamed from major publishing companies and the many smaller publishers that specialize in the Civil War era. Desktop computer publishers transcribed family documents and printed and bound them in booklike format. Civil War journals and magazines included personal narratives as regular features. And the periodicals of professional historical associations and state and local historical societies included eyewitness narratives as they were relevant to the geographical or topical concerns of the publication.

Reasons for the continuing interest in these writings are numerous, but several explanations—popular and scholarly—merit consideration. The narratives of individuals who recorded their travails in the midst of emotional distress and national unrest possess inherent drama for readers of every generation. But during the past decade that enduring appeal has been tapped by several successful television and motion picture productions which focused on the individual and utilized first-person narration for dramatic technique. Thus, many viewers who previously might have been uninterested in the Civil War were attracted to the conflict by being able to "see" the war and listen to passages of personal experiences that were excerpted from the writings of actual participants. Also, the research of genealogists into family documents have uncovered narratives that might have remained unread. The genealogist probes into the broader field of family history often sheding light on usually unanswered questions about the identity of these writers beyond their Civil War experiences.

During the decade covered by this bibliography, historians demonstrated greater appreciation for the value that personal writings possess for interpreting the totality of America's experience with civil war. By delving into Civil War narratives and sharing the research techniques and conclusions of other disciplines, historians have a clearer understanding of the war and also the United States at the middle of the nineteenth century. While scholars still attempt to determine and explain the outcomes of battles from the soldiers' descriptions, researchers have increasingly probed the soldiers' accounts for such related themes as motivation, morale, conduct under fire, and group cohesion. Others have gleaned these narratives for ideological, economic, and cultural distinctiveness within the North and South for causes that initiated the war and both prolonged and undermined dedication to the war effort. Still other scholars have incorporated gender studies to explain the interrelatedness of home and camp and the impact of the war on the home front, especially as it altered the roles of women.

Civil War Eyewitnesses II concludes with items published through 1996. However, between the brief period of 1997 and October 1998 some 180 Civil War personal narratives were published as books! And scholarship that utilizes these accounts to explore varied themes about America and Americans of the Civil War era has also continued. Examples of recent studies are: James M. McPherson, *For Cause & Comrades: Why Men Fought in the Civil War* (1997); Earl J. Hess, *The Union Soldier in Battle: Enduring the Ordeal of Combat* (1997); James Marten, *The Children's Civil War* (1998); William C. Davis, *Lincoln's Men: How President Lincoln Became Father to an Army and a Nation* (1999); and Jeffry D. Wert, *A Brotherhood of Valor: The Common Soldiers of the Stonewall Brigade, C.S.A., and the Iron Brigade, U.S.A.* (1999). Many more accounts and scholarly studies seem likely to appear in coming years, and hopefully they will all appear in *Civil War Eyewitnesses III*.

SIGNIFICANCE

This bibliography continues the major earlier bibliographies that contain Civil War personal narratives: *Civil War Books* (Allan Nevins, James I. Robertson, Jr., and Bell I. Wiley, 1967–1969); *Military Bibliography of the Civil War* (Charles E. Dornbusch, 1961–1987); *Travels in the Confederate States* (E. Merton Coulter, 1948); and *Civil War Eyewitnesses* (Garold L. Cole, 1988). These four bibliographies, together with *Civil War Eyewitnesses II,* provide reference guides to the most important personal accounts published from the era of the Civil War up to 1996.

Three recently published bibliographies that include selective listings and essays about Civil War narratives should be noted. They are *The Civil War in Books: An Analytical Bibliography* (David J. Eicher, 1997); *The American Civil*

War: A Handbook of Literature and Research (Steven E. Woodworth, 1996); and *Guide to Civil War Books: An Annotated Selection of Modern Works* (Domenica M. Barbuto and Martha Kreisel, 1996).

ARRANGEMENT

The items in this bibliography are assembled, annotated, and indexed in an arrangement that is intended to lead students of the Civil War to desired information. They are gathered in three sections, "The North," "The South," and "Anthologies, Studies, and Foreign Travelers."

The annotations identify the individuals, summarize their activities, and offer a glimpse at the writers' feelings and attitudes about the war and themselves. Quotations are used liberally to allow readers of today to appreciate the language of the Civil War era, the writers' human qualities, and their distinctiveness and commonality. Wherever possible, the annotations are intended to help place the Civil War in the complete fabric of the participants' lives.

The annotations indicate: (1) the period during which the document was written; (2) the type of document (letter, diary, or memoir); (3) the soldiers' ranks (usually the highest attained within the time covered by the document); (4) the unit (or units) in which the individuals served; (5) detailed descriptions of the military engagements and/or places the individuals served (listed in order of their occurrence); (6) civilians' occupations, the nationalities of foreign travelers, and places both groups lived or visited; and (7) comments about the individuals' actions or responses to their experiences on the battlefield or at home.

The index includes names of all authors of the accounts; the battles they described; places from which they wrote; the units in which they served; a selection of subjects about which they wrote; titles of books; and editors of the accounts.

SCOPE

Civil War Eyewitnesses II contains personal narratives first published as books and articles between 1986 and 1996. However, publications from the year 1986 are divided between the first volume of *Civil War Eyewitnesses* and this volume. Thirty items published in 1986 that are not included in the earlier volume are included here. Accounts published in earlier years with significant new editorial amendments have been included, but reprints with brief new introductions have been excluded. An exception to this guideline is that reprints of accounts that were first published in the late nineteenth and early twentieth centuries, but have long been out of print, are included. Many other reprinted editions of popular Civil War accounts are currently available, and most can be found in *Books in Print*.

PROCEDURE

This bibliography was compiled in much the same manner that any specialized collection of books is accumulated. General print and computer records as well as brief notices in periodicals all provided clues to the existence of pertinent publications. For book-length accounts, the computerized databases of *WorldCat* and *Books in Print* provided broad coverage, but less obvious were book reviews and advertisements in Civil War publications. Many periodical articles were found in the quarterly index *America: History and Life.* Other bibliographies, such as "Southern History in Periodicals," which appears annually in the *Journal of Southern History,* and "Recent Scholarship," a quarterly listing of the *Journal of American History,* were also helpful. Finally, a methodical issue-by-issue search of some fifty professional historical journals, state and local historical society publications, and specialized Civil War publications yielded articles not found in other sources.

ACKNOWLEDGMENTS

Dr. James I. Robertson, Jr., encouraged this volume, just as he did my earlier *Civil War Eyewitnesses.* His insight into Civil War soldiers remains unsurpassed. I especially want to acknowledge the moral support provided by members of Dr. Robertson's annual "Campaigning With Lee" seminar, sponsored by Virginia Tech. For most of the 1990s their inquiries about a second volume of *Civil War Eyewitnesses* kept me aware that another such volume would be welcomed by the Civil War community.

At Illinois State University my colleague Dr. Mark Plummer promoted my earlier work to his graduate Civil War Seminar and indicated similar interest in my progress with this volume.

A grant from the American Library Association and a sabbatical leave from Illinois State University provided funding for travel and time for accumulation and organization of materials.

Without the assistance of the Interlibrary Loan Division of Illinois State University's Milner Library—the best such service in the state—this bibliography might have floundered into the future. Carol Ruyle, Cindy Lee, and Carol Hartzell processed hundreds of requests routinely and hounded other libraries to lend obscure items.

Ginny Schmult proofread my manuscript promptly and efficiently. Because I knew that she was interested in reading what I had written about these accounts, she provided me with yet another source of encouragement.

My dog and my wife deserve special recognition. Pete has been my constant companion during the over three years I worked on this bibliography. Now fifteen years old, he is no longer able to step nimbly over and between stacks of books and piles of papers with the same consideration and agility he possessed three years ago. Now I guide him to a safe spot where he lies for hours, sleeping with one eye half open watching me. I sometimes flatter myself that he is wondering what I am doing; but I know he is only contemplating his next treat or walk. As I watch him, I marvel and am jealous at his contentment.

Betsy is less inclined to be content than Pete. But then, she spends an enormous amount of time "typing and griping." Nevertheless, just as she did at the end of my previous bibliographies, she has already asked what my next project will be. She remains my most vocal critic and my devoted supporter. Everyone needs one of those—and a dog. Once again, thanks, love.

I. THE NORTH

A. Union Military
Items 1–277

1. **ABBOTT, CHARLES FREDERICK.** *Civil War Diary of Cpl. Charles Frederick Abbott, Co. B, 44th Massachusetts Infantry. Expedition to North Carolina, October 1862–June 1863.* Transcribed by John Tucker Abbott. Bedford, Mass.: Whin Bush Associates, 1994. 50 pp.
    August 29, 1862–August 10, 1863. Diary. Corporal. Forty-fourth Massachusetts Infantry. Duty in North Carolina, including the battle of Rawle's Mill and Foster's expedition to Goldsboro. Abbott left unflattering descriptions of the inhabitants of Plymouth and commented on the cold, rainy living conditions, other engagements, and the idleness of encampment. When the regiment returned to Boston in June, the jubilant Abbott wrote: "FREE. Our Time is up" (p. 28). But a synopsis of his later service record reveals that he served again as acting assistant paymaster aboard the USS *Memphis* between April 24 and December 10, 1865.

2. **ABBOTT, HENRY LIVERMORE.** *Fallen Leaves: The Civil War Letters of Major Henry Livermore Abbott.* Edited by Robert Garth Scott. Kent, Ohio: Kent State University Press, 1991. 266 pp.
    May 1861–April 24, 1864. Letters. Major. Twentieth Massachusetts Infantry. Ball's Bluff; the Peninsular campaign, especially Seven Pines and the Seven Days' Battles; second Bull Run; the Antietam campaign and battle; Fredericksburg; Chancellorsville; Gettysburg; the Bristoe campaign; and the Mine Run campaign. Abbott was a Harvard-educated son of an upper-class Lowell, Massachusetts, family. While he supported the Union, as a Democrat, he opposed abolitionists and all of the Lincoln administration's transgressions: for example, restraint of civil liberties, conscription, and the Emancipation Proclamation. Abbott joined the "Harvard Regiment" because of a sense of duty, but he also desired "a speedy engagement in order to try myself" (p. 45). Scarcely a superior officer escaped Abbott's criticism. After Fredericksburg he agreed with Robert E. Lee, who had said of the Union leaders that "the men who ordered the crossing of the river are responsible to God for murder" (p. 155). Abbott frequently praised the soldiers he commanded. After Seven Pines he wrote: "Our men showed wonderful discipline, firing & ceasing to fire just as they were ordered" (p. 127). Proof that Abbott led by example was evident at Gettysburg. When a position in the rail fence was left uncovered during Pickett's Charge, Abbott and his men rushed to plug the gap. He also praised the Confederate soldiers for exhibiting such "pluck," but he said that he and everyone else knew that they "should give them Fredericksburg" (p. 188). Abbott used disparaging terms when he referred to lower classes and the foreign-born. While he blamed foreigners for the high rate of desertion, his opposition to conscription may in part be attributed to the fact that he thought being drafted served to erode the self-pride of the immigrant soldiers. And it should be noted that in the fall of 1863, as he trained the recent volunteers, many of whom were foreign born, he was convinced that "upon the whole, our new men will fight decently . . . since discipline is socked into them from the old soldiers, as well as the officers" (p. 206). Abbott opposed the conscription of black units. The death of Robert Gould Shaw proved to Abbott's satisfaction that using black soldiers was "an experiment I think that has demonstrated niggers won't fight as they ought" (p. 199). Abbott's letters reveal that he was a loving family member. After his brother was killed

at Cedar Mountain, Abbott searched for the exact spot where he died and then wrote a touching letter to his father. Abbott was killed at The Wilderness on May 6, 1864.

3. **AKER, WASHINGTON.** "Washington Aker's Civil War Letter." Edited by George F. Schultz. *Whitley County Historical Society Bulletin* 28 (October 1990): 3–11.

July 21, 1863. Letter. Private. One-hundredth Indiana Infantry. Siege of Jackson. Aker relates incidents of the fighting in Mississippi to the *Columbia City (Indiana) News*, the town in which the regiment was raised.

4. **ALFORD FAMILY.** *The Alford Brothers: "We All Must Dye Sooner or Later."* Edited by Richard S. Skidmore. Hanover, Ind.: Nugget Publishers, 1995. 356 pp.

May 9, 1861–October 29, 1862. The primary Alford family correspondents represented here are the father, Franklin, and brothers James Warren (Warren), Wayne, and Lafayette. However, the mother, Mary, other brothers and sisters and relations, and soldiers from Alfordsville are all contributors. The Alfords owned a farm in Alfordsville (Daviess County), in southwestern Indiana. Warren joined the Fourteenth Indiana Infantry in May 1862. He saw duty in the Cheat Mountains (including battles of Cheat Mountain and Greenbrier River) and in Maryland and Virginia (including first Kernstown and Harrison's Landing). Wayne and Lafayette enlisted in the Sixth Indiana Infantry the following October. They served together in Kentucky and Tennessee, and both fought on the second day of Shiloh. Wayne also participated in the siege of Corinth. This family's love for one another is central to this correspondence. Warren set the tone in an early letter when he told Wayne and Lafayette: "You do not know how much I mis your society. Home society is a vary desireable thing With me" (p. 29). Several months later he advised his brothers to stay at home out of harm's way, "for I think farmers will be needed worse than soldiers by far" (p. 65). News about each other and friends from Alfordsville, the home front (especially activities on the farm and local opposition to the war), and patriotic and religious expressions fill the letters. Writings about military matters are generally devoted to troop movement and living conditions. However, Warren did provide a rousing account of first Kernstown: "We came up through a Showr of bullets but there was not a man faultered. We went in at a bayonett charge and drove them like a flock of sheep before us" (p. 235). And Wayne described Shiloh. Franklin's rather formal letters to Warren contain information about farm prices, crop yields, business entanglements, etc., and expressions of religion and affection. Immediately after Shiloh, Lafayette and then Wayne were taken ill and died in May and June 1862, respectively. At Antietam, near the "Bloody Lane," Warren was shot through the lung and mortally wounded. In April, Franklin had assisted Lafayette to leave a hospital in Evansville to return home, where he died. In May, Franklin went to Corinth in a futile attempt to retrieve Wayne's remains. In September, Franklin traveled to Maryland to transport his third son's remains back to Alfordsville for burial. The editor concludes with an "Epilogue" in which he summarizes the lives of the surviving immediate family. Throughout *The Alford Brothers . . .* the editor's wide-ranging research presents pertinent background information on the Alfords, the state of Indiana, and the Civil War, especially as it affected the Alford family.

5. **ANDERSON, PETER DANIEL.** *Marching Barefoot: A Collection of Civil War Letters Written by Peter Daniel Anderson to His Wife and Children in Scandia, Minnesota.* Compiled by Ralph C. E. Peterson. Minneapolis, Minn.: Bind-a-Book, 1991. 81 leaves (unpaged).

September 7, 1864–May 25, 1865. Letters. Fourth Minnesota Infantry. The Atlanta campaign, including Allatoona; the March to the Sea; the Carolinas campaign, including Bentonville; and the Grand

Review. Anderson's letters maintain an even-tempered blend of comments on his military experiences; requests for, and news about, soldiers from Scandia; and advice to his wife on how to run the farm. Family and religion sustained Anderson throughout his ordeal, and he constantly encouraged his wife to maintain her faith in God. Nevertheless, the ugly realities of war tested his personal relationship with the Almighty. After he heard how Union prisoners were allegedly mistreated near Savannah, he wrote: "May the gracious God have mercy on our nation's people . . . but punishments can also be of some good, for we chastise those we love" (December 26, 1864). Later, during the march through the Carolinas, he approved of greater retribution when still more Union prisoners were butchered. He was convinced that "We have had to pay them back with the same punishment," but at the same time he was aware that "this is so hideous" (undated). The title of the book refers to the ragged condition of the Union soldiers. Curiously, Anderson never mentioned his rank, and he requested that letters to him be addressed as "Mr." Translated from Swedish.

6.   **ANDES, JOHN WESLEY, and WILLIAM ANDERSON MCTEER.** *Loyal Mountain Troopers: The Second and Third Tennessee Volunteer Cavalry in the Civil War.* Edited by Charles S. McCammon. Maryville, Tenn.: Blount County Genealogical and Historical Society, 1992. 386 pp.
1861–1865. Memoirs. Lieutenant, Second Tennessee Cavalry (U.S.), and Major, Third Tennessee Cavalry (U.S.). The editor has combined these regimental histories written by Andes and McTeer, which were published separately in the *Knoxville Daily Chronicle* during 1878 and 1879. He has arranged the combined accounts chronologically, divided them into chapters, added endnotes, and indexed the work. The regimental rosters from the *Report of the Adjutant General of the State of Tennessee . . .* (Nashville: S.C. Mercer, 1866) and photographs are also appended. The two men relate myriad accounts of their regiments' battles, skirmishes, expeditions, and raids in Tennessee and northern Georgia, Alabama, and Mississippi between mid 1862 and the end of the war.

7.   **ANONYMOUS.** *A Yankee Raid to East Tennessee by the Lochiel Cavalry Christmas 1862: An Eyewitness Account.* Format and new material by Lincoln B. Young. Knoxville, Tenn.: Fine Arts Press, 1991. 27 pp.
December 20, 1862–January 5, 1863. Memoir. Ninth Pennsylvania Cavalry. Carter's raid from Winchester, Kentucky, to East Tennessee and southwest Kentucky. This account was taken from Frank Moore's compilation *The Civil War in Song and Story* (New York: P. F. Collier Co., 1889).

8.   **BACON, JAMES B.** "Reminiscences of War Time Service: With the 24th Wisconsin." *Milwaukee History* 14, no. 2 (1991): 66–69.
1862–1863. Memoir. Kentucky. Twenty-fourth Wisconsin Infantry. Bacon's rambling anecdotes include a story about his taking doughnuts from the cook that were meant for an officer. In another tale he tells of crossing enemy lines to get a drink of fresh water and encountering another thirsty Union soldier. Many years after the war the two men met accidentally again.

9.   **BAILEY, GEORGE W.** *The Civil War Diary and Biography of George W. Bailey.* Transcribed by Charles Post. Colleyville, Tex.: G. R. Post, 1990. 144 pp.
March 31, 1863–December 14, 1864. Diary. Private. Third Michigan Infantry. Chancellorsville; Gettysburg (including pursuit of Lee); the New York draft riots; The Wilderness; and Andersonville and Florence Prisons. Brief entries recorded camp life, the weather, marches, battles, and imprisonment after he was captured at The Wilderness. This work also includes newspaper articles by and about

George Bailey, genealogical materials about Bailey's descendants, and information regarding the Third Michigan Infantry. An article about Bailey's experiences is Albert Castel's "From Allegan to Andersonville: Private George Bailey Sees the Civil War," *Michigan History* 76 (July/August 1992): 34–40.

10.   BAKER, JOEL B. *Letters Home.* Delevan, N.Y.: N. B. Baker, 1996. 254 pp.

August 23, 1862–June 23, 1865. Letters and diary. Colonel. Eighth New York Heavy Artillery. Duty at the forts around Baltimore and the Virginia campaign, including Spotsylvania, North Anna, Cold Harbor, the siege of Petersburg, Deep Bottom, and second Hatcher's Run. Until spring 1864 Baker wrote his wife about the routines of garrison and picket duty. On December 13, 1863, he remarked that he had served one half of his enlistment and wrote that he would be pleased if the remainder of his service would pass safely. However, beginning in May 1864 circumstances changed dramatically. At Spotsylvania he wrote: "I have stood my first fire without flinching & fear I think I am good for another" (p. 175). As his company charged the Confederate lines at Cold Harbor, he recorded how "the storm of lead & iron" caused "The Company to melt away" (p. 185). Letters from the next few months relate similar details. In July, before Petersburg, he was still able to tell his wife that he had "gone into every battle perfectly cool," but he added, "I hope this field charging will soon play out" (pp. 196–97). Between March and May 1865, a period for which few letters exist, details of Baker's service are uncertain. He was forced to face a court-martial (of which he was acquitted), but during the Appomattox campaign he was in command of his regiment.

11.   BALDWIN, FRANK DWIGHT. "A Soldier's Education: Frank Dwight Baldwin's Civil War Experience in the 19th Michigan Volunteer Infantry." By Robert M. Carriker. *E. C. Barksdale Student Lectures* 11 (1989/1990): 288–317.

1861–1865. Diary and memoir. Lieutenant Colonel. Nineteenth Michigan Infantry. While serving in Tennessee, Baldwin was captured and incarcerated in Libby Prison. Later he was sent to Richmond's dreaded Castle Thunder for dumping a bucket of cockroaches ("Johnny Greybacks") on the prison guards. Following his parole he went back to Tennessee, where he was again briefly captured. He later served in the Atlanta campaign, the March to the Sea, and the Carolinas campaign. The Emancipation Proclamation caused Baldwin to realize that his reaction to the war had changed in favor of the new war policy. Earlier he said that he preferred to leave the Union as it was and "let Negro remain where he is and as he is" (p. 289). During the Atlanta campaign he mentioned the unwritten rules of fraternization between enlisted men. If an officer should appear while the men were bartering, one side or the other would fire a stray round to distract the officer. At Peachtree Creek, Baldwin reported hand-to-hand fighting with bayonets, the only time he saw the weapon used in combat. In the same battle he chased and captured two Confederates and was awarded the Congressional Medal of Honor. During the March to the Sea he was placed in charge of foraging. Baldwin maintained that he paid for provisions taken from civilians. However, when he looted the Georgia State Treasury at Milledgeville of unsigned Confederate notes, he used the stolen tender to pay for provisions. Outside Savannah he confiscated a rice mill and processed grain for the soldiers. Following the Grand Review and his discharge, Baldwin reenlisted. He retired with the rank of brigadier general in 1906.

12.   BARBER, CHARLES. *The Civil War Letters of Charles Barber, Private, 104th New York Volunteer Infantry.* Edited by Raymond G. Barber and Gary E. Swinson. Torrance, Calif.: Gary E. Swinson, 1991. 248 pp.

December 2, 1861–November 1, 1864. Letters. Private. 104th New York Infantry. Duty in Virginia and Maryland; and battles of Cedar Mountain, Thoroughfare Gap, second Bull Run, South Mountain, Antietam, Fredericksburg, Burnside's "Mud March," Chancellorsville, Gettysburg, the Bristoe campaign, Rappahannock Station, the Mine Run campaign, and Spotsylvania. Once Barber attempted to explain to his wife just how much mail meant to all of the soldiers. He said that all the men gathered for mail call; some left happy and others were disappointed. One soldier learned from a letter that his wife had died. Even though the soldier's three children were without means of support, the army still refused to grant him a furlough. As a result of that experience, Barber remained apprehensive about opening his own letters. Barber's first battles were at Cedar Mountain and at Antietam. He said that he was pleased and somewhat surprised at being so cool under fire. His spirits remained high until the early spring of 1864, but for the remainder of his service he seems to have been preoccupied with the ugliness of war. When the military offered promotion and bounty money to induce reenlistments, Barber was unswayed. He said that he was confident he had fulfilled his duty for three long, hard years. At their Cedar Mountain encampment in March 1864, Barber observed poor white women and children and blacks begging for food, which proved to him that "southern pride and haughty rebellious spirit is now terribly mortified . . . for the great moral and political sin of slavery" (p. 167). Barber also criticized the damage that prostitution was doing to the army. The hospitals were filled with men "sick with diseases contracted at the houses of ill fame" (p. 170). After Barber was wounded at Spotsylvania, he spent the summer and early fall of 1864 recuperating at hospitals in Alexandria. The editor has appended additional information about the 104th New York Infantry.

13. **BARD, DAVID D.** *Friend Alice: The Civil War Letters of Captain David D. Bard, 7th and 104th Regiments, Ohio Volunteer Infantry, 1862–1864.* Edited by James T. Brenner. Kent, Ohio: Scholar of Fortune, 1996. 112 pp.

January 1862–October 17, 1864. Letters. Sergeant, Seventh Ohio Infantry, and Captain, 104th Ohio Infantry. Jackson's Shenandoah Valley campaign, including first Kernstown; duty in Kentucky and Tennessee; the Atlanta campaign, including Dallas, the battle of Atlanta, Utoy Creek, Jonesboro, and operations against John B. Hood in north Georgia and north Alabama. Bard wrote freely about his experiences and personal feelings to a lady friend from his home in Brimfield, Ohio. He described how the campfires glowed beautifully at night. He told her that he loved picket duty and the sound of the artillery's martial music. In Kentucky he enjoyed watching the "darkies" dance and believed that "a negro has the very soul of music in him." Still, he labeled their dance "ugly contortions." He doubted that the blacks had sufficient "brains" to carry out the slave insurrection so widely anticipated by the local civilians (pp. 43–44). Bard wrote that the soldiers felt they had been forgotten, and he complained that newspaper reporters had made civilians unable to comprehend "the horrid scenes of the field which had become commonplace to the soldiers" (p. 64). Bard frequently reflected on how the war had changed him: "I do actually believe that I have forgotten how to act look or walk like a civilian" (p. 63). Later he said that he had not read a book in over three years and doubted that he would feel comfortable in normal society, "especially lady society" (p. 84). During the Atlanta campaign he summarized the meaning of the couple's lengthy period of correspondence; it represented a valuable relationship of the brother and sister that neither possessed. Then he reflected on what he had just written and self-consciously dismissed it with: "But what a stupid letter this is proving to be" (pp. 84–85). Near the end of 1864, as he described the beauty of eastern Tennessee and northern Georgia, he wrote optimistically of a future without slavery in which a "superior class" of "enlightened" people would populate the South and bring change (p. 99). Bard was killed at the battle of Franklin.

14. **BEAUDRY, LOUIS N.** *War Journal of Louis N. Beaudry, Fifth New York Cavalry: The Diary of a Union Chaplain, Commencing February 16, 1863.* Edited by Richard E. Beaudry. Jefferson, N.C.: McFarland & Company, 1996. 248 pp.

February 16, 1863–July 18, 1865. Diary. Chaplain. Fifth New York Cavalry. Duty near Washington, D.C., and the march to Gettysburg, including the battle of Hanover. Captured at Monterey Gap, Pennsylvania, on July 5, he spent July 18 through October 27, 1863, in Libby Prison. He returned to duty in the fall of 1863 and participated in the Virginia campaign, Sheridan's Shenandoah Valley campaign, including third Winchester, Cedar Creek, and winter camp at Winchester. Perhaps because this Methodist minister was compiling a history of the regiment, Beaudry's journal is filled with details. Weather conditions were often noted. Just prior to the march to Gettysburg he wrote: "Mercury in the shade 98 degrees, in the sun 122 degrees" (p. 44). At Libby Prison he preached, engaged in debates, taught a French class, carved bone rings, and helped publish a newspaper (the "Libby Chronicles"). Still, his entire entry of August 14, 1863, reads: "Life is monotonous" (p. 61). One diary entry expresses his abhorrence of the drinking, gambling, and profanity. When he observed a man reading a book with "unbecoming and indecent engraving," Beaudry purchased and burned the book. Beaudry blamed such vices on the fact that men were separated from "respectable female society, and the sacred influences of home," as well as on the individual's character before coming into the army (p. 25). Beaudry was optimistic about the progress of the war, but he criticized the army following Gettysburg. After the battle of Williamsport, while he was a prisoner, he observed the Confederate army and thought it was "demoralized and dispirited." He concluded that "Had General Meade attacked them there . . . I cannot see how the 'REBS' could have avoided entire annihilation" (p. 52). Entries written during the Virginia campaign and with Sheridan in the Valley are filled with descriptions of fighting. Much of 1865 was spent in headquarters in Winchester, where he gathered facts and subscriptions for his regimental history, *Historic Records of the Fifth New York Cavalry . . .* (Albany, N.Y.: S. R. Gray, 1865).

15. BENJAMIN, SAMUEL N. "We Cleared the Way . . . Firing Canister." Edited by Curt Johnson. *Civil War Times Illustrated* 32 (March/April 1993): 20, 22–23.

August 29–September 1, 1862. Report. Lieutenant. Second U.S. Artillery, Battery E. Second Bull Run and Chantilly.

16. BENNECKE, HERMAN. "German Immigrants at Antietam." By C. Eugene Miller. *Maryland Historical Magazine* 87 (Fall 1992): 309–15.

September 17, 1862. Poem. Captain. Twentieth New York Infantry. Antietam. Bennecke's poem relates the role of German-American regiments in the fighting around the Dunker Church. Here Miller has translated Bennecke's "In der Schlacht am Antietam."

17. BENSON, CHARLES E. *The Civil War Diaries of Charles E. Benson, Corporal, Company I, Seventh Regiment, Michigan Infantry Volunteers.* Edited by Richard H. Benson. Decorah, Iowa: Anundsen Publishing Company, 1991. 119 pp.

August 12, 1861–December 31, 1862. Diary. Corporal. Seventh Michigan Infantry. Induction in Monroe, Michigan; train trip to Washington, D.C.; duty along the Potomac and at Harpers Ferry; and the Peninsular campaign, including the siege of Yorktown and battle of White Oak Swamp. Among Benson's brief notations is information about a typical day and picket duty. On March 1, 1863, he wrote: "It has been a pleasant day. The boys had a game of Base Ball to stir up our stagnant blood. Countersign Montreal" (p. 47). During the last half of 1862 Benson suffered from an undisclosed illness. He was first hospitalized in Virginia, then shipped to a hospital in Brooklyn. Several letters from Benson are included with the diary entries.

18. **BIGELOW, EDWIN B.** "Sergeant Edwin B. Bigelow's Exciting Adventures." By Frank L. Klement. *Blue & Gray Magazine* 8 (August 1991): 36–38.
January 1, 1863–June 14, 1865. Diary. Fifth Michigan Cavalry. Brief excerpts include Bigelow's two escapes from Confederate captors.

19. **BIRCHER, WILLIAM.** *A Drummer-Boy's Diary, Comprising Four Years of Service with the Second Regiment Minnesota Veteran Volunteers, 1861 to 1865. With History of William Bircher and History of Drummer-Boys.* Edited by Newell L. Chester. Saint Cloud, Minn.: North Star Press of Saint Cloud, 1995. 129 pp.
July 1861–July 1865. Memoir. Second Minnesota Infantry. Logan's Cross Roads; Shiloh (aftermath); Perryville; the Tullahoma campaign; Chickamauga; Missionary Ridge; the Atlanta campaign; Sherman's March to the Sea; the Carolinas campaign; the Grand Review; and his return trip home. This narrative of a fifteen-year-old (at enlistment) focuses on troop movements and anecdotes of battle and camp life. While some idea of the range of activities drummer boys performed is apparent in Bircher's comments, the editor's introduction of their overall duties is more informative. Originally published: Saint Paul, Minn.: Saint Paul Book and Stationery Co., 1889.

20. **BIRMINGHAM, THEODORE.** *Yours in Love: The Birmingham Civil War Letters.* Edited by Zoe von Ende Lappin. Grawn, Mich.: Kinseeker Publications, 1989. 255 pp.
August 17, 1862–May 10, 1865. Letters. Twenty-third Michigan Infantry. This work, which is primarily a Birmingham family history, contains letters from family members and friends, most of whom lived in Duplain (Clinton County), Michigan, between 1862 and 1902. The fifty-three letters written by (and to) Theodore constitute the bulk of this work. Several letters from brothers Orlo (Tenth Michigan Cavalry) and James (Second Michigan Infantry) are also included, as are those from other correspondents. Theodore's duty was in Kentucky (including pursuit of Nathan Bedford Forrest in the summer of 1863); Tennessee (including Campbell's Station and the siege of Knoxville); the Atlanta campaign; operations against Hood in northern Alabama; duty at Nashville (but not the battle); and capture of Wilmington, North Carolina. While Theodore described some battles, the focus of his letters is on his immediate circumstances and exchange of news about acquaintances. On several occasions he mentions his duties as a bugler. The value of this body of letters is that it provides evidence of how family and community and soldiers retained their cohesiveness while being separated by the war. The editor has appended family group sheets, lists of lineage, biographical sketches, regimental histories, and photographs.

21. **BLANCHARD, IRA.** *I Marched with Sherman: Civil War Memoirs of the 20th Illinois Volunteer Infantry.* San Francisco, Calif.: J. D. Huff and Company, 1992. 170 pp.
April 1861–August 1, 1865. Memoir. Sergeant. Twentieth Illinois Infantry. Enlistment at Joliet; duty in Missouri; Forts Henry and Donelson; Shiloh; Britton's Lane; the Vicksburg campaign, including passage of the Vicksburg blockade (on April 22, 1863), Port Gibson, Raymond, Jackson, Champion Hill, the assaults of May 19 and 22, and the siege of Vicksburg; the Meridian campaign; and the Atlanta campaign. Blanchard's preface reads: "This little book is not designed to be a history of the great rebellion. It is intended to simply relate in the shortest manner possible the events I actually saw" (p. 11). He described troop movements, battles, local inhabitants (especially slaves in Mississippi); held conversations with "Rebs"; watched the levee at Lake Providence cut and the bayous flooded; and attended a

ball put on by black high society after the fall of Vicksburg. He also observed how the strongest man in the regiment "Had a peculiar knack of getting sick just as the bullets began to fly" (p. 112). Blanchard received his reenlistment bonus and his leave home but returned to battle during the Atlanta campaign. He was wounded in the July 22 battle for the city and spent the remainder of the war in hospitals.

22. **BOBST, ISAAC.** *A Soldier's Journey: An Account of Private Isaac Bobst, 128th Pennsylvania Volunteer Infantry and 1st Pennsylvania Cavalry, from Antietam to Andersonville.* Edited by Daniel V. Biles III. Gettysburg, Pa.: Thomas Publications, 1990. 168 pp.

August 28, 1862–March 14, 1865. Memoir. 128th Pennsylvania Infantry and First Pennsylvania Cavalry. Antietam; duty near Harpers Ferry; and Chancellorsville, where he was captured and exchanged. Bobst was discharged on May 20, 1863, but reenlisted in the First Pennsylvania Cavalry on February 6, 1864. He was captured at White House Landing on June 21, 1864, imprisoned at Belle Isle and Andersonville, and exchanged on March 3, 1865. This work is primarily a narrative of the regiment's military actions, written by Biles, while Bobst was a member.

23. **BOLINGER, PHILIP, and HENRY HUDSON.** *Civil War Sketchbook and Diary.* Edited by Nancy S. Shedd. Huntingdon, Pa.: Huntingdon County Historical Society, 1988. 94 pp.

August 30, 1864–August 12, 1865. Diary. 202nd Pennsylvania Infantry. Duty guarding railroads in northern Virginia; the defense of Washington, D.C., and Alexandria; and after the war, duty in northeastern Pennsylvania. This book consists of journal notations by Philip Bolinger and drawings by Henry Hudson. Both men enlisted in Company K, which was recruited in Huntingdon County, Pennsylvania. The editor explains that the nature of this compilation is "more complementary than parallel" (p. 10). The younger Bolinger's entries are a sparse record of daily routines, news about Abraham Lincoln's assassination and John Wilkes Booth's capture, and the concluding events of the war. In the editor's opinion Hudson's sketches indicate the broader perceptions of an older man. In addition to illustrating such aspects of camp life as picket duty, writing home, and prayer meetings, he also sketched political and social themes. The editor's footnote explains that the regiment was deployed to the coal district of northeastern Pennsylvania after the war because of fear of civil unrest.

24. **BOOTH, BENJAMIN F.** *Dark Days of the Rebellion: Life in Southern Military Prisons.* Edited by Steve Meyer. Garrison, Iowa: Meyer Publishing, 1996. 261 pp.

1861–1865. Memoir. Twenty-second Iowa Infantry. Organization of regiment; the Vicksburg campaign; and Sheridan's Shenandoah Valley campaign, including Booth's capture at Cedar Creek and imprisonment at Libby and Salisbury Prisons. In the introduction to his memoir, written thirty-odd years after the events, Booth states that he was not writing to "ask for vengeance or retribution for the thousands of heroic men who died from murder, starvation, cruelty and disease in these prison pens of the Confederacy." Rather, he desired that their "noble heroism and loyalty to their country and their flag shall not be forgotten or treated as a mere trifle" (p. xiii). The editor comments that Booth's privately printed work was not popular because of "its stark revelation of the exacting toll taken upon Union soldiers at Salisbury, and Booth's prejudice and bitterness towards the southern people" (p. vii). While Booth blamed the entire South for the poor handling of the prisoners, he was unwilling to hold the Lincoln administration culpable for the decline of the exchange and parole policy. In addition to relating the same depressing aspects of prison life that most other captives wrote about, Booth often mentioned the blacks held at Salisbury. He reported that they suffered more than the white prisoners, their garments were more frequently stolen, and they were given smaller rations than other prisoners. According to Booth, the black soldiers' will to live was nearly nonexistent, and by March 1865 only about sixty of the original three hundred at Salisbury had survived. Before Booth left Salisbury Prison he was allowed to copy the camp's "death list." The editor indicates that it is among the few extant records of the camp. In his final chapters Booth relates his arrival home and subsequent illness and recovery. Originally published in Indianola, Iowa: Booth Publishing Company, 1897.

25.   BOWEN, ROLAND E. *From Ball's Bluff to Gettysburg . . . and Beyond: The Civil War Letters of Private E. Bowen, 15th Massachusetts Infantry, 1861–1865.* Edited by Gregory A. Coco. Gettysburg, Pa.: Thomas Publications, 1994. 268 pp.

August 20, 1861–April 23, 1864. Letters. Private. Fifteenth Massachusetts Infantry. Ball's Bluff; duty near Harpers Ferry; the siege of Yorktown; Seven Pines; Seven Days' Battles; Antietam; Fredericksburg; and Gettysburg, where he was captured, imprisoned at Belle Isle, exchanged, and held at Camp Parole until April 1864. Bowen wrote in a sincere, dramatic style, frequently utilizing self-deprecating and dark humor to convey his experiences. He depicted how the men acted during the chaos and confusion of the Union rout at Ball's Bluff. Bowen said that he escaped by throwing away all of his equipment and swimming to safety clad only in his shirttails. When shock of the previous twelve hours hit him, he "wept like a child" (p. 50). Bowen would again confess to crying when he learned of his brother's death. After Ball's Bluff, as he described winter camp and constructing defenses, he anticipated the battle. He wrote to his mother: "Maybe we will have a little *Fun* in the shape of *Smashing* each others *Brains* out." Perhaps he was attempting to allay her concerns for his well-being, for in the same letter he assured her that hardships were "exceptions," not "common things," and that "guard duty was the worst thing" (p. 58). Bowen freely confessed to stealing civilian property in Harpers Ferry, ransacking Fredericksburg, and being concerned for his own needs over those of other prisoners at Belle Isle Prison. He told his friend Guild that nine out of every ten words that came out of a soldier's mouth were either profane or vulgar. As if to offer proof, he lambasted the "God damned set of Infernal Politicians" for not giving George McClellan enough men to win the Peninsular campaign (p. 115). The regiment suffered heavy losses at Antietam; thus, he was only partially joking when he advised Guild: "Enlist if you want to. Come in the 15th so that I can Bury you. I don't know of any body that can do it quicker or with less cerimony" (p. 122). The remainder of Bowen's career after he returned to duty during the Virginia campaign, including a second capture at Jerusalem Plank Road, is recounted by another soldier.

26.   BOWEN, ROLAND E. "'Nothing But Cowards Run': Gettysburg, July 2, 1863. Question of the Life and Death . . . Made on the Spur of the Moment." *Civil War: The Magazine of the Civil War Society* 50 (April 1995): 42–49.

July 1–3, 1863. Memoir. Fifteenth Massachusetts Infantry. Battle of Gettysburg.

27.   BRADLEY, KERSEY. "A Soldier's Report: The Battle on Missionary Ridge and Lookout Mountain." Annotated by Marlin H. Bradley. *Journal of the Lancaster County Historical Society* 92 (Hilarymas 1989/1990): 15–17.

December 13, 1863. Letter. Seventy-ninth Pennsylvania Infantry. Battles of Lookout Mountain and Missionary Ridge. Writing shortly after the battles, Bradley related the poor condition of the Union army, especially its horses and mules. Also, he recognized the army's reliance on steamboats for transporting supplies.

28. BRENDEL, JOHNNY. *Swamp Hogs: The Civil War Journals of Johnny Brendel.* By William Thomas Venner. Goshen, Ohio: Larrea Books, 1995. 325 pp.

July 29, 1861–July 28, 1864. Journal. Nineteenth Indiana Infantry. Enlistment at Camp Morton and travel to northern Virginia; Lewisville; duty in northern Virginia; John Pope's Virginia campaign; Cedar Mountain (aftermath); Gainesville; second Bull Run; South Mountain; Antietam; Fredericksburg; Ambrose Burnside's "Mud March"; Chancellorsville; Gettysburg, including pursuit of Lee; the Bristoe campaign; the Mine Run campaign; The Wilderness; Spotsylvania; Cold Harbor; assaults on Petersburg; and the siege of Petersburg. Thomas Venner states in his introduction that these journals were the Civil War experiences that his great-grandfather recorded. However, in his concluding section—"Denouement"—he confesses: "This story was constructed, using the diaries, journals, reminiscences, letters, and reports which have survived the ravages of passing time" (p. 321). Venner lists some of the writings of members of the Iron Brigade that he consulted and states that regimental records, newspaper accounts, etc., "cement" the actual accounts together. Thus, Johnny Brendel never existed. But, Venner writes, "Everything written, did happen, and was included in someone's recollections" (p. 322). Venner's purpose in composing this work was to emphasize the similarity of the experiences of American soldiers from the Civil War to the Vietnam War, of which he (according to his introduction) was a veteran.

29. BREWSTER, CHARLES HARVEY. *When This Cruel War Is Over: The Civil War Letters of Charles Harvey Brewster.* Edited, with an introduction, by David W. Blight. Amherst: University of Massachusetts Press, 1992. 366 pp.

July 17, 1862–October 27, 1864. Letters. Lieutenant. Tenth Massachusetts Infantry. Duty around Washington, D.C.; the Peninsular campaign, especially the siege of Yorktown and Seven Pines; Chancellorsville; Gettysburg, including the pursuit of Lee; the Bristoe campaign; Rappahannock Station; The Wilderness; Spotsylvania; Cold Harbor; and recruiting duty in Norfolk, Virginia. When Brewster wrote to his mother and two sisters in Northampton, Massachusetts, he told them how other boys from home were faring, about their living accommodations, and about the ever-present mud. He described the noise of battles, the destruction and stench of the aftermath of a big battle (especially Williamsburg and Spotsylvania), as well as the beauty of the Virginia landscape. In expressions of his desire to be promoted, he seems to have been more anxious to improve his status and self-esteem than to achieve acclaim. Brewster wrote favorably about slaves and blacks during the winter of 1861–1862, when his unit was stationed in Maryland. Brewster called slavery a "vile stain" on the country. He complained that the issue was not being faced squarely and said that it must be: "Nigger has got to be talked, and talked thoroughly to, and I think niggers will come out of this scrape free" (p. 64). He and others in his company protected runaway slaves from their masters until the issue of fugitive slaves threatened to create a revolt in the regiment. But despite his initially favorable remarks about the slaves, Brewster never again wrote highly of blacks as a race. On several occasions during the battle of Williamsburg he noted, without further comment, that blacks were serving as armed soldiers in the Confederate army. Brewster often used the words *courage, bravery,* and *cowardice* broadly, applying them to both events and people. But he no longer seems to have been concerned with convincing others that he was brave by the beginning of the Virginia campaign. He told one sister: "You are mistaken about their being nothing cowardly about me. I am scared most to death every battle we have" (p. 308). After he was discharged Brewster returned to service as a recruiter of black troops for the state of Massachusetts in Norfolk, Virginia. Between July and November 1864 he wrote of the many other recruiters and agents seeking to enlist the few available blacks, as well as of the social conditions in Norfolk. Appended are four letters transcribed by his daughter in the 1880s which, the editor says, possess the style of "sentimentalized memory." The editor's expansive introduction is an essay on the historical importance of Brewster's letters, especially as they apply to recent trends in social history.

30. **BROOME, JOHN LLOYD.** "My Own Account of the Fall of New Orleans." Edited by J. Michael Miller. *Civil War Times Illustrated* 26 (May 1987): 38–41.
April 25–29, 1862. Letter. Captain. United States Marine Corps detached to Farragut's flagship, the USS *Hartford*. Capture of New Orleans. This letter to Gideon Wells (written September 13, 1875) attempts to rectify the error in the report concerning which military body really hoisted the United States flag over the New Orleans Custom House on April 29, 1862. Broome asserts that his marines should have received the credit, rather than the navy, and provides details of how the marines pacified New Orleans.

31. **BROOMFIELD, WILLIAM.** "An Englishman in Union Service Writes Home and Describes 'My Imprisonment Down in Dixie.'" Edited by Richard E. Shue. *Civil War Times Illustrated* 27 (January 1989): 26–33.
May 13–December 1864. Letter. First New York Cavalry. Broomfield was captured during a raid around New Market. He spent the next five months at Danville and Andersonville Prisons before being shipped to Charleston. He was exchanged on December 8.

32. **BROWN, ROBERT CARSON.** *The Sherman Brigade: The Civil War Memoirs of Colonel Robert Carson Brown.* Edited by Charles G. Brown. Mansfield, Ohio: Brownlea Books, 1995. 163 pp.
1861–1865. Memoir. Colonel. Sixty-fourth Ohio Infantry. Organization and training at Camp Buckingham; Shiloh; the siege of Corinth; Don Carlos Buell's pursuit of Braxton Bragg in Kentucky; Stones River; Chickamauga; Missionary Ridge; the relief of Knoxville; the Atlanta campaign; and the Franklin and Nashville campaign. Brown's memoir, which constitutes a rough history of the Sixty-fourth Ohio, blends wartime events with postwar perspective. The marches and hardships of the common soldier predominate, but incidents of camp and battle are also included. One example of camp entertainment was a fight between a horse and a jackass in which the horse was put to flight. In an entry written in late 1863 Brown describes how he helped to establish the "Cracker line," and in a passage written during the Atlanta campaign he relates topics of fraternization between opposing pickets. On a march near Chattanooga in 1864 the soldiers came upon a community composed of female slaves who had been placed there by a slave owner. The only occupants were black and mulatto women. Brown wrote, "The children seemed to be from 3 to 12 years of age and a large per cent of them were red haired" and concluded, "The object being to enrich the master producing slaves for the market" (p. 69). Brown resigned from the regiment in February 1865 but continued to write the unit's history. These memoirs originally appeared in installments of the *Mansfield (Ohio) News* in 1896.

33. **BUCK, ERASTUS.** *Buck's Book: A View of the 3rd Vermont Infantry Regiment.* Edited by John E. Balzer. Bolingbrook, Ill.: Balzer and Associates, 1993. 84 pp.
July 30, 1861–May 10, 1864. Letters. Captain. Third Vermont Infantry. In these letters Buck relates duty from various places in Virginia, including battles of Lee's Mill, Fredericksburg, and The Wilderness. His few correspondences include his feelings about his wife and children, the activities of his regiment, and his devotion to the Union. He made only a brief comment on what proved to be a fatal wound he received at The Wilderness.

34. **BURBANK, JEROME.** *Jerome: To My Beloved Absent Companion. Letters of a Civil War Surgeon, to His Wife at Home, Caring for Their Family.* Edited by Sylvia Burbank Morris. Cullman, Ala.: Sylvia Morris, 1996. 250 pp.

August 25, 1862–August 1, 1894. Letters. Surgeon. Twenty-second Wisconsin Infantry and Thirty-third Wisconsin Infantry. Duty in Kentucky, Tennessee (including the battles of Thompson's Station and Nashville and the pursuit of Hood), Arkansas, Missouri (including the pursuit of Sterling Price), and the Mobile campaign. Thirty-five-year-old Burbank, from Rock County, Wisconsin, served two tours of duty. Between September 1863 and July 1864 he was discharged for medical reasons. Throughout his writings he sought to bolster the confidence of his "absent companion." He assured her that she was the best mother that their four (then five following a furlough) children could have, gave her a stern pep talk about the importance of disciplining the children, prescribed specific medications when the children were sick, and told her not to worry about the one son who was growing more slowly than another. Burbank instructed his wife on how to handle a tenant who was taking advantage of her. He also gave her advice on planting crops, chopping wood, collecting debts, and paying bills. Burbank believed that the importance of the war—whether men were capable of self-government—was not limited to the United States, but that it had relevance to other nations as well. Although Burbank recognized that doctors were held in low esteem in the army, this served only to make him work harder and gave him more reason to be proud that he had a good reputation. His letters are filled with details of hospital routines, movement of medical wagons, treatment of the sick, and procurement of healthful food that would hasten the recovery of his patients. Burbank wrote critically about the food. When he described the grease-laden beans, the fat pork, and pancakes (as "heavy as so much hammered sole leather"), he said they would "tax the digestive organs of a sallamander" (p. 162). During his second period of duty Burbank complained less about his circumstances, perhaps because he was surgeon in charge of the regiment.

35. **BURNETT, ALVIN.** *Glimpses of Alvin Burnett Featuring Civil War Letters to His Mother, Josephine.* Compiled by Raymond E. Watkins (a great-grandson). Arlington, Tex.: Published by the compiler, 1995. 1 vol. (various paging).

August 7, 1862–June 11, 1865. Letters. Ninety-first Illinois Infantry. Enlistment at Camp Butler; duty in Kentucky guarding the Louisville and Nashville Railroad and attempting to locate John Hunt Morgan (his regiment was captured by Morgan at Elizabethtown on December 28, 1862, and paroled to Benton Barracks until June 5, 1863); and duty at Vicksburg and Port Hudson after the sieges of those cities. In Louisiana he served at New Orleans and in the battles at Morgan's Ferry and Morganza. In Texas he saw frontier and garrison duty at Brownsville and Brazos Santiago, among other places, and he concluded his service with the Mobile campaign. Obtaining postage was an early problem for Burnett. He told his correspondents that if they wanted to hear from him they would have to furnish him with stamps. He was also concerned with settling outstanding debts and other unresolved affairs back home in Henderson County, Illinois, including a relationship with a woman friend. At Vicksburg, Burnett reported on the conditions under which the civilians lived during the siege. At Port Hudson he described the medication he concocted to fight diarrhea: "blackberry roots and sweet gum bark gum boiled down to a syrup and sweetened" (pt. 2, p. 3). In Louisiana he was pleased that he was making more money by "pressing things from the rebs and selling them" than he was receiving in pay (pt. 2, p. 8). Burnett exhibited pride in the fact that he seldom got the "blues." However, it is obvious that he was not immune to the emotion because he wrote that he tried not to think about coming home and thus avoided being overcome by homesickness. After the battle of Mobile Bay, he was among the minority of his comrades willing to be sent to the Texas border to fight Maximilian.

36. **BURNS, WILLIAM S.** *Recollections of the 4th Missouri Cavalry.* Edited by Frank Allen Dennis. Dayton, Ohio: Morningside House, 1988. 162 pp.
1861–November 24, 1864. Memoir. Captain, Fourth Missouri Cavalry, and Acting Assistant Inspector General, Third Division, XVI Corps. Duty in Missouri, Arkansas (including Pea Ridge and Old River Lake), Mississippi (including the Meridian campaign, Tupelo, and A. J. Smith's expedition from La Grange, Tennessee, to Oxford, Mississippi), and Louisiana (second Red River campaign, including Fort De Russy, Pleasant Hill, Marksville Prairie); and mustering-out duty in Saint Louis. On the first page of this memoir Burns offers readers of *The Steuben Courier* (Bath, New York) a disclaimer to the possibility that after twenty-odd years his memory had faded and he would not be able to write vividly. By consulting his wartime journal and conversing with participants, Burns was able to reconstruct a creditable account of the above battles and present as well some unique aspects of his duties as a staff officer.

37. **BUSWELL, BRIGHAM.** (Part I) "A Sharpshooter's Seven Days." *Civil War Times Illustrated* 34 (February 1996): 20, 22–28.
––––––. (Part II) *Civil War Times Illustrated* 35 (April 1996): 22–24, 26–27, 30, 32, 76–77.
June 1–July 1, 1862. Memoir. First U.S. Sharpshooters. Seven Days' Battles, especially Mechanicsville and Malvern Hill. Buswell recalls the common soldier's faith in George McClellan and such scenes as a Union officer, who had been hit by a shell fragment, sitting against a stump with his bowels protruding. Buswell watched one of Thaddeus Lowe's balloons spy on the enemy until their artillery got the balloon's range and forced it to descend. He said that he and the other sharpshooters were ordered to aim at only officers and color bearers and not to waste shots on other Confederate soldiers. Between the morning of June 26 and June 30 Buswell's unit was on the move, receiving little sleep and almost no food. He said the men subsisted on coffee, grinding it between their teeth and washing it down with muddy water. When they located a granary, the men lapped the cornmeal with their tongues like barnyard animals. They discovered beehives and fought the bees for the honey, suffering numerous stings in the process. Buswell told how he shot a Confederate officer at Malvern Hill but was immediately hit in return. He struggled back to the Union rear through the mass of confusion before he passed out. He awoke as a captive held in a barn. Because he had been placed on a feather tick mattress, his body was covered in dried blood and feathers. Shortly Buswell was loaded onto a baggage wagon and was on his way to a Richmond prison.

38. **BYERS, S. H. M.** "How Men Feel in Battle." *American History Illustrated* 22 (April 1987): 11–17.
1861–1865. Memoir. Major. Fifth Iowa Infantry. Battle of Corinth; the siege of Vicksburg; and Missionary Ridge.

39. **CAMPBELL, JAMES H.** "'Lee Has Escaped!': Civil War Letters of Lt. Col. James. H. Campbell, 39th Regiment, Pennsylvania Volunteer Militia." *Pennsylvania History* 61 (January 1994): 102–11.
July 5–July 25, 1863. Letters. Lieutenant Colonel. Thirty-ninth Pennsylvania Infantry (Militia). Organized to contest Lee's invasion, the militia spent part of the month anticipating Confederate movements. After Lee had returned to Virginia, the militia encamped near Greencastle, Pennsylvania. In several letters Campbell mentioned to his wife apprehension over the possibility of antidraft riots in their home of Pottsville (Schuykill County), which was a stronghold of Copperhead activity. The unit was mustered out on August 2, 1863.

40. CARLETON, HERBERT. "A Year at Sea: The Civil War Memoirs of Herbert Carleton." *America's Civil War* 58 (August 1996): 34–39.

1864–1865. Memoir. USS *Circassian.* The underage Carleton served on the dispatch and supply vessel *Circassian* between April 2, 1864, and April 12, 1865. His first voyage was from Boston to the Rio Grande, with stops at Hilton Head and New Orleans, and then a return trip to Boston. Subsequent episodes included a chase of the CSS *Florida,* participation in the Mobile Bay campaign, exchange of Union prisoners at Hampton Roads, and a raging storm off Cape Hatteras.

41. CARPENTER, GEORGE BRADFORD. "War and Other Reminiscences." Introduction by Kris Van Den Bossche. *Rhode Island History* 47 (November 1989): 109–47.

September 1861–October 1864. Memoir and letters. Fourth Rhode Island Infantry. Enlistment and training at Camp Greene; duty outside Washington, D.C.; Burnside's North Carolina expedition, including the capture of New Bern; South Mountain; Antietam; Fredericksburg; the siege of Suffolk; provost duty at Point Lookout Prison; and the siege of Petersburg, including the Petersburg Mine Assault. Carpenter recalled with pride that, early in their training, his unit did not break and run when Gen. Oliver O. Howard tested their discipline by charging the men while brandishing his sword. He remembered the capture of a pig (against orders) on Roanoke Island with greater clarity than he did the rough ocean voyage or the fighting. Carpenter retained a vivid recollection of "the Crater." He was ordered into the breech, but upon realizing the impossibility of the task, he escaped just as the Confederates were recovering. However, Carpenter lost an arm in the assault. His hospital treatment included cleansing the stump with sulfuric acid. His wife was informed that he had been killed at "the Crater," and her few letters contemplate his death, then express her joy. Carpenter concluded his memoir with his return home in time to cast his vote for Abraham Lincoln.

42. CHAMBERLAIN, JOSHUA LAWRENCE. *"Bayonet! Forward": My Civil War Reminiscences.* Gettysburg, Pa.: Stan Clark Military Books, 1994. 328 pp.

1862–1865. Lieutenant Colonel, Twentieth Maine Infantry, to Major General, V Corps, Army of the Potomac. This work contains seventeen articles, reports, addresses, and letters written or delivered by Chamberlain. Nearly all came from published sources. The selections cover Chamberlain's reflections on military actions from Fredericksburg to Appomattox, the Grand Review, and tributes to units he had commanded and Abraham Lincoln. One selection has also been republished, with additional illustrations, as *Through Blood and Fire at Gettysburg: General Joshua Chamberlain and the 20th Maine* (Gettysburg, Pa.: Stan Clark Military Books, 1994).

43. CHAMBERLAIN, JOSHUA LAWRENCE. *Through Blood & Fire: Selected Civil War Papers of Major General Joshua Chamberlain.* By Mark Nesbitt. Mechanicsburg, Pa.: Stackpole Books, 1996. 226 pp.

July 14, 1862–July 31, 1865. Papers. Lieutenant Colonel, Twentieth Maine Infantry, to Major General, V Corps, Army of the Potomac. Enlistment and duty in northern Virginia; Fredericksburg; Chancellorsville; Gettysburg; assault of Petersburg; the Weldon Railroad expedition to Hicksford; Gravelly Run; Five Forks; and acceptance of the Confederate arms at Appomattox on April 12. Mark Nesbit has blended Chamberlain's official and private papers with historical narrative to shed light on both Chamberlain's personality and military actions. In his initial letters to Gov. Israel Washburn of Maine, Chamberlain expressed his patriotic desire to serve his country, even though he anticipated objections among the faculty at Bowdoin College to his departure. But on October 10, 1862, he felt pleasure at having escaped academia. Although he admitted to the "care & vexations" of the field, he adamantly wrote: "but let me say no danger & no hardship ever makes me wish to get that college life again. . . . One thing though I *wont* endure again" (p. 24). While Chamberlain's letters to those in authority are stiff and formal, when he wrote to his family he expressed caring and affection. Once he told his wife that he found himself unconsciously humming a love song—"First to my dear one first to my love—because I am always thing of first of you" (p. 52). Later he implored her to write of "dreamy love" (p. 107). In a letter written to his young daughter he describes the look of the Chancellorsville battlefield in the manner that a child could understand without being horrified. But this work primarily concerns military matters. Chamberlain wrote several accounts of his actions at Little Round Top. He described how he was wounded in the June 18, 1864, assault of Petersburg and again at Gravelly Run. And he composed a lengthy report of the Appomattox campaign. In other letters Chamberlain recommended promotions for officers of Maine units, as well as punishments for soldiers who had not measured up at Gettysburg. Several letters to the governor of Maine in June 1863 were sympathetic to the mutinous soldiers of the Second Maine of whom he had been put in charge. As he led his brigade on the Weldon Railroad expedition to destroy the rails in December 1864, the destruction of civilian property became excessive and a guerrilla was hung in retribution for the murder of Union stragglers. In letters written to his brother and sister Chamberlain reveals how deeply these events disturbed him. In January 1865 Chamberlain was offered a civil service position as a customs collector in Maine. After Appomattox he expressed to his wife that he was glad that he had not taken the position because it would have prevented him from seeing the conflict to its conclusion. Throughout his papers Chamberlain wrote of honor, manliness, duty, and the belief that God had predestined the future.

44.   CHAMBERLAIN, SAMUEL OSCAR. *Civil War Letters of an Ohio Soldier: S. O. Chamberlain and the 49th Ohio Volunteer Infantry.* Edited by Dick Chamberlain and Judy Chamberlain. Flournoy, Calif.: Walker Lithograph, 1990. 67 pp.

September 11, 1861–November 3, 1865. Letters. Forty-ninth Ohio Infantry. Duty in Kentucky and Tennessee; the siege of Corinth; pursuit of Bragg in Kentucky; the Atlanta campaign, operations against Hood in north Georgia and north Alabama; and duty in Texas. Chamberlain wrote his parents about camp life and troop movements rather than battles. He mentioned such activities as Union and Confederate soldiers fraternizing while swimming near Battle Creek, Alabama; his duties as orderly sergeant; and a description of the landscape and people of San Antonio. He described postwar occupation duty in Texas. He called Gonzales "one of the most Rebelious holes in all Texas" (p. 52). Women shook their fists at the Union flag, and the men of the town appeared crestfallen. Chamberlain described a street fight in which a drunken civilian boasted that he "could whip any Yankee son of a B— from the North" (p. 52). After Union soldiers beat the man, Chamberlain wanted the folks at home to know that "the old Regt. will fight for its Honor as well in a Street Row as in Battle Army" (p. 52). In November 1865 he wrote that a great many of the blacks in Texas continued to be held in servitude. Their masters told them that they would not be free for another seven years.

45.   CHAPIN, SAMUEL. *Memorandum and Journal of Samuel Chapin of South Wilbraham, Massachusetts, Company I, 46th Regt., M.V.M.* Typed and transcribed by Beryle C. Doten and Gertrude M. Lyons. Hampden, Mass.: Historical Society of the Town of Hampden, 1987. 133 leaves.

September 20, 1862–July 29, 1863. Diary. Forty-sixth Massachusetts Infantry. Organization of unit in Springfield; duty in North Carolina, including Gum Swamp; duty in Maryland; and pursuit of Lee after Gettysburg. While in Massachusetts, Chapin noted receipt of uniforms, weapons, and rubber blankets; drilling and watching others drill (for some unexplained reason one company wore their drawers outside their pants); and assorted camp high jinks. In North Carolina he recorded the appearance of the land around New Bern; the great number of "contraband"; and such details as men washing their greasy dishes by scouring them with sand, cleaning his rusty rifle, studying the manual of arms, and drilling. Once he remarked that "the Captain had something to say about the boys 'cracking beans' when on battalion drill" (p. 29). As Chapin reflected on the destruction in North Carolina, he wrote that people of the North did not realize what it was to have war on their soil. Chapin heard a lot of rumors; thus, when news of Stonewall Jackson's death was circulated, he was skeptical, writing: "he has been killed so many times and turned up again, he may do so again" (p. 104). Chambers's nine-month unit was mustered out in July 1863.

46. **CHAPMAN, IRA HARRISON.** *The Diary of Ira Harrison Chapman, Company G, 100th Illinois Volunteers 2nd Brigade, 2nd Division, 4th Army Corps, Army of the Cumberland, February Through September 1864.* Nashville, Tenn.: J. R. Cole, 1995. 1 vol. (various paging).
February 1–September 25, 1864. Diary. One-hundredth Illinois Infantry. Duty around Athens, Tennessee, until April, and then the Atlanta campaign. Chapman wrote this portion of his diary in fragments that reveal what he did but not how he felt about his circumstances. Between February and April he was in camp selling the paper, pens, and envelopes he had brought from a recent leave home. He was mending his trousers; listening to preachers; and making rings, inkwells, and stools. Chapman often mentioned the food and weather, and he kept an expense account, which is appended. He learned of the deaths of both parents, but his terse entries offer no comment. As soon as the Atlanta campaign got under way, Chapman recorded the continual movement and fighting.

47. **CHASE, SAMUEL B.** "The Civil War Letters of Lieutenant Samuel B. Chase." By Harry H. Anderson. *Milwaukee History* 14, no. 2 (1991): 38–62.
January 1863–Autumn 1865. Letters. Lieutenant. Twenty-fourth Wisconsin Infantry. Duty in Kentucky, Tennessee, Mississippi, and Georgia. Chase's duties as quartermaster required that he provide the soldiers with such basic needs as living accommodations, commissary stores, mules and horses, etc. Chase reluctantly foraged from civilians because he knew that they would be left with little on which to subsist. Chase helped to maintain the "Cracker line" during the Chattanooga campaign and was glad when river transportation replaced the necessity of crossing the Cumberland Mountains with mules to feed the troops in Chattanooga. The health of the soldiers was of constant concern to Chase, and he maintained an awareness of the men available for duty. Chase was a refreshingly blunt-spoken man and possessor of numerous biases. Military life had a peculiar attraction for Chase. In one passage that raises questions about his personal life, Chase wrote the following: "The sound of Cannons and rifles is far preferable to many other griveances that com upon us outside the battlefield" (p. 54).

48. **CHESTER, HENRY WHIPPLE.** *Recollections of the War of the Rebellion: A Story of the 2nd Ohio Volunteer Cavalry, 1861–1865.* Edited by Alberta R. Adamson, Robert I. Girardi, and Roger E. Bohn. Wheaton, Ill.: Wheaton History Center, 1996. 257 pp.
September 1861–June 20, 1865. Memoir. Captain. Second Ohio Cavalry. Enlistment, organization, and shipment to the western frontier; duty in Missouri, Kansas, and Indian Territory; Kentucky, including Rocky Gap; Morgan's Kentucky, Ohio, and Indiana raid; Burnside's east Tennessee campaign; pursuit of Longstreet following the siege of Knoxville; the Virginia campaign, including Hanover Court House, Ashland, and Wilson's and Kautz's Petersburg raid; Sheridan's Shenandoah Valley campaign, including third Winchester, Tom's Brook, Cedar Creek, Newtown, and Waynesboro; and the Appomattox campaign, including Dinwiddie Court House, Five Forks, and Sayler's Creek, where he was wounded

and removed from the war; and the Grand Review. Chester directs his recollections (written between 1912 and 1915) to his grandchildren. He wanted his experiences to serve as a reminder of the struggle that he (and others like him) had made to preserve the United States as a single nation against those who would have left it fragmented. He emphasizes that "The war was not fought to free the slaves but their freedom was recognized as a military necessity and was used as a means to save the Union" (p. 2). Chester frequently refers readers to accounts by other members of the regiment and reports in the *Official Records.* In addition to incidents of the regiment's raids, engagements, and battles (according to the editors, there were ninety-seven in fourteen states spread over some twenty-seven thousand miles), other events mentioned are the return of loyal Indians from Kansas to Indian Territory in the spring of 1862; how men were detailed to the Twenty-fifth Ohio Light Artillery, although they "objected strongly"; the destruction of a Copperhead newspaper, *The Crisis,* in Columbus, Ohio, on May 5, 1863, by members of the Second Ohio Cavalry; Chester's rise from private to captain; an unsuccessful saber charge at third Winchester; and the wound he received at Sayler's Creek. The editors have included a detailed map of the regiment's travels and battles, as well as photographs of the soldiers and the Chester family.

49.   CHISHOLM, DANIEL, and SAMUEL A. CLEAR. *The Civil War Notebook of Daniel Chisholm: A Chronicle of Daily Life in the Union Army, 1864–1865.* Edited by W. Springer Menge and J. August Shimrak. New York: Ballantine Books, 1989. 202 pp.

February 25, 1864–July 21, 1865. Diary and letters. 116th Pennsylvania Infantry. The Virginia campaign; siege of Petersburg; and the Appomattox campaign. After the war Daniel Chisholm copied the diary of Sgt. Samuel A. Clear into this notebook format. He added his own letters, together with several by his brother Alex, which were written between March 2, 1864, and June 3, 1865. Clear blended anecdotes of daily routines of camp with those of battle. In an early notation he tells of a fight in which one man mistakenly stabbed another man. Clear claims that he was so near the incident that he could hear the knife cut the victim's bones. In December 1864 Clear described how soldiers were forced to stand outside in the cold weather and witness the execution of three deserters. He recorded details of the construction of the gallows and the insults that observers heaped upon the doomed soldiers. Clear attended a horse race on Saint Patrick's Day in 1865. Although observers and participants (both horses and men) were killed and injured, the accidents failed to halt the celebrations. Clear wrote that it was a "crazy day" and added: "I will have to alter my mind if I ever go to see another Irish fair" (p. 69). At The Wilderness, his first battle, Union soldiers retreated, dragging their wounded from the burning undergrowth. Then they hastily dug defensive positions with their bayonets and bare hands. Clear wrote that at Cold Harbor the Yankee troops had withstood several Confederate assaults when a two-hour truce was called to enable each side to claim its casualties. Clear also wrote of the fighting during Reams' Station, Five Forks, and the Appomattox campaign. He concluded his account with the Grand Review, the wait to be discharged, and the trip back home. Daniel Chisholm's letters to his parents relate many of the regiment's similar experiences. Chisholm, who was wounded on June 16, 1864, wrote from several hospitals through the remainder of 1864 and part of 1865. Excerpts from brother Alex's letters are interspersed with Daniel's. Other documents and lists pertaining to the 116th Pennsylvania Infantry are also included. Samuel, Daniel, and Alex were all members of Company K from the community of Uniontown in southeastern Pennsylvania.

50.   CHURCH, CHARLES H. *Civil War Letters by Sgt. Major Charles H. Church, Co. G, 3rd Regt., Michigan Volunteers Written to His Parents at Williamston, Michigan.* Rose City, Mich.: Rose City Area Historical Society, 1987. 52 pp.

May 14, 1861–May 1, 1864. Letters. Sergeant. Third Michigan Infantry. Duty in Virginia (including first Bull Run, the siege of Yorktown, and Fredericksburg) and in North Carolina. Early in Church's account he repeats the report of a soldier who had been captured at first Bull Run. The man testified that the Confederates were numerous and well armed. He alleged that, in an unspecified location, he saw seven hundred Indians being drilled as skirmishers and four hundred blacks also "a—drilling" (p. 8). During the fall and winter of 1861–1862 Church's unit constructed forts around Washington and saw duty near Fortress Monroe. Church recorded the festivities on Saint Patrick's Day of 1862. A horse-racing event in an Irish brigade resulted in the deaths of "only" four horses. Near the end of 1862 Church wrote that the soldiers still supported McClellan but had little faith in Burnside. Nevertheless, he later approved of the tactics of Burnside's "Mud March" and blamed the weather for its failure. Church held negative feelings about blacks and the Republican Party. The "Black abolition party & that rotten congress" were one and the same to him (p. 32). Documents pertaining to Church's death on May 8, 1864, at The Wilderness are included.

51.   CLARK, WILLIAM ALLEN. "'Please Send Stamps': The Civil War Letters of William Allen Clark." (Part I) Edited by Margaret Black Tatum. *Indiana Magazine of History* 91 (March 1995): 81–108.

———. (Part II) Edited by Margaret Black Tatum. *Indiana Magazine of History* 91 (June 1996): 197–225.

———. (Part III) Edited by Margaret Black Tatum. *Indiana Magazine of History* 91 (September 1995): 288–320.

———. (Part IV) Edited by Margaret Black Tatum. *Indiana Magazine of History* 91 (December 1995): 407–36.

August 17, 1862–February 19, 1865. Letters. Corporal. Seventy-second Indiana Infantry. Duty in Kentucky, Tennessee (including the Tullahoma campaign, Chattanooga, and Chickamauga); and the Atlanta campaign. The editor characterizes Clark as being critical of both the North and the South. Clark objected to the abolitionists' antislavery policies, but he opposed secession even more. In time he became increasingly critical of the Republican administration and military censorship. While he held out hope for compromise between the warring sections, he dismissed rumors that this had occurred. Clark also opposed equality of the races and frequently made degrading remarks about blacks. Clark described the countryside from the point of view of the farmer he was and attempted to avoid foraging because of what it did to the rural population. Other topics of his letters include his lack of opportunity to practice religion, requests for sewing materials and stamps, concern about the war spreading to Indiana, and refusal to take a "French leave" for fear of being labeled a deserter. His writing from the summer of 1864 is focused on picket duty and skirmishing during the Atlanta campaign. The editor notes a change in the letters following Clark's leave at home between August and December 1864. Clark wrote less about politics, battles, and camp life and more about returning home permanently. No letters exist for the period between March and June 1865, when he received his discharge.

52.   COMSTOCK, CYRUS B. *The Diary of Cyrus B. Comstock.* Compiled and edited by Merlin E. Sumner. Dayton, Ohio: Morningside, 1987. 408 pp.

January 6, 1861–December 23, 1865. Diary. Brigadier General. Instructor at West Point; Assistant Inspector General of the Military Division of the Mississippi; and Aide-de-camp to Ulysses S. Grant, Army of the Potomac. Comstock was teaching at West Point as the war began. In Tennessee he served as assistant inspector general between November 1863 and March 1864. He was aide-de-camp to Grant in Virginia in 1864 and 1865. He also served as an engineer in the defenses of Washington, D.C., in 1861 and in both attacks on Fort Fisher, as well as in the Mobile campaign. Portions of the diary for 1861 through 1863 are not extant. Comstock's responsibilities in Tennessee allowed him to comment with authority on such aspects as the general state of the army and the specific condition of the telegraph and rail lines. During the spring and summer of 1864 he carried written messages (as well as verbal explanations) from Grant to generals engaged in the Virginia campaign and to Secretary of War Edwin Stanton in Washington. Because of his proximity to the high command, he was in a position to observe the capabilities and personalities of generals. About William S. Rosecrans Comstock wrote, "Rosecrans is adroit" when the general attempted to avoid sending Grant five thousand troops he had requested, and he added, "He does not obey an order if he can avoid it" (p. 263). Soon after the failure of the Petersburg Mine Explosion, Comstock wrote that Burnside was "not competent to command a Corps" and added, "[Gen. George] Meade & Burnside managed to quarrel again" (p. 285). A typical comment about Benjamin Butler was that "Butler has the ability to be more dangerous, sharper . . . more disagreeable than any man I have ever seen" (p. 271). Comstock thought Sheridan was an energetic fighter and efficient officer, but he wrote that, as a man: "Don't think his calibre very great & wish he did not drink so much. Would probably be a good corps commander" (p. 257). Comstock was selected to the jury to try the Lincoln assassination conspirators but was released because Grant was initially thought to also have been a target. Comstock dreaded the duty and thought that it should have been a civil trial, not a "secret" commission (p. 317). The entire diary covers the years 1851 through 1885.

53.   CORBY, WILLIAM. *Memoirs of Chaplain Life: Three Years with the Irish Brigade in the Army of the Potomac.* Edited by Lawrence Frederick Kohl. New York: Fordham University Press, 1992. 412 pp.

December 1861–September 1864. Memoir. Chaplain. Eighty-eighth New York Infantry. The Peninsular campaign, especially Seven Pines and the Seven Days' Battles; Antietam; Fredericksburg; Chancellorsville; Gettysburg; The Wilderness; Spotsylvania; and the siege of Petersburg. Writing from memory in the early 1890s, Corby recalled his duties as a Catholic chaplain with the Irish Brigade in camp and in the field. He conducted masses, listened to confessions, counseled soldiers, and served as an intermediary between soldiers and their families by writing letters and sending money and other valuables to the soldiers' homes. But Corby also advanced onto the battlefield while the fighting was in progress. During the Peninsular campaign he aided the wounded at Seven Pines, as well as those who fell ill with malaria. A passage written at Gettysburg by another soldier recorded how Corby gave absolution to the Irish Brigade on July 2. As battles raged on both sides, Catholic and non-Catholics fell to their knees in prayer; then they rose and charged into "The Wheatfield." In April 1864 Corby attempted to stop what he felt was an unjust execution. He pleaded the case with Abraham Lincoln, who agreed to a pardon, but only under the condition that General Meade also give his consent. Meade refused, and the soldier was hung. Corby, who was content that the man had died a Christian, reconciled the event with: "Had he been pardoned he might not in the end have died as excellent dispositions" (p. 228). Corby also utilized these memoirs to defend Catholics from "bigots" who sought to stir up animosity against the Church (p. 66). Corby concludes his work with chapters written by other Catholic chaplains. This is a facsimile reprint (Notre Dame, Ind.: Scholars Press, 1894), which contains an introduction, a biographical sketch, and an index by the editor. It also includes photographs and copies of documents pertinent to Corby's military career.

54.   CROWDER, JOHN H. "The Civil War Through the Eyes of a Sixteen-Year-Old Black Officer: The Letters of Lieutenant John H. Crowder of the 1st Louisiana Native Guards." Edited by Joseph T. Glatthaar. *Louisiana History* 35 (Spring 1994): 201–16.

November 20, 1862–May 5, 1863. Letters. Lieutenant. First Louisiana Native Guards. The editor values this correspondence as being among the few personal letters of black officers from the Louisiana Native Guards regiments. He adds that researchers of these units are generally forced to rely on only official records. Crowder's letters are unique in what they reveal about his military and private life.

Appointed second lieutenant at the age of sixteen, he excelled in drill, leadership, and general efficiency. However, Crowder aroused the ire of less dedicated comrades. In addition, Glatthaar says that Crowder was a victim of Gen. Nathaniel Banks' s declaration to purge the black officers from the army. Crowder was accused by the military of a variety of unfounded charges, but he professed to his mother that he was free from vices and misconduct. (On one occasion he defended a woman from the obscenities of one of his antagonists.) Crowder successfully retained his rank. Crowder's private life is revealed in his love for his mother, as well as in his affection for a female slave whom he sent home (along with the girl's mother) to assist his mother. Since he intended to marry the girl after the war, he pleaded with his mother to speak well of him. Crowder was killed at Port Hudson on May 27, 1863. The editor's preface places the issues raised in these events in perspective.

55. **CROWELL, LEVI.** *History of Levi Crowell as Written by Himself, Including the Diary of His Incarceration in a Confederate Prison, 1862.* West Dennis, Mass.: Privately printed, 1990. 114 pp.

December 10, 1861–October 16, 1862. Diary. Acting Master. USS *Sumter.* Crowell recorded blockading activities off the South Carolina coast, including capturing and sometimes losing prizes. On May 11 he and part of the crew were taken as prisoners while sailing a cutter to visit Fort Pulaski. Crowell was first removed to Atlanta, where he reported he was treated as a curiosity but exceptionally well. He recalled that outside his room he saw the railroad raider John Andrews being put into a carriage for transport to his hanging as a spy. After about one month Crowell's period of luxury ended. He was shipped to Madison, Georgia, and held in a filthy cotton factory. He was joined by Gen. Benjamin M. Prentiss and others who had been captured at Shiloh. Unionist civilians from eastern Tennessee were detained on the floor above, but the two groups were not allowed to converse. As the conditions at Madison worsened, Crowell attributed the maltreatment to the Confederate officer in charge of the prison—none other than Captain Calhoun, "a nephew of the noted traitor John C. Calhoun" (p. 47). Until October, Crowell wrote entries describing such daily prison pastimes as making bone rings and canes, hearing the guards' rumors that the war was going poorly for the Union, and awaiting the eventual exchange of troops. Crowell's military service appears to have been more of a continuation of his seafaring merchant's life than an expression of patriotism. Other portions of this work indicate that he rejoined the U.S. Navy after his exchange and returned to blockading duty.

56. **CUMMINGS, CHARLES.** "Letters of Charles Cummings, Provost-Marshal of Fairfax Courthouse, Winter 1862–1863." *Yearbook: The Historical Society of Fairfax County, Virginia* 22 (1989/1990): 45–69.

October 29, 1862–March 21, 1863. Letters. Lieutenant Colonel. Sixteenth Vermont Infantry. Fairfax County, Virginia. Cummings was proud that he was becoming a good officer. He wrote that he was proficient at drilling and riding despite saddle sores, piles, and diarrhea. His health was good except for colds, which he treated with the opium he requested from his wife. He called the opium "my sheet anchor in such complaints" (p 51). Cummings seldom commented about the progress of the conflict. He once wrote, "We do not know half as much as the N.Y. correspondents pretend to about the war" (p. 60). The whole camp looked forward to spending the winter of 1862–1863 at Camp Vermont (Fairfax County), and Cummings even sent his wife sketches of their intended quarters. But on the evening of December 12 orders were issued to move out early the following morning. He and the rest of the men objected to being forced to leave their comfortable quarters. In Cummings's words: "Accordingly some tall swearing was indulged in rather freely" (p. 63). Soon after, the Union army occupied a county courthouse, and Cummings found comfort using an old record book for a pillow. Throughout his letters Cummings gave his wife advice on which bills to pay, as well as suggestions on how to handle other household matters. His tone was consistently cheery. Her letters were apparently as encouraging to him, since he assured her how much they meant to him.

57. CUTLER, JEROME. *Letters of Jerome Cutler, Waterville, Vermont, during His Enlistment in the Union Army, 2nd Regiment Vermont Volunteers, 1861–1864.* N.p.: N. pub., 1990. 132 leaves.

July 14, 1861–June 7, 1864. Letters. Second Vermont Infantry. First Bull Run; the Antietam campaign; Chancellorsville; Gettysburg; the New York draft riots; and Spotsylvania. Cutler discusses war-related themes in letters he wrote to his aunt and uncle. For example, in correspondence from early 1862 he informs them of his opposition to the popular sentiment in the North that the army should get moving. He was undoubtedly contemplating being a participant in a military disaster and retorts sarcastically, "do they want another Bull Run" (February 3, 1862). He also discusses the investigations of the Committee on the Conduct of the War and the successes and failures of George McClellan. Cutler's letters to his fiancée are more personal; in them he expresses concerns about his health, mentions his struggle to practice his religion, describes his immediate duties, and occasionally expresses feelings of endearment. To both parties, however, Cutler was extremely vague about details of battles. He avoided the subject with such comments as "But enough, you this is a war letter and nothing else" (May 4, 1862) and "Well enough of war matters" (June 3, 1862). He described to his fiancée how it felt to be under fire at first Bull Run. He wrote that he was not afraid but, rather, felt indifferent. He inferred that others reacted in the same manner. One soldier fired his weapon until it was too hot to handle; nonchalantly put the weapon aside; and lit up his pipe, which he smoked until the piece was cool enough to be fired again. Cutler was somewhat ambivalent about the purpose of the war. In his early letters he wrote that his goal as a soldier was to wipe out the rebellion, and he consistently expressed his feeling that the war was necessary to keep the Union together. However, in a cosmic sense, Cutler saw the hand of God at work. He believed that the war reflected the wickedness of the whole country and that "our nation when sufficiently punished will eventually become a purer a holier and a better people" (April 22, 1863).

58. DAVIS, ELMER. "'The Consequence of Grandeur': A Union Soldier Writes of the Atlanta Campaign." Edited by William C. Niesen. *Atlanta History* 33 (Fall 1989): 5–19.

June 12–September 1, 1864. Letters. Corporal. First New York Light Artillery, Battery M. Atlanta campaign. During fraternization a Confederate picket shot a Union soldier. Out of a sense of fairness the Confederates sent the guilty man through the lines for punishment. However, the Union soldiers returned the culprit, saying that they could not commit cold-blooded murder. Davis, who was a veteran of the Eastern Theater, commented somewhat cryptically about Confederate soldiers of the Western Theater: "We don't care much for the rebs down here. They don't fite like the Virginia rebs" (p. 6). But his description of Georgia women was much less mysterious: "They are all tall, sparse, thin, tawny, starved looking objects to pity" (p. 18). Davis occasionally gave his wife advice about the farm and expenditures. He was exceptionally parsimonious and profited from the sale of paper and envelopes his wife sent to him. He calculated that after he received his discharge he would have accumulated more money by being a soldier than by staying home and working himself to death on a farm. Davis's letters were often affectionate but were far from mushy. In one he slipped into a romantic mood before abruptly catching himself: "I am getting off the track. Love and war don't go well together. My business is killing in stead of talking love" (p. 13). Davis's letters also reveal another soldier's familial relationship. His tentmate Dave and his wife were in constant disagreement. The woman did not write Dave often, and when she did it was for the purpose of asking for money. Davis observed: "She did not even sine her name to it. Dave was mad and said the damed bitch mite go to hell before he would send her any money" (p. 13). However, Dave relented when he received a "soft soap" letter from his "dear" wife (p. 16). Davis quipped, "she may well be called dear since it has cost him twenty-five dollars per month" (p. 16).

59. DAVIS, WILLIAM. *The Civil War Journal of Billy Davis: From Hopewell, Indiana to Port Republic, Virginia.* Edited by Richard S. Skidmore. Greencastle, Ind.: Nugget Publishers, 1989. 179 pp.

April 12, 1861–June 12, 1862. Diary. Private. Seventh Indiana Infantry. Duty in West Virginia, including battles of Philippi (Davis's company was not involved) and Corrick's Ford; first Kernstown; and Port Republic. Billy's first entries record civilian reaction to the news of Fort Sumter and are followed by the reasons why he volunteered for the three-month Seventh Indiana Infantry. He described his physical examination at Camp Morton, the train trip to West Virginia, and the skirmishes during June and July. Shortly after his discharge Billy returned home and helped raise the three-year Seventh Indiana Infantry. During the fall and winter of 1861–1862 his unit slogged through rain, snow, and mud in the Cheat Mountain region of Virginia. Like the rest of the men, Billy never understood the reasons for, or direction of, their next march. Terse mention of names of those who died appear in his entries with regularity. When Billy suffered from a toothache, he was persuaded to take a chew of tobacco. While it did alleviate the pain temporarily, the tobacco made him violently ill: "it prostrated my nervous system" (p. 125). During this dismal period of duty the "blues" were commonplace. For some men it was debilitating. Billy described one soldier who became so "homesick" that he cried constantly, which provoked the laughter of his comrades. Billy never railed against other soldiers' vices, and he committed a few of the soldier's usual transgressions himself. He saw nothing wrong with stealing fence rails against official orders, and shooting "secessionist" hogs was fair game. Billy was a good Christian soldier in the broadest sense. For example, at first Kernstown he stayed behind all night with the wounded Confederates. He visited hospitals and swept the installations' floors because he felt it was needed. He proved his bravery on the battlefield at Port Republic when he volunteered to rescue deserted Union artillery pieces. In the spring of 1862 as the unit moved eastward, Billy noted that the food supply was much improved. The millers in the regiment took over a grist mill, making flour for flapjacks and biscuits plentiful. In May 1862 President Lincoln reviewed the troops. Although Lincoln revealed himself to be "a very awkward horseman," Billy said that it did not lessen the soldiers' admiration for him (p. 124). Billy Davis's transcribed journal ends abruptly in 1862, although extant manuscripts continue through the middle of 1863.

60. DAWES, EPHRAIM CUTLER. "An Indomitable Will." By L. J. Kozlowski. *Timeline* 9 (June/July 1992): 18–29.

May 28, 1864–May 28, 1889. Diaries and letters. Major. Fifty-third Ohio Infantry. Dawes was shot in the jaw and the back of the head on May 28 outside Dallas, Georgia. He was unable to eat solid food or speak. His transfer to a hospital in Nashville on jostling carts and overpacked trains prolonged his agony. Medical treatment included having the dead skin tissue burned away with a solution of chlorinated soda. The article includes graphics of the reconstructive surgery performed on Dawes. Kozlowski adds that Dawes overcame his disfiguring wound and lived a long, successful life.

61. DEGRESS, FRANCIS. "Report of the Battle of Atlanta." *Blue & Gray Magazine* 11 (April 1994): 28–30.

July 22, 1864. Report. Captain. First Illinois Light Artillery, Battery H. Battle of Atlanta.

62. DENNISON, JAMES H. *Dennison's Andersonville Diary: The Diary of an Illinois Soldier in the Infamous Andersonville Prison Camp.* Notes and transcription by Jack Klasey. Kankakee, Ill.: Kankakee County Historical Society, 1987. 107 pp.

March 3, 1864–February 21, 1865. Diary. Sergeant. 113th Illinois Infantry. Samuel D. Sturgis's expedition to Guntown; Dennison's capture at Brice's Cross Roads; and imprisonment at Andersonville

(June 19 to September 29, 1864), Savannah, Camp Lawton Prison, Florence, and Richmond. He was paroled on February 24, 1865. Dennison's brief, phonetically spelled entries record the growth of Andersonville and the frequency of deaths that occurred there. On August 22, 1864, he wrote: "the men dys verry fast hear now from 75 to 125 per day" (p. 61). The editor adds that on that date, the worst day in the camp's history, there were actually ninety-seven deaths. Topics of his diary include the poor quality of the food that was served in inadequate amounts, men suffering from heat and rain, the prisoners' inhumanity toward each other, the execution of the "raiders," and incidents of guards shooting those who came too near the "dead line." Dennison comments on the prisoners' petition to Washington, which sought a change in Union policy of exchanging prisoners. A mock election held by the prisoners was won by Lincoln, but he apparently did not get Dennison's vote. During October and November, Dennison noted that on three occasions prisoners took the oath of allegiance to the Confederacy. On March 13, 1865, he wrote to his wife from Baltimore General Hospital informing her that he was "in the land of the loving once more" (p. 97).

63. **DEPLEDGE, WILLIAM.** *". . . do just as you think best": The Civil War Letters of William Depledge.* Edited by Paul M. Leone. Jamestown, N.Y.: Fenton Historical Society, 1995. 81 pp.

October 15, 1862–March 26, 1865. Letters. 112th New York Infantry. Duty at Suffolk, Virginia; the Charleston harbor islands; the siege of Petersburg; and the capture of Wilmington. William joined the army to provide a better life for his wife, Jenie, and their three young sons, who lived on a rented farm in Chautauqua County, New York. When William was ill, he considered applying for a medical discharge but was dissuaded by the fact that he would lose the bounty money. He sent Jenie the extra money he earned by working as a hospital steward and chopping wood for the sutler. When one young son died, William was filled with remorse and lamented his decision to join the army. During William's leave home Jenie conceived another boy. After the completion of his leave, William expressed little interest in the war. Confederate prisoners told William that they were fighting to protect their homes, and that convinced him that the Northern abolitionists were mistaken in thinking that they could defeat the South. William seldom mentioned battles, but he did write descriptive letters of his duty in Charleston harbor and the Union entry into Wilmington, and he related the poor condition of the Union soldiers who were released from prisons in Wilmington. William died of typhoid fever in March 1865. Several letters of condolence are appended. Six letters from his wife, Jenie, are also included.

64. **DEXTER, SEYMOUR.** *Seymour Dexter, Union Army: Journal and Letters of Civil War Service in Company K, 23rd New York Volunteer Regiment of Elmira, with Illustrations.* Edited by Carl A. Morrell. Jefferson, N.C.: McFarland & Co., 1996. 158 pp.

April 26, 1861–December 30, 1864. Letters and journal. Twenty-third New York Infantry. Organization of unit and duty in northern Virginia, including second Bull Run, South Mountain, and Fredericksburg. Dexter enlisted "to defend the cause of truth, humanity, and justice" (p. 11). But even before he had left training camp at Elmira, those pristine goals were tainted by more swearing and drinking than Seymour said he had heard and seen in his life until then. Then, only two months later at first Bull Run, Dexter wrote that the army that had been so stimulated by patriotism and the justice of its cause "was now retreating with blasted hopes, disgraced arms and gloomy spirit" (p. 35). Dexter frequently commented on how change in leadership affected the morale of the soldiers. After the Peninsular campaign, he wrote that the soldiers still retained their faith in McClellan and were glad when "Little Mack" again took command from Gen. John Pope after second Bull Run. Just prior to Fredericksburg, Dexter felt that McClellan's next replacement, Ambrose Burnside, had the confidence of the men. After Fredericksburg, however, he wrote: the men "think even more than ever of General Burnside as a high-toned, honorable man, but less as a General" (p. 124). In March 1863 Dexter commended Gen. Joseph

Hooker for exhibiting energy that was gaining him the confidence and esteem of the troops. In May 1863 the regiment returned to Elmira to be mustered out.

65. DICKERSON, FRANK. *Dearest Father: The Civil War Letters of Lt. Frank Dickerson, a Son of Belfast, Maine.* Edited and narrated by H. Draper Hunt. Unity, Maine: North Country Press, 1992. 216 pp.

August 30, 1862–December 31, 1865. Letters. Lieutenant. Fifth U.S. Cavalry. Antietam; cavalry raids in northern Virginia; Burnside's "Mud March"; and detached duty at several places in Maryland (including Point Lookout Prison), Madison, Wisconsin, and Nashville. Dickerson wrote a little about Antietam; more about the weather conditions during Burnside's offensive (his unit carried supplies to grateful soldiers who were stuck in the mud); but nothing about Brandy Station, where he suffered a head wound. During the summer of 1862 he was incapacitated by diarrhea. To prevent its reoccurrence he wore an "aromatic belt or soldiers life preserver," which was made of "flannel inside of which there are placed aromatic stimulants such as cayenne. It completely protects the stomach, keeping it warm all the time, etc." (p. 22). He approved of Hooker's appointment to command the Army of the Potomac and particularly praised the promotion of Gen. George Stoneman to head the cavalry. After Chancellorsville, however, Dickerson found fault with Hooker when Hooker tried to make Stoneman the scapegoat for the Union loss. Following the summer of 1863 much of Dickerson's service was spent on detached duty and in and out of hospitals. While at Point Lookout Prison he wrote that the Union guards were preparing for a rumored Confederate assault to free the captives. For most of 1864 Dickerson was hospitalized. In January 1865 he was well enough to serve as a recruiting and mustering-out officer in Madison, Wisconsin. He served his last few months with the quartermaster corps in Nashville and died in January 1866 of tuberculosis and chronic diarrhea while on his way home.

66. DOLPHIN, WILLIAM. *William Dolphin's Civil War Diary, August 15, 1863 Through April 4, 1864.* Transcribed and edited by C. M. Crisfield. Ossining, N.Y.: Ossining Historical Society, 1991. 121 pp.

August 15, 1863–April 4, 1864. Diary. Second New York Cavalry. Duty in Virginia, including imprisonment at Belle Isle. Dolphin's expressions of annoyance with his military experiences are repetitive and brusque and ring with honesty. For example, following an inspection he wrote: "Devil of an inspection Am Mad as Hell. & Damnation" (p. 8). On September 21 the Second New York Cavalry was involved in a skirmish at White's Ford. Dolphin related the day's events with characteristic brevity. "Revilie at day Light March for Orange CH get in a fight a D—D hot Place & am taken Prisoner" (p. 19). His incomplete sentences written at Belle Isle Prison are revealing: "Wish I could write home, a hard Cold & Feel Miserable. Puss & Pains" (p. 23). Later he wrote, "Cold weary Oh So lonesome" (p. 44). Even when he was released on March 20, his joy was constrained but to the point: "Great News. We have all Been Parolled to Day" (p. 77). Appended is Dolphin's diary record of "Monies Owed and Received," "Cash account," and "Bets won and Lost."

67. DOMSCHCKE, BERNHARD. *Twenty Months in Captivity: Memoirs of a Union Officer in Confederate Prisons.* Edited and translated by Frederic Trautmann. Teaneck, N.J.: Fairleigh Dickinson University Press, 1987. 175 pp.

1863–1865. Memoir. Captain. Twenty-sixth Wisconsin Infantry. Domschcke described the hard march to Gettysburg, his capture on July 1, the march back to Richmond, and imprisonment at several Confederate prisons. He was placed in Libby until May 1864 and then moved to Danville, en route to Macon's Camp Oglethorpe, where he remained until the end of July. The rest of the fall and winter he spent in prisons in Savannah, Charleston, Columbia's Camp Sorghum, Goldsboro, and Wilmington, where he was exchanged on February 28, 1865. Among his themes are observations of the American character, as well as how men behaved while in captivity. Domschcke, who was German-born and lived in Milwaukee, noted "some Americans' venom for Germans" (p. 42). Domschcke said that despite his many excellent qualities, the American "finds it hard to free himself of nativistic prejudices" and "He likes to sink his teeth of scorn into the 'Dutchman'" (p. 42). He also pointed to the American propensity to raise hell. At Libby, when all lights were extinguished, a racket spread throughout the prison. Domschcke concluded that "no doubt the American appetite for foolishness and love of mischief will create bedlam" (p. 48). But Domschcke also praised the American: "Gifted and sensitive, he makes much of every small advantage" (p. 108). The only Southerners whom Domschcke observed from prison were either of the aristocratic slaveholding class or the slovenly state militia who, he felt, had suffered from the results of the plantation system. Domschcke watched the different ways men reacted to captivity. At Libby he despised a group known as the "Royal Family," who "toadied favor" by their compliant association with guards and other authorities (p. 51). At Savannah, after having spent many months in captivity, Domschcke concluded that prison life simply "imitated the world at large" (p. 92). Some prisoners easily fell into groups, while others preferred seclusion. Each prisoner moved into "his narrow orbit of grouchy self-centeredness and, over time, had unlearned all concern and every sympathy for anybody else" (p. 93). First published as *Zwanzig monate in kriegs-gefangenschaft* (Milwaukee: W. W. Coleman, 1865).

68. DOWNEY, JOHN. "The Drummer Boy and the Ghost." Edited by Leland W. Thornton. *Michigan History* 75 (March/April 1991): 24–28.
August 1864. Memoir. Eleventh Michigan Infantry. Atlanta campaign. According to Downey, the apparition of his best friend appeared and led him to the spot where the friend and another Union soldier lay dead.

69. DUNN, ARLINGTON. "Civil War Letters of Arlington Dunn, 123rd Ohio Volunteer Infantry." Edited by Richard Manion. *Northwest Ohio Quarterly* 63 (Winter/Spring 1991): 17–25.
November 5, 1863–February 17, 1865. Letters. Private. 123rd Ohio Infantry. Duty in Martinsburg, West Virginia, with the provost marshal and quartermaster offices. His letters consist of camp routines involving his regiment and events in Martinsburg. Several companies of the 123rd Ohio guarded the B & O Railroad in small squads. During March 1864 he wrote that nonresidents, including merchants, were not allowed into Martinsburg. Also, federal authorities made residents of the city clean up their properties. Dunn blamed the high rate of inflation in the region on the Confederacy. The final letter was written from the Bermuda Hundred, where he reported that Confederate desertion was increasing.

70. EARLY, JACOB. *Letters Home: The Personal Side of the American Civil War.* Compiled and edited by Robert A. Driver and Gloria S. Driver. Rev. ed. Roseburg, Oreg.: Robert A. & Gloria S. Driver, 1993. 106 pp.
September 1, 1862–May 11, 1865. Letters. Ninety-ninth Ohio Infantry and Fiftieth Ohio Infantry. Duty in Kentucky and Tennessee (including Stones River, Chickamauga, the Chattanooga campaign, and Lookout Mountain); the Atlanta campaign; and duty in North Carolina. Jacob filled his letters to his wife, Sarah, with details about battles and his daily existence. Jacob described the stench and unhealthy conditions created by decaying animals and human remains that littered the ground near his Murfreesboro camp. He was fascinated with Nickajack Cave and wrote, "the bat shit is about two feet deep" and "It seems just like walking over a bed of sawdust" (p. 50A). Jacob probably heightened Sarah's concern for his safety when he told her that Union soldiers near Raleigh were found tied to trees "with there throats cut out and some cut in to quarters" (p. 102). Jacob repeatedly expressed concern for Sarah and

his young daughter. He praised his wife's management of the farm and supported her even when she opposed his wishes. On one occasion Jacob sought to protect his and the family's reputation. Jacob could have reenlisted and received a furlough; however, he decided against such action because it might have endangered his position of relative safety with the commissary corps. Jacob asked Sarah to keep his decision quiet, "for fear it might make a heap of talk" (p. 88). In his letters he seldom let Sarah know when he was in need of anything, except for the occasional box that contained "powders" for his diarrhea. Jacob refused to allow himself to become disconsolate. But in December 1863 he came close as he was lulled into daydreams about home. Suddenly his writing stopped short: "Hush, hush. I must not say anymore about it or els I will get homesick" (p. 48).

71. EDRINGTON, WILLIAM E. "True Glory." Introduction by Alan D. Gaff. *Blue & Gray Magazine* 7 (April 1990): 45.
October 12, 1863. Letter. Fifty-fourth Massachusetts Colored Infantry. In this letter a member of Company K recounts the disastrous assault on Battery Wagner on July 18, 1863. He also mentions the later Confederate evacuation of the battery.

72. EDWARDS, ABIAL HALL. *Dear Friend Anna: The Civil War Letters of a Common Soldier from Maine.* Edited by Beverly Hayes Kallgren and James L. Crouthamel. Orono: University of Maine Press, 1992. 161 pp.
November 16, 1861–June 30, 1866. Letters. Tenth Maine Infantry and Twenty-ninth Maine Infantry. Duty in Maryland and West Virginia guarding the B & O Railroad; Jackson's Shenandoah Valley campaign, including first Winchester; Cedar Mountain; Antietam, and Burnside's "Mud March." Discharged in May 1863, Edwards reenlisted in September and served in Banks's second Red River campaign; in Sheridan's Shenandoah campaign, including Cedar Creek; and in the Shenandoah Valley. After the war he served in the army of occupation in South Carolina. While Abial and Anna L. Conant had worked together at a textile mill in Lewiston, Maine, before the war, their relationship was nurtured solely through their letters during the war. In January 1863 he anticipated coming home after the expiration of his first term of enlistment. He wrote to her: "So I shall want your promise to remain *free* until then" (p. 44). However, the couple never met that summer, nor throughout the war. Abial wrote favorably about most of his generals but discerned that the reason McClellan was so well liked "by his army is because he was so kind to them not because he was a great general" (p. 39). Abial also related the white soldiers' begrudging acceptance of black soldiers. In Louisiana he wrote that although he thought the blacks would make good soldiers, "we still have gut that dislike which can not be overcome at once" (p. 79). In his next letter he wrote "our Regt. has come to the conclusion that they can and ought to fight as well as white folks but as for cheering them they cant do it" (p. 80). In South Carolina he did not feel the former slaves were ready for the vote because they would be too easily influenced by the "Southern gentlemen." After the war he expressed disappointment that the Johnson administration was giving away all that the soldiers had gained by issuing so many pardons. The editors' final chapter summarizes later letters and explains why the couple did not marry until 1869.

73. ELLIOTT, FRANCIS MARION. "'Dear Friends': The Civil War Letters of Francis Marion Elliott, a Pennsylvania Country Boy." Edited by Peter G. Boag. *Pittsburgh History* 72 (Holiday Issue 1989): 193–98.
August 10, 1862–March 17, 1864. Letters. Second Pennsylvania Cavalry. Virginia, including Pope's Virginia campaign, Reams' Station, and first Hatcher's Run. On one hand, Elliott questioned the excessive foraging ordered by General Pope in July 1862 because he wondered what the people of Virginia would eat during the coming winter. On the other hand, he also believed that, had the Union army pursued the same tactics earlier, the war would have been over. Among other topics was Elliott's opposi-

tion to serving with black soldiers. In 1864 he begged his parents and the folks at home to vote for McClellan if they cared for the soldiers. Several times Elliott said that he wanted to be "free from this hel of A war" (p. 194). After Reams' Station he remarked: "I am tired of Fighting in this unjust war" (p. 196). The editor adds that Elliott deserted shortly after August 1862. He was arrested in January 1864 but was apparently allowed to return to his regiment without punishment. Boag points out that, because these letters are written in an unschooled hand, they provide a sample of nineteenth-century southern Pennsylvania vernacular and speech patterns.

74. ENSMINGER, SAMUEL. *Letters to Lanah: A Series of Civil War Letters Written by Samuel Ensminger, a Drafted Union Soldier.* Compiled and edited by Clarence M. Swinn Jr. Gettysburg, Pa.: C. M. Swinn Jr., 1986. 73 pp.
November 11, 1862–July 29, 1863. Letters. Sergeant. Fifty-eighth Pennsylvania Infantry. Duty in Suffolk, Virginia, and New Bern, North Carolina; Dix's Peninsular campaign; and the pursuit of Lee after Gettysburg. Samuel described the countryside and camps, especially winter quarters at New Bern and the strangeness of the town. He said he liked the military and told his wife, Lanah, that if he were single he would stay in the army. He often gave her advice about tending the farm and instructed her to do the butchering herself if he could not get home to help. He also consented to her moving; however, he urged her to remember to take "allong feede troof henroost boards" and other similar farm items (p. 26). Samuel congratulated Lanah on the quality of one letter: "I am astonished at how well it was rote & spelt. If you rote it" (p. 16). Samuel sent Lanah a smallpox scab from his arm with these instructions: "You waxnate yourself & your childer with it" (p. 20). While Samuel wrote little about the war, during the pursuit of the Confederate army after Gettysburg he concluded: "I think old Lee is too sharp for our men" (p. 50). The editor has appended Ensminger's military records and summarized his subsequent life.

75. EWING, GEORGE HENRY, and JAMES M. EWING. *The Ewing Family Civil War Letters.* Edited by John T. Greene. East Lansing: Michigan State University Press, 1994. 239 pp.
September 7, 1862–December 17, 1865. Letters. George (Private, Twentieth Michigan Infantry) wrote to his parents and sister, Susan, between September 7, 1862, and November 13, 1863. He described duty in Virginia, including Fredericksburg; Maryland; Kentucky; the sieges of Vicksburg and Jackson; and duty in east Tennessee, including the Confederate siege of Knoxville. George's letters concern mention of troop movements; his need for supplies from home; news of the men from Stockbridge, Michigan; the effect of foraging on civilians in both Virginia and Kentucky; occasional incidents of fighting; and comments about affairs at home. Several letters from other soldiers describe how George was killed during the Confederate assault on Fort Sanders (Knoxville) on November 29, 1863. A cousin, James (Lieutenant, Twelfth Michigan Infantry), also corresponded with Susan between January 9, 1863, and December 17, 1865. His service consisted of duty in Tennessee; the siege of Vicksburg; and duty in Arkansas, especially at Duvall's Bluff, Little Rock, and Camden. James's letters, fewer than those written by George, contain comments about social occasions in Tennessee and Arkansas, the weather, reenlistment in a veteran volunteer unit, and, after the war, the wait to be mustered out.

76. FORBES, EUGENE. *Death Before Dishonor: The Andersonville Diary of Eugene Forbes, 4th New Jersey Infantry.* Edited by William B. Styple. Kearny, N.J.: Belle Grove Publishing Co., 1995. 215 pp.
May 1, 1864–February 5, 1865. Diary. Fourth New Jersey Infantry. This diary includes details of capture at The Wilderness and imprisonment at Andersonville (until September 11) and Florence Prisons. Forbes was not judgmental toward his Confederate captors, and he understood why fellow prisoners

took the oath of allegiance to the Confederacy. Writing from Andersonville, after recording that some sick men had been found who had not eaten in three days, Forbes explained: "The rebels are doing all in their power to alleviate these unfortunates and have ordered our internal police to seek out all such cases . . . over 400 extra rations were issued to the sick yesterday" (p. 120). Forbes also forgave the Union soldiers who became "galvanized" because he felt that they were hungry. He mentioned the villain of other accounts, Henry Wirz, only once. Even when Forbes blamed Abraham Lincoln for sticking to his refusal to exchange prisoners, he did so in a reserved manner. Forbes often mentioned the means by which prisoners punished other prisoners. The most prominent prosecutors of justice were members of the "prison court," who tried offenders, and the "regulators," who were responsible for hanging the raiders. On several occasions the "galvanized Yankees" had their possessions stolen by other prisoners as punishment. In one instance the white prisoners supported a group of captured black soldiers when the "galvanized Yankees" had seized the black soldiers' possessions. Beginning with entries written in November, Forbes's diary is a chronicle of his personal decline. His writings gradually became shorter and increasingly ominous as the harsh winter and inadequate rations took their toll on his health. Forbes, who often wrote with a touch of humor, evinced lightheartedness for the final time on January 15, 1865, when a friend gave him a "huge plate of beans and dumplings, which astonished my 'innards' considerably" (p. 162). On February 1 he wrote: "No improvement in our condition—terrible coughs and cramps in the bowels. . . . Drew meal, salt and beans" (p. 164). Entries for February 3 through February 5 are repetitive: "No better. Same rations" (p. 164). On February 7, 1865, Forbes died. This work also includes two earlier letters written by Forbes, and several other accounts by members of the Fourth New Jersey are appended. Originally published in limited numbers as a sixty-eight-page pamphlet: *Diary of a Soldier and Prisoner of War in the Rebel Prisons*. Trenton, N.J.: Murphy & Bechtel, 1865.

77.   FORDYCE, BENJAMIN ALLEN. *Echoes from the Letters of a Civil War Surgeon.* Edited by Lydia P. Hecht. Longboat Key, Fla.: Bayou Publishing, 1996. 287 pp.

July 7, 1863–January 15, 1865. Letters. Surgeon. 160th New York Infantry. Louisiana, including second Red River campaign (he was captured April 9, 1864, at Pleasant Hill while treating the wounded and was released on June 19) and Sheridan's Shenandoah Valley campaign (including third Winchester and Cedar Creek). This forty-year-old surgeon departed Venice Township (New York), leaving behind a wife (Emeline), two daughters, and a young son. The couple maintained a positive attitude about their circumstances throughout the war. Benjamin offered his wife advice about farm matters and medical care of the children. Emeline kept Benjamin informed about the children and their home. Only once did Benjamin chastise Emeline for being despondent, and he did so then because it made him miss home. The letters of the two precocious daughters (ten and twelve years of age in 1863) are mostly chats about a home life with a mischievous young brother and without their father. Benjamin occasionally lashed out against supporters of slavery and Copperheads, but he expressed most of his feelings more casually. While en route to Louisiana, Benjamin wrote of touring the newly opened New York Central Park and seeing the New York City draft riots firsthand. From Louisiana he commented on such topics as fertile soil. And he noted that huge profits were being made on cotton, especially from the plantations operated by the federal government. Benjamin repeatedly asserted that the slaves would be able to take care of themselves after they attained their freedom. In Virginia, Benjamin was placed in charge of the XIX Army Corps Hospital at Winchester. Benjamin recognized that the war was expanding his medical knowledge, and he modestly mentioned his proficiency in the art of amputation. Benjamin's account of the battle of Pleasant Hill and his ten-week captivity is contained in a speech that he delivered on Decoration Day of 1886. Also included is Benjamin's report of an amputation close to a soldier's shoulder, which merited inclusion in *The Medical and Surgical History of the Civil War*.

78. **FORRY, MICHAEL.** "'Enough to Make a Preacher Sware': A Union Mule Driver's Diary of Sherman's March." Edited by W. R. Johnson. *Atlanta History* 33 (Fall 1989): 20–36.

May 1–December 31, 1864. Diary. Sixty-sixth Ohio Infantry. Atlanta campaign and March to the Sea. Forry detailed the back-breaking work involved in driving heavy wagons and testy mules across difficult terrain. The weather was always either too hot and dusty or too cold. The drivers were constantly packing and unpacking wagons and caring for their animals. Although Forry was not at the front, he could hear the sounds of battles and see the wounded being transported to the rear. While his diary documents Sherman's relentless drive to capture Atlanta and Savannah, Forry did not record the surrender of Atlanta. Even when the city was being burned, he wrote only: "City on Fire" (p. 33). He described the Confederate evacuation of Savannah in slightly more detail.

79. **FREY, EMIL.** *An American Apprenticeship: The Letters of Emil Frey, 1860–1865.* Edited and translated by Hedwig Rappolt. Afterword by Hans Rudolf Guggisberg. New York: Peter Lang, 1986. 227 pp.

November 8, 1860–July 7, 1865. Letters and memoir. Lieutenant, Twenty-fourth Illinois Infantry; then Captain, Eighty-second Illinois Infantry. Duty in Missouri, Kentucky, and Tennessee, including Mitchel's expedition to Huntsville and Decatur, Alabama. Frey was captured at Gettysburg and incarcerated in Libby Prison. Writing in 1894, Frey gave three reasons for joining the Union army after arriving in America from Switzerland in 1860. He said that he came from a long line of soldiers; he wished to preserve the Union and the universal cause of liberty; and he wanted to abolish slavery. However, in his letters of the 1860s he was less idealistic, indicating his desire for more money than he was earning as a farmhand in Highland, Illinois (Madison County). In his letters the war seems to have been the irritating backdrop of a young man's struggle to find his niche in life. Frey wrote bluntly: "I am sick and tired of the war . . . no blindly self-destructive patriotism for America exists inside me" (p. 122). Frey was contemptuous of Northern leaders. He wrote: "Lincoln is a dunderhead and a traitor; his wife governs, and his wife is a Secessionist by kinship" (p. 99). He rated William Seward and Henry Halleck no higher but praised John C. Fremont and Franz Siegel. He had little to say about the common soldiers; one exception was: "We don't get along so well with our Irish and Yankee colleagues" (p. 94). Frey wrote loving letters to his family back in Switzerland and wanted to return home when he resigned from the army in June 1862, but his father apparently dissuaded him. In August 1862 he raised a company for the Eighty-second Illinois and received a captaincy. At that time Frey's mood seems to have changed, and he felt responsible for the company of men he had recruited. Frey wrote few letters while in prison between July 1863 and January 14, 1865. Frey returned to Switzerland soon after the war and later became his nation's president. His memoir, "My American Experiences, by the President of the Swiss Republic," is appended.

80. **FREYBURGER, MICHAEL.** *Gold Rush & Civil War Letters to Ann from Michael Freyburger.* Shelbyville, Ill.: Shelby Co. Historical and Genealogical Society, 1986. 79 pp.

October 1, 1861–August 1865. Letters. Lieutenant. Seventh Illinois Cavalry. Induction and training at Camp Butler; the siege and battle of Corinth; Grierson's raid; the siege of Port Hudson; and the battle of Nashville. Freyburger's letters to his wife offer constant encouragement but no expressions of love. He addressed their absence once with: "You can write such good love letters, but I am sorry to say that I am a bit hard at it" (p. 27). His letters are filled with requests for clothing, reports of the weather, brief mention of fighting, information about the health of his horses, a description of an execution, information on the men from home, and advice on how to run the farm. On several occasions he commented on slaves and the performance of the black soldiers. Freyburger favored the Emancipation Proclamation on the grounds that, if any slaves were set free, the need for manpower on the Southern home front would be increased. The black soldiers' stubborn resistance in the siege of Port Hudson convinced him that "The problem of whether the Negroes will fight or not has been solved" (p. 47). After an unidentified battle in northwest Mississippi during the late summer of 1864, he commented again about the black soldiers: "We did not take many prisoners. The Negroes remembered 'Fort Pillow'" (p. 65).

81. **FURST, LUTHER C.** "A Signal Sergeant at Gettysburg: The Diary of Luther C. Furst." *Gettysburg Magazine* 10 (January 1994): 42–52.
June 12–July 14, 1863. Diary. Sergeant. VI Corps, Army of the Potomac. Gettysburg campaign, including the battle of Gettysburg and the pursuit of Lee. While Furst was critical of Meade for not engaging Lee before the Confederate army could return across the Potomac, he also recorded that Union soldiers were fatigued and short of clothing and food, and that their horses were dying by the hundreds.

82. **GANGEWER, HENRY WILLIAM.** "'And Three Rousing Cheers for the Privates': A Diary of the 1862 Roanoke Island Expedition." Edited by Mary Seaton Dix. *North Carolina Historical Review* 71 (January 1994): 62–84.
November 23, 1861–April 7, 1862. Diary. Private. Fifty-first Pennsylvania Infantry. Burnside's expedition to North Carolina. Gangewer's entries begin with the long voyage from Annapolis to Hatteras Inlet and then to Pamlico Sound. On the voyage the men suffered privation of food and water and were buffeted by gales. After the fighting Gangewer commented on the results: "Horrid, Horrid war" (p. 75). He wrote of the truce that allowed the Confederates to retrieve their dead and how he and other Union soldiers gathered battlefield relics. Gangewer described the amphibious attack on New Bern, and although he continued to record events of the expedition, he was removed from duty as a result of an accidental injury.

83. **GANTZ, JACOB.** *Such Are the Trials: The Civil War Diaries of Jacob Gantz.* Edited by Kathleen Davis. Ames: Iowa State University Press, 1991. 122 pp.
March 12, 1863–April 1, 1865. Diary. Fourth Iowa Cavalry. Vicksburg campaign; duty in Mississippi (including Brice's Cross Roads, A. J. Smith's expedition to Tupelo, and the battle of Tupelo); Price's Missouri raid (including Mine Creek); and duty in northwestern Alabama. Gantz recorded few details of the fighting, but he noted the dangers of picket duty and foraging. Because he was a cook, he frequently drew large amounts of rations and baked many loaves of bread and pies in preparation for a march. During one march he ground the corn that was intended for the horses into meal and baked corn bread for the hungry soldiers. Gantz often mentioned the health and serviceability of the horses. During one expedition forty mounts died. Gantz explained, "the nats killed them" (p. 21). During the pursuit of Price in November 1864, Gantz recorded that "this month we marched 607 miles, we then started on" (p. 77). The editor adds that the Fourth Iowa Cavalry logged 1,952 miles between September and December 1864 and wore out two sets of horses. But soldiers, as well as horses, suffered from overexertion. While chasing Forrest in Mississippi, Gantz made the notation: "found one of our men dead at noon laying by the fence. He had been marched so hard that he fell over dead" (p. 69). Most of Gantz's entries concern routine activities: writing letters to his wife, washing clothes, attending church, and keeping an account of his health, for example. Several camp accidents are mentioned without comment. One man "shot himself through the hand axidently while fishing" (p. 21). Another man "shot himself steeling. He tried to open a truck with his revolver & it went off and shot him through" (p. 72).

84. GARFIELD, JAMES A., and LUCRETIA R. GARFIELD. *Crete and James: Personal Letters of Lucretia and James Garfield.* Edited by John Shaw. East Lansing: Michigan State University Press, 1994. 397 pp.

August 22, 1861–December 13, 1863. The complete collection of letters in this work runs between November 16, 1853, and June 30, 1881, from the beginning of the couple's five-year courtship to a few days before President Garfield was fatally shot. The editor has selected these letters to "tell a story of a marriage" (preface). Thus, domestic matters, not military, or public affairs, are the predominate themes. During the Civil War period (pp. 118–98) Garfield rose from colonel (Forty-second Ohio Infantry) to major general (Eighteenth and Twentieth Brigades, Sixth Division, Army of the Ohio). He was elected to the U.S. House of Representatives in 1863, resigned from the army, and took up residence in Washington in December 1863. Although his letters do not contain descriptions of military events, Garfield comments on his duty in eastern Kentucky against Gen. Humphrey Marshall; at Shiloh (he was not involved) and in the beginning of the siege of Corinth; and in northern Alabama, where he sat on the court-martial of Gen. Basil Turchin. The debilitating effect of bloody piles and dysentery caused him to take a sick leave during the late summer of 1862. He resumed duty in Washington as General Rosecrans's chief of staff and served on the court-martial of Gen. Fitz John Porter. He was sent to Tennessee in spring 1863 and later mentioned the fighting around Chattanooga. Lucretia ("Crete"), who wrote primarily from Hiram, Ohio, related news about their young daughter, "Trot" (Eliz), and how much she missed James. One example of the ebbs and flows of the Garfield relationship concerns James's affairs with other women. The couple, with their daughter, had enjoyed the period in 1862 when James was back in Ohio regaining his health. James called their time together a "baptism into a new life"; he said that, as he wrote, his pen was "in the hand of my heart" (pp. 157–58). Throughout that fall Lucretia responded with words in kind. Late in 1862 the couple was separated while James was posted in Washington. During that time he insisted on seeing a lady friend who had previously been the reason for discord. The letters reveal how the Garfields discussed the problem and that they smoothed it over for the time being. But the letters from 1864, written while James was serving in the United States Congress, treat another incident of James's infidelity, which again was followed by Lucretia's forgiveness.

85. GATES, THEODORE B. *The Civil War Diaries of Col. Theodore B. Gates, 20th New York State Militia.* Edited by Seward R. Osborne. Highstreet, N.J.: Longstreet House, 1991. 179 pp.

December 15, 1861–December 30, 1864. Diary. Colonel. Eightieth New York Infantry. Defenses of Washington; duty in northern Virginia; Beverly Ford; second Bull Run; Chantilly; South Mountain; Antietam; Gettysburg; provost duty, including transportation of Confederate prisoners from Gettysburg and later those taken during Grant's Virginia campaign; and commandant of City Point. Gates's terse journal entries record little of the regiment's activities and almost nothing of his reactions to his experiences. Even when he lost a congressional bid in November 1864 he simply reported that he attended the election. Following Fredericksburg he expressed his frustration over the way the Army of the Potomac was being used and believed that the Emancipation Proclamation would be effective in wiping out slavery. Gates often refers to visits to Washington, New York City, and home and mentions meeting prominent individuals. In his preface the editor explains that the men of the Twentieth New York State Militia preferred to be known by that designation rather than the unit's state designation, the Eightieth New York Volunteer Regiment, because their unit predated the war.

86. GEARY, JOHN WHITE. *A Politician Goes to War: The Civil War Letters of John White Geary.* Edited by William Alan Blair. Selections and introduction by Bell Irvin Wiley. University Park: Pennsylvania State University Press, 1995. 259 pp.

July 30, 1861–April 29, 1865. Letters. Colonel, Twenty-eighth Pennsylvania Infantry, and Brigadier General (then Brevet Major General), Second Division, XII Corps, Army of the Potomac and Army of the Cumberland and XX Corps, Army of the Cumberland. Duty along the Potomac, including Bolivar Heights, where he was wounded; duty in northern Virginia guarding the Manassas Gap Railroad; Gettysburg; Wauhatchie Station; Lookout Mountain; Missionary Ridge; the pursuit of Bragg to Ringgold, Georgia; the Atlanta campaign, including Rocky Face Ridge, Resaca, and Peachtree Creek; the March to the Sea; and the Carolinas campaign. In letters to his wife, Mary, who spent most of the war in Philadelphia and New Cumberland, Pennsylvania, Geary wrote in glowing terms about military successes against overwhelming odds, often implying that his actions were the reasons for victory. However, the editor, in his introductions and footnotes, regards many of Geary's claims as exaggerations or partial presentations of facts. The battles on the second day at Gettysburg, at Lookout Mountain, and at Peachtree Creek serve as examples. In the editor's opinion, Geary was a mediocre to competent military strategist. When he was promoted to major general in February 1865, Geary considered the honor overdue by two years. However, Geary was recognized by superiors as a good administrator, an evaluation that led to his appointment in administrative positions at the cities of Murfreesboro, Atlanta, and Savannah. Geary's love for his wife and constant desire to be kept informed about his children are persistent themes in his letters. Two sons served with him for a time during the war. When his son Eddie, a lieutenant in Knap's Battery, was killed at Wauhatchie Station, Geary was devastated. His letters written over a period of months mention Eddie's death. Geary trusted Mary's abilities to collect rents and purchase a new house. Throughout his letters Geary expresses contempt for the common people of the South. In Virginia, Tennessee, Alabama, and South Carolina he referred to Southerners as "ignorant" or "slovenly," conditions he blamed on the "vile curse of slavery." Geary made few references to the slaves. After the war Geary utilized his skills at self-promotion to switch from being a war Democrat to obtain election as the Republican governor of Pennsylvania between 1867 and 1873. He died in 1873.

87. GODFREY, JOHN FRANKLIN. *The Civil War Letters of Capt. John Franklin Godfrey.* South Portland, Maine: Ascensius Press, 1993. 90 pp.

March 18, 1862–April 23, 1864. Letters. Lieutenant, Maine Light Artillery, First Battery; then Captain, First Louisiana Cavalry, Company C. Duty in Louisiana, including Godfrey Weitzel's operations in the La Fourche District, the siege of Port Hudson, and duty in the La Fourche District. In Godfrey's first letter to his parents he summarizes his recruiting duty in Maine and shipment to Louisiana, where he recruited a cavalry company composed of mixed nationalities. In Louisiana, Godfrey's spirits remained high until Benjamin Butler was replaced by Nathaniel Banks. Godfrey praised Butler for instilling a spirit of mutual trust. He said that under Butler the soldiers felt that they were fighting for a cause. Godfrey initially believed that Banks was too conciliatory toward the civilians of Louisiana; later, however, he commended Banks's willingness to take the advice of others. Godfrey pondered the reasons why Americans found it difficult to develop a great military commander like Napoleon. While he felt that Butler was the best leader of the war, Godfrey conceded that the animosity toward the general precluded such recognition. Godfrey lamented that the freed slaves' happiness was only temporary: "those whom they now looked upon as deliverers, were men more or less like those they had left and they like many before them were only to exchange masters" (p. 33). Letters written between July 4, 1863, and April 23, 1864, are not included. Godfrey's final letters mention an illness and a surgeon's suggestion that he resign from the service. In his final letters, which were written after he had returned to civilian life, Godfrey is convinced that he had served his country well.

88. GOODE, PHILIP H. "'My Dear Wife': A Soldier's Letters." Transcribed by Edward W. Vollertsen. *Palimpsest* 72 (Summer 1991): 68–69.

April 12, 1862–December 24, 1864. Letters. Lieutenant. Fifteenth Iowa Infantry. Shiloh. Goode arrived at Pittsburg Landing on April 6, 1862, at 4:30 A.M., just a few hours before the Confederate attack. He was proud of his bravery under fire, especially because he was wounded and had two fingers amputated. Goode resigned from service with the Fifteenth Iowa in May 1862, but a final letter indicates that he was serving with the Fourth Iowa Battery in 1864.

89. GOODE, PHILIP H. "'A Pretty Hard Business': The Civil War Diary of Philip H. Goode." Transcribed by Edward W. Vollertsen. *Palimpsest* 72 (Summer 1991): 51–67.
March 15–May 22, 1862. Diary. Lieutenant. Fifteenth Iowa Infantry. Goode wrote of being transported down the Mississippi and his duty in Tennessee, including the battle of Shiloh.

90. GOODING, JAMES HENRY. *On the Altar of Freedom: A Black Soldier's Civil War Letters from the Front, Corporal James Henry Gooding.* Edited by Virginia M. Adams. Foreword by James M. McPherson. Amherst: University of Massachusetts Press, 1991. 139 pp.
March 3, 1863–February 22, 1864. Letters. Corporal. Fifty-fourth Massachusetts Colored Infantry. Organization and training at Camp Meigs; and duty in South Carolina, Georgia, and Florida, including the burning of Darien, Georgia, the siege of Charleston, battle on James Island (July 16, 1863), the assault of Battery Wagner, and the Olustee campaign. Gooding, a free black and former sailor, wrote these forty-eight letters to his hometown newspaper, the abolitionist *New Bedford (Mass.) Mercury*. In his first several letters, as he was promoting recruitment for the Fifty-fourth, Gooding emphasized that everyone needed to be aware that blacks were willing to fight for their freedom. If the institution of slavery were to die without the help of black soldiers, Gooding feared that "language cannot depict the indignity, the scorn, and perhaps violence, that will be heaped upon us" (p. 13). Near the end of his letters, when he observed that the Sea Island slaves had taken care of themselves after "Massa" had left, Gooding was more specific about how freed slaves could contribute to society. Gooding assured his readers that former slaves would be good for the economy, both as workers in the "looms of New England" and as purchasers of goods and products. Gooding's stance on the inequity of pay for black soldiers is enunciated in a letter to President Lincoln that is appended by the editor. Writing on September 28, 1863, Gooding forcefully attacked the crux of the problem of pay: "Now the main question is, Are we *Soldiers,* or are we *Labourers?*" (p. 119). Gooding usually related the activities of the Fifty-fourth in relation to the broader context of the war. He was totally without remorse after the Fifty-fourth was ordered to raze Darien, Georgia, and even mocked the Confederate press when it criticized the action. He wrote about the assault of Battery Wagner in detail, and when he learned that Colonel Shaw had been buried in a trench with his men, without respect for his rank, Gooding was outraged. On August 16, 1863, Gooding penned a well-balanced appraisal of Shaw's personality, including the high esteem in which the regiment held him, and evaluated Shaw's contributions to the Fifty-fourth. In November 1864, after suggesting that Fort Sumter might be retaken by dowsing it with oil and setting it ablaze, Gooding rationalized that "War is nothing but barbarism at the best, and those who can excel in that, to put an end to a longer train of barbarisms, are in the end the most humane of the two" (p. 82). Gooding seldom revealed his intimate feelings, except that he was proud to be contributing to the conflict. Captured at Olustee, Gooding was sent to Andersonville Prison, where he died on July 18, 1864. The editor has appended several of the poems that Gooding wrote while he was a sailor.

91. GOODWIN, FAIRFIELD. "Doubly Paid for Any Sacrifice." Edited by Ann Gebhard. *Michigan History* 74 (March/April 1990): 10–16.
October 15, 1861–May 1862. Diary. First Illinois Light Artillery, Battery I. Pea Ridge and Shiloh. In April 1861 Goodwin was among a group of men in a unit known as "Wilson's Mechanic Fusiliers" who enlisted under the impression that they would serve as a special regiment of mechanics and would

receive more pay than regular enlisted men. The unit assembled in Chicago and waited until February 1862 for official recognition, which never materialized. Goodwin wrote that the captain "Told how he had worked for us but he lied like hell" (p. 14). The men, believing that the army had duped them, rebelled in the midst of an unusually cold winter. Some were arrested because they refused to drill. All of the men wanted to leave the service, but they hesitated because they received conflicting assessments about how being mustered out would reflect on their military futures. Throughout the whole ordeal Goodwin remained good-natured, writing and singing to pass the time.

92. **GORDON, EDWIN A.** *The Civil War Diary of Capt. Edwin A. Gordon, 57th Ohio V.V.I., 1865.* Transcribed by Paula Cash. Upper Sandusky, Ohio: Wyandot County Historical Society, 1988. 42 leaves.
January 1–December 26, 1865. Diary. Fifty-seventh Ohio Infantry and Thirty-fifth New Jersey Infantry. Gordon's first entries were written in a Cleveland hospital while he was recovering from a wound received near Atlanta. At the end of January he returned to duty at Pocotaligo, South Carolina. As acting adjutant general with the Thirty-fifth New Jersey, he was assigned to administer the oath of allegiance to Southerners. In one entry he alludes to having to officiate at a "rank mutiny." Apparently a soldier from the Twentieth Ohio was tied up by his thumbs for stealing. When friends attempted to rescue him, one soldier was killed and twenty-two others were held up on charges. Just as the war was ending, Gordon rejoined his old regiment near Raleigh. The unit marched to Richmond, then on to Washington for the Grand Review. From Washington he traveled by train and boat to Little Rock, Arkansas, where he was discharged on August 14; he then returned home to Ohio. The fragmented sentences conceal much of what Gordon experienced.

93. **GOSSETT, JOSEPH B.** "A Letter from the Front: Vicksburg, 1863." By Erich L. Ewald. *Indiana Magazine of History* 91 (September 1995): 321–25.
June 6, 1863. Letter. Eighth Indiana Infantry. Vicksburg campaign, including Champion Hill, Big Black River, and the assault of May 22. Gossett summarizes recent battles and predicts a quick end to the siege.

94. **GRAHAM, JAMES E.** "'Had a Pleasant Time': Excerpts from the Diary of a Yankee in Dixie." Edited by Albert Castel. *Blue & Gray Magazine* 3 (February/March 1986): 32–37.
July 4, 1863–April 24, 1865. Diary. Eightieth Ohio Infantry. Sherman's March to the Sea.

95. **GREENE, J. HARVEY.** *Letters to My Wife: A Civil War Diary to My Wife.* Compiled by Sharon L. D. Kraynek. Apollo, Pa.: Closson Press, 1995. 105 pp.
September 10, 1861–September 1865. Letters. Captain. Eighth Wisconsin Infantry. Enlistment and organization at Camp Randall; duty in Missouri, including the battle of Fredericktown; the siege of Island No. 10; the siege of Corinth; Farmington; Iuka; Corinth; duty in Mississippi and Tennessee; duty at Young's Point; the siege of Vicksburg; the second Red River campaign, including Pleasant Hill; and Old River Lake. Greene wrote several revealing passages about how men behaved in battle. At Farmington, after a canister shot passed through his blouse and "something else" knocked him down, he wrote: "I am satisfied—my curiosity to be in a battle I think will never trouble me again" (p. 23). Many battles later his experiences led him to believe that every soldier expected to be shot, although few actually were. "Still, away down in every soldier's heart there is a sneaking hope that he may be wounded so as to have an 'honorable scar' for his service" (p. 82). He wrote about blacks in several circumstances. In Missouri the soldiers tried to protect the runaway slaves against their owners. He described

the "white slaves" (mulattos) in Mississippi. And when he observed that many soldiers sought promotions by joining the new black regiments, Greene concluded that the whole brigade had "nigger on the brain" (p. 60). Greene approved of the black regiments, although he described them in a condescending manner. Greene also addressed numerous other battles, topics, and activities. He often commented on the antics of "Old Abe," the eagle that was the regimental mascot. He related the homesickness that occurred during times of idleness; his annoyance that the drum corps was going crazy over "a new piece of secesh music ["Bonnie Blue Flag"], and they beat it to death" (pp. 48–49); being ordered to burn Southern properties at Jackson, Mississippi; and the peculiarities in people and vegetation that he observed everywhere he traveled. Following his reenlistment and furlough in the summer of 1864, Greene briefly summarized the final year of the regiment's service at such places as the battle of Nashville and during the Mobile campaign.

96. **GREENE, WILLIAM B.** *Letters from a Sharpshooter: The Civil War Letters of Private William B. Greene, Co. G., 2nd United States Sharpshooters (Berdan's), Army of the Potomac, 1861–1865.* Transcribed by William H. Hastings. Belleville, Wis.: Historic Publications, 1993. 329 pp.

December 7, 1861–March 31, 1865. Letters and journal. Private. Second U.S. Sharpshooters. Duty at Camp Instruction; Virginia, including The Wilderness; Spotsylvania; the siege of Petersburg; and stays in various hospitals around Washington. Greene's letters to and from his mother, as well as a brother and other friends, focus more on his efforts to obtain a discharge from the army than on the unique aspects of being a sharpshooter. In his initial letters he reveals how the volunteers were disgruntled because they were not issued the new model Sharps rifles right away. Greene always had a plan to get a discharge, if he "played his cards right," as he wrote on several occasions. He managed to leave the army between fall 1862 and December 1863. Greene was arrested in Wisconsin, but he received only minimal punishment because of an administrative technicality involving his medical records. With pride he wrote: "I had play so shrewd a game that they could not prove any thing against me" (p. 172). His widowed mother worried about her son. When Greene was arrested and sent back to the army, she was outraged at the person who had reported him to military authorities. Greene's letters (and memorandum book), written during the summer of 1864, are informative. He was a good soldier during the siege of Petersburg, where he related details from the trenches and fraternization with a Confederate soldier. From November 1864 until the end of the war he was in Lincoln General Hospital (Washington, D.C.). In late March 1865 he received a furlough for "emaciation consequent to Typhoid Fever," and he never returned to the army. The editor has added a sketch of Greene's later years in Kansas and Civil War illustrations that are pertinent to Greene's career.

97. **GRIFFIN, DAVID BRAINARD.** *Letters Home to Minnesota: 2nd Minnesota Vol.* Compiled by Joan W. Albertson. Spokane, Wash.: P. D. Enterprises, 1992. 1 vol. (unpaged).

September 30, 1861–September 11, 1863. Letters. Corporal. Second Minnesota Infantry. Organization and training at Fort Snelling; duty in Kentucky, including the battle of Logan's Cross Roads, pursuit of Bragg, and Perryville; the siege of Corinth; and duty in Tennessee, including the Tullahoma campaign. Writing on April 28, 1862, David set the tone for his correspondence. He told his wife, Nerva, that "fretting" only made a man and everyone around him miserable. He implored her to consider this period as a dark time in her life and to try to put up with it. He constantly offered her such advice as when to have barrels made, when to cut the hay, when to plow, and when to pay bills and taxes, but he also expressed confidence in his wife's ability to handle these problems. He told her that she performed "first rate" (letter no. 9). To David these matters were insignificant compared to his love for her. He assured Nerva that every living thing on the farm could die if only she and the two children were well. Nerva must have supported him in a similar manner because he said that her letters brought tears to his eyes and that he shared her letters with the other men. David provided Nerva with many details about his style of living and the food. He told her how he needed large quantities of coffee and that his head would ache when he could not get it. David liked the blacks he met, even though he depicted their physical characteristics in unflattering terms. Once he boasted that he had learned to "talk niger" (letter no. 51). David knew that the situation for the former slaves after the war looked bleak, but his only solution was that they should be removed from the United States. He wrote: "this country was made for the white men to till and every man to be his own master" (letter no. 82). Griffin was killed on the first day of Chickamauga. Several descriptive letters from friends and officers are included.

98. **HACK, LESTER G.** ". . . This Thing Will Never Be Settled. . . ." By James E. Peterson. *Vermont History News* 40 (March/April 1989): 40–42.
December 17, 1862. Letter. Sergeant. Fifth Vermont Infantry. Battle of Fredericksburg. Hack arrived at the conclusion quoted in this title as a result of conversations with Confederate soldiers along the skirmish line following Fredericksburg.

99. **HALL, EDWIN C.** "A Brookfield Soldier's Report: The Civil War Recollections of Edwin C. Hall." Edited by Norbert A. Kuntz. *Vermont History* 57 (Fall 1989): 197–225.
December 1863–May 1865. Memoir. Tenth Vermont Infantry. The Virginia campaign, including The Wilderness, Spotsylvania, Cold Harbor, and the siege of Petersburg. Among this foot soldier's recollections was the expedition to Danville following the Confederate surrender at Appomattox.

100. **HALSEY, THOMAS J.** *Field of Battle: The Civil War Letters of Major Thomas J. Halsey.* By K. M. Kostyal. Washington: Book Division, National Geographic Society, 1966. 156 pp.
August 28, 1862–June 4, 1865. Letters. Major. Eleventh New Jersey Infantry. Defenses of Washington; Fredericksburg; Burnside's "Mud March"; Kelly's Ford; Payne's Farm; The Wilderness; Cold Harbor; and the assaults of Petersburg (June 15–18, 1864). Halsey was captured on July 22, 1864, imprisoned at Camp Sorghum, and exchanged in March 1864. This work combines brief excerpts from Halsey's letters to his wife and five children with text and illustrations on the Civil War in general. Passages from Halsey's letters demonstrate the spectrum of soldiers' concerns: his love for his family and consideration of matters dealing with the farm; camp life; arresting a drunken soldier and burying another; a hard winter march, the purpose of which remained a mystery to Halsey; illnesses, primarily diarrhea; a review by President Lincoln; and attendance at religious and temperance meetings. Halsey wrote one letter to his son explaining what he expected of him as a man. Also included is a letter from his wife, Sarah, in which she comments on conditions on their farm in Monroe County, New Jersey. Halsey never wavered in his support of the preservation of the Union or in his opposition to Copperheads. His descriptions of battles are brief.

101. **HAMMOND, JOHN.** "A Civil War Letter." By William Moore Peterson. *Vermont History News* 44 (May/June 1993): 38–42.
July 17, 1863–April 23, 1864. Letters. Brigadier General. Fifth New York Cavalry. In the first letter Hammond expresses his frustration over the Union army's less-than-aggressive pursuit of the Army of Northern Virginia following Gettysburg. Hammond's regiment had just captured Hagerstown, Maryland, and was awaiting Meade's arrival. In the second letter Hammond expresses regret at the loss of veteran cavalrymen with the approach of the spring Virginia campaign.

102. HAND, GEORGE. *The War in Apacheland: Sergeant George Hand's Diary, California, Arizona, West Texas, New Mexico, 1861–1864.* Edited by Neil B. Carmony. Silver City, N.M.: High-Lonesome Books, 1996. 215 pp.
August 19, 1861–October 3, 1864. Diary. Sergeant. First California Infantry, Company G. Hand recorded duty with the "California Column," which was recruited to discourage an invasion by the Confederate army but instead fought the desert, each other, and the Indians. The initial march was from Fort Yuma to Tucson across the heat and deep sand of the Sonoran Desert. A later trek was from Tucson to the Rio Grande. The soldiers were always alert for Apache raids, especially during the march to west Texas. Disciplining and punishing unruly men occurred almost daily. Hand described the terrain, wildlife, Mexican and Indian populations, and such places as Fort Yuma, Tucson, the mission of San Xavier del Bac, and El Paso. Hand wrote in an interesting manner and utilized anecdotes of daily camp life, thus concealing many of the hardships of his service. The editor has expanded on Hand's entries and included information about his subsequent life and other writings about the Southwest.

103. HARRIS, JOSEPH K. "A Soldier's Narrative: I Escaped from Andersonville Prison." *Civil War Times Illustrated* 27 (May 1988): 36–41.
February 20–October 16, 1864. Corporal. Seventh New Hampshire Infantry. Harris describes his capture during the battle of Olustee, life at Andersonville, and his escape following the capture of Atlanta.

104. HARRIS, LOYD G. "With the Iron Brigade at Gettysburg." Edited by Lance J. Herdegen and William J. K. Beaudot. *Gettysburg Magazine* 1 (July 1989): 29–34.
July 1–3, 1863. Lieutenant. Sixth Wisconsin Infantry. Battle of Gettysburg.

105. HARTER, FREDERICK ADOLPH. "'Those Exciting Times': A Soldier from the Eighth Illinois Cavalry Regiment Recalls His Experiences While Camped Outside of Washington, D.C., During the Civil War." Translated by Frederic Trautmann. *Chicago History* 16 (Spring 1987): 38–50.
September 1861–March 1862. Memoir. Eighth Illinois Cavalry. Harter recalled the flush of patriotism at the beginning of the war and the mobilization of civilians at Camp Kane from a variety of civilian occupations. At the ceremony honoring the soldiers, a flag made by the local ladies tore when unfurled. A cannon was fired, but it burst. Eventually the men were issued horses and departed for Washington via Chicago and Pittsburgh. Harter wrote that in October 1861 the capital appeared to be a sea of tents. The men busied themselves learning to cook and ride, but the repetition of drilling and caring for the horses soon became boring. In December the large army moved to Alexandria. Harter noticed that the Virginia city was quiet and old, very different from the newer western cities he had seen. Sectional tensions peaked when some citizens of Alexandria criticized the Union soldiers and pro-Union civilians responded by burning the offices of the local newspaper. The pastor of the Episcopal church was temporarily arrested for encouraging the Confederacy, which Harter thought was appropriate because "he had used the pulpit for vulgar political ends and downright treason" (p. 50). This is a translated chapter from *Erinnerungen aus dem Amerikanischen Bürgerkrieg . . .* (Chicago: F. A. Harter, 1895).

106. HASKELL, FRANK ARETAS. "A Union Officer at Gettysburg." *American History Illustrated* 23 (Summer 1988): 12–21, 46–48.
July 3, 1863. Lieutenant. Second Division, II Corps, Army of the Potomac. A member of Brig. Gen. John Gibbon's staff recounts Pickett's Charge.

107. HAWKINS, ISAAC R. "West Tennessee Unionists in the Civil War: A Hawkins Family Letter." By Charles L. Lufkin. *Tennessee Historical Quarterly* 46 (Spring 1987): 33–42.

October 11, 1864. Letter. Colonel. Seventh Tennessee Cavalry (U.S.). Hawkins first reveals the reasons why he favored Lincoln in the upcoming presidential election. Then he denies the charge that he surrendered his cavalry regiment at Union City to Forrest's troops on March 24, 1864, because of "pure cowardice" (p. 34). Hawkins concludes with a description of his brief imprisonment by the Confederates.

108. HAYDON, CHARLES B. *For Country, Cause & Leader: The Civil War Journal of Charles B Haydon.* Edited by Stephen W. Sears. New York: Ticknor & Fields, 1993. 371 pp.

April 21, 1861–February 21, 1864. Journal. Lieutenant Colonel. Second Michigan Infantry. Duty around Washington, D.C.; Blackburn's Ford; first Bull Run (observed); the Peninsular campaign, especially the siege of Yorktown, Williamsburg, Seven Pines, and the Seven Days' Battles; second Bull Run; Fredericksburg; Burnside's "Mud March"; duty in Kentucky; the Vicksburg campaign; and the siege of Jackson, where he was wounded and removed from action until December 1864. Haydon, a lawyer from Kalamazoo, recorded the rowdiness, vice, and absence of order that reigned during six weeks of training. He admired good officers who were able to enforce discipline, such as Gen. Phil Kearny, and criticized poor leaders. Common soldiers, with all their flaws, are the heroes of Haydon's journal. Following the debacle at Bull Run, Haydon lamented: "When our officers are equal to the soldiers we will have the best army the world ever saw" (p. 69). He said that as men on the Virginia Peninsula struggled with the mud and cold April rain, it took only the rumor of the arrival of coffee, sugar, and biscuits to make the men "happy as larks" (p. 217). Six weeks later the weather had turned hot and dusty and the Peninsular campaign had stalled. Haydon wrote that the soldiers, who lived on "two cups of muddy coffee & a few squares of hard tack per day," were driven by their hatred of secession. And on the Fourth of July 1862 the men cheered lustfully "for country, cause & leader" (p. 263). Haydon was only speculating when he wrote that pride sustained most men at the start of a battle, but that "was soon followed by excitement & rage which so completely occupies the mind that their is no chance for anything else" (p. 112). After Williamsburg his first reaction to danger verified his speculation. Haydon was annoyed at the prevalence of vices but found them to be more uncouth than immoral. Coffee was his personal vice. While he knew it was addictive, he found it comforting and stimulating. He justified his craving, asserting that "it prevents disease" (p. 217). The soldiers' sexual proclivities and off-color humor pop up throughout. In training camp Haydon was sure that "If the men pursue the enemy as vigorously as they do whores they will make very efficient soldiers" (p. 4). Everyone laughed when one soldier with a case of clap exchanged drawers with another man, thus transmitting the disease. In Tennessee a woman who "granted an indulgence" for only five cents complained to Haydon when the man did not pay her (p. 354). Another Tennessee woman became a laughingstock when she attempted to milk a male goat. In Cincinnati, on his way home on a veteran volunteer leave in February 1865, Haydon contracted pneumonia, from which he soon died.

109. HEG, HANS C. "Twelve Civil War Letters of Col. Hans C. Heg to His Son." Edited by E. Biddle Heg. *Norwegian-American Studies* 32 (1989): 177–97.

December 9, 1861–July 28, 1863. Letters. Colonel. Fifteenth Wisconsin Infantry. Kentucky and Tennessee. These letters to Heg's eldest son reveal a mixture of high expectations for a young boy (eight to ten years of age) and doting affection. Heg told Edmund to sell the ponies and sheep, learn Norwegian and German, prepare himself to be a military aide to his father, and expect to become a coproprietor in Heg's store after the war. Heg admonished his son for staying out too late and teasing his younger brother. From these letters, together with scraps of letters to the other children, Heg emerges as a loving but strongly paternalistic figure. He was killed at Chickamauga.

110. **HENRY, JOHN N.** *Turn Them Out to Die Like a Mule: The Civil War Letters of John N. Henry, 49th New York, 1861–1865.* Edited by John Michael Priest. Leesburg, Va.: Gauley Mount Press, 1995. 471 pp.
September 29, 1861–June 8, 1865. Letters and diary. Forty-ninth New York Infantry and hospital steward in various VI Corps hospitals in northern Virginia. Duty around Washington, D.C.; the Peninsular campaign; Antietam; Fredericksburg; Chancellorsville; the Gettysburg campaign; the Bristoe campaign; Rappahannock Station; the Mine Run campaign; the Virginia campaign, including The Wilderness, Spotsylvania, North Anna, and Cold Harbor; the siege of Petersburg; and duty in the Shenandoah Valley. Henry was a thirty-nine-year-old Methodist Episcopal circuit rider from Forrestville, New York, who admitted that he joined the army to provide a better life for his wife and family and to secure the Union, in that order. Henry often expressed his love for his family and was especially homesick during the winter of 1862 and 1863. Although he was granted two furloughs in 1863, the couple's relationship became strained. There are indications that marital discord preceded the war. For example, when his wife wanted to buy a new carpet, he told her to go ahead if she preferred carpets to clothing, as long as she was "suited." Henry broadened the rift when he complained: "For Some years my conduct neither Suited you or your mother. She used to say that you had no chance for your life" (p. 354). He said that he loved married life "but prefer death in the army to future complaints from your friends" (p. 354). Early in these letters he told his fifteen-year-old daughter that she was not going to get by in the world on her looks and that she had a "sour temper" (pp. 188–89). He advised her to concentrate on the domestic arts, develop a pleasant disposition, and learn something every day. In a much more positive tone, he later encouraged her to aspire to a high level of learning. He said that it was a mistake to think that women should only toil in the kitchen, and he added that men who have any "sense" hold a woman with an education in high regard (pp. 384–85). Henry related his military experiences openly, and in his position as a hospital steward he seemed fulfilled. Near the end of the war he was allowed to participate in several postmortem examinations, which he proudly described in a letter to a doctor at home. The editor adds that after the war Henry became a doctor and opened a practice for a short period.

111. **HILL, WILLIAM.** *Civil War Diary of William Hill.* Sterling Heights, Mich.: Sterling Heights Genealogical & Historical Society, 1992. 66 pp.
January 1–May 19, 1865. Diary. Seventeenth Wisconsin Infantry. The Carolinas campaign, including the battle of Bentonville; travel through Virginia to Washington for the Grand Review; then back to Louisville to be mustered out; and finally return to Kenosha, Wisconsin. Following the "ordors" of the day, Hill recorded the army's trek through the swampy Carolina low country during the rainy season. Not only was the march arduous, it was dangerous: "There was 7 men found kild yesterday 2 was shot & 2 had their throats cut . . . there was one of the 20th Ills found kild & all mangled. the First Brigade shot a Reb prisoner for it. they were made to draw chits to see who would dye" (p. 25). Some of Hill's entries remain unexplained, for example: "there was a man of the 12th New York Cavalry shot for murdering a young girl in Kingston" (p. 35). However, references to foraging and destroying railroad tracks are easily understood. Hill conveyed the soldiers' lament about the assassination of "our good old President Abram Lincoln" (p. 40). On April 20 he repeated a camp rumor that Lincoln was not dead but only badly wounded and expected to live. He also recorded "nuse of the attempt to take the Life of General John A. Logan" (p. 40). Hill was a fife major, but he did not describe his specific duties.

112. **HITCHCOCK, ROBERT.** "One Marine's Brief Battle." Edited by David M. Sullivan. *Civil War Times Illustrated* 31 (March/April 1992): 14, 16, 18, 20–21, 57–60.
May 7–July 20, 1861. Letters. Lieutenant. U.S. Marine Battalion attached to the Fifth U.S. Artillery, Battery D. First Bull Run. Hitchcock wrote his parents that the recruits were poorly trained as they pre-

pared for the war's first major battle. The editor fills in the details about the marines' performance at Bull Run, in which Hitchcock was killed.

113. HODGKINS, JOSEPH E. *The Civil War Diary of J. E. Hodgkins, 19th Massachusetts Volunteers from August 11, 1862 to June 3, 1865.* Edited by Kenneth C. Turino. Introduction by Dr. Steven C. Eames. Camden, Maine: Pecton Press, 1994. 178 pp.

August 11, 1862–July 3, 1865. Diary. Lieutenant. Nineteenth Massachusetts Infantry. Fredericksburg; the Mine Run campaign; and the Virginia campaign, including The Wilderness, Spotsylvania, Totopotomy, Cold Harbor, second Hatcher's Run, and the April 2 assault on Petersburg. Hodgkins was shot twice during the assault on Marye's Heights. The first minié ball hit him in the knapsack but was partially deflected by a plate, a spoon, and a rolled-up copy of his hometown newspaper, the *Lynn Reporter* (Massachusetts). The second shot, in his left arm, necessitated his rehabilitation at home for six months. He became irked by transportation officers whose indifference to a wounded soldier forced him to wait while they drank beer and smoked cigars. At Cold Harbor, Hodgkins was awarded a lieutenant's commission for delivering a dispatch under a hail of fire. He was captured at Jerusalem Plank Road on July 22 and sent to Andersonville via Libby and Belle Isle Prisons. His first entry written at Andersonville describes both the wretched conditions and his unfavorable impression of Henry Wirz. In other brief entries Hodgkins exhibits some despair but usually comments only on the poor food and shelter and his deteriorating physical condition. He mentions the mock presidential vote conducted by the Confederates in which Lincoln was the overwhelming victor. Hodgkins was later transferred to the prison pen at Camp Lawton. Paroled on November 25, his first meal of Union hard tack, raw pork, and raw onion represented a "good supper" to Hodgkins (p. 111). In the Grand Review, Hodgkins proudly commanded one of the divisions of his reduced regiment.

114. HOLT, DANIEL M. *A Surgeon's Civil War: The Letters and Diary of Daniel M. Holt, M.D.* Edited by James M. Greiner, Janet L. Coryell, and James R. Smither. Kent, Ohio: Kent State University Press, 1994. 314 pp.

September 5, 1862–October 8, 1864. Letters and diary. 121st New York Infantry. Duty in Maryland and Virginia, including Crampton's Gap (aftermath), Fredericksburg, Salem Church, Lee's retreat from Gettysburg (described), the Mine Run campaign, The Wilderness, Petersburg, the expedition to Snicker's Gap, Jubal Early's Washington raid, and Sheridan's Shenandoah Valley campaign. Holt was a forty-three-year-old country doctor with a wife and five children when he left his Herkimer County, New York, practice to become a soldier. He believed that "I could do more good to my country in the capacity of Surgeon, than in any other" (p. 5). Only two weeks after its induction, the regiment marched from Washington, D.C., into Maryland, where the doctor saw how quickly men could die of sunstroke. At Crampton's Gap he received his first view of battlefield carnage. At Antietam he saw piles of limbs lying in the sun for miles around and wrote, "still the knife went steadily in its work adding to the putrid mess" (p. 28). At Spotsylvania bodies were so riddled that "they were complete jelly" and had to be rolled into holes (p. 190). Throughout his letters Holt grumbles about the inefficient quartermasters, other surgeons, inadequate supplies, and military politics. Holt firmly believed that the reason he was able to help cure the sick and wounded was because both he and his patients knew that he cared for them. During his brief captivity at Salem Church he was exhilarated by the hard work of ministering to his patients. As a result of this experience, he renewed his covenant with God to "do all in my power to give relief, and solace the pillow of death" (p. 97). He was gratified that Robert E. Lee visited him several times and that the two men exchanged comparisons of Union and Confederate medical treatments. Holt deplored slavery; however, in his later writings he reveals honest ambiguity. He wrote: "for all my love for a black skin I never yet saw one with whom I would be willing to be on *perfect* equality" (p. 61). Holt went on to say that he knew he was not better by nature, but his feelings were derived from "my education—early as life itself is against it. It is engrafted in me—I can not help it" (p. 61). Holt considered himself a regular soldier. After Gettysburg he criticized Meade's failure to pursue Lee. He understood Ulysses S. Grant's flanking movements of the Virginia campaign, and he could not fathom why the Confederates continued to make frontal assaults on Union positions when they always got the worst of them. But with a soldierly exuberance Holt exclaimed, "I like such charges" (p. 196). His ever-present respiratory problems worsened during Sheridan's Shenandoah Valley campaign. Long before the regiment was discharged in October 1864, his decimated condition was obvious to others. Holt died in 1867 of tuberculosis. A diary that he kept from May 1 through October 21, 1864, supplements the few letters he wrote during this period.

115. HOLWAY, SUMNER ANSEL. *To Let Them Know: The Civil War Diaries of Sumner Ansel Holway, Pvt., Company H, 1st Maine Cavalry.* Edited by Peter Carl Haskell. N.p.: Arcadia Lodge Press, 1990. 84 pp.
March 21, 1862–November 24, 1863. Diary. Private. First Maine Cavalry. Duty in Virginia, including the battles of Middletown, second Bull Run, Antietam (observed), Stoneman's raid during the Chancellorsville campaign, Brandy Station (rear guard duty), and Aldie, where a wound removed him from the war. Holway's early complaints about inactivity and the repetition of drilling and boring camp routines immediately disappeared when Stonewall Jackson launched his Shenandoah Valley campaign. After early 1862 Holway always seemed to be going on or coming off picket duty; he was frequently aroused in reaction to false alarms; and he was mustered for pay four times before eventually receiving any money. For part of his service Holway was an orderly assigned to carrying dispatches. Holway often said that he felt sick of the war, but he repeatedly reminded himself that he was a soldier and had to make the best of the situation. He seldom indicated patriotic fervor or hatred of the enemy.

116. HOPKINS, CHARLES. *The Andersonville Diary & Memoirs of Charles Hopkins, 1st New Jersey Infantry.* Edited by William B. Styple and John J. Fitzpatrick. Kearny, N.J.: Belle Grove Publishing Co., 1988. 220 pp.
May 1861–March 1865. Memoir and diary. First New Jersey Infantry. Writing in 1890, Hopkins first recounted the battles of first Bull Run and Gaines' Mill, where he was briefly captured. He resumed his account on May 6, 1864, with his capture at The Wilderness and imprisonment at Andersonville (until mid September) and Florence (until March 1865). The editor has inserted portions of Hopkins's 1864 diary between sections of the memoir. Hopkins dwells on the horrible conditions of the prisons and attributes blame for their existence. He provides examples of how commandant Henry Wirz and Gen. John Winder purposefully inflicted suffering and death on Union captives at Andersonville. Hopkins wrote that Winder boasted that he had selected the spot for the "Bull Pen" in a location "where disease and death would come more quickly by 'natural causes'" (p. 77). Hopkins asserts that death by "natural causes" soon became "systematic causes" when the prisoners were ordered to be vaccinated for smallpox with "impure vaccine matter" (pp. 96–97). One example of Wirz's contemptible acts was his diversion of the clean water of "Provident Spring" away from the prisoners' reach. Hopkins's account of life at Florence follows the same pattern. Poor living conditions were aggravated by the cold weather. In December 1864 gangrene was widespread. One man had both feet amputated with a knife only four inches long. Many years later at a prisoners' reunion Hopkins met the amputee, who was walking steadily on two cork feet. The editor has included an abundance of information on Hopkins's postwar life, photographs, essays about Hopkins's efforts in creating tributes to soldiers (especially the statue of Gen. Phil Kearny), and how in 1892 Hopkins was awarded the Congressional Medal of Honor for bravery at Gaines' Mill.

117. HOUTZ, JOHN W. *Diaries of Pvt. John W. Houtz, 66th Ohio Volunteer Infantry, 1863–1864.* Homer, N.Y.: Robert T. Pennoyer, 1995. 123 pp.

January 1, 1863–December 31, 1864. Diary. Private. Sixty-sixth Ohio Infantry. Duty at Dumfrees, Virginia; Chancellorsville; Gettysburg, including the pursuit of Lee; duty at Bridgeport, Alabama; the Atlanta campaign; and the March to the Sea. This work includes primarily brief daily entries about camp life and battles. The lengthiest accounts were written during the Atlanta campaign and the March to the Sea. Between January and March 1864 Houtz and others who chose not to reenlist were transferred to the Seventh Ohio Infantry. A letter and "Memoranda" that describe his service between July and August 1864 precede the diary.

118. HUBBELL, HENRY P. "A Democrat in Lincoln's Army: The Civil War Letters of Henry P. Hubbell." By Simon P. Newman. *Princeton University Library Chronicle* 50 (Winter 1989): 155–68.

April 1861–January 26, 1863. Letters. Lieutenant Colonel. Third New York Infantry. The editor utilizes these letters to examine the reasons why a Northern Democrat would join the Union army in the summer of 1861 and then resign two years later. Hubbell was always a supporter of the Union and an opponent of secession. However, as the war progressed it became clear to him that he had enlisted in a crusade with which he did not sympathize. He believed that the Republicans were seeking to alter the initial war aim of preserving the integrity of the Union to pursuing abolition of the slaves. When Lincoln criticized McClellan's performance on the Peninsula, Hubbell remarked that the war could be won in short order if the soldiers "would go at it in earnest and let politics & the niger alone" (p. 161). The Emancipation Proclamation signaled to Hubbell a profound change in the reason the war was being fought and constituted an egregious misuse of executive power for partisan purposes.

119. HUDSON, JOHN W. "Tired Soldiers Don't Go Very Fast." Edited by John M. Priest. *Civil War Times Illustrated* 30 (January/February 1992): 36–41.

September 17, 1862. Lieutenant. Aide to Brig. Gen. Edward Ferrero. Second Brigade Second Division, IX Corps, Army of the Potomac. Antietam. The title of this article provides Hudson's rationale for why it took Union soldiers so long to cross Burnside's Bridge.

120. HULBERT, SIMON BOLIVAR. *One Battle Too Many: An American Civil War Chronicle. The Writings of Simon Bolivar Hulbert, Private, Company E, 100th New York State Volunteers, 1861–1864.* Compiled and interpreted by Richard P. Galloway. Gaithersburg, Md.: Olde Soldiers Book, 1987. 348 pp.

December 11, 1861–August 9, 1864. Letters and diary. Private. One-hundredth New York Infantry. Induction and training at Camp Morgan; the Peninsular campaign, including Williamsburg and Seven Pines (he was captured the morning of the battle and sent to Salisbury and Belle Isle Prisons); duty in North Carolina; bombardment of the Charleston harbor islands, including both assaults on Battery Wagner; and Butler's operations on the south side of the James River against Petersburg and Richmond, including Drewry's Bluff. Captured again on May 16, 1864, Hulbert was shipped to Andersonville. Hulbert lent money freely and wrote letters for those who could not; however, he was no saint. He constantly complained about his slovenly, illiterate tentmate, "My old Slut, Mrs. Winters" (p. 187). "She" ran around for two weeks with the seat of "her" pants out and wore no shirt for three or four days. The tentmate became the "fool Ignoramus Winters" when he expounded on Whig politics. Scurvy caused Hulbert to suffer: "My gums are all drove from my teeth & I can see the roots of them" (p. 85). In the fall of 1862 he wrote: "this everlasting never ending dysentery. I suppose I am to be travelling again all night with the back doors trot" (p. 118). A hernia was Hulbert's most painful ailment. He said that any heavy weight "brings it down, in my left testicle," and he added that the hot weather "brings the left one down some eight inches, or nearly half way to my knee" (p. 193). A medical discharge was thwarted by his captain, "a kind of a mean shit" (p. 166). Hulbert hired a lawyer in Buffalo who unsuccessfully pleaded his case. A sympathetic surgeon eventually gave him a truss which reduced the pain. In Salisbury Prison his firsthand acquaintance with Confederate soldiers was favorable. The Confederates were "generally tall, slim & wiry, quick as cats, real American people" (p. 125). He also noted that as soldiers they were obedient and quiet in ranks. He contrasted their behavior to that of Union soldiers, who spoke "ten different Languages" and reacted to orders with confusion or "like geese" (p. 125). The Southern soldiers, he observed, did not care for spit and polish: "if the gun is only clean inside so that it will go off, it does not make any difference how rusty it is outside" (p. 125). Throughout his writings the observant Hulbert describes geographical and cultural differences. Hulbert died at Andersonville in August 1864.

121. **HUNT, LEONARD H.** "Return to Spotsylvania." By Bob Korroch. *Michigan History* 78 (March/April 1994): 8–17.
1864. Diary. Lieutenant. Twenty-sixth Michigan Infantry. Spotsylvania. Korroch blends his grandfather's diary, his own research (during which a photograph of Hunt was located), and secondary sources to relate military events of early 1864.

122. **HUNTER, ALVAH FOLSOM.** *A Year on a Monitor and the Destruction of Fort Sumter.* Edited, with an introduction, by Craig L. Symonds. Columbia: University of South Carolina Press, 1987. 184 pp.
December 1862–December 1863. Memoir. USS *Nahant,* South Atlantic Blockading Squadron. Enlistment, training, and repairs en route to Port Royal; bombardment of Fort McAllister; Samuel F. Du Pont's naval bombardment of Charleston harbor (especially Fort Sumter); capture of the CSS *Atlanta* by the USS *Weehawken;* bombardment and siege of Battery Wagner (including references to the assaults of July 11 and 18, 1863); bombardment of Fort Sumter on August 17, 1863; and the accidental sinking of the USS *Weehawken.* In the 1920s Hunter wrote with the same boyish enthusiasm he apparently displayed in 1862. As an undersized sixteen-year-old from New Hampshire, he pestered naval authorities in Boston into accepting him for duty. He became a first class boy and was assigned to the monitor USS *Nahant,* which spent nearly the whole of 1863 in the vicinity of Charleston harbor. Hunter's curiosity led him to observe and record the details of his surroundings and experiences: his duties and the punishments that other boys received; the excitement of battle; and disbelief as he watched the overloaded USS *Weehawken* sink. Never bored, Hunter fished, swam, gathered blackberries, scraped barnacles, and explored his surroundings. When the CSS *Atlanta* was captured after a brief fight, Hunter went aboard and visited with the Confederate seamen. They told him that the citizens of Savannah participated in the construction of the *Atlanta* and that it was an object of civic pride. Hunter would later receive prize money for being a member of a vessel that supported the attack of the *Atlanta.* After the Confederates evacuated Battery Wagner, Hunter spent a whole day's liberty exploring the earthworks, declining the offer of his mates to get drunk. During the April 7 attack on Fort Sumter, Hunter witnessed his first battle casualty. A shell fired from Fort Sumter hit the *Nahant,* forcing a nut to fly across the vessel and kill one man and seriously wound two others. Hunter often related problems with the monitor's mechanical operations. On several occasions the men below became ill ("physical depression") because of their confined quarters and the smoke and foul air. Hunter described the various types of torpedoes (mines) that the Confederates used to defend against Union ships. Hunter ended the year back in Boston with his aunt, but within the text he refers to later service with the signal corps on the James River.

123. **HUPP, ORMOND.** *In Defense of This Flag: The Civil War Diary of Pvt. Ormond Hupp, 5th Indiana Light Artillery.* Transcribed and annotated by John Lee Berkley. Bradenton, Fla.: McGuinn & McGuire Publishing, 1994. 313 pp.

September 16, 1861–November 1864. Diary. Private. Fifth Indiana Light Artillery Battery. Duty in Kentucky, Tennessee, and Alabama. Wounded at Perryville, Hupp spent the next eighteen months in a hospital at New Albany, Indiana. He rejoined his regiment for the Atlanta campaign, including Rocky Face Ridge, Dallas, Kennesaw Mountain, Peachtree Creek, Atlanta, Jonesboro, and Lovejoy Station. Near Stevenson, Alabama, Hupp wrote of burning the homes of guerrillas and feeling sympathy for the women. In Kentucky he wrote that the water had an inch of green scum on top, but since the men needed it for their coffee, "of course we would use it in preference to our going without" (p. 31). At Perryville he was wounded when a shell hit an ammunition box, which he said blew him ten feet in the air. He struggled back to a makeshift hospital, where he was treated by a surgeon who "was so frightened that he knew nothing, as he wanted to take my arm off when there was no bone injured. I left him at once" (p. 34). Hupp was sent to the hospital in New Albany, Indiana, and served as a nurse. The entries he wrote after he joined his regiment in April 1864 are devoted to the fighting. Hupp's diary was originally published as *My Diary* (Odessa, Mo.: Ewing Printers, 1923). This edition contains a lengthy section by the editor: "The Narrative: A Biographical and Historical Perspective."

124. HYDE, SOLON. *A Captive of War.* Edited, with a preface, by Neil Thompson. Shippensburg, Pa.: Burd Street Press, 1996. 201 pp.
October 1863–February 1865. Memoir. Hospital steward. Seventeenth Ohio Infantry. Captured at Chickamauga, Hyde spent the next seventeen months at Richmond, Danville, Andersonville, and Salisbury Prisons. Some thirty-five years later he published his experiences. A constant theme of Hyde's memoir is his low opinion of the Confederacy. Hyde wrote that a gentleman from Charleston admitted to him that the Confederate goal was neither states' rights nor the retention of slavery but, rather, the establishment of an aristocracy. Hyde said that when Southern soldiers buried their own dead at Chickamauga, they left the Union troops to rot and bleach in the sun. Hyde reacted with indignation: "No Confederate spade should dig the trench, no hand be raised to give them Christian burial. Shame, shame, boasted chivalry!" (p. 18). But he leveled his most damning charge toward the administrators of the Confederate prison system. The "rebel prisons seemed to be a studied, systematized mode of torture intended to offset the arming of the negro in the north" (pp. 191–92). To Hyde, proof of this conclusion was that Confederate soldiers held in Northern prisons did not suffer and die to a similar degree. But he was equally critical of General Grant's refusal to exchange prisoners: "We were abandoned to our fate simply as a military necessity" (p. 14). At Chickamauga, Hyde treated and exchanged the wounded before and after his capture. He described the hospital, doctors, and medicines that were available at Andersonville. As a hospital steward Hyde was permitted to travel outside Andersonville to gather the Confederacy's primary medicines, "roots and yarbs" (p. 125). For each prison he recorded descriptions of the facilities, the number of prisoners held, the means of communication between prisoners, topics of popular interest, and punishment and ill-treatment at the hands of the guards. He also described his aborted escape from Danville. Hyde was paroled at Wilmington, North Carolina, on February 27, 1865. Original publication: New York: McClure, Phillips & Co., 1900.

125. IRWIN, GEORGE WASHINGTON. *George Washington Irwin: The Civil War Diary of a Pennsylvania Volunteer.* Compiled and edited by Jane B. Steiner. Lafayette, Calif.: Hunsaker Publishing Co., 1991. 221 pp.
September 18, 1861–July 3, 1863. Diary. Twenty-eighth Infantry and 147th Pennsylvania Infantry. Duty in northern Virginia; second Bull Run; Antietam; Chancellorsville; and Gettysburg. This work is primarily a terse record of troop movements and comments about the weather, camp accidents, recreation, punishments, rumors, and incidents of skirmishes and battles. Appendixes include letters of Col. Airo Pardee Jr. and the memoir of Lt. Joseph Addison Moore, both of whom continued their accounts with the 147th into the Atlanta campaign. Chapters from Samuel P. Bates's *History of the Pennsylvania Volunteers* (1869) are among other documents appended.

126. **JONES, JOSHUA.** "'absent So long from those I love': The Civil War Letters of Joshua Jones." Edited by Eugene H. Berwanger. *Indiana Magazine of History* 88 (September 1992): 205–39.

August 11, 1861–September 6, 1862. Letters. Corporal. Nineteenth Indiana Infantry. Peninsular campaign; Cedar Mountain (aftermath); and second Bull Run. Family and monetary matters are the main themes of these letters. Jones frequently expressed his longing to see his wife and son and often gave her advice on how to raise the boy. Jones admitted he was stingy. He routinely sent his pay home with instructions that it was to be saved. In addition, he lent his comrades money at interest and washed their clothes. When Jones purchased a watch for twelve dollars and sold it for eighteen dollars, he boasted: "Some is Smart and Some aint Smart" (p. 222). Jones's goal was for his family to improve themselves financially as a result of their hardships. Or, in his words, "I want to have a big pile when I get home" (p. 219). He often congratulated his wife for possessing the same goals about their future. He told her to purchase feathers and pork at good prices and to sell the dog. After the Iron Brigade became engaged in heavy fighting, Jones mentioned matters of love less frequently. Also included are letters that describe how Jones was fatally wounded at Antietam.

127. **KAUCHER, JOSEPH E.** "Letters Home . . . Written by a Union Soldier from Reading." Compiled by Harold E. Yoder Jr. *Historical Review Berks County* 51 (Spring 1986): 57–62, 70–75.

August 10, 1862–June 1, 1865. Letters. 128th Pennsylvania Infantry; Twentieth Pennsylvania Infantry (Emergency); and Durrell's Independent Battery D, Pennsylvania Light Artillery. Battles of Antietam, Chancellorsville, The Wilderness, and the siege of Petersburg.

128. **KAUFFMAN, HENRY.** *The Civil War Letters (1862–1865) of Private Henry Kauffman: The Harmony Boys Are All Well.* Edited by David McCordick. Lewiston, N.Y.: Edwin Mellen Press, 1991. 110 pp.

October 15, 1862–May 31, 1865. Letters. Private. 110th Ohio Infantry. Duty in West Virginia and Virginia, including in the Shenandoah Valley, along the Rappahannock and Rapidan Rivers, and the siege of Petersburg. Kauffman frequently wrote his sister about the condition of the boys from Harmony, Ohio, and the receipt of boxes, and he requested news of other family members. He was captured at second Winchester but mentioned neither the battle nor his captivity. After he was returned to Union lines and was placed in a parole barracks at Annapolis, he revealed that he had been arrested and fined for starting home. He rejoined his regiment during the Bristoe campaign and described fording the Rappahannock, but he treated the skirmishing with only: "On last Wednesday eve had a right smart of a fight" (p. 37). Even after he was wounded at Cedar Creek, Kauffman wrote only of routine matters from the hospital. During the siege of Petersburg he related his conversations with Confederate soldiers and added that a group of deserters came over while he was on picket duty. Near Winchester in 1863 he was a member of a scouting expedition that shot and burned the home of a bushwhacker who refused to surrender his guns. Kauffman agreed that it had to be done, "though it looks rather hard" (p. 25). Kauffman preferred that Lincoln be reelected and recorded the regiment's overwhelming vote in his favor. Later Kauffman lamented Lincoln's assassination.

129. **KEARNY, PHILIP.** *Letters from the Peninsula: The Civil War Letters of General Philip Kearny.* Edited by William B. Styple. Foreword by Brian C. Pohanka. Kearny, N.J.: Belle Grove Publishing Co., 1988. 240 pp.

March 4–August 31, 1862. Letters. Major General. First Division, III Corps, Army of the Potomac. Peninsular campaign, including Williamsburg, Seven Pines, Malvern Hill, and second Bull Run.

Kearny was an experienced officer prior to the Civil War. He had been an observer with the French in the Algerian War of 1840, served as an aide to Gen. Winfield Scott in the Mexican War (he lost his left arm at the battle of Churubusco), fought Indians on the western frontier, and won the Honor of Legion in 1859 while fighting with the French during their war with Italy. When the American Civil War began, Kearny was frustrated that his accomplishments were not sufficiently recognized by the Union army. He was convinced that he should have been appointed to command the New Jersey volunteers, instead of being relegated to command the First New Jersey Brigade. Also, he complained that he remained brigadier general for too long. Kearny related examples of his bravery and leadership in action, which, he believed, went unobserved by his superiors, though not by other officers or the enlisted men. Kearny was highly critical of George B. McClellan, whom he considered an incompetent "engineer." He criticized McClellan's timidity, his strategy of getting to Richmond via the Virginia Peninsula, and McClellan's praise for Gen. Winfield Scott Hancock's actions at Williamsburg when Kearny felt that the greater credit belonged to his own troops. Kearny commended the Confederacy for placing its best officers—many of whom he knew from the war with Mexico—in important commands. When Kearny wrote to his wife Agnes, he said that her letters cheered him and often made him feel like returning home. Kearny occasionally offered Agnes advice and expressed his love, but the focus of his letters is his own circumstances. Kearny was killed at the battle of Chantilly. The editor's introduction includes a summary of Kearny's relationship with Agnes, whom he met in France, and his divorce from his first wife and suggests that Kearny's private life may have hampered his military advancement. Additional information consists of testimonials from comrades and photographs of memorials to Kearny.

130. KELLOGG, FREDERIC HENRY. *From Your Affectionate Son: The Civil War Letters of Frederic Henry Kellogg.* Compiled by his great-granddaughter Kathi Mac Iver. Cripple Creek, Colo.: Columbine Press, 1996. 171 pp.

May 21, 1861–July 21, 1865. Letters. Private, Fifteenth Illinois Infantry, and Sergeant, Third Ohio Cavalry. Duty in Missouri; Fort Donelson (aftermath); Shiloh; duty in Tennessee; the Atlanta campaign, especially Kilpatrick's raid to Jonesboro; duty at Louisville and Gravelly Springs, Alabama; and Wilson's raid to Macon. These letters, primarily to Kellogg's mother, mention camp life, troop movements, anticipation of battles, condition of his health, and requests for news about his brothers, but they contain few details of the fighting. After Kellogg was wounded at Shiloh, he was placed in a hospital in Nashville. He was discharged in October 1862 suffering from typhoid fever and pneumonia. A few letters written during 1863 indicate that he tried his hand at farming before reenlisting in the Third Ohio Cavalry in January 1864. The editor explains that Kellogg's father had deserted his mother and ten children in the late 1840s, leaving her to raise them on their North Fairfield, Ohio, farm. Fred later went to live with his father in Illinois. As the editor points out, his initial letters to his mother begin tentatively but soon warm up with referrals to himself as "Your Affectionate Son." His letters often mention his brothers, three of whom were in the army and often served near each other. Although he seldom told anecdotes, Kellogg did relate how "Mizs Sue Monday" (the guerrilla who passed as a woman) stole his horse while he was having dinner with a farmer near Bardstown, Kentucky, on Christmas Day of 1864.

131. KEMP, DANIEL F. "Navy Life on the Mississippi River." *Civil War Times Illustrated* 33 (May/June 1994): 16, 66–73.

September 1862–January 1863. Memoir. Kemp recounted his daily duties aboard the ironclad USS *Cincinnati*. The highlight of this period was the navy's role in the capture of Arkansas Post.

132. KENNEDY, CHARLES W. "Garrison Duty in Alexandria: The Red River Campaign Letters of Lt. Charles W. Kennedy, 156th New York Volunteer Infantry." Edited by Ed Steers. *Civil War Regiments* 4, no. 2 (1994): 104–17.
March 27–May 23, 1864. Letters. Lieutenant. 156th New York Infantry. Second Red River campaign. This staff officer (Third Brigade, Second Division, XIX Corps, Army of the Gulf) wrote about the Union attempt to capture Shreveport. Kennedy was in charge of transporting the brigade from Baton Rouge to Alexandria. His duties entailed shipping the horses and mules, establishing a warehouse for stores, foraging for rations, etc. Eventually he wrote, "I have gotten out of the grocery business" (p. 114). After the Union defeats at Mansfield and Pleasant Hill, Kennedy described the construction of the dam at Alexandria that allowed the Union fleet to raise the water level of the Red River and escape to the Mississippi River.

133. KENT, WILLIAM. "A Wilderness Memory." *Civil War Times Illustrated* 28 (March 1989): 34–39.
May 4–5, 1864. Memoir. First U.S. Sharpshooters (Berdan's). Kent recalled many details about the first day of The Wilderness. He remembered rushing across the same terrain where Stonewall Jackson had been shot a year earlier at Chancellorsville. When the Union troops clambered through the tangle of bush and small growth, they encountered the enemy. As his unit retreated, he watched comrades (whose names he barely remembered) shot. Kent was also wounded. For nearly twenty-four hours he had nothing to eat and was unable to smoke. Years later Kent regarded being able to sleep for three hours early in the morning of May 5 as his "sweetest" memory.

134. KIRK, ALVAH. "The Civil War Letters of Alvah Kirk." By Jeffrey Scheuer. *New York History* 73 (April 1992): 169–92.
1862–1864. Letters. Private. Ninety-fifth New York Infantry. Kirk's letters to his wife are practically devoid of his battle experiences. He mentions Chancellorsville, requests goods, comments about the weather, and makes cryptic references to himself and his family. The editor feels that Kirk was probably illiterate and that the letters were written for him. Scheuer believes Kirk had an uncertain relationship with his wife and children, and that he seemed imbued with a spiritual bleakness. Kirk died of wounds during The Wilderness. This article is not as much about what Kirk did or did not say as it is about Scheuer himself. The editor conducted an extensive genealogical hunt, interviewed elderly descendants, and visited Kirk's grave. However, the historical records and interviews were as unrevealing about "Kirk the man" as were Kirk's personal writings. Nevertheless, Scheuer believes that his efforts were not in vain. His quest made him realize that Kirk's hold on his imagination was a metaphor for his own need—not simply to remember the past, but to connect personally with what came before. For Scheuer, the letters of Alvah Kirk represented such a bridge.

135. LADLEY, OSCAR DEROSTUS. *Hearth and Knapsack: The Ladley Letters, 1857–1880.* Edited by Carl M. Becker and Ritchie Thomas. Athens: Ohio University Press, 1988. 414 pp.
May 13, 1861–February 11, 1865. Letters. Private, Sixteenth Ohio Infantry, and Captain, Seventy-fifth Ohio Infantry. Duty in West Virginia and Maryland; McDowell; Cedar Mountain (described); duty near Washington, D.C.; Chancellorsville; Gettysburg; duty in Florida during 1864, including Gainesville (not present); and duty at Pocotaligo, South Carolina. The letters that Oscar and his mother and two sisters exchanged between September 7, 1862, and July 27, 1863, provide unique insights into a close-knit family. All parties asked and answered each other's questions. Oscar remained as interested in events at home in Yellow Springs, Ohio, as the family did about his experiences in the field and the war in

general. Oscar once stopped in midsentence to write excitedly, "here comes the mail" (p. 7). After he read his letters, he described the melee mail call prompted. "You cannot imagine how we act when the letters come in to camp some of the boys run and jump, yell like Indians, and others take it cool" (p. 8). Oscar and his mother were disseminators of news for concerned parents and soldiers. His mother evinced concern about Oscar's safety, but she did not burden him with expressions of excessive worry. The girls often wrote about the community. When he read that someone had put a cow in a cellar at Antioch College, Oscar replied that he was glad he was not at home because this time the college could not blame him. He reminded them that several years earlier he "was blamed for egging that *Nigger* student" (p. 102). One sister wrote about a black lady from Oberlin who had come to attend school at Antioch only to have the students draft a petition to have her expelled. The whole family shared negative opinions of Germans. On September 13, 1862, Oscar wrote that "dutch blood is below par with us" (p. 45). He explained why his XI Corps was routed at Chancellorsville: the ignorance of the generals, the inexperienced men, and the presence of New York "dutch" regiments. Oscar expressed pride in his brigade's performance at Gettysburg but wrote: "I do not expect that we will get the credit for it as Schurtz is in Command" (p. 143). For the period after late 1863 only Oscar's letters have survived. He continued to write about details of his service: the vegetation in Florida (he sent sprigs of holly and honeysuckle); why the Confederate mines were strung across Charleston harbor; and several expeditions in Florida to capture wild horses. Oscar was mustered out in February 1865, but he reenlisted in April 1866. He continued to write his family from posts in the West until his natural death in 1880.

136. LAMSON, WILLIAM. *Maine to The Wilderness: The Civil War Letters of Pvt. William Lamson, 20th Maine Infantry.* Edited by Roderick M. Engert. Orange, Va.: Publisher's Press, 1993. 107 pp.

August 4, 1862–May 3, 1864. Letters. Private. Twentieth Maine Infantry. Induction and training at Camp Bangor; and battles of Aldie, Gettysburg (including pursuit of Lee), and the beginning of the Virginia campaign. These letters consists primarily of incidents of camp life and requests for news (and stamps) from home. Lamson's early letters indicate the different ways men of the regiment became accustomed to each other and military life and include descriptions of such activities as fistfights, getting drunk, having their pictures taken, raiding sutler's stores, and receiving punishments. He frequently recorded camp accidents. One soldier's gun went off in camp, wounding a man in the bowels, two others in the arms, and a fourth in the nose. On Saint Patrick's Day 1863 another accident occurred during a horse race in which two horses and one man suffered broken necks. Soldiers climbing a greased pole received no injuries. When his regiment was reviewed by Lincoln and McClellan early in October 1862, Lamson noted: "Lincoln is not *very* handsome and not so *very* homely. I thought that Mc Looked a little cross" (p. 28). On March 29, 1863, he fired his first shot in battle, and thereafter fighting became more intense. During May 1863 Lamson mentioned that members of the disgruntled Second Maine Infantry were added to the unit. At Gettysburg, Lamson was a member of Company B, which executed the surprise bayonet attack on the right and rear of the advancing Fifteenth Alabama Infantry at Little Round Top. Later that year in winter camp at Rappahannock Station, Lamson observed the extensive guard and picket defense around VI Corps headquarters. He quipped that the officers were "afraid that Mosby will come and carry them off" (p. 85). Lamson was killed at The Wilderness.

137. LAUDERDALE, JOHN VANCE. *The Wounded River: Civil War Letters of John Vance Lauderdale, M.D.* Edited by Peter Josyph. East Lansing: Michigan State University Press, 1993. 241 pp.

April 15–August 28, 1862. Letters. Surgeon aboard the hospital steamer *D.A. January,* which carried the wounded to hospitals along the Mississippi, Ohio, and Tennessee Rivers. Shortly after graduating from the Medical College of the University of New York, Lauderdale signed up as a contract surgeon with the United States Sanitary Commission. His letters to his sister reveal more about his personal reactions to the sick and wounded than they do about the medical treatments he performed. As he looked at the shipload of wounded from Shiloh, he understood that they were suffering from the trauma of battle in addition to their physical wounds. He moved from cot to cot administering medications but realized the impossibility of treating each man on the overcrowded ship. Lauderdale felt helpless but knew that it was the duty of the shipboard doctors to stabilize the wounded, "to render our patients as comfortable as possible, and promise them more thorough treatment at the hospitals" (p. 133). Still, Lauderdale was frustrated at not being able to observe the results of his efforts. After Shiloh he watched how the dead were piled in a trench as wide as a man and some ten to twenty feet long without ceremony. Lauderdale's letters assume the form of a travel account as he portrays scenes along the rivers and compares Memphis with Saint Louis and Milwaukee. Section 1 of this book (pp. 41–140) is devoted to Lauderdale's Civil War service. Section 2 relates to his practice at New York's Bellevue Hospital and includes an account of the New York draft riots. Section 3, which covers his duty in Utah among the Mormons, contains Lauderdale's comments in favor of Lincoln in the 1864 election, as well as his reaction to the president's assassination. The editor adds that Lauderdale formally entered the military in 1866 and served until 1896.

138. LECLEAR, LOUIS RUSSELL. "A Soldier's Letters, 1864." By Philip M. Reitzel. *Maryland Historical Magazine* 83 (Fall 1988): 254–67.
July 28–September 1864. Ninety-third New York Infantry (National Guard). Howard County, Maryland. These letters were written by one of the one-hundred-day enlistees called to protect against Jubal Early's summer threat of Washington, D.C. Sixteen-year-old Russell spent all of an abbreviated tour guarding the B & O Railroad lines at Washington Junction and Ellicotts Mills, Maryland. Young Louis frequently received parental admonitions that ranged from the need for him to wash clothes regularly to the proper conduct of his life. For example, after Louis simply mentioned the prevalence of thievery in camp, his parents warned him to watch over his possessions. They told him to remain a good man: "Do not let the low morals of your associates affect you in the least" (p. 256). Louis casually commented about the girls who worked in the local mills. His mother responded with her desire that he not have social intercourse with any of them. She told him to "Have a clear conscience when you come home to your fond, and proud, parents" (p. 260). When Louis became ill in September, Mrs. LeClear nursed him in the hospital and took him back home to Staten Island, thus ending Louis's military career.

139. LEE, GEORGE R. "Wagonmaster's Letter: A Witness to the War in Mississippi." *Civil War Times Illustrated* 27 (March 1988): 30–33.
August 17–21, 1863. Letter. Third Brigade, Third Division, XV Corps, Army of the Tennessee. Quartermaster. Lee describes how he lived and fought during the Vicksburg campaign as Sherman's men moved through Mississippi to Jackson. He mentions the problems of moving the wagons and the destruction of Jackson by Union troops.

140. LEGATE, GEORGE H. "Never Defeated Yet." Edited by Paul Kallina. *Lincoln Herald* 89 (Fall 1987): 117–22.
November 25, 1862–January 27, 1863. Letters. Sergeant. Second Wisconsin Infantry. Fredericksburg and Burnside's "Mud March." In his first letter Legate says that the uproar among the troops over McClellan's removal had subsided but that neither Burnside nor any other general held the soldiers' confidence. After the battle of Fredericksburg he admitted that he had feared that the Union army would delay its attack until the rebels were too well entrenched, and he added that he did not know what prevented the Confederates from destroying the whole Union army. Legate wrote that the Army of the Potomac was so demoralized that he was worried over what might happen if the soldiers' insubordination did not cease.

141. **LIEB, HARRY W.** *Harry Lieb's Diary.* Transcribed and edited by Richard
L. Tritt. Boiling Springs, Pa.: Boiling Springs Civic Association, 1993. 1 vol.
(unpaged).

January 1–December 20, 1862. Diary. Corporal. Thirty-sixth Pennsylvania Infantry (Seventh
Reserves). Peninsular campaign, including Gaines' Mill, White Oak Swamp, and Malvern Hill; second
Bull Run; Antietam campaign, including South Mountain and Antietam; and Fredericksburg. Lieb's
most interesting entries are of his medical treatment at Fredericksburg, where he was wounded on
December 13. He lay on the field the first night. The next day he was loaded onto a wagon and moved
half a mile, where he was unloaded. On the 14th he was moved to another open field for the night. On
the 15th he was picked up and again unloaded in still another open field, where he again lay overnight
in the cold and rain. On the 16th the process was repeated. On the 17th his wounded leg was treated for
the first time. On the 19th he commented that the hospital was unheated and that the wounded were still
arriving. By the 19th his condition had improved. The wounded men were fed crackers and soup and
given straw on which to lie. By December 20 the stoves had still not arrived.

142. **LINCOLN, ALFRED LYMAN.** "Missing in Action: The Civil War Letters of Private Alfred Lyman Lincoln." Edited by Edwin G. Lincoln. (Part I)
New Jersey History 106 (Fall/Winter 1988): 52–77.

————. (Part II) *New Jersey History* 107 (Spring/Summer 1989): 58–75.

January 12, 1862–January 13, 1863. Letters. Private. First New Jersey Infantry. Massachusetts and the
battle of Gaines' Mill. Most of this selection of letters is written by Alfred's brother Edwin M., his sister Mary, and a comrade, Edwin H. Hollinger. The theme of this correspondence revolves around the
family's reaction to Alfred's being wounded and reportedly killed during the fighting at Gaines' Mill.
However, he was only wounded and briefly held captive. He was soon paroled and spent several months
in Fortress Monroe Hospital before rejoining his unit on December 27. Expressions of bereavement and
condolence were exchanged until Edwin eventually received a letter from Alfred that had been written
much earlier, on August 10. Expressions of joy followed, as did a plea for Alfred to seek a medical discharge. Other themes of the article address economic conditions of the Connecticut home front, family
problems, and Edwin's personality.

143. **LIND, WILLIAM WILSON.** *The Long Road for Home: The Civil War*
Experiences of Four Farmboy Soldiers of the Twenty-Seventh Massachusetts
Regiment of Volunteer Infantry as Told by Their Personal Correspondence,
1861–1864. Edited by Henry C. Lind. Rutherford, N.J.: Fairleigh Dickinson
University Press, 1992. 210 pp.

April 2, 1861–September 3, 1864. Letters. Twenty-seventh Massachusetts Infantry. Burnside's expedition to North Carolina, including Roanoke Island; duty in North Carolina until fall 1863, especially the
Confederate siege of Washington and the expedition from New Bern to Winton; duty in Virginia at
Portsmouth and Norfolk, battles of Drewry's Bluff and Cold Harbor, and the siege of Petersburg. This
is a collection of letters written to and from the families and friends of William Lind (Berkshire Center, Vermont), Alfred and Chauncey Holcomb (Southwick, Massachusetts), and Christopher Hudson.
The majority of the letters are from William, but several lengthy letters were written by Alfred. The
other men wrote fewer letters. The editor has interspersed all the correspondence with secondary and
primary sources and added his own historical narrative. The first letters included were written during
summer 1861 when William and Christopher were traveling in Massachusetts in search of employment.
After the men enlisted, the regiment spent the fall at Annapolis and then endured the rough voyage to
North Carolina. After the capture of Roanoke Island their lengthy duty in North Carolina was the "lazy

life," as they called it. Highlights include Alfred's graphic descriptions of the removal of his toenail and how taking too much quinine for ague had made his teeth and gums sore. They related episodes of misconduct by officers and soldiers alike, although William and Alfred insisted that they were free from vices. Both men remarked on the women of North Carolina. William wrote, "they look like a dog when he gets a whipping. They can't look you right in the face" (p. 78). Alfred was more explicit: "I have not seen one yet but what looked pale and sickley and had either red or white hair and chawed snuff and that is a nough to turn the stomach of a dog" (p. 111). Routines were occasionally interrupted by skirmishes and expeditions, especially in the summer of 1863. The regiment returned to Virginia in autumn 1863. Chauncey was killed at Drewry's Bluff, and Alfred was wounded at Petersburg. William was wounded at Cold Harbor but returned to duty in the trenches before Petersburg. Christopher Hudson had deserted in 1862. William's letters reflect the dilemma his family faced after the death of his father. At issue was whether the family farm should be sold, a course of action that William opposed. Advice came from as far away as Scotland, where an uncle lived, and the matter went unresolved until 1867, when the property was sold.

144. **LINN, JOHN B.** "A Tourist at Gettysburg." *Civil War Times Illustrated* 29 (September/October 1990): 26, 57–65.
July 6–11, 1863. Memoir. Lieutenant. Fifty-first Pennsylvania Infantry. While recuperating at his home in Lewisburg, Pennsylvania, Linn traveled to the Gettysburg battlefield. Along his route Linn observed graves, bodies of dead men and horses, and soldiers and civilians coming and going from the town. At Gettysburg he saw soldiers still in need of care, the carnage of the battlefield, and the battle sites. Linn also related incidents that were told to him by those present during the battle.

145. **LOOP, CHARLES.** "Your Charlie." *Civil War Times Illustrated* 31 (January/February 1993): 20, 62–69.
July 26–December 20, 1864. Letters. Major. Ninety-fifth Illinois Infantry. Atlanta campaign, including the battle for the city; and Nashville.

146. **MAHER, THOMAS E.** "'I Hardly Have the Heart to Write These Few Lines. . . .'" Edited by Brian C. Pohanka. *Civil War Regiments* 1, no. 2 (1991): 42–43.
October 9, 1862. Letter. Corporal. Fifth New York Infantry. Maher informs the mother of Pvt. James McCarthy of the circumstances of her son's death at second Bull Run.

147. **MAJORS, JOHN S.** *A Civil War Family.* By Bert McQueen Jr. Brownsville, Ind.: Exponent Publishers, 1987. 115 pp.
January 19, 1863–November 18, 1864. Letters. Private. Thirteenth Indiana Infantry. Siege of Charleston harbor; and the Virginia campaign, including Cold Harbor, assaults on Petersburg (June 15–18, 1864), and the siege of Petersburg (including the Petersburg Mine Assault). John's early letters convey a tone of desperation over his inability to take care of his family. Money problems instigated family arguments; John once asserted that his wife, Carrie, lived better than he did. But his wife was encountering additional problems that also contributed to John's feelings of helplessness. One George Cooks was pestering her for an undefined reason. John's anger boiled over, and he wrote that Cooks had better leave town before he got home "for I will mighty near take his life" (pp. 33–34). When separation and despair led his wife to worry about his marital fidelity, John assured her of his constancy. "You spoke like you were afraid that I would bother other women. Carrie that is something I won't do, as long as you live" (p. 26). John unsuccessfully sought release from military service because he believed that his

turn of enlistment had expired. All of these problems, in addition to the persistence of diarrhea and the strain of combat, caused John to wonder if he or any man would emerge from the war alive. Near the end of the period in which these letters were written, John had been removed from the line of fire and detached to a brigade headquarters as "brigade saddler" (repairer of officers' bridles). With the change in duty John's health and spirits improved.

148. **MCCARTER, WILLIAM.** *My Life in the Irish Brigade: The Civil War Memoirs of Private William McCarter, 116th Pennsylvania Infantry.* Edited by Kevin O'Brien. Campbell, Calif.: Savas Publishing Co., 1996. 266 pp.
August 23, 1862–May 12, 1863. Memoir. Private. 116th Pennsylvania Infantry. Organization and march to Washington, D.C.; duty at Harpers Ferry; and battles at Charlestown, Snicker's Gap, and Fredericksburg. Wounded at Fredericksburg, McCarter spent six months at hospitals in Washington and received a medical discharge on May 12, 1863. McCarter's memoirs capture the minutiae of soldier life: marches, weather, humor, fighting, and characteristics of leaders and comrades, etc. McCarter praises Gen. Thomas F. Meagher, for whom McCarter served briefly as adjutant, and his portrait includes Meagher's bouts with drunkenness. McCarter awards Gen. Winfield Scott Hancock top honors in proficiency with profanity but wrote that he was only slightly more accomplished than Gen. Phil Kearny. McCarter was among the many soldiers who thought that McClellan had been unfairly treated. As McCarter observes how differently men acted in battle than they acted in camp or on the drill grounds, he singles out the desire for self-preservation exhibited by a specific lieutenant and a certain colonel. Yet McCarter emphasizes that all men experienced "dread, fear and suspense" before they heard the command "Charge, forward, march" (p. 28). McCarter's description of the Fredericksburg campaign is the highlight of his account. He included the details of all that he saw: the month-long preparation for the attack; the bravery of the soldiers under fire; and the dead and wounded Union soldiers who blanketed the approaches to Mayre's Heights. McCarter received numerous wounds (he later emptied some three dozen projectiles from his protective blankets), but Confederate volleys prevented him from getting off the battlefield. Later he described the field hospital where he saw the results of numerous amputations that were performed unnecessarily by inexperienced physicians. His own recovery was only partially successful. Portions of the battle of Fredericksburg were published by the editor as "The Breath of Hell's Door," *Civil War Regiments* no. 4 (1994): 47–66.

149. **MCCLEERY, ROBERT W.** "A Marylander's Eyewitness Account of the Battle of Port Royal, South Carolina, 7 November 1861." By Alexandra Lee Levin. *Maryland Historical Magazine* 85 (Summer 1990): 179–83.
November 7, 1861. Letter. Chief Engineer aboard the USS *Wabash*, Adm. Samuel F. Du Pont's flagship of the South Atlantic Blockading Squadron. Battle of Port Royal.

150. **MCCLELLAN, GEORGE B.** *The Civil War Papers of George B. McClellan: Selected Correspondence, 1860–1865.* Edited by Stephen W. Sears. New York: Ticknor & Fields, 1989. 651 pp.
December 27, 1860–July 4, 1865. Major General. Army of the Potomac. These official documents and personal letters begin with McClellan as president of the Ohio & Mississippi Railroad and continue with his Civil War service, his bid to become president of the United States, through to the immediate postwar period. The majority of the 813 documents are military letters and dispatches and his personal correspondence. Many were previously unpublished. In addition, another 192 letters to his wife, Mary Ellen, "appear here uncensored for the first time" (p. x). The editor deems these letters to McClellan's wife particularly valuable because "he told her everything of his emotions and opinions and motives" (p. xii). Themes included in the correspondence are McClellan's messianic complex and conviction that

the fate of the nation depended on him; self-praise of his battlefield victories and denial of defeat (or failure to achieve greater successes); and feuds with the Lincoln administration, especially Stanton and Halleck. After he was relieved of command of the Army of the Potomac in November 1862, he wrote his wife that "No cause was given" and added, "alas for my poor country" (p. 520). McClellan said that he was sorry for his successor, Ambrose Burnside, and wrote a letter to Mary Burnside assuring her that cordial relations between him and her husband continued. The correspondence written during 1863 and 1864 reveals his inactivity within the military, his eventual resignation from the army (just prior to the November 1864 election), and his unsuccessful pursuit of the presidency. His few letters near the end of the war were written from Italy. The editor divided the correspondence into eleven chapters, each preceded by an introduction. He compiled indexes of addresses and a general index, which includes a year-by-year listing of topics about which McClellan wrote. Sears utilized this correspondence in his 1988 biography, *George B. McClellan: The Young Napoleon* (New York: Ticknor & Fields).

151. MCCONNELL, HENRY A. "Volunteer's Tour of Duty." By Larry Wakefield. *Military History* 5 (April 1989): 42–49.

1862–1865. Letters. Private. Tenth Minnesota Infantry. This includes McConnell's military activities during Sibley's 1863 expedition against the Sioux in the Dakota Territory and at the battle of Nashville.

152. MCDONALD, ANDREW. *Daily Diary of Andrew McDonald during the Civil War Years.* Edited by Niels T. Andersen. Cedar Springs, Mich.: Cedar Springs Rotary Club, 1987. 172 pp.

August 1862–April 1865. Memoir and diary. Twenty-first Michigan Infantry. Pursuit of Bragg in Kentucky; Chickamauga; duty in Tennessee; the March to the Sea; the Carolinas campaign (including the battle of Bentonville); and the Grand Review. Among the brief notations are reports of duty with an engineer brigade that built bridges around Chattanooga, the burning of Atlanta, bushwhacker activity against Union soldiers in North Carolina, and a postwar tour of Libby Prison.

153. MCILVAINE, SAMUEL. *By the Dim and Flaring Lamps: The Civil War Diaries of Samuel McIlvaine.* Edited by Clayton E. Cramer. Monroe, N.Y.: Library Research Associates, 1990. 157 pp.

February 5–June 10, 1862. Diary and letters. Tenth Indiana Infantry. Duty in Kentucky, including Logan's Cross Roads; and the siege and evacuation of Corinth, Mississippi. McIlvaine recorded incidents of camp life and marches, usually in the mud and rain, without offering the slightest complaint. Much of his diary reads like a travel account. He noted the crops that were grown and differences between the poorer and richer sections of Kentucky. He conversed with slaves and civilians of both Union and Confederate sympathies. He devoted one page to a cotton gin, a machine about which he had previously only heard. He explored a saltpeter cave in Kentucky and described the shorelines of the Ohio, Cumberland, Tennessee, and Mississippi Rivers from boats, noting the differences in vegetation and terrain. During the last month covered by this account McIlvaine was ill. He recorded the exact medications he was given and related events of the time he spent in recuperation with a civilian family of Confederate sympathies.

154. MCMAHAN, ROBERT A. "Conduct and Revolt in the Twenty-fifth Ohio Battery: An Insider's Account." By Dennis K. Boman. *Ohio History* 104 (Summer/Autumn 1995): 163–83.

1861–1864. Diary. Second Ohio Cavalry and Twenty-fifth Ohio Light Artillery Battery. Boman utilizes McMahan's diary to "consider the attitudes and circumstances that caused the Twenty-fifth Ohio

Artillery to revolt" (p. 165). The underlying issues in the revolt were the enlisted men's lack of confidence in their commander, the citizen-soldiers' rights to consider the appropriateness of an officer's command, and the need for officers to accommodate those men who had elected them. The first part of the article treats the army's practice of democratic elections of officers and how the process undermined the officers' authority. McMahan's diary provides examples of enlisted men ignoring officer's orders regarding the confiscation of private property and the emancipation of slaves. The second part of the article addresses the issue of whether companies of the Second Ohio Cavalry could be legally transferred to the Twenty-fifth Ohio Light Artillery and, if they could, for what length of time. The revolt in late 1862 by the enlisted men took the form of refusal to muster. While the men were being threatened with courts-martial, the issues were referred to higher military authorities. The men ultimately agreed to serve.

155. MCMAHON, JOHN T. *John T. McMahon's Diary of the 136th New York, 1861–1864.* Edited by John Michael Priest. Shippensburg, Pa.: White Mane Publishing Co., 1993. 142 pp.

September 27, 1861–December 3, 1864. Diary. Sergeant. 136th New York Infantry. Fredericksburg (observed); Burnside's "Mud March"; Chancellorsville; Gettysburg, including pursuit of Lee; Lookout Mountain; the Atlanta campaign; and the March to the Sea. The first eleven months of this diary contain events of McMahon's civilian life on his western New York farm. On August 7, 1862, he weighed the pros and cons of volunteering or waiting to be drafted. He chose volunteering because he would receive both a bonus and additional pay. However, he felt that it was equally important for it to be said that he had willingly volunteered to fight for his country. McMahon recorded events in a straightforward style. He was shot on two occasions, but he merely described the events. He was promoted to sergeant but betrayed no sense of pride. He did note such incidents as hearing a great amount of swearing in camp, taking his first bath in three years shortly after enlisting (he recorded another the following June), seeing a Confederate sign which read "Burnside's stuck in the mud," marching in knee-deep mud during the winter of 1862, recording receipt of pay, performing routine duties, and moving from place to place. McMahon described the frequency of the fighting, but he often remarked that his unit was not involved. At Gettysburg, however, clearly he was engaged as he wrote "Today I was in it" (p. 53). Later he called Resaca the regiment's hardest fight. McMahon was a staunch Methodist, and he frequently criticized chaplains and the lack of substance in their sermons. On one occasion he summarized his feelings: "I have come to the conclusion that our Chaplains are a class of men that could not get employment at home and by underhanded work have got to be Chaplains" (p. 60). The concluding portions of McMahon's diary are not extant.

156. MARKLE, DEWITT C. "'. . . The True Definition of War': The Civil War Diary of DeWitt C. Markle." Edited by Erich L. Ewald. *Indiana Magazine of History* 89 (June 1993): 125–35.

January 2–August 17, 1863. Diary. Fifty-seventh Indiana Infantry. This article includes the battle of Stones River, where Markle was wounded in the leg. His recuperation at a series of hospitals—Nashville, New Albany, Indiana, and the Soldier's Home in Indianapolis—was slow. The quotation in the title of the article is Markle's lament about those friends at home who were enjoying the blessings of peace that were provided at the expense of the soldiers.

157. MARTIN, HIRAM H. "Service Afield and Afloat: A Reminiscence of the Civil War." Edited by Guy R. Everson. *Indiana Magazine of History* 89 (March 1993): 35–56.

1861–1864. Memoir. Duty in Kentucky, Mississippi, on the Tennessee River, and in Louisiana. Martin recalled his induction into the Twenty-ninth Indiana Infantry and shipment to Camp Nevin for training and picket duty. The various illnesses from which many other Indiana soldiers in Kentucky died between November 1861 and February 1862 also affected Martin. He received a medical discharge from the army in June 1862. His service aboard ironclads with the Western Flotilla began in April 1863. As a member of the Mississippi River Marine Brigade, he related how the guerrillas on the shore fired on the vessels and described the skirmishes that followed. In March 1864 his boat captured a large amount of cotton on the Black River in Louisiana, and later that spring he participated in Banks's second Red River campaign.

158. MATRAU, HENRY. *Letters Home: Henry Matrau of the Iron Brigade.* Edited by Marcia Reid-Green. Foreword by Reid Mitchell. Lincoln: University of Nebraska Press, 1993. 166 pp.

July 22, 1861–July 23, 1865. Letters. Captain. Sixth Wisconsin Infantry. Second Bull Run; Antietam; Fredericksburg; Chancellorsville; Gettysburg; the Mine Run campaign; The Wilderness; Spotsylvania; the siege of Petersburg; and the Appomattox campaign. During the period of these letters Matrau rose from a sixteen-year-old private to a battle-hardened captain. His letters indicate that he was a good son who was intent on describing his battle experiences in a manner that would protect his parents from worry. For example, he related the execution of a soldier for desertion in detail but did so without emotion. And although Matrau was fiercely patriotic, he criticized Copperheads, deserters, draft dodgers, and bungling generals without endless ranting. Matrau never mentioned his feelings on the cause of the war; and he exhibited only admiration, never rancor, toward Confederates. He seldom referred to blacks or slavery. Nevertheless, Matrau's human qualities do emerge from his writings. Once he told his parents that all soldiers would read anything available to pass the time, even if "it tends towards vice & immorality," but asked that his parents not think of such reading choices as "strange" (p. 40). Another time he obtained a leave of absence on the pretense of having a sick relative at home. In addition he attempted to have his uncle use his influence as a state legislator to obtain an appointment to West Point. Matrau's first and last letters were written from Camp Randall. On July 23, 1865, he reflected on himself back then. Earlier, as he held his old flintlock, he had felt "a proud feeling of satisfaction, what a 'man' I am and I won't make a brave soldier though" (p. 124).Throughout the war it remained important to Matrau that he become a "brave soldier" and a stalwart man. On October 23, 1864, he wrote that "soldering teaches one hard lessons, but they will last a man for his life time" (p. 98). He felt that he was "able to present so clear a record of my services and I believe that my Parents will be proud of their son" (p. 98). The foreword by Reid Mitchell is a thoughtful essay on the evolution of personal narratives in writings on the Civil War during the past fifty years.

159. MATTERN, DAVID WILLIAM. "A Pennsylvania Dutch Yankee: The Civil War Letters of Private David William Mattern 1862–1863." Edited by Carolyn J. Mattern. *Pennsylvania Folklife* 36 (Autumn 1986): 2–19.

August 20, 1862–March 18, 1863. Letters. Private. 128th Pennsylvania Infantry. Duty in Washington, D.C., and Maryland, including South Mountain (aftermath) and Antietam; and duty at Harpers Ferry. Soon after enlistment the poorly equipped and inadequately trained nine-month unit was engaged in "the Cornfield" at Antietam, where Mattern received a head wound. Family matters fill most of his letters. He berated his family for not writing him three times a week, but thanked them for loans. He especially appreciated the boxes and gave advice on how to keep the eatables from spoiling in the future. Although Mattern thought that Virginia was beautiful, he felt that the land could be much more productive if worked by Pennsylvania farmers.

160. MATTESON, ELISHA C. "Dear Sister: They Fight to Whip." *Civil War Times Illustrated* 30 (May/June 1991): 16–17, 58–59.

January 12–March 3, 1863. Letters. Ninth Iowa Infantry. Vicksburg campaign. A separate letter by Elisha's brother recounts how Elisha was killed in the assault of May 22.

161. MATTOCKS, CHARLES. *"Unspoiled Heart": The Journal of Charles Mattocks of the 17th Maine.* Edited by Philip N. Racine. Knoxville: University of Tennessee Press, 1994. 446 pp.

April 18, 1863–June 14, 1865. Diary and letters. Major. Seventeenth Maine Infantry and First U.S. Sharpshooters. Chancellorsville; Gettysburg; Kelly's Ford; and the Mine Run campaign, including Payne's Farm. After being captured at The Wilderness, Mattocks was imprisoned at Camp Oglethorpe in Macon, Georgia, and at Camp Sorghum in Columbia, South Carolina, from which he escaped. After his recapture he was imprisoned at Charleston and then exchanged in February 1865. He returned to duty in time for the Appomattox campaign. Mattocks enlisted in the Seventeenth Maine immediately after his graduation from Bowdoin College in 1862. He had risen to the rank of major and acting commander of the Seventeenth Maine by spring 1864 and then was given command of the First U.S. Sharpshooters. The supremely self-confident Mattocks believed that discipline led to success on the battlefield. Thus, in each unit he commanded, inspections and reviews were the order of the day. Officers were courts-martialed and classes were held to insure proper execution of duties. Enlisted men were punished and campgrounds meticulously policed. Mattocks accepted his unpopularity without concern. However, he valued recognition by his superiors. For several weeks he wrote entries about Chancellorsville that glow with pride because he had led a midnight bayonet charge that merited official praise. At the end of July 1863 he returned to Maine on recruiting duty. Transporting a shipload of unruly conscripts from Portland to Virginia had proven hazardous to others in authority, but Mattocks reserved no qualms about punishing the "New Hampshire trash" (p. 67). Throughout his nine months of captivity Mattocks refused to allow imprisonment to alter his character. Mattocks observed that there were men who would rather stay imprisoned for fear of being exchanged and sent back into battle. He knew that the prison authorities feared escapes and was aware that many of the militia who were forced to serve as prison guards preferred to be back home. Mattocks was sincerely concerned about the enlisted men at Andersonville and frustrated with the federal policy that was allowing thousands of white prisoners to die in prison camps because the Confederacy refused to exchange the few hundred black Union soldiers it held captive. Mattocks's aborted escape from Columbia ended in recapture just short of the Tennessee border. Along the way he learned to distinguish assistance from field slaves, who could be trusted, from that of house slaves, who were more likely to report the escapees to their masters. Mattocks also discovered that the anti-Confederate communities of North Carolina were composed of Unionists, escaped Confederates, and others who simply did not want to be involved in the war. After Mattocks was exchanged in February 1865, he returned to lead his Seventeenth Maine at Sayler's Creek in a courageous charge for which he later received the Congressional Medal of Honor. During the action Mattocks characteristically detected some "stragglers & skulkers." He wrote that they "will have a dose of discipline at the first regular halt" (p. 271). Letters that Mattocks wrote to his mother are also included.

162. MELCHER, HOLMAN S. *With a Flash of His Sword: The Writings of Major Holman S. Melcher, 20th Maine Infantry.* Edited by William B. Styple. Kearny, N.J.: Belle Grove Publishing Co., 1994. 331 pp.

September 1, 1862–July 22, 1865. Letters and diary. Major. Twentieth Maine Infantry. Fredericksburg; Chancellorsville; Gettysburg, including the pursuit of Lee; the Mine Run campaign; The Wilderness; the siege of Petersburg, including second Hatcher's Run; the Appomattox campaign; Lee's surrender at Appomattox Court House; and the Grand Review. In these letters to his brother (and a diary for 1865) Melcher reveals pride that he was resisting temptations. Melcher describes Fredericksburg but did not mention that he was appointed sergeant major for meritorious service. He describes combat with bayonets at The Wilderness. At second Hatcher's Run he brought order to panicked troops. At Laurel Hill on May 8, 1864, Melcher was wounded and removed from action until the following October. He served most of the rest of the war as an aide to Gen. Gouverneur K. Warren. At Appomattox Court House he was on the V Corps headquarters staff as it accepted Confederate arms and ordnance, distributed rations, and paroled more than twenty thousand Confederate soldiers. The focal point of this work is the controversy surrounding the role of the Twentieth Maine at Little Round Top. In chapter 3, "Gettysburg: One Wild Rush" (pp. 36–143), the editor examines documents and speeches by those present during the fight for Little Round Top. Among the editor's conclusions is that the charge that routed the Confederate troops was "an impulsive and spontaneous effort in order to protect their wounded comrades in their front" (p. 143). Also, the editor believes that it was Lt. Holman Melcher, not Col. Joshua Chamberlain, who led the charge down the slope. No letters from Melcher written during this period exist; however, in an account written for a newspaper in 1885 Melcher implies that the event was spontaneous.

163. MESSER, TIMOTHY B. *Civil War Letters of Timothy B. Messer, Tenth Vermont Volunteers.* Edited by Edward C. Phelps. Greenfield, Mass.: E. A. Hall, 1986. 77 pp.
July 7, 1861–April 1, 1865. Letters. Private. Tenth Vermont Infantry. Duty in Maryland and Virginia, including the Virginia campaign (especially the assault on Fort Stedman). Messer avoided writing to his wife, Susan, about battles. He concentrated on troop movements, requests for and receipt of items from home, his frequent illnesses and stays in hospitals, and matters regarding the family's finances. With the passage of time he expressed greater confidence in his wife's judgment about affairs at home. Once he even apologized for giving her advice; he told her to do what she thought was "best and proper" (p. 61). He admitted that he had been away from home for too long to know how to help her or even how to make her happy. He wrote bluntly: "I merely write about it thinking that you would like to hear about it" (p. 60). Also included are documents regarding his death at Petersburg on April 2, 1865, as well as several letters from his wife, Susan, written in early 1864.

164. MOBUS, WILHELM. "The Life of 'Wilhelm Yank': Letters from a German Soldier in the Civil War." By David L. Anderson. *Michigan Historical Review* 16 (Spring 1990): 73–93.
September 23, 1864–May 28, 1865. Letters. Private. Thirteenth Michigan Infantry. March to the Sea and the Carolinas campaign, including battle of Bentonville. This German American entered the service in September 1864 as a substitute volunteer for another resident of Saint Joseph County, Michigan. He wrote about camp life, news of other German Americans, the receipt of boxes, and cheating that occurred when the soldiers tried to vote in the presidential election. While he was able to vote for McClellan, he said procedures prohibited many other soldiers from casting their votes for the Democrats. Mobus was usually even-tempered, but on one occasion he unleashed a tirade against doctors. He wrote: "for the doctors are all worth no more than that one would shoot him dead. They let the sick soldiers lie in camps so long until they are half dead and then they put him in the hospital" (p. 86).

165. MOLYNEUX, JOEL. *Quill of the Wild Goose: Civil War Letters and Diaries of Private Joel Molyneux, 141st P.V.* Assembled and edited by Kermit Molyneux Bird. Shippensburg, Pa.: Burd Street Press, 1996. 327 pp.
August 27, 1862–June 5, 1865. Letters and diary. Private. 141st Pennsylvania Infantry. Fredericksburg (observed); Burnside's "Mud March"; Chancellorsville; Gettysburg, including pursuit of Lee; Kelley's Ford; the Virginia campaign, including The Wilderness, Spotsylvania, and Cold Harbor; the siege of Petersburg; and the Appomattox campaign. For thirty-four months of his service Molyneux was

detached to headquarters on provost guard duty with the First Division, III and then II Corps. In his letters to his parents, who lived near Millview, Pennsylvania, and his future wife, Elvira, he mentions such everyday activities as the arrest of deserters, courts-martial, executions, the fighting during the Virginia campaign, the surrender, and the unrest that followed Lincoln's assassination. Many of his comments address matters at home, as the relationship with his former student progressed to a formal engagement. Molyneux was a strong Lincoln supporter who readily accepted freedom for the slaves as an additional war aim. Although Molyneux maintained high spirits, he hated the war. Just prior to the Virginia campaign he told Elvira that he longed for the day that he could be away from "This cruel, cruel war! . . . Vilie, I am so tired of hearing the drum, fife, and bugle—seeing white tents and white covered army wagons" (p. 181). His final entry indicates that Molyneux had realized his dream: "Are home at last, safe and sound, and my own man again!" (p. 294). The editor's research, explanations, and essays expand the scope of Molyneux's writings.

166. **MORROW, LESLIE G.** *Journal of Leslie G. Morrow, Captain's Clerk of the U.S. Steamer Galena.* Introduction by Albert P. Morrow. Yorba Linda, Calif.: Specialty Services Co., 1988. 59 pp.

February 18–November 5, 1864. Diary. USS *Galena.* Battle of Mobile Bay. Morrow's first entries describe the ship's problems getting through the ice of Philadelphia harbor. In Norfolk he contrasted the bustling, businesslike appearance of the city, which was now characterized by the "Yankee goaheaditiveness which invariably attends the march of this free and enterprising people," with the "lazy, slovenly appearance of everything in the land where the peculiar institution exists" (pp. 7–8). He also described the appearance of the Portsmouth Naval Shipyard, which federal authorities had burned when they abandoned it in April 1861. After the ship was repaired in Baltimore, it stopped in Nassau to take on coal and then continued on to Mobile Bay. Morrow recorded the attack on Mobile Bay in detail. Following the surrender of Fort Morgan, the *Galena* served with the East Gulf Blockading Squadron until its return trip to Philadelphia.

167. **MORSE, DEWITT C.** "A Fighting Sailor on the Western Rivers: The Civil War Letters of 'Gunboat.'" Edited by Jeffrey L. Patrick. *Journal of Mississippi History* 58 (Fall 1996): 255–83.

February 28–November 1, 1864. Letters. Acting Masters Mate. USS *Curlew.* Mississippi and Tennessee Rivers. Morse wrote these eight letters to his cousin, who, as editor of the *Enterprise* (Mishawaka, Indiana), published them for his readership. Morse related the presence of other ships, the landscape along the rivers, and his impressions of many cities. In his first letter he provides a favorable description of Mound City but reports that Cairo was such a mud hole that it should have been cut loose and allowed to "wash away down the river" (p. 258). In Vicksburg he saw the effects of the Union bombardment and visited the Yazoo River site of Sherman's failed Chickasaw Bluffs attack. While in Memphis he observed a "genuine rank Secesh Lady" who "merely glanced at us, with a faint smile on her face, and at the same time a most bitter curl on her lip" (p. 261). His other experiences included capturing a steamer that was smuggling cotton; being set ashore to chase guerrilla bands near Vicksburg; exchanging fire with a Confederate battery at Gaines' Landing, Arkansas; shelling Fort Henry (which Nathan Bedford Forrest's troops were thought to occupy); and then moving on to Johnsonville, Tennessee, where Forrest was in the process of bombarding the Union supply base. Soon after writing his last letter, Morse died of typhoid fever.

168. **MORTON, PHILO S., and JOHN P. WILSON.** "A Scratch with the Rebels." Edited by Carolina P. Scribner. *Civil War Times Illustrated* 32 (January/February 1994): 49.

June 16, 1862. Letter. Lieutenant and Private. One-hundredth Pennsylvania Infantry. Battle of Seces-sionville. Two soldiers of James McCaskey's regiment describe how he was killed during a bayonet charge on the fort at Secessionville.

169. MOSHER, CHARLES C. *Charlie Mosher's Civil War: From Fair Oaks to Andersonville with the Plymouth Pilgrims (85th New York Infantry).* Edited by Wayne Mahood. Highstreet, N.J.: Longstreet House, 1994. 378 pp.
October 11, 1861–April 23, 1865. Diary and letters. Eighty-fifth New York Infantry. Defenses of Wash-ington, D.C.; the Peninsular campaign, especially Seven Pines; duty in Suffolk, Virginia, and in North Carolina, including Foster's expedition to Goldsboro and the siege of Washington. Mosher was cap-tured during the Confederate siege of Plymouth, North Carolina, and imprisoned in Andersonville and Florence Prisons. He said that in North Carolina the soldiers sought amusement by sneaking up on blacks and throwing flour in their faces. The men also dropped cartridges down the chimneys of the black troops' houses. Mosher tersely remarked: "Fun for us" (p. 77). At Seven Pines a wounded man insisted that his arm be amputated, although the surgeons believed that the operation was unnecessary. Mosher administered the chloroform; however, because he gave the soldier an insufficient amount, the man threw up his arm as the surgeons were cutting. Mosher said that another man in the hospital com-plained that his heel ached and insisted that he needed to stand on it. In reality, Mosher wrote, "His heel was in a field with other legs and arms" (p. 58). When the regiment was captured at Plymouth, the men shredded their flag and distributed the small pieces. Soldiers of another regiment, the Second North Car-olina Infantry (U.S.), traded uniforms with dead men of other regiments so that Confederates would not discover that they were serving in the Union army. One white captain who was serving with the United States Colored Troops exchanged his uniform to prevent being identified as an officer of black troops. As it became obvious to the black troops that Plymouth was about to fall, they fled and were shot on sight. Mosher commented: "It was a massacre" (p. 205). Mosher was at Andersonville between April 30 and September 16, 1864; then he was sent to Charleston for six weeks. He spent the period of Octo-ber 6, 1864, through March 1, 1865, at Florence Prison. Among his entries about prison life is a descrip-tion of how black troops at Florence had their "blankets and stuff" stolen by the "galvanized Yankees." The Union officers gave the black soldiers permission to recover their possessions. Of the fight that ensued, Mosher wrote: "It is needless to say that the 'darks' gained the day as well as their goods" (p. 277). Mosher concluded his diary with his exchange at Wilmington and travel home to Seneca Falls, New York.

170. MOSMAN, CHESLEY A. *The Rough Side of War: The Civil War Journal of Chesley A. Mosman, First Lieutenant, Company D, 59th Illinois Volunteer Regiment.* Edited, with biographical sketch, by Arnold Gates. Garden City, N.Y.: Basin Publishing Co., 1987. 442 pp.
January 24, 1862–January 13, 1866. Journal. Lieutenant. Ninth Missouri Infantry and Fifty-ninth Illi-nois Infantry. Duty in Arkansas, including Pea Ridge; Kentucky, including Perryville; Tennessee, including the Tullahoma campaign, the siege of Chattanooga, and Lookout Mountain; the Atlanta cam-paign; operations against Hood in northern Georgia and Alabama; and the battles of Franklin and Nashville, where Mosman was wounded. He served the remainder of the war in Alabama and east Ten-nessee and in Texas after the surrender. Hardly a day went by that the observant Mosman failed to make notations on a variety of themes, but the grime and drudgery implicit in soldiering appear repeatedly. In September 1863 he wrote that the "Dust was just awful, filling eyes, nose, and throat, and settling down on clothes that were wet with perspiration" (p. 82). By December it was "Rain, rain, rain. Will it never stop. . . . Cloudy and the mud stands in seas" (p. 141). His brief entry of August 3, 1864, bespeaks volumes: "Sanitary conditions are bad and the stench in camp is awful" (p. 253). Mules that had starved

to death were scattered all around Chattanooga. Flies were everywhere during the Atlanta campaign, but Mosman outsmarted them. He lured them into "a column" with sugar and then "blew up 2000 of them by using cartridges as a cannon" (p. 260). Mosman read constantly, swam when he was able, played chess rather than chuck-a-luck, learned to play the scale on a flute, and remarked uncritically on vices such as drunkenness. Mosman's sensitive nature is frequently revealed. He was aware of the beauty of the landscape. In December 1863, when he saw snow and ice frozen on trees, he called them "the prettiest Christmas trees I ever saw—my what visions memory raises at mention of those words." Then he stopped abruptly, writing: "Put it away. There is no such thing as Christmas recognized by U.S. Army regulations, so quit your dreaming" (p. 145). In November 1864, after having written a letter of condolence to the family of a man he hardly knew, Mosman mused: "Poor fellow; somebody's darling. But there are lots of darlings here engaged in a bloody work in which there is no place for sentiment" (p. 307). But when his war-long comrade was killed at Nashville, Mosman mourned and composed two lengthy eulogies to his friend. During his last six months of duty in Texas, Mosman, unlike other troops of occupation, apparently enjoyed himself.

171. MUNHALL, LEANDER WHITCOMB. *Letters Home, 1862–1865.* By George A. Smyth III. N.p.: George A. Smyth Publishing Company, 1992. 107 pp.

August 10, 1862–April 17, 1865. Letters. Seventy-ninth Indiana Infantry. Duty in Kentucky and Tennessee; Stones River; the Tullahoma campaign; Chickamauga; the siege of Chattanooga; Missionary Ridge; the Atlanta campaign; Nashville and the pursuit of Hood; and duty in east Tennessee. Munhall signed his letters to his mother with variations of "From your obt. (obedient) Son." He apologized for enlisting without requesting her permission, and when a woman named "Gussie" wrote him a "Dear John" letter, Munhall asked his mother and brother not to blame Gussie's "kind, good" parents because their daughter "has proven herself unworthy of me" (p. 60). Soon after that Munhall feared that his mother had also forgotten him, but he quickly explained that it was Gussie's deception that led him to "sometimes think that a Mother's Love is *apt* to retract" (p. 77). The religious Munhall described how on a Sunday morning the "glad songs of Zion" at one end of the camps competed with the unintentional "blaspheming or singing some vulgar song" at the other (p. 91). Munhall also wrote of other aspects of camp life and his duties as quartermaster and postmaster. At Stones River he described his participation in a bayonet charge. During the Atlanta campaign he wrote on June 25 that he had been out of the line of fire for only six of the previous thirty-four days. Munhall saw the bloody spot where Confederate general (and Episcopal bishop) Leonidas Polk was killed, but he exhibited only disdain. Munhall was impressed by the effectiveness of black soldiers at the battle of Nashville; he wrote, "No one kneed tell me they won't fight for I know better. They fought like demonds" (p. 94). Abraham Lincoln's assassination was "threatening," and Munhall called it the greatest calamity "that has ever happened to the government" (p. 102). Some letters written to his brother at home expand on topics mentioned in letters to his mother. Munhall's diary entries for the summer of 1864 flesh out events for that active period when he was able to write few letters.

172. MURPHEY, JOSIAH FITCH. *The Civil War: The Nantucket Experience, Including the Memoirs of Josiah Fitch Murphey.* By Richard F. Miller and Robert F. Mooney. Nantucket, Mass.: Wesco Publishing, 1994. 196 pp.

August 1862–August 1864. Memoir. Private. Twentieth Massachusetts Infantry. Second Bull Run; South Mountain (aftermath); Antietam; Fredericksburg; Chancellorsville; the Mine Run campaign; The Wilderness; Spotsylvania; and the siege of Petersburg. Murphey's recollections begin with indoctrination into military life. Chaos reigned at Camp Cameron as men of different backgrounds grouped together. Although the unit had received almost no training, it soon undertook a hard march to Maryland, disposing of unneeded clothing along the way. Murphey's first observation of men who had been killed in battle was at South Mountain, where he gathered battlefield souvenirs. His regiment's baptism of fire came the next day at Antietam. Murphey wrote that he never felt real fear because of the excitement of the moment, the need to obey orders under penalty of death, and the threat of being considered a coward by others. Murphey related a pleasant conversation with a wounded rebel and the horrors of the hospital after he was shot in the face at Fredericksburg and again when he contracted typhoid fever en route to Gettysburg. He recounted the story of a soldier who was arrested for leaving the battle after having witnessed his father's death. (Because of the circumstances, the son was only discharged.) Murphey declined reenlistment in July 1864. In addition to editing this account, the two authors have also composed an economic and historical sketch of Nantucket at midcentury which reveals the impact of the war on the community. Many of the men from Murphey's Company I were from Nantucket.

173. MUSSER, CHARLES O. *Soldier Boy: The Civil War Letters of Charles O. Musser, 29th Iowa.* Edited by Barry Popchock. Iowa City: University of Iowa Press, 1995. 260 pp.

December 14, 1862–July 25, 1865. Letters. Sergeant. Twenty-ninth Iowa Infantry. Duty in Helena, Arkansas; the Yazoo Pass expedition; the battle of Helena; Steele's expedition to Little Rock, including the battle of Little Rock; duty at Little Rock; the Camden expedition, including Jenkins' Ferry; the Mobile campaign, including Spanish Fort and Fort Blakely; and duty at Brazos Santiago, Texas, and New Orleans. Musser attempted to explain to his parents why he enlisted against their wishes. Because his father was experiencing difficulty maintaining the family farm near Council Bluffs, Musser felt guilty. He wrote: "I ought to have stayed home on your account" and later "I Know it is hard for you to See to every thing there. I done wrong in enlisting" (pp. 70, 95). But he emphasized that it was his duty to serve his country. Always eager for action, Musser was restricted to relative inactivity. However, guerrilla actions were constant. He mentioned how guerrillas who had been captured had "misteriously disappeared" while being escorted back to Union lines (p. 53). And later during a skirmish, "some raised a white rag, but no such thing was in the thoughts of our boys" (pp. 99). At Jenkins' Ferry he narrowly missed being killed, but he shot his attacker. When Musser returned to the spot he remarked, "there lay the dead rebbel just as he fell, his face white as a sheet, the life Blood all drained out. Poor fellow—he showed bravery worthy of a better cause" (p. 140). As Musser attempted to analyze the bond between soldiers, he compared the camaraderie to "the ties of a Secret Brotherhood." He believed that the army brought out the "weak and strong points in a man's Character" and that "if a man is a friend to you here, he is a friend that you can depend on anywhere" (p. 152). Musser remained enthusiastic throughout his service, but he was glad when the war was over. He said that he was tired of marching and fighting; of hearing the drum, fife, and bugles; and of the musketry and cannons. On June 9, 1865, he wrote apologetically: "I cannot write anymore long letters like I used to. I do not feel like the same person I was a year ago" (pp. 211–13).

174. NEIL, ALEXANDER. *Alexander Neil and the Last Shenandoah Valley Campaign: Letters of an Army Surgeon to His Family, 1864.* Edited by Richard R. Duncan. Shippensburg, Pa.: White Mane Publishing Co., 1996. 156 pp.

February 28–December 18, 1864. Letters. Surgeon. Twelfth West Virginia Infantry. Franz Sigel's expedition to New Market, including the battle of New Market; Hunter's Shenandoah Valley campaign, including Piedmont and Lynchburg; Early's Washington raid, including second Kernstown; Snicker's Ferry; Sheridan's Shenandoah Valley campaign, including third Winchester, Fisher's Hill, and Cedar Creek; and the Appomattox campaign. Shortly after his graduation from medical school Neil wrote to his family in Ohio about the struggle for control of the valley. He described Union soldiers fleeing in panic at both New Market and at second Kernstown. At Piedmont he detailed how a Union bayonet charge helped to secure victory, and as he worked among the wounded on the battlefield, he saw how the men begged for his help. He regretted that there was little a field surgeon could do except "to administer a little cordial occasionally or ligate a bleeding artery & see that they are carefully handled by the stretcher bearers" (p. 35). After one year of medical service Neil was well aware of how much medical experience he had obtained, "particularly in the branch of operative surgery" (p. 52). By fall 1864 Neil described fewer of his experiences. Perhaps, as he explained after Cedar Creek, it was because he felt: "To go over the battlefield the next day after the battle was a *great,* but *common* sight to me, as it was the 10th battle I have been in this summer & fall" (p. 73). Neil wrote that David Hunter's campaign of destruction was excessively brutal and thought that it reflected the general's personality: "I must say that I am ashamed to belong to an army under such a *tyrant.* Loose reign was given to the soldiers in all kinds of vice, robbery, and murder" (p. 39). Only a few months later, however, the battle-hardened Neil approved of Sheridan's policy of destruction. The editor summarizes Neil's activities of 1865 around Richmond and includes Neil's letter from Appomattox of April 10, 1865, in which he wrote about the preceding ten days.

175. NEMO. "Shiloh: Where Death Knows No Distinction: 'Nemo,' 6th Ohio Infantry at the Battle of Shiloh." Edited by Gary L. Ecelbarger. *Civil War: The Magazine of the Civil War Society* 50 (April 1995): 66–69.

April 5–7, 1862. Letter. Officer. Sixth Ohio Infantry. Battle of Shiloh. First published in the *Cincinnati Daily Commercial* on April 10, 1862.

176. NICKERSON, MARK. *Recollections of the Civil War by a High Private in the Front Ranks.* N.p.: N. pub., 1991. 109 pp.

1861–1865. Memoir. Tenth Massachusetts Infantry and Thirteenth New York Cavalry. Peninsular campaign; second Bull Run; Antietam; Fredericksburg; Chancellorsville; Gettysburg; and the Virginia campaign, including The Wilderness, Spotsylvania, Cold Harbor, and the siege of Petersburg. Nickerson was certain why he enlisted: "a mighty wave of patriotism was sweeping over the North and West. . . . The war fever was raging. . . . It got hold of me strong. I must go to war. . . . The Union must be preserved" (p. 3). After Bull Run he knew that "it was not going to be a picnic, but that it meant serious business" (p. 7). As he wrote many years later, all of the inexpressible, horrid forms of war he had experienced were awakened in him: "You have got to be in it, walk over a battlefield after a big battle and witness the buring of the dead and visit a field hospital" (p. 14). Before entering the battle at Malvern Hill, Nickerson destroyed the letters of a lady friend in case he was killed. At Antietam he recalled that a woman acting as a rebel soldier was found among the Confederate dead. Also at Antietam, Nickerson assisted a wounded man to a field hospital where he observed arms and legs piled three feet high. His recollection of the ghastly operations going on inside the tent filled one complete page. When the VI Corps learned that their assignment was to storm Maryes Heights at Chancellorsville, he said that the men again felt that they were going into a death trap: "A feeling of weight came over me, as though I was held down by some weight which I was unable to throw off" (p. 57). After Nickerson's enlistment with the Tenth Massachusetts Infantry had expired, he was uncomfortable as a civilian, as "uneasy as a fish out of water" (p. 105). Three months later he enlisted in the Thirteenth New York Cavalry, which Nickerson thought fun by comparison with the infantry. His final entries relate a cavalry dash from Maryland to Washington following Lincoln's assassination to protect the nation's capital.

177. NORTON, OLIVER W. "Vincent's Brigade on Little Round Top." Edited by James R. Wright. *Gettysburg Magazine* 1 (July 1989): 41–44.

July 1–3, 1863. Memoir. Private. Eighty-third Pennsylvania Infantry. Brigade bugler and color bearer (Third Brigade, First Division, V Corps, Army of the Potomac). Battle of Gettysburg. This is a description of the battle written to the editor of *Appleton's Cyclopedia of American Biography* on September 28, 1888.

178. **NUGENT, WASHINGTON GEORGE.** *My Darling Wife: The Letters of Washington George Nugent, Surgeon, Army of the Potomac.* Compiled and annotated by his great-granddaughter, Marice Randall Allen. Cheshire, Conn.: Ye Olde Book Bindery, 1994. 363 pp.

January 17, 1861–July 17, 1865. Letters. Major. Fourteenth Pennsylvania Infantry (three-month), Ninety-sixth Pennsylvania Infantry, and 126th Pennsylvania Infantry. Duty in Pennsylvania, Maryland, Virginia (including the Peninsular campaign, Fredericksburg, and Burnside's "Mud March"); and Fort Delaware Prison. A sense of duty to his country induced this thirty-nine-year-old Pennsylvania doctor to leave his wife and child. He expressed his reasons with such phrases as "chastisement of the enemies of our beloved institution" (p. 112) and "teaching the rascals a lesson that they were unwise in expounding the rebellion" (p. 123). As late as February 6, 1865, he thought an appropriate conclusion to the war would be "a delivery over of the leaders to expiate their crimes with a rope about their necks" (p. 310). But Nugent's patriotism was coupled with his recognition that his wartime experiences would make him a better doctor, as well as improve his financial status. Nugent seldom wrote about the slave issue, but in a letter written shortly after the issuance of the Emancipation Proclamation his feelings are clear: "I have no fancy for emancipating a lot of uneducated wild, ferocious and brutal negroes, I hate it" (pp. 163–64). As a doctor he felt helpless that all he could do was offer his patients the temporary relief of good cheer or an opium-laced powder. Aboard the hospital ships off the Virginia Peninsula he was concerned about being able to keep the wounded covered from the rain and preventing them from slipping overboard. He enjoyed being an administrator of a field hospital in charge of all aspects of its operation. Although he abhorred paperwork, as head surgeon of Fort Delaware Prison, Nugent left detailed descriptions of his duties and the management of the prison hospital. Among his observations was that the Southerners seemed to have little immunity to childhood diseases, a disposition which rendered them vulnerable to pneumonia. They also exhibited a particular aversion to the cold weather. Nugent's relationships with the other doctors was distant. He tried to explain his sense of incompatibility when he wrote: "I am wrongly made up"; "I do not enjoy society in general"; and "I was not formed for such enjoyment" (February 22, 1864). Nugent said he cared only to be back with his wife, Sarah, and daughter, Minnie. Many of his letters express that desperate longing for his family.

179. **ODELL, THOMAS GOLDSBOROUGH.** *The Civil War Correspondence of Judge Thomas Goldsborough Odell.* Edited by Donald Odell Virdin. Introduction and historical footnotes by Brian C. Pohanka. Bowie, Md.: Heritage Books, 1992. 133 pp.

September 4, 1862–January 8, 1865. Letters. Seventy-eighth Illinois Infantry. Duty in Kentucky and Tennessee, including the battle of Chickamauga. Letters to his wife, Beliscent, and his four children reveal Odell's devotion to them and describe places he was posted, as well as news about the men from Adams County, Illinois. The family's economic problems appear early in the correspondence. The rent on the house in which the family was living was increased soon after Odell was inducted. Beliscent had to decide whether she should move or stay. Odell did not conceal his anger toward his landlord: "I have had about as much to do with that man as I am going to have" (p. 21). Odell frequently expressed a yearning to see his family, and Beliscent became despondent about their separation. Odell reminded her that part of the reason for his being away was for her benefit. Odell was fighting the war to demolish slavery and the potential enslavement of others, which in mid 1863 he described as "That *institution*, that principle, which had crushed the freedom of the black man, & placed him on a level with the brute, and which was making rapid strides toward the enslavement of the entire poor class of whites" (p. 74). Thus, it was with pride in late 1864 that he pointed to the progress of the "downtrodden," not only on "the *National* sky" but by all nations: "God is the respecter of persons, and he is not always going to permit man to oppress his fellow man" (p. 127). Odell liked all the blacks he met and took pride in teaching his cook to read and write. Wounded at Chickamauga, Odell avoided amputation, but he required treatment for fourteen months in army hospitals at Chattanooga, Murfreesboro, and Quincy, Illinois. Odell served as a judge following the war.

180. **OSBORN, THOMAS WARD.** *No Middle Ground: Thomas Ward Osborn's Letters from the Field (1862–1864).* Edited by Herb S. Crumb and Katherine Dhalle. Hamilton, N.Y.: Edmonston Publishing, 1993. 199 pp.

March 6, 1862–March 20, 1864. Letters. Captain, First New York Light Artillery, Battery D; then Major, Chief of Artillery, XI Corps. Peninsular campaign, including the siege of Yorktown, Williamsburg, Seven Pines, Oak Grove, and Savage's Station; Fredericksburg (observed); Chancellorsville; pursuit of Lee after Gettysburg; and the siege of Chattanooga, including Wauhatchie, Lookout Mountain, and Missionary Ridge. At Williamsburg, Osborn and his cannoneers volunteered to man guns that had been deserted by another battery. In December 1862, after his Battery D had been commended by the regimental chief of artillery, Col. Charles S. Wainwright, Osborn explained to one brother how his hard work and philosophy of leadership had contributed to the unit's recognition. Osborn said that the first time he was under fire he did not feel "the sickening anxiety so often spoken of as affecting men going into battle" (p. 30). After Seven Pines he described the stench of dead men and horses and the sight of the mutilated wounded and dead. Osborn was aware of George McClellan's strengths and weaknesses. He remained an apologist for Joe Hooker. However, he found no redeeming qualities in Burnside's leadership. Osborn believed Ulysses S. Grant to be "head and shoulders above any other General under whom I have served" (p. 182). Osborn also assessed the Confederate military. At first he thought that Stonewall Jackson was the South's best general. After Chancellorsville, however, he transferred that accolade to Lee. Osborn believed that the Confederacy's propensity for massing troops at one point for an attack was an effective battle plan on the Peninsula because McClellan reacted slowly. But later in the war Osborn felt that the tactic had cost the Confederacy more men than it could afford to lose. Osborn described the melee at Chancellorsville as he attempted to force his artillery forward through the retreating XI Corps on the night of May 2. Osborn initially wrote that a battery of his command was responsible for wounding Stonewall Jackson, but he later corrected himself when he learned that Gen. A. P. Hill had been wounded instead. During June and July 1863 Osborn wrote few letters about the Gettysburg campaign, but in the fall he penned considerably more about the performance of his batteries at Chattanooga. During the Atlanta campaign he was assigned as chief of artillery, Army of the Tennessee. An account of the later year of his service was published as *The Fiery Trail . . .* (Knoxville: University of Tennessee Press, 1986) and was edited by Richard Harwell and Philip N. Racine. Osborn's several accounts of Gettysburg were published as *The Eleventh Corps Artillery at Gettysburg . . .* (Hamilton, N.Y.: Edmonston Publishing, 1991) and were edited by Herb S. Crumb.

181. **PAGE, WILLIAM H.** "I Shall Be a Prisoner." *Civil War Times Illustrated* 30 (September/October 1991): 42–52, 65, 67–73, 75.

1862. Memoir. Surgeon. Peninsular campaign. When the federal army withdrew from the Peninsula, this civilian surgeon decided to stay with the wounded at Savage's Station's field hospital. He described how the men were soon captured, imprisoned in Richmond, and paroled after about six weeks. Throughout the ordeal Dr. Page continued to care for the wounded prisoners.

182. **PALMER, JOHN, WILLIAM T. PALMER, and EDWARD L. PALMER.** *"Thy Affectionate Son . . .": A Collection of Letters of Three Brothers: John Palmer, William T. Palmer, and Edward L. Palmer from the 1860's.* Compiled and edited by James B. Stabler. Colorado Springs, Colo.: James B. Stabler, 1993. 78 leaves.

1862–1865. Letters. John (124th Pennsylvania Infantry) wrote between May 29, 1862, and October 6, 1865, and described Antietam. William (Sixteenth Pennsylvania, three-month) wrote between September 17 and November 8, 1862, when his militia regiment was called up during the Antietam campaign. Edward (Fifteenth Pennsylvania Cavalry) wrote between October 27, 1864, and June 22, 1865. He described his duty around Chattanooga, pursuit of Hood's army following Franklin and Nashville, and Stoneman's raid into southwest Virginia and northern North Carolina. All of the soldiers' letters focus on day-to-day activities. John was mustered out May 15, 1863, but several postservice letters were written from Cincinnati. Edward related public reaction to Lincoln's death. He said that people feared the assassination was only the preliminary of something even more dreadful yet to come. He felt that the atmosphere of that period was comparable to the one that existed at the beginning of the war.

183. **PARDEE, GEORGE K.** *"My Dear Carrie": The Civil War Letters of George K. Pardee and Family.* Edited by Robert H. Jones with Caroline J. Pardee. Akron, Ohio: Summit County Historical Society Press, 1994. 286 pp.
August 5, 1862–September 21, 1864. Letters. Captain. Forty-second Ohio Infantry. Sherman's Yazoo expedition, including Chickasaw Bluffs; Arkansas Post; duty at Milliken's Bend and Young's Point; the Vicksburg campaign; and staff duty in Louisiana and at Saint Charles, Arkansas. The editor estimates that of the approximately 760 days Pardee was in service, some 660 were spent in routine duty. During the Vicksburg campaign Pardee saw that the rivalry between Generals Grant and Sherman on one side and McClernand on the other was hampering military success. Pardee exhibited almost no feelings toward blacks, and while he did call them "Nigs" or "darkies," his usual terms of reference were "of African descent" or "colored." Pardee's letters to Carrie always contained expressions of affection for his wife and son. Unfortunately, he found a much-longed-for furlough to be bittersweet. He could scarcely withstand the agony of having to say good-bye. His letters written after his return to duty speak less of devotion to his country and more of love for his family and expectations for a good life after the war. Pardee was insightful. When he observed a fight between "two darkies" who were being cheered on by a ring of soldiers, Pardee did not share their enthusiasm; rather, he blamed their actions on the war: "It almost makes a man wild, and uncivilized to be a soldier" (p. 136). Pardee was apprehensive about the great number of single women that would exist after the war. According to the history of all wars, Pardee wrote, the loss of so many young men led to degradation. Thus, "it must surely follow after the war females will become demoralized" (p. 222). Pardee believed that the solution rested with the males: "men must be men and blot all mean thoughts from their minds forever as the rules of society will be trampled under foot" (p. 222). The editor provides information about the family's subsequent lives.

184. **PARKER, ISAAC NEWTON.** *A Seneca Indian in the Union Army: The Civil War Letters of Sergeant Isaac Newton Parker, 1861–1865.* Edited by Laurence M. Hauptman. Shippensburg, Pa.: Burd Street Press, 1995. 120 pp.
October 9, 1861–April 1, 1865. Letters. Sergeant. 132nd New York Infantry. Duty at Suffolk, Virginia, and near New Bern, North Carolina, including the battle of Batchelder's Creek. Parker, a Seneca from the Tonawanda Indian Reservation in New York, was educated at the Baptist Mission school and attended New York State Normal School at Albany. When the war began, he was a farmer and teacher. Parker's first attempt to enlist was denied because, as he wrote on October 9, 1861, "there is no regulation, that is no law for accepting the 'red man' in the 'U.S.' law" (p. 47). But the following summer he and twenty-four other Indians enlisted as members of the integrated Company D (the Tuscarora Company) of the 132nd New York, after serving briefly with the Fifty-third New York. Parker's initial letters to his wife relate some of the problems in the recruitment of Indians in New York state. In writings from North Carolina he mentioned daily camp routines, his assignment of signaling, and promotion to company color-bearer. He provided news about the other Indians and implied that a har-

monious relationship existed with the white soldiers. Parker expressed a desire to protect the Union and the Constitution and fought to quell the rebellion. He wrote love letters to his wife, but she seldom wrote to him, especially after late 1863. By May 7, 1864, he was desperate. He begged her to tell him what was wrong: "Must a rupture occur between *you* and me?—Oh! *God* forbid!" (p. 99). His later correspondence contains no references to his wife. In June 1864 he asked his sister to send him moccasins (army boots were too hot) and gifts for a North Carolina family. He wrote little about fighting, but he mentioned several marches and the presence of Confederate scouts around the Union pickets. In a letter to his sister-in-law he described the fatal wounding of a friend and how the Confederates stripped their captives of all possessions. The letter of condolence he wrote to the parents of the friend is included. The editor's introduction and footnotes contribute considerably to this scattered collection of letters.

185. **PARKHURST, CLINTON.** "Corinth: Tenting on the Old Camp Ground: A Soldier Summers in Mississippi." Edited by Allyn R. Vannoy. *Civil War Times Illustrated* 25 (January 1987): 30–35.
Summer 1862. Memoir. Corporal. Sixteenth Iowa Infantry. Parkhurst reflects on a quiet summer in Corinth absorbed in camp routines.

186. **PARKS, GEORGE.** *The Civil War Letters of Private George Parks, Company C, 24th New York Cavalry Volunteers.* By Joseph M. Overfield. Buffalo, N.Y.: Gallagher Printing, 1992. 109 pp.
January 25, 1864–July 28, 1865. Letters. Private. Twenty-fourth New York Cavalry. Duty at the forts around Washington, D.C.; the Virginia campaign; and the siege of Petersburg. Although the Twenty-fourth was not organized until late in the war, the regiment was involved in approximately thirty battles after May 1864. Members of the unit were initially upset because they were not paid their bounty money promptly. Also, they remained unmounted until October 1864. In the 1864 elections Parks's regiment favored a peace candidate. He explained to his wife his reasons for having changed his mind about favoring Lincoln: "I cannot go for a man who thinks more of the niger than a white man" (p. 41). Other aspects of Parks's letters include requests for news about the farm, his sense of humor and use of affectionate terms for his wife, and reports of gathering clothing from the battlefield, which he sent home to be made into garments for his children. When Abraham Lincoln was assassinated, Parks reported the tension that existed between the victors and the vanquished at City Point, Virginia, and that many Union soldiers believed the killing was a Confederate plot. One foolhardy Confederate officer openly praised the assassination and was unceremoniously hung by the Union soldiers. Additional information on Parks's postwar life is appended.

187. **PARTRIDGE, GEORGE W., JR.** *Letters from the Iron Brigade: George Washington Partridge, Jr., 1839–1863, Civil War Letters to His Sisters.* Edited by Hugh L. Whitehouse. Indianapolis: Guild Press of Indiana, 1994. 117 pp.
October 13, 1861–June 24, 1863. Letters. Seventh Wisconsin Infantry. Duty around Washington, D.C.; second Bull Run; South Mountain; Antietam; Fredericksburg; and Burnside's "Mud March." In his early letters Partridge relates the uneventful routines of duty in northern Virginia. His descriptions of battle are limited to experiencing the enemy's shelling, hearing bullets whiz over his head, firing at the enemy without knowing if he hit anyone, and marching in mud ankle deep during the "Mud March." In winter camp during 1863 Partridge was among the many Union soldiers who suffered from low morale. He wrote that he did not want to fight to free the slaves and that if he were an officer he would resign. During this period he said that five soldiers were drummed out of the service for desertion. In

his final letter he tells of Union forces that were tracking Lee northward. Partridge was killed at Gettysburg on the first day.

188. PARTRIDGE, JOHN W. *Boylston, Massachusetts, in the Civil War: The Letters Home of Pvt. John W. Partridge with Biographical Sketches of Other Boylston Soldiers.* Compiled and edited by Frederick G. Brown, William O. Dupuis, and Norman H. French. Bowie, Md.: Heritage Books, 1995. 182 pp.
November 3, 1861–January 28, 1864. Letters. Private. Twenty-fifth Massachusetts Infantry; then, U.S. Signal Corps. These letters relate travel from Massachusetts to Annapolis; the ocean voyage to North Carolina with Burnside's expedition; the battle of New Bern; and duty at and around New Bern, including Foster's Goldsboro expedition, the siege of New Bern, and Gum Swamp. Partridge's repetitious duties in North Carolina provided few opportunities for him to relate to his parents and sister more than news of the Boylston boys, the weather, and occasional expeditions and skirmishes. Partridge admitted to his mother that vices were ever present. However, he considered "On the whole the morals of the army as safe as that of society at home" (p. 96). He told her that when the war was over, civilians would find changes in the soldiers' behavior to be equally divided between good and bad. Partridge believed that one advantage of the war was that it represented "one of the checks which an all wise Creator has placed in an evil world" (p. 121). But Partridge found disadvantages to be more numerous and elaborated by pointing to "the demoralization of the principals of the army and the community at large" (p. 99). Partridge conceded that blacks were smart and attended church with no coaxing. However, he believed that they had no idea how hard they would have to work for themselves once they were freed. He agreed that blacks should serve as soldiers because "That is the only way they can know the value of liberty"; but with his personal well-being in mind, he added, "I don't see any other way for me to get out of this scrape" (pp. 74–75). To Partridge the appearance of the white population of New Bern was unsightly. Their propensity for tobacco was especially abhorrent. Particularly disgusting was the "chewing stick," the opposite ends of which had been dipped in snuff and were chewed by men and women. In fall 1863 Partridge was transferred to the signal corps, and he described his signaling duties in several letters. Partridge was captured at the battle of Batchelder's Creek and died at Andersonville in April 1864. The editors have added letters of condolence and photographs and appended regimental, genealogical, and other materials, such as the Boylston Town Council minutes.

189. PATTERSON, WILLIAM ELWOOD. *Campaigns of the 38th Regiment of the Illinois Volunteer Infantry, Company K, 1861–1863: The Diary of William Elwood Patterson.* Edited by Lowell Wayne Patterson. Bowie, Md.: Heritage Books, 1992. 58 pp.
July 1861–September 1864. Diary. Thirty-eighth Illinois Infantry. Missouri, including duty at Pilot Knob, operations around Fredericktown, and an expedition against Jeff Thompson; the siege of Corinth; Buell's pursuit of Bragg in Kentucky; Perryville; Stones River; the Tullahoma campaign, and the Chickamauga campaign and battle. Wounded at Chickamauga, Patterson was captured when the Union hospital was overrun, but he was paroled soon after. On the last two pages he summarizes his stays at several hospitals and eventual arrival back home in Olney, Illinois.

190. PECK, DANIEL. *Dear Rachael: The Civil War Letters of Daniel Peck.* Compiled and annotated by Martha Gerber Stanford. Freeman, S.D.: Pine Hill Press, 1993. 76 pp.
January 17, 1862–April 18, 1864. Letters. Corporal. Ninth New York Cavalry. Duty at the defenses of Washington, D.C.; the early stage of the Peninsular campaign; and the battle of Williamsport and duty in northern Virginia that included unidentified cavalry clashes. Daniel described few of his military

encounters, camp activities, or illnesses to his sister, Rachael. Several times he mulled over reenlistment, but most of his correspondence concerned news of people from home. In his early letters Daniel refers to the problem of financing the schooling of a younger brother. Daniel's pay as a private was thirteen dollars a month. Rachael was a schoolteacher who earned approximately two dollars a month. Later Daniel recalled with tenderness the last time he saw Rachael's fiancée marching into battle, never to return. In a letter written a short time later Daniel tactlessly remarked how old Rachael looked (the editor assumes that the aged look was caused by the combination of the loss of her fiancée and worry about Daniel). Following his reenlistment in 1864, Daniel was wounded at Todd's Tavern and discharged that August.

191. **PECK, MARCUS.** *Letters of a Civil War Soldier and His Family.* Edited by Eve H. Gemmill and Marie E. Hoffman. Poestenkill, N.Y.: Poestenkill Historical Society, 1993. 70 pp.

September 28, 1862–March 19, 1863. Letters and diary. Sergeant. 169th New York Infantry. Duty at the defenses of Washington, D.C. During his brief period as a soldier Peck related his trip from home to Staten Island and the nation's capital, guard duties around Washington's "Chain Bridge," camp entertainment, war news, receipt of pay, the routines of camp life, and general living conditions. Letters from family members are included. Marcus contracted typhoid fever and died at Armory Hospital in Washington on March 25, 1863. Among the items appended to this work are a history of the 169th New York Infantry, a map of Washington, a genealogical chart, and a newspaper article about these letters.

192. **PETTIT, FREDERICK.** *Infantryman Pettit: The Civil War Letters of Corporal Frederick Pettit, Late of Company C, 100th Pennsylvania Veteran Volunteer Infantry Regiment, "The Roundheads," 1862–1864.* Edited by William Gilfillan Gavin. Shippensburg, Pa.: White Mane Publishing Company, 1990. 214 pp.

July 14, 1862–July 9, 1864. Letters and diary. Corporal. One-hundredth Pennsylvania Infantry. Mustered in at Camp Curtin; South Mountain; Antietam; duty in Kentucky; siege of Vicksburg; siege of Jackson; Burnside's east Tennessee campaign, including Blue Springs; the siege of Knoxville, including the assault on Fort Sanders; The Wilderness; Spotsylvania; Cold Harbor; and the siege of Petersburg. Pettit's letters to his family in Hazel Dell, Pennsylvania, provide lengthy descriptions of camp life, the geographic features he observed while on the march or being transported, and several battles. His concern for family matters is apparent, as is his religious nature and opposition to Copperheads and slavery. Pettit was usually even-tempered, but while in Kentucky he launched a tirade (for him) against the "utter disregard of morality and virtue" he found so apparent in that state (p. 108) The source of the flaw was the "idleness" created by slavery, which he approved of abolishing with war and bloodshed. He wrote that after the war "the whole south will be a ruined physically, intellectually and morally. What a wide field it will open for those engaged in for the education of the masses" (p. 108). He later identified "the masses" as the "poor whites who will need to be educated and christianized," adding that "The Negroes must be colonized sooner or later" (p. 113). Pettit deplored the prevalence of vice among the soldiers, but he understood why it flourished. For him the undesirable conditions were a test of character. He wrote: "A person who withstands all these influences will certainly not come out of the contest weakened in moral principle" (p. 138). Pettit always portrayed the war as going well and his determination, as well as that of the other men, to be strong. He portrayed the soldiers in eastern Tennessee as being willing to suffer the hardships without complaint. And after he was wounded at Cold Harbor, he returned to his regiment early because he thought it would be a "disgrace" to go home when men were needed in the field (p. 160). On the night of July 9, 1864, he was killed by a Confederate sharpshooter in the trenches before Petersburg. Letters of condolence are included. Pettit's diary for the period of September 18, 1863 through January 24, 1864, is written from east Tennessee.

193. PHILLIPS, JOHN R. "The Diary of a Union Soldier from Alabama." *Alabama Heritage* 28 (Spring 1993): 20–25.

1861–1862. Memoir. First Alabama Cavalry (U.S.). Phillips relates how he opposed secession during the early war years. He escaped Confederate conscription and hid in the woods of Winston County, Alabama, with other Unionists before eventually joining the United States Army.

194. PHIPPS, PORTER. *Porter Phipps' Letters Home from the Civil War: Other Family Letters, 1862 Diary (Partial), Account Book.* Edited by Nancy Byers Romig. Export, Pa.: N. B. Romig, 1994. 148 pp.

September 25, 1862–June 10, 1865. Letters and diary. Sixteenth Pennsylvania Cavalry. Organization at Harrisburg, Pennsylvania; and duty in Maryland. Battles in Virginia include Dranesville (written by another soldier); Chancellorsville; Lee's retreat from Gettysburg, including Shepherdstown; the Bristoe campaign; the Mine Run campaign; the Virginia campaign, including Dinwiddie Road, Reams' Station, and first Hatcher's Run; the Appomattox campaign; and the expedition to Danville. Phipps's pride in the Union cavalry increased after June 1863, and in time he felt that the Union cavalry was superior to the legendary Confederate cavalry. Phipps's references to cavalry duty included the frequency with which the cavalry had to dismount to fight the opposing infantry on foot and embark on long, dusty rides. Phipps never complained about living conditions or food. He especially praised coffee. At the end of the day, in order of importance, tents sprang up, fence posts disappeared, and the soldiers gathered pails of water to brew their coffee. He wrote: "it does the tired soldier more real good than any other thing he can get," and "Coffee is our real nourishment" (pp. 31–32). After the hotly contested battle of Shepherdstown, he wrote: "If Meade had attacked Lee in his chosen position we might of met with a repulse for Lee had the best position that the country could afford and it might of proved bad for us" (p. 31). The activities of Copperheads at home perturbed him. Phipps said he held no ill feelings toward McClellan and considered him a "fine man" who simply got into "such bad company as [Clement] Vallandigham" (p. 75). Phipps was fighting to restore the Union, and he opposed slavery. He retained faith in Abraham Lincoln's ability to guide the Union war effort and was optimistic about the difficult period that he knew would follow the war. Phipps was able to find some good in the war: "in the end we will as a nation come out purified & will be the grand centre from which will emenate justice & equality to mankind" (p. 85). One interesting aspect of the letters from, and to, friends in Venago County, Pennsylvania, is evidence of the prosperity of the region. The drilling of oil wells and the high price of land were reportedly encouraging many residents to sell their farms.

195. PIERCE, BENJAMIN FRANKLIN, and HARRIETT JANE GOODWIN PIERCE. *An Enduring Love: The Civil War Diaries of Benjamin Franklin Pierce (14th New Hampshire Vol. Inf.) and His Wife Harriett Jane Goodwin Pierce.* By Sheila M. Cumberworth and Daniel V. Biles III. Gettysburg, Pa.: Thomas Publications, 1995. 180 pp.

January 1, 1863–June 8, 1865. Diaries. This work consists of two parts. The first is a narrative which combines a history of the Fourteenth New Hampshire Infantry, the progress of the war, and information about the family with photographs and excerpts from the diaries. The second part contains the full text of the diaries. Frank's diary (January 1, 1863–January 7, 1864) was written from Poolesville, Maryland, and Washington, D.C. His terse entries mention camp routines, drilling, and guard duty at Old Capitol Prison. "Hattie's" equally brief entries (January 1, 1864–June 8, 1865) record events of her life in Bradford, New Hampshire: visits to and from friends and relatives, cooking, sewing (she made and sold women's "drawers"), attending church and political meetings, and longing for Frank's return. Both parties mention the loss of a daughter to diphtheria. The editors add that Frank was shot in the ankle at Cedar Creek and spent the rest of the war in hospitals. He received his discharge on June 2, 1865.

196. PINGREE, SAMUEL E., and STEPHEN M. PINGREE. "The Civil War Letters of S. E. and S. M. Pingree, 1862–1864." By Kelly A. Nolin. *Vermont History* 63 (Spring 1995): 80–94.

January 1862–June 1864. Letters. Lieutenant Colonels, Third (Samuel) and Fourth (Stephen) Vermont Infantries. In August 1863 Samuel explained why he had changed his mind about the war policy. He had become a vociferous supporter of emancipation and favored using blacks as soldiers, even if it meant "hanging a rebel for everyone of them executed or sold into slavery" (pp. 82–83). Samuel also included lengthy descriptions of the Vermont Brigade's participation at Spotsylvania and at Cold Harbor. In Samuel's last letter he expresses the belief that another draft was necessary to crush the rebellion. In correspondence from July 1863 Stephen expresses the need for more troops and suggests that the New York draft rioters should be quelled by canister. He asserts that blood should run in the streets before mob reaction to conscription spread. Stephen relates the battle of Rappahannock Station in detail. Samuel and Stephen both describe a review by President Lincoln and what combat was really like for the two young sons of the recipient of these letters, a cousin named Augustus P. Hunton.

197. PORTER, JOHN A. *76th Regiment Pennsylvania Volunteers, "Keystone Zouaves": The Personal Recollections, 1861–1865, of Sergeant John A. Porter, Company "B."* Edited by James A. Chisman. Wilmington, N.C.: Broadfoot Publishing Co., 1988. 141 pp.

September 2, 1861–August 12, 1865. Memoir. Seventy-sixth Pennsylvania Infantry. Organization at Harrisburg, Pennsylvania; transfer to South Carolina (including duty at Hilton Head, the battle of Secessionville, the expedition to Pocotaligo in 1862, and both assaults on Battery Wagner); and duty in Virginia (including Drewry's Bluff, Chaffin's Farm, and Fair Oaks). Thirty-odd years after the war Porter remained proud of how easily the Union veterans had been assimilated back into society, when many civilians feared that the returning soldiers would create a crime wave. However, he seems to have been ambivalent toward the slaves. He recalled that at Hilton Head the "darkies" were having a glorious time: "they had loafing reduced to a science and could keeping moving and do as little work as any lot of men I ever saw" (p. 15). After he had taken an interest in his cook and taught him to read, Porter generalized that "all the colored folks were extremely apt scholars, anxious and quick to learn" (p. 15). But Porter called those blacks who rose to political power during Reconstruction "ignoramuses." While he said that he understood the indignation of white Southerners during the era, he felt that Reconstruction was just punishment for having embraced slavery. Porter often recalled minute occurrences. In South Carolina a dog, which had been shot, was nursed back to health by Union soldiers. Two years later, while the animal was barking at the top of the breastworks at Petersburg, it was killed by a Confederate sharpshooter. More than three decades later the killing of an innocent dog still caused Porter to bristle with anger. He recalled that entertainment during Christmas of 1862 included soldiers attempting to climb a greased pole or catch a greased pig. Also, two "darkies" were encouraged to dig a coin from a barrel of white meal with their teeth, which was considered hilarious by the Union soldiers. Porter criticized Benjamin Butler for his poor leadership at Drewry's Bluff. However, he commended the general for returning a Confederate soldier who had been surrendered to the Union troops by the rebels in return for one of their men having violated the rules of fraternization by capturing a Union soldier. When Porter was wounded, he had part of his leg amputated. The skin eventually shrank from around the leg stump, exposing an inch of bone. He said he was grateful when he found a surgeon who was willing to saw off the protruding bone. Porter also described the treatment of gangrene. The process involved burning away the dead flesh with "Brumalian wash" (the editor explains that this was a mixture of nitric and hydrochloric acids).

198. POTTER, WILLIAM W. *One Surgeon's Private War: Doctor William W. Potter of the 57th New York.* Editor-in-chief, John Michael Priest. Shippensburg, Pa.: White Mane Publishing Co., 1996. 158 pp.

Summer 1861–May 1865. Memoir. Surgeon. Forty-ninth New York Infantry and Fifty-seventh New York Infantry. Organization of the Forty-ninth New York; defenses of Washington, D.C.; the Peninsular campaign; Antietam; Fredericksburg; Chancellorsville; Gettysburg, including the pursuit of Lee; the Bristoe campaign; the Mine Run campaign; The Wilderness; Spotsylvania; North Anna; Totopotomy; Cold Harbor; the siege of Petersburg; and Reams' Station. Potter was in charge of the First Division (II Corps) field hospital from August 1863 until September 1864. Although Potter based these memoirs on letters to his wife, most of the account is devoted to military matters and his medical responsibilities. On June 29, 1862, he stayed behind with the wounded Union soldiers on the Peninsula while the army retreated. He was captured, sent to Libby Prison, and released on July 17, 1862. Potter often mentioned officers killed and wounded and the number of sick and wounded he treated. During the Virginia campaign—between May 3, 1864, and his departure on September 19, 1864—his field hospital had treated eight thousand patients, six thousand of whom were wounded. While Potter seldom revealed personal feelings, he commented on several leaders. He did not like his brief service under Gen. John Pope. He blamed Gen. Reynolds for precipitating the "chaos" at Gettysburg. Potter thought that Meade's decision not to pursue Lee after Gettysburg would be judged a wise decision by history. And he often praised Gen. Winfield Scott Hancock. At Reams' station Potter said that the II Corps behaved disgracefully: some "ran like sheep." However, he emphasized that it was the first time the unit had behaved in such a manner. His wife apparently asked him to resign on several occasions. Potter refused and labeled such action "disgraceful." In a brief appendix Potter relates his civilian life between his release from active duty in September 1864 and the Grand Review.

199. PRICKITT, DANIEL J. *Daniel J. Prickitt, Sergeant, Company H., Third Ohio Cavalry, 1861–1865.* Edited by Col. E. D. Stoltz.. Archbold, Ohio: E. D. Stoltz, 1988. 208 pp.

September 10, 1861–December 31, 1865. Diary. Sergeant. Third Ohio Cavalry. Duty in Ohio; Indiana; Tennessee, including operations against Wheeler; the Atlanta campaign, including operations against Hood and Forrest in northern Georgia and Alabama; and Wilson's raid to Macon. The author seldom wrote about battles, the war in general, or even the cause of the war. Also, Prickitt wrote relatively little about home. His specific duties are unclear, but he occasionally mentioned performance of clerical work. At the start of his service Prickitt recorded the confusion attendant when men from all walks of life are thrown together. Profanity, drunkenness, fistfights, and gambling were rampant. Both before and just after muster the men slept and ate wherever and whatever they could. Prickitt's group assumed that they would serve in the same unit together. However, when they found that they were to be separated, they simply marched to another place of enlistment and became a part of Company H, Third Ohio Cavalry. The regiment's horses are a constant theme of Prickitt's journal notations. He related their distribution and the quality of the animals, the accidents that occurred as men became familiar with their mounts, and the requisition and distribution of hay and oats. Prickitt maintained high moral standards but said that he simply could not resist playing cards. At the war's end Prickitt kept a record of his role in the process of mustering out and paying the soldiers. The daily entries of the postwar period describe his transition to civilian life. Prickitt's journals for February 22–September 2, 1862; October 5–November 5, 1862; and May 3–September 1, 1864, are missing.

200. PUTERBAUGH, JOHN W. *March and Countermarch: Letters from a Union Soldier, May 14, 1861–April 3, 1862. A Collection of 72 Letters from 2nd Lt. John Puterbaugh, Co. K, 15th Infantry Regiment, Illinois Vols. to His Wife and Friends.* Compiled and (slightly) edited by his great-granddaughter, Ruth H. Kilbourn. Grants Pass, Oreg.: R. H. Kilbourn, 1995. 121 leaves.

May 14, 1861–April 3, 1862. Letters. Lieutenant. Fifteenth Illinois Infantry. Organization and training at Freeport and Alton, Illinois; duty at several camps in central Missouri; Fort Donelson (aftermath);

and encampment at Pittsburg Landing. Early in his letters Puterbaugh related the dissension among many recruits who assumed they had volunteered for three months but instead found that they were bound for three years of service. Puterbaugh's letters written by July reveal that he and his family were suffering from monetary hardships. Apparently his wife had asked him what she should do about getting some clothing; she and their little boy "were nearly naked" (p. 19). Puterbaugh replied that he did not know how to respond because he had received only $5.30 in pay and he still needed to buy his uniform and equipment. He often mentioned people with whom they were both familiar but asked his wife not to let anyone else see his letters. He feared that his comments might be misunderstood and result in dissension at home. Puterbaugh escaped many of the illnesses with which others were afflicted, but he did develop a large boil on his hand and a painful toothache. The tooth hurt him for eight days before he went to the surgeon. But his visit brought little relief because during the extraction "the Damned old Fool broke it off and it is ten times worse than before" (p. 56). As the exceptionally cold winter lengthened, his complaints about fighting the war by guarding bridges in Missouri increased. Eventually the regiment moved to Fort Donelson in February, arriving there only hours after the Confederates had surrendered. The unit was soon transferred to Pittsburg Landing. While Puterbaugh and the rest of the army were wondering about its next move, the Confederates attacked. Several final letters describe how Puterbaugh was killed at Shiloh.

201. RANSOM, JOHN L. "Johnny Ransom's Imagination." By William Marvel. *Civil War History* 41 (September 1995): 181–89.

March–December 1864. Memoir. Ninth Michigan Cavalry. Andersonville Prison. The veracity of the journal that Johnny Ransom purportedly maintained while held in several Confederate prisons and later published as a book has long been regarded as suspect by historians. When Marvel compared significant dates and events mentioned in Ransom's journal with other prisoners' diaries and hospital and pension records, he found that Ransom's account contained errors in sequence, dates, and numbers of prisoners. Despite Ransom's insistence that his original manuscript was burned in a fire after the war, Marvel believes that no journal ever existed. Rather, "it was not the product of an 1864 journal at all. It was, instead, a postwar creation relying partly on memory, partly on published material, and partly on imagination" (p. 182). Marvel attributes Ransom's purpose for publishing his account to the promotion of a congressional bill designed to provide pensions for former prisoners. In fact, Ransom's first edition was published with the text of the proposed bill included. In addition Ransom had filed a pension claim in 1879, for the loss of teeth from scurvy, at about the time he began writing. Marvel concludes with the statement that because of the success of Ransom's book, despite his "exaggerations and misrepresentations," he and many other prisoners received pensions for many years. Ransom's first edition was published as *Andersonville Diary, Escape, and List of the Dead . . .* (Auburn, N.Y.: 1881).

202. RATH, JOHN. *Left for Dixie: The Civil War Diary of John Rath.* Edited by Kenneth Lyftogt. Parkersburg, Iowa: Mid-Prairie Books, 1991. 100 pp.

August 2, 1862–July 2, 1865. Diary. Thirty-first Iowa Infantry. The Vicksburg campaign (including Chickasaw Bluffs, Arkansas Post, and the siege of Vicksburg); the Atlanta campaign; Lookout Mountain and Missionary Ridge; Sherman's March to the Sea; the Carolinas campaign (including Bentonville); and the Grand Review. Rath's notations are primarily devoted to battles and movements. He accepted trying weather conditions and bad food without complaint. Rath criticized Hooker's leadership at Missionary Ridge, but he did so discreetly. Even after Rath experienced the death and burial of his brother in the same battle, he showed little emotion. The chapter on the Carolinas campaign is a most engaging section, perhaps (the editor adds) because Rath rewrote it later. On January 31, 1865, he revealed the soldiers' mood. The men sought vengeance upon the "hotbed of rebellion"; they swore "to burn everything that would burn" (p. 71). Between February 15 and 19 Rath recorded the events that led to the burning of Columbia and its aftermath. In the final chapter Rath tells of mustering out, the soldiers' complaints about the slowness of the process, and their itinerary back to Dubuque.

203. REID, JOHN B. *Civil War Letters of John B. Reid.* Greenville, Ill.: Bond County Genealogical Society, 1991. 98 leaves.

November 1862–February 18, 1865. Letters. Major. 130th Illinois Infantry. Duty at Memphis (Fort Pickering); the Vicksburg campaign, including Port Gibson and the siege and assaults of Vicksburg on May 19 and 22; duty at New Iberia, Louisiana, and Pass Cavallo, Texas; the second Red River campaign, including Mansfield; and duty in New Orleans. Early in his service Reid was annoyed at the paymaster's delay because the shortage of money was creating hardships for his wife and children, as well as other soldiers of all ranks. To Reid, his children were "cubs" and "cubbies" or "those who inhabit our home." He tried to send his boy a colt and a sword and provided money for his girl's piano lessons. He often sent his wife money with instructions to do with it whatever she wished. Reid was saving his own money to realize a "good many plans to fix up the house and make things more pleasant and comfortable for my family" (p. 42). Reid was fighting the war out of a sense of duty and to abolish slavery. He criticized the North and asserted that it might need to be "chastened" because it also had been guilty of many sins. He wrote, "We have all winked at slavery and were willing, for the sake of peace, to let it stand"(p. 39). Reid often observed the vegetation and the uniqueness of the South, including alligators and the blacks in Louisiana who spoke French. At Mansfield he was severely wounded and captured. Without reservation he described how he was shot through the left shoulder, the ball passing through his right side. He lay on the battlefield still conscious while he was stripped of his sword by a Confederate officer and relieved of his other accoutrement by an enlisted man. He was eventually picked up by the Confederates, only to suffer a tortuous ride in a Confederate ambulance to a makeshift hospital, which soon burned to the ground. Fortunately Reid had secreted money in a belt and was able to pay townspeople for his care. In January 1865 Reid returned to New Orleans to prepare for the Mobile Bay campaign and keep the decimated 130th Illinois from being consolidated with the Seventy-seventh Illinois.

204. REYNOLDS, ELMER. "On the Road to Atlanta: Observations of a Yankee Soldier." Edited by Lewis N. Wynne and Barbara Ann Grim. *Atlanta History* 31 (Winter 1987/1988): 53–55.

May 27, 1864. Letter. Tenth Wisconsin Light Artillery Battery. Atlanta campaign.

205. RICH, JAMES B. "Quaker Soldier: Letters of James B. Rich to Sue J. Sheppard (1862–1864.)" Edited by Edward T. Addison. *Bulletin of the Historical Society of Montgomery County* 25 (Spring 1987): 275–307.

September 28, 1862–June 7, 1864. Letters. Virginia and Pennsylvania. Eighty-fourth New York Infantry and Fifth New York Infantry. These chatty missives primarily treat conditions at home and address few comments to the fighting. Although Rich avoided details of combat—he even neglected to mention how he was wounded at Gettysburg—his letters reveal a great deal about him. For example, he set aside his pacifist Quaker beliefs to fight a bully who had hurt a twelve-year-old boy. In 1864 his pleasant nature seems to have undergone a change after he was separated from his original unit. He was reassigned to serve with the Fifth New York Veteran Infantry. He hated the predominantly Irish regiment and its terrible food. He considered the unit to be "coarse" and suffered abuse in some undisclosed manner. His final writings touch on the early fighting of the Virginia campaign, in which he was killed on June 18, 1864, at Petersburg.

206. RICHARDS, JOHN V. *From Wisconsin to the Sea: The Civil War Letters of Sergeant John V. Richards, Thirty-first Regiment of Wisconsin Volunteer Infantry 1862–1865.* Edited by Richard C. Rattenbury. Houston, Tex.: D. Armstrong Company, 1986. 111 pp.

December 31, 1862–January 2, 1865. Letters. Sergeant. Thirty-first Wisconsin Infantry. Duty in Kentucky and Tennessee; the Atlanta campaign, including the battle of Atlanta; and the March to the Sea. Throughout his letters to his mother, father, sister, and brother Richards stressed everyday activities. Early in his service he developed a carbuncle on his knee that "swelled as big as four knees" and "bled like ox" when it was lanced (p. 10). Richards's unique brand of humor appears frequently. When the regiment was issued Enfield rifles, he professed to be mystified at how he aimed at a tree across the river but hit a hog instead; after all, "The tree and the hog was a good ways apart" (p. 26). Richards was almost free of vices. The editor found occasional profanity (Richards referred to a captain as having "acted the Shitass with us" [p. 14]), and Richards was not above petty thievery. He failed in an attempt to pilfer a coat to send home to his brother, but he successfully relieved another soldier of a chicken. Richards expressed no high-minded philosophy about the cause of the war nor any clearly defined reason why he was fighting. Freeing the slaves was not a war aim for Richards; he was pleased to see the contrabands being put to work for the government. News about members of Company E (which was raised in LaFayette County, Wisconsin) was exchanged between the battlefields and home, but some information was kept secret. Richards wrote to his parents about a man who had been severely punished for sleeping on duty. The man's parents, who were unaware of the situation, wrote to Richards regarding their son's whereabouts. Richards did not disclose his reply, but he told his own mother: "I would not say any about it to the folks" (p. 72). Richards felt proud that he was surviving his military experience, but he discouraged his brother from volunteering.

207. RIPPLE, EZRA HOYT. *Dancing Along the Deadline: The Andersonville Memoir of a Prisoner of the Confederacy.* Edited by Mark Snell. Novato, Calif.: Presidio Press, 1996. 168 pp.

July 3, 1864–March 1865. Memoir. Private. Fifty-second Pennsylvania Infantry. Captured on James Island and imprisoned at Andersonville (between July 3 and September 13, 1864) and Florence Prisons (between September 1864 and March 1, 1865). Ripple wrote these memoirs in 1896 for lectures to the Scranton, Pennsylvania, YMCA. He illustrated his talks with a series of sketches (or "lantern shows") executed by the noted Civil War artist James E. Taylor for this purpose. Ripple begins and ends his memoir with statements that he purposefully avoided the horrid details of the prisons, as well as rancor toward the South. As a result Ripple's account is a good-natured story that focuses on his survival. He wrote satirically about mock battles with fleas at Andersonville. At Florence during the cold winter when men slept tightly packed next to each other in "spoon fashion," if one man felt the urge to scratch, the man next to him might be hit in the nose or the ribs. Ripple used his skills as a violinist at Florence to form a band that performed for extra rations. He said that in the cold weather the men saved their rations until the evening so they could go to sleep having eaten a hot meal. They concocted recipes from the meager rations, savored those peas that contained little black bugs, and pooled their cornmeal to make hot mush, which they shared. Ripple described the only fresh water in the camp at Andersonville, the "Providence Springs," which ran just on the other side of the perilous "deadline." Without dwelling on the suffering, Ripple wrote: "Prisoners of war died in a very matter-of-fact way, there was no struggle, no regrets, no fears" (p. 66). Ripple stressed acts of kindness between the prisoners, as well as between the prisoners and the guards. Henry Wirz was referred to only in a humorous comparison between Wirz and a dog, although Ripple said it was unfair to the dog. Ripple reserved his harsh words for the "cruel, bloodthirsty monster," Gen. John H. Winder (p. 43). Ripple accepted Gen. Grant's refusal to exchange prisoners on the grounds that if a general exchange had occurred, the sickly Union captives would have been placed in hospitals, whereas the "rebel prisoners, well fed, well cared for, in as good condition as when they were captured," would have been sent back into battle, prolonging the war indefinitely (p. 71). In February 1865 Ripple attempted an escape, but he was pursued by the dogs and recaptured. On March 1, 1865, he was one of the last to be paroled from Florence.

208. ROBERTS, CYRUS MARION. *Captain Cyrus Marion Roberts, 78th Ohio Volunteer Infantry and U.S. Army Signal Corps: Civil War Diaries.* Transcribed by Bradley T. Lepper and Mary E. Lepper (Sweeten). N.p.: B. T. Lepper, 1993. 99 leaves.

September 1, 1863–May 1865. Diary. Captain. Seventy-eighth Ohio Infantry and service with the Department of Kansas. Following the Vicksburg campaign, where Roberts had been on detached duty with the signal corps, he was sent to Kansas to establish a signal corps under Gen. Samuel R. Curtis. At Fort Leavenworth and Fort Scott he established a signaling unit that consisted of five officers, twenty enlisted men, and twenty-five horses. When Sterling Price invaded Missouri, Roberts was engaged in the repulse. He described the battles of Westport, Big Blue River, and Mine Creek and the Union pursuit of Price into Arkansas. In December 1864 Roberts terminated his detached service and rejoined the main body of the Seventy-eighth Ohio in South Carolina. He participated in the Carolinas campaign, leading a party of foragers. On April 10 he was detailed to the headquarters staff of the XVII Army Corps to serve as commissary of musters. Throughout his diary Roberts exhibits a keen eye for detail. He expresses surprise that the people of New Orleans all seemed to speak French. He describes river travel in Louisiana and then on the Mississippi and Missouri Rivers. He portrays the prairie landscape in Kansas and Missouri and comments on the Indians at the Catholic Osage Mission. In South Carolina, Roberts felt sorry for a forty-five-year-old Confederate soldier with six children who was unlucky enough to have had his lot randomly drawn for execution in retribution for the killing of a Union forager. And he lamented the fate of clusters of people outside Columbia who were clutching their belongings and watching the fire. He wrote, "I hope I never have to see such again" but added, "such are the consequences of Secession" (p. 83).

209. ROGERS FAMILY. *Patriots in Blue: Civil War Letters of the Mark E. Rogers Family of Fairfax, Vermont.* By Mark Curtis Wilson. Fairfax, Vt.: Fairfax Historical Society, 1987. 88 pp.

1861–1865. In this combination of letters, family lore, and narrative Wilson attempts to reconstruct the lives of the fourteen-member Rogers family, who lived on a small farm in northwestern Vermont. The letters, few in number, were primarily written by the four sons, who served with the First (three-month) Infantry and Fifth Vermont Infantry and the First Vermont Cavalry. Edward (Fifth Vermont), who was the most prolific and thoughtful writer, occasionally commented on such topics as Lincoln's reelection. The cavalrymen, William and Mark, wrote letters about Gettysburg and Sheridan's Shenandoah Valley campaign. Another son, Mote, was killed in The Wilderness. The author probes the economic hardships caused at home by the absence of four laborers. The condition of the frail mother, who wrote three letters, was an issue for family concern. Wilson continues the family history up to 1900. Edward, who had been badly wounded at Cedar Creek, was severely depressed over the prospect of being incapacitated in civilian life. Shortly after returning home he committed suicide by ingesting an overdose of strychnine. By the 1870s members of the Rogers family had scattered far from their childhood home. Genealogical information is appended.

210. ROLFE, EDWARD. *A Civil War Union Soldier Describes His Army Life of "Hard Marches, Hard Crackers, and Hard Beds, and Pickett Guard in a Desolate Country."* Transcribed and compiled with additional text by Edward Rolfe's great-grandson, Laurence F. Lillibridge. Prescott Valley, Ariz.: Lillibridge Publishing Company, 1993. 183 pp.

August 31, 1862–July 7, 1865. Letters and diary. Corporal. Twenty-seventh Iowa Infantry. Duty in Tennessee; foraging and guarding railroads at Jackson and later duty at Memphis and Nashville, including the battle of Nashville; Arkansas, including the capture of Little Rock; Mississippi, including the Meridian campaign, A. J. Smith's expedition to Tupelo, A. J. Smith's expedition to Oxford, and the Mobile Bay campaign; Louisiana, including Banks's second Red River campaign; and Missouri, including the pursuit of Price. When forty-three-year-old Rolfe went to war, he left his wife and four children on a farm in Delaware County, Iowa. The welfare of the family and the maintenance of the farm are the foci of these letters. Charlotte was unquestioningly head of the family back home in Iowa, but Edward, the fourteen-year-old son, was also held responsible for making decisions regarding the crops, farm animals, farm implements, and house painting and for maintaining the emotional stability of his mother and sisters. Rolfe and Charlotte had prepared themselves for the emotional hardships of being apart. On one occasion young Edward was feared ill. Rolfe wrote his wife: "but My Dear we must try to bear up against all such trials with fortitude. We have been highly favoured so far in this Seperation. I have done my Duty to my country" (p. 107). Eventually military service took its toll on the middle-aged Rolfe. After suffering a severe sunstroke and ague in 1863, he was assigned duties behind the lines in the commissary and as a provost clerk. Rolfe abhorred drunkenness, but he often regarded a "sup" of whiskey while on picket duty to be "very acceptable" (pp. 104, 106). The editor's introductory material is useful for placing Rolfe and Iowa farming in historical context.

211. ROY, ANDREW. *Fallen Soldier: Memoir of a Civil War Casualty.* Edited by William J. Miller. Medical commentary by Clyde B. Kernek. Montgomery, Ala.: Elliott and Clark Publishing, 1996. 158 pp.

June 27, 1862–November 1863. Memoir. Private. Thirty-ninth Pennsylvania Infantry (Tenth Reserves). Roy describes how he was wounded in the groin at Gaines' Mill. He was taken prisoner and treated by Confederate doctors, who informed him that he would probably die. He spent the next sixteen days in a field hospital combating flies, maggots, and mosquitoes before he was transferred to the hospital at Libby Prison. Paroled on July 25, 1862, Roy was sent to the hospital at Fortress Monroe, to the General Hospital at Annapolis, and, in late December, to the General Hospital in Clarysville, Maryland. Twice during the spring of 1863 he begged surgeons for an operation that would remove the bone fragments from his wound. On both occasions he was advised that such an operation would kill him and that he should be patient and let nature take its course. Roy persisted, however, and eventually received two operations, both of which were performed without anesthesia. By late 1863 he thought that his wound was healed; however, he suffered from its complications for the rest of his life. In his afterword the editor summarizes how the United States government begrudgingly allotted a medical disability pension to Roy. The editor indicates that despite his physical impairment, which worsened every year, Roy lived a fruitful life until his death in 1914. Dr. Kernek's "Medical Commentary" provides a modern-day clinical analysis of Roy's ordeal. This work is a revision of Roy's *Recollections of a Prisoner of War,* 2nd. ed., revised (Columbus, Ohio: J. L. Trauger, 1909). The editor slightly reorganized some chapters to focus on Roy's struggle with his wound.

212. RUDULPH, JAMES K. "The Rudulph Collection of Civil War Letters." Edited by Dan R. Brook. *West Virginia History* 50 (1991): 129–52.

April 22, 1862–June, 22, 1864. Letters. Private. Twenty-third Ohio Infantry. Duty in West Virginia and the battles of South Mountain and Antietam. These are primarily love letters to Rudulph's fiancée in which he reassures her of his devotion and insists he will not reenlist. His reflections on courage following Antietam indicate that Rudulph was proud of his conduct.

213. RUSSELL, IRA, and FRED RUSSELL. "The Aftermath of Prairie Grove: Union Letters from Fayetteville." Edited by William L. Shea. *Arkansas Historical Quarterly* 47 (Winter 1988): 345–61.

December 29, 1862–February 7, 1863. Letters and a report by a Union surgeon and his son. The two men were deployed to Fayetteville to head the U.S. General Hospital, District of Western Arkansas. Ira related the deplorable situation that resulted from the battle of Prairie Grove, as well as the efforts of civilian groups to assist the wounded. Fred wrote about the general conditions around Fayetteville.

214. SACHS, JOHANNES M. *Captain John M. Sachs: His Long Road Back to Gettysburg.* By John B. Horner. Gettysburg, Pa.: Horner Enterprises, 1994. 42 pp.

June 1863–November 1864. Memoir. Lieutenant. Fifth Maryland Infantry. After being captured at second Winchester, Sachs spent the next twenty months being shuttled between Confederate prisons. He escaped from Camp Sorghum (Columbia, South Carolina) in early November 1864 and embarked on a two-month trek back to Baltimore. Soon after returning home he related his experience to Rev. Jacob Blas. The translated version appears here.

215. SCHMALZRIEDT, FREDERICK. "The Civil War: A Young German Joins the Cavalry." By Edward G. Longacre. *Manuscripts* 40 (Fall 1988): 323–25.

September 10–20, 1861. Letters. First Michigan Cavalry. Schmalzriedt explained that he had two reasons for enlisting. One was to get away from his abusive employer (he worked as a hired hand on a farm), and the other was to do his part in "keeping freedom and the Union" (p. 325).

216. SCHOYER, SAMUEL C. *The Road to Cold Harbor: Field Diary, January 1–June 12, 1864, of Samuel C. Schoyer, Captain, Company G, 139th Pennsylvania Volunteer Regiment, Supplemented by Accounts of Other Officers and a Brief History of the Regiment.* Edited by William T. Schoyer. Apollo, Pa.: Clossen Press, 1986. 117 pp.

January 1–June 12, 1864. Diary. Captain. 139th Pennsylvania Infantry. During the first four months of this account Schoyer scribbled brief entries of his activities and living conditions at and around Harpers Ferry. He served on courts-martial, made social visits, and recorded weather conditions. Schoyer's terse notations made after Grant's army crossed the Rapidan follow the heavy fighting at The Wilderness, Spotsylvania, North Anna River, Totopotomoy, and Cold Harbor, where he was wounded and removed from the war. This work is augmented by the editorial material and contemporary accounts. The editor reveals that Schoyer's ankle wound left him almost completely paralyzed.

217. SCHWARTZ, EZEKIEL KOEHLER. *Civil War Diary of Ezekiel Koehler Schwartz, March 1863 to June 1865, and History of E. K. Schwartz Family.* Shelbyville, Ill.: Shelby County Historical & Genealogical Society, 1989. 90 pp.

March 28, 1863–June 9, 1865. Diary. Lieutenant. 115th Illinois Infantry. Duty in Tennessee; Chickamauga; the siege of Chattanooga; the Atlanta campaign, including Rocky Face Ridge and Resaca; and duty in Alabama and at Nashville. Although Schwartz seldom revealed his feelings or attitudes, he did lambaste the South for starting the war. And after visiting disabled men in a hospital, he was moved to write that the hospital was the "worst feature of the war" (p. 17). Schwartz was detached from his regiment guarding the railroads and attending to administrative and quartermaster duties. During the winter of 1864–1865 he wrote of participating in several camp debates. The men explored such issues as whether women should be as highly educated as men, if capital punishment should be abolished, and intemperance as a societal evil. In his last months of the war Schwartz recorded his furlough home and the news of the final Union victories. Just after Lincoln's assassination Schwartz mentioned that a soldier from a Kentucky regiment who cheered was sentenced to one year in a military prison.

218. **SHANKLIN, JAMES MAYNARD.** *"Dearest Lizzie:" The Civil War As Seen Through the Eyes of Lieutenant Colonel James Maynard Shanklin. . . .* Edited by Kenneth P. McCutchan. Evansville, Ind.: Friends of Willard Library Press, 1988. 321 pp.

November 14, 1861–May 24, 1863. Letters. Lieutenant Colonel. Forty-second Indiana Infantry. Duty in Kentucky, Tennessee, and Alabama, including the battle of Wartrace, Tennessee; occupation of Decatur, Alabama; pursuit of Bragg in Kentucky; Perryville; and Stones River, where he was captured and imprisoned at Libby Prison. Shanklin's letters are a mixture of affection for his wife, concern for affairs at home, and army matters. During his first winter in Kentucky, Shanklin attempted to depict camp life. He wrote that the soldiers moved about the camp like shadows. Sometimes they sang, and the band sometimes played "Gentle Annie." He once said that as he wrote, illumination was provided by the "light of a candle fixed in the handle of a bayonette" (p. 42). Shanklin, who was a lawyer and war Democrat, often struggled to make sense of the conflict and predict what the future might bring. As Tennesseans watched their dead soldiers being returned home, Shanklin could see that hatred toward the North was increasing. He wrote: "How are we to woo this people back to their old love for the Union is a mystery to me" (p. 191). One thing Shanklin was certain of was that after the war, "There must be a new era in the manners and morals of this Country" (p. 178). He believed that "our national misfortunes" should have humbled everyone and that the United States' "arrogance toward other nations, as well as each other, had always been a national flaw" (p. 178). On May 6, 1863, Shanklin was released from Libby Prison. He died of natural causes soon after he reached home in Evansville, Indiana. The editor has added footnotes to each letter, as well as extensive genealogical information.

219. **SHAW, ROBERT GOULD.** *Blue-Eyed Child of Fortune: The Civil War Letters of Colonel Robert Gould Shaw.* Foreword by William S. McFeely. Edited by Russell Duncan. Athens: University of Georgia Press, 1992. 421 pp.

April 5, 1861–July 18, 1863. Letters. Private, Seventh New York Militia; Captain, Second Massachusetts Infantry; and Colonel, Fifty-fourth Massachusetts Colored Infantry. Duty at Harpers Ferry and Frederick, Maryland; Jackson's Valley campaign, especially Front Royal; Cedar Mountain; second Bull Run (aftermath); Antietam; organization and training of the Fifty-fourth Massachusetts at Camp Meigs; duty on the South Carolina–Georgia Sea Islands, including the razing of Darien, Georgia, the battle on James Island (July 16, 1863), and preparation for the assault of Battery Wagner on July 18. These letters to his family and friends are preceded by a sixty-eight-page biography of Robert Gould Shaw, the son of a wealthy abolitionist family from Boston. The editor summarizes Shaw's life from his boyhood education in Europe and two years at Harvard College to leadership of the Fifty-fourth Massachusetts Colored Infantry. The letters Shaw wrote while serving with the Second Massachusetts between May 1861 and February 1863 comprise the majority of this work. During this period he wrote on such topics as visiting the engine house in which John Brown had holed up, dissatisfaction with the political manner in which officers were elected, death on the battlefields during the summer of 1862, skepticism about the Emancipation Proclamation, and his dedication to his comrades of the Second Massachusetts. Shaw first declined and then accepted Gov. John A. Andrews's invitation to command the Fifty-fourth Massachusetts, although Shaw never embraced abolition as intensely as did his parents. On February 8, 1863, he wrote a letter to his future bride, Annie Haggerty, in which he reveals the role that his desire for personal achievement assumed as motivation for accepting the commission. Although Shaw used common nineteenth-century derogatory references toward blacks, he was certain that they could be developed into a well-disciplined regiment. From training camp at Camp Meigs he wrote about the arrival of recruits of high quality, the selection of competent white officers, and the regiment's progress in drilling. He advocated strong disciplinary measures, which, on one occasion, elicited complaints from the soldiers. Shaw believed that his unit of free blacks from Northern states was superior to the units from South Carolina that were comprised of former slaves. He also considered his soldiers to be more willing to accept discipline than the Irish in other regiments. Shaw opposed the proposal that companies of the Fifty-fourth be sent into combat in piecemeal fashion. Such deployment, he felt, would lessen the impact of an entire regiment of black fighting men on the public mind. The regiment left Boston amid great ceremony and in May 1863 was sent to the South Carolina–Georgia Sea Islands. It was placed under the command of Col. James Montgomery, a prewar Kansas jayhawker, and ordered to take part in an expedition that plundered and razed the town of Darien, Georgia, on June 11, 1863. Shaw objected to burning the town, in part because the black soldiers might be discredited in Northern and Southern newspapers. However, Shaw remained fascinated by Montgomery's personality and his concept of waging war. On July 1, 1863, Shaw wrote his mother that the Fifty-fourth was to be paid only ten dollars a month, of which three dollars were appropriated for clothing. At the time of their enlistment it was agreed that they would receive an amount equal to that of white soldiers, thirteen dollars a month. Shaw said that he would tell his men to refuse any less pay. And if they did not receive the thirteen dollars, he thought the regiment should be mustered out of service. (The editor adds that the pay issue would not be settled until 1864.) On July 16 the Fifty-fourth helped to repel a Confederate attack on James Island. On the evening of July 18, 1863, the Fifty-fourth was in the vanguard of the assault on Battery Wagner. Shaw led his men to the top of the Confederate parapet before being killed. The Fifty-fourth held its position for about an hour before being forced to withdraw. The following morning Shaw was buried by the Confederate defenders in a trench with his black soldiers. A portion of these letters was also published as "The Letters of Robert Gould Shaw at the Massachusetts Historical Society," edited by Brenda M. Lawson, *Proceedings of the Massachusetts Historical Society* 102 (1990): 127–47.

220. SHEARER, SILAS I. *Dear Companion: The Civil War Letters of Silas I. Shearer.* Edited and published by Harold D. Brinkman. Ames, Iowa: Sigler Printing and Publishing, 1995. 164 pp.

September 3, 1862–August 10, 1865. Letters. Sergeant. Twenty-third Iowa Infantry. Duty in Missouri; the siege of Vicksburg; Louisiana, including the second Red River campaign; duty in Texas and Arkansas; and the Mobile campaign, including the siege of Fort Blakely. Shearer seldom complained to his wife, Elizabeth, about camp conditions, troop movements, battle experiences, or the war that kept them apart. His health was usually good, and he liked many places in the South. But he did not like General Banks. Shearer wrote: "This battle up Red River was foolishly lost by Banks mis management Cotton is what Banks is after and he will loose men to get it" (p. 79). At a review of the troops a few days later the proceedings were rained on. Shearer scribbled: "If the oald General got his Ass wet I dont care for the weting" (p. 82). By September 1863 he announced that his attitude toward blacks and slavery had changed. He praised the "Negros" and thought that "Taking the Negros from the South and arming them is one of the greatest blowes that was Struck" (p. 56). In the 1864 election he favored Abraham Lincoln, not because he thought that Lincoln was an exceptional man but because he had experience at being president. In mid 1864 Shearer speculated that even when the Union had won the war, troops would still be needed for several years to quell guerrilla actions. Even on May 8, 1865, he wrote about the possibility of going across the river to fight the "rebs." Instead the unit was sent to Columbus, Texas, where the Union army encountered unruly civilians and slave owners who were reluctant to grant their slaves freedom or negotiate new labor agreements. Shearer's relationship with Elizabeth was obviously strong. Once he teased her about getting "Fleshy" and kiddingly told her, "You must have Someone that takes care of you when I was home" (p. 106). Another letter, which contained personal matters, Shearer marked "Keep this to yourself" (pp. 95–96). On August 10, 1865, Shearer was in Vicksburg administering oaths of loyalty.

221. SHENKEL, JACOB. "The Last Shot? Jacob Shenkel's Gettysburg Diary." By Timothy R. Brookes. *Timeline* 4 (June/July 1987): 46–54.
May 11–November 19, 1863. Diary. Sixty-second Pennsylvania Infantry. Battle of Gettysburg. The matter-of-fact entries in Shenkel's diary verify that the whole series of supposedly dead soldiers photographed by Gettysburg photographer Peter S. Weaver were staged several months later. Shenkel's November 11 entry reads: "Went to Round Top with an artist to take some scenes of the battlefield. Took one scene of dead men, then as skirmishers, then on Picket" (p. 52). The editor adds that Weaver was anticipating a demand for such images since the Gettysburg battlefield was soon to be dedicated.

222. SHERMAN, WILLIAM T. "The New Sherman Letters." By Joseph H. Ewing. *American Heritage* 38 (July/August 1987): 24–32, 36–37, 40–41.
1861–1865. Letters. Major General. Military Division of the Mississippi. Ewing describes a previously unpublished collection of twenty-four letters that Sherman wrote to Thomas Ewing, Sherman's foster father, and his foster brother, Philemon B. Ewing. These men were Joseph Ewing's great-grandfather and grandfather. In "The Letters in Perspective" Shelby Foote expresses the belief that they do little to deepen our portrait of Sherman but do serve to "broaden it to closer to life-size" (p. 28). While Sherman's war-long battle with the press takes center stage, Foote was most struck by the human qualities Sherman exhibited. He points to Sherman's remorse over the death of his nine-year-old son by typhoid fever just after the family had spent a delightful visit near Vicksburg in summer 1863. In another passage Sherman admired the extent to which Southerners would go to support the Confederacy. Northerners, on the other hand, "seem more intent on getting Negroes and vagabonds to take the place of soldiers" (p. 40). In conclusion, Ewing returns to the question of whether Sherman's antagonism against newspaper reporters was well founded. He finds it to have been appropriate and offers as evidence the memoirs of Civil War newspaper correspondent Henry Villard, who, some forty years after the events, agreed with Sherman's stance.

223. SHERMAN, WILLIAM T. "Sherman Reveals Something About His Strategy." *Civil War Times Illustrated* 33 (July/August 1994): 28–29, 76.
1864. Letter. Major General. Military Division of the Mississippi. March to the Sea. Writing in 1888, Sherman explained to an Augusta newspaper editor why he spared the Georgia city from destruction. After passing Augusta, Sherman reasoned that since the military supply lines to both Lee in Virginia and Hood in Tennessee had been severed, Augusta was sufficiently isolated from military concerns.

224. SHORTELL, MICHAEL. *The Civil War Letters of Corporal Michael Shortell, Company G, 7th Wisconsin Volunteer Infantry.* Compiled and printed by Mary Wanty Frazier. Bowie, Md.: N. pub., 1992. 90 pp.
October 22, 1861–December 22, 1862. Letters. Seventh Wisconsin Infantry. Duty in Virginia, including winter camp at Arlington and the battle of Fredericksburg. Shortell describes his adjustment to military life and asserts his determination to avoid playing cards and drinking, even though he found the winter encampment boring. Colds were rampant, but when a doctor gave Shortell quinine, he threw the powder into the fire and selected his own form of medication; Shortell "went out in the fields and got some penneroil, which I made tea of" (p. 26). His sparse letters, filled with apologies for not knowing what to write, tell of two reviews by President Lincoln, rumored troop movements, and financial matters. Shortell was constantly concerned for his parents' health. He admitted that his worry resulted in his feeling blue, which was rare for him. Facsimiles of Shortell's letters are included, as are service records and letters describing his death along the North Anna River.

225. SMITH, WILLIAM FARRAR. *Autobiography of Major General William F. Smith, 1861–1864.* Edited by Herbert M. Schiller. Preface by Edwin Cole Bearss. Dayton, Ohio: Morningside House, 1990. 164 pp.
1861–1864. Memoir. Major Gen.. Smith recounts his experiences as division and corps commander (Army of the Potomac) during the Peninsular campaign, Antietam, and Fredericksburg; chief engineer of the Department of the Cumberland; and commander of the XVIII Corps (Army of the James) at Cold Harbor and the assaults on Petersburg. The editor points to Smith's often stormy role in military politics, which involved Joe Hooker's "unscrupulous ambition," Ambrose Burnside's "ineptitude," and Ulysses S. Grant's "alcohol problems." Among the major military activities that Smith recounts is "his" plan to establish the "Cracker line" from Bridgeport, Alabama, to supply the besieged federal troops in Chattanooga. Smith also included his official "Report on Action at Cold Harbor and Petersburg, May 27–June 15, 1864," his record of an attack he was criticized for failing to press more vigorously. This autobiography was addressed to his daughter after his death, but both Schiller and Bearss point out that portions are included in Smith's other publications and reports.

226. SPENCER, NEWTON B. "The Court-Martial of Private Spencer." Edited by R. G. Merrill. *Civil War Times Illustrated* 27 (February 1989): 34–40.
July 1864. Private. Letter. 179th New York Infantry. Spencer's letter to his hometown newspaper, the *Pen Yan Democrat,* was critical of the army's conduct of the Petersburg Mine Assault. Because of his letter Spencer was court-martialed and fined. Part of the trial proceedings is included.

227. STILES, CHARLES B. *Grandfather Was a Drummer Boy: A Civil War Diary and Letters of Charles B. Stiles.* Edited by John Stiles Castle. Solon, Ohio: Evans Printing Company, 1986. 145 pp.
September 9, 1861–October 2, 1864. Diary and letters. Thirty-sixth and Eighty-eighth Illinois Infantries. Duty in Missouri; Arkansas, including Pea Ridge; Mississippi; pursuit of Bragg in Kentucky, including Perryville; Tennessee, including Stones River, the Tullahoma campaign, the siege of Chattanooga, Missionary Ridge, and the relief of Knoxville; Chickamauga; and the Atlanta campaign, including Rocky Face Ridge, Resaca, Kennesaw Mountain, Peachtree Creek, the siege of Atlanta, and Jonesboro. Seventeen-year-old Charles, who was slightly over five feet tall and weighed 105 pounds at enlistment, quickly put on weight. He was especially pleased when he could boast that he weighed more than his father. However, the diminutive Stiles still had to ask for shoes to be made for him at home; size five was not available as military issue. Charles assured his parents that all boxes, or "tokens of love," from home were appreciated by the soldiers (p. 35). He was proud of his improvement at drumming and mentioned that drummers were often utilized as assistants in hospitals. Although musicians were held out of some battles, they served on picket duty and made the same hard marches as the regular soldiers. Just after Lincoln issued the Emancipation Proclamation, Stiles wrote that he was not quite the abolitionist he was when he entered the service. Still, he insisted that if the slaves were to be freed, they should be allowed to fight. Later he felt that slaves needed to be released slowly because they "were ignorant and comparatively helpless" (p. 67). Stiles's entries on the Atlanta campaign are brief and lack his usual sense of humor.

228. STOWELL, MARTIN. "A Nebraska Cavalryman in Dixie: The Letters of Martin Stowell." Edited by James E. Potter. *Nebraska History* 74 (Spring 1993): 22–31.
October 16, 1861–March 10, 1862. Letters. Sergeant Major. Curtis' Horse Cavalry (later Fifth Iowa Cavalry). These letters relate the company's journey from Omaha to Keokuk, then down to Benton Bar-

racks. Stowell describes the battle of Fort Donelson, although his cavalry unit did not participate, and he relates the concentration of Union troops readying for the Shiloh campaign. He wrote that his cavalry unit was anxious to "see the elephant" before the war was over. Stowell was killed in a battle outside Paris, Tennessee, on March 11, 1862. Contempt for slavery and the Confederacy is a persistent theme of his letters. Stowell was a soldier-correspondent for the *Nebraska Advertiser,* in which these letters were published.

229. STRATHERN, JOHN H. *The Civil War Letters of Cpl. John H. Strathern: Eighth Pennsylvania Reserve Volunteer Corps.* Compiled by Marlene C. Bumbera. Apollo, Pa.: Clossen Press, 1994. 93 pp.

August 3, 1861–January 3, 1863. Letters. Corporal. Thirty-seventh Pennsylvania Infantry (Eighth Reserves). Duty around Washington, D.C., and in northern Virginia. John's letters to his parents, brother, and sister reveal little detail about his military experiences or his feelings on the war. He was pleased that Lincoln released the Emancipation Proclamation, but most of his letters contain requests for clothing, money, news about soldiers the family knew, and descriptions of places he visited. In one letter he warns his younger brother about the wiles of women. In another letter he thanks a friend for a bottle of hair oil but admits that it was little used by soldiers. Several letters concern the whereabouts of his brother-in-law, who had been killed at Seven Pines. John encouraged his sister to believe that the man would appear on some prisoner-of-war list. John was detailed to Gen. McDowell's construction corps building bridges during the spring and summer of 1862 and, thus, was not present at the regiment's battles on the Peninsula, second Bull Run, and the Antietam campaign. He apparently saw no action until Fredericksburg, after which he wrote that he had "received two flesh wounds in the left leg" but added, "My wounds are doing well" (p. 91). John died of some combination of his wounds and typhoid fever on January 7, 1863.

230. STUCKENBERG, JOHN H. W. *I'm Surrounded by Methodists . . . Diary of John H. W. Stuckenberg, Chaplain of the 145th Pennsylvania.* Edited by David T. Hedrick and Gordon Barry Davis Jr. Gettysburg, Pa.: Thomas Publications, 1995. 140 pp.

October 6, 1862–September 28, 1863. Diary. Chaplain. 145th Pennsylvania Infantry. Antietam (aftermath); Fredericksburg; Chancellorsville; and Gettysburg. Stuckenberg was a young German-born Lutheran chaplain with congregations in Erie, Pennsylvania. During September and October 1862 he experienced many "firsts." En route to Harpers Ferry he was nearby when a private attempted suicide by stabbing himself and cutting his throat. At Antietam he witnessed his first battlefield carnage and his first wounded soldier, a Confederate who had lain unattended in the sun for two days. As a part of the Irish Brigade, Stuckenberg recorded his activities among the unruly Irish soldiers. Stuckenberg noted the many vices: profanity, card playing, and men who experienced "frequent nocturnal emissions, foul dreams, etc.," which he blamed on "the pernicious effects of early indulgences" (p. 17). Stuckenberg was a soldiers' chaplain who worked tirelessly on the men's behalf. The soldiers entrusted him with their money, which he took to Washington and sent to their families. He ministered to the spiritual needs of all denominations and frequently visited hospitals. After Fredericksburg one badly wounded man asked Stuckenberg to kill him. The man pleaded: "It is cruel to let me suffer so—it is a mercy to kill me" (p. 43). Stuckenberg penned lively accounts of the fighting. He said that at Chancellorsville he tried to turn back the panicked XI Corps, which was fleeing from the Confederate advance. At Gettysburg, on July 2, just after Father William Corby's emotional Service of Absolution, Stuckenberg held a similar worship for non-Catholics of the Irish Brigade. Stuckenberg often second-guessed the decisions of Union commanders. At Fredericksburg he could not understand why Union forces had not attacked earlier. And after Gettysburg he criticized Gen. Meade for failing to engage the retreating Army of Northern Virginia in full-scale battle. Stuckenberg returned to his congregation in Erie in October 1863.

231. SULLIVAN, JAMES P. *An Irishman in the Iron Brigade: The Civil War Memoirs of James P. Sullivan, Serg., Company K, 6th Wisconsin Volunteers.* Edited by William J. K. Beaudot and Lance J. Herdegen. New York: Fordham University Press, 1993. 189 pp.

July 1861–1864. Memoir. Sergeant. Sixth Wisconsin Infantry. Organization and training at Camp Randall; defenses of Washington, D.C.; Gainesville; second Bull Run; South Mountain; Fitzhugh's Crossing; Gettysburg; and Globe Tavern. Sullivan wrote these memoirs as columns for the *Milwaukee Telegraph* in the 1880s. He reminded readers that the Sixth Wisconsin, which suffered devastating casualties in heavy fighting through Gettysburg, had made a great contribution to the Union victory. And he emphasized the nation's unpaid debt to all veterans. "Mickey's" columns are a mixture of humorous anecdotes and bitter invectives. He criticized most generals, especially John Pope, but praised Phil Kearny, "the one armed devil." Also, he minced no words when he referred to the "blundering war department" and "blood-thirsty" newspaper editors. His battlefield descriptions are realistic. At South Mountain, where he fought despite having the mumps, he was wounded in his already sore jaw. Then he was hit in the foot. He received brief treatment at a field hospital and was housed temporarily in the House of Representatives. Following an operation and recuperation in a Washington hospital, he was released and told to go home, although he had little money. He enlisted in the Sixth Wisconsin again a few months later. The editor says that Sullivan's most popular newspaper column involved the regiment's role in the fighting at the Railroad Cut at Gettysburg. Sullivan was wounded and captured and spent two days in the Confederate-held town of Gettysburg before the Southerners withdrew. Sullivan spent the rest of 1863 in a Philadelphia hospital, where he met his future wife, after which he again reenlisted. Sullivan's last piece describes the fighting along the Weldon Railroad, especially at Globe Tavern in August 1864.

232. SWEETLAND, EMORY. "Emory Sweetland Remembers November 19, 1863." By Mark H. Dunkelman. *Lincoln Herald* 96 (Summer 1994): 44–51.

November 19, 1863. Memoir. 154th New York Infantry. Sweetland, who was serving on detached duty as hospital steward at the Camp Letterman Hospital (Gettysburg), described the events of the day. He recalled being so close to Lincoln that he could see "the tears trickling down the face of the great emancipator" (p. 44). The editor quotes from and paraphrases Sweetland's other letters, which describe his duty with the 154th New York Infantry.

233. TAYLOR, JOHN HENRY, JR., and MARY ANN TAYLOR. *The Family of John Henry Taylor, Jr., Featuring Family Letters Written During and After the Civil War.* By Alice Paula Perkins Mortensen and Edward Hjalmar Mortensen. Baltimore, Md.: Heritage Press, 1995. 136 pp.

1861–1863. Letters. John was a first-class fireman aboard the screw steamer USS *Dragon*. The gunboat served with the James Flotilla and the Potomac Flotilla enforcing the blockade between Maryland and Virginia. The *Dragon* was hit in the boiler during the naval battle of March 8, 1862, off Hampton Roads. John's letters (December 26, 1861–December 17, 1863) describe the battle and his duties. But most of his letters involve the family. John often expressed his love for Mary Ann and instructed his children about what he expected of them in his absence. On several occasions he asked his wife to keep aspects of his letters to herself because he did not want their acquaintances at home to know what he had written. John kept a close accounting of the money that he sent home and set goals for how much he wanted to have saved when he received his discharge. He spent money sparingly, once rejecting the opportunity to come home because it would have cost $20. On another occasion Mary Ann apparently asked for money to pay a doctor bill. He agreed to send her $2 of the $3.50, "as it is for such an old chum," but added, "all I shall ask of you will be a little interest" (p. 73). He further advised her to keep her "account straight with me for fear I might jew you." His few letters in the last half of 1863 were written from hospitals, and he was discharged for poor health in December 1863. The seven letters from Mary Ann (June 1–November 2, 1863) were written from their home in Nyack, New York. She mentioned daily routines, her undying love for John, and concern for his illness. Letters written in the 1870s between the children and Mary Ann are included, as is a section on "Family Genealogy."

234. TAYLOR, JOSEPH KNIGHT. "Two Years in Blue: The Civil War Letters of Joseph K. Taylor." By Kevin Murphy. *Historical Journal of Massachusetts* 24 (Summer 1996): 145–63.

August 1862–1864. Letters. Sergeant and Lieutenant. Thirty-seventh Massachusetts Infantry. Duty in Virginia. Murphy believes that Taylor's letters are important documents because they "express many of his values, shed light on the meaning of courage and duty to an ordinary soldier in the ranks, and illuminate the social history of the war" (p. 144). Murphy compares Taylor's expression of these themes with studies of Union soldiers by historians Bell I. Wiley, George M. Fredrickson, Michael Barton, and Gerald Linderman, among others. Murphy was baffled as to why Taylor enlisted. In mid 1862 the patriotic fervor of the previous year had waned. Taylor was not an abolitionist, nor did he speak favorably of blacks. And he was not in need of the bounty money. Murphy conjectures that one reason Taylor enlisted was because he had inherited a value system common to Victorian-age children. Within that value system the concepts of honor, morality, and restraint were major components. Because rebellion exemplified a lack of restraint, Northerners felt duty-bound to repress the Confederate threat to the Union. Taylor's letters indicate that he possessed such a value system, and Murphy suggests that it would have been reinforced by serving with others from his social class. Still another reason why Taylor might have enlisted at this time is addressed by that part of the Victorian value system which held that an individual needed to experience adversity in order to become a better person. (This concept applied to nations and individuals alike.) Taylor's letters often indicate pride in his and his regiment's ability to endure suffering. Another theme that Murphy scrutinizes is the belief held by some historians that as the war lengthened, the veteran soldiers felt that the overall quality of the army, as well as the concept of personal courage, was being diminished by the influx of volunteers, recruitment of blacks, and changes of leadership. In 1864 Union soldiers are said to have become inured to bloodshed and developed a fatalistic attitude about the war. Taylor exhibited some degree of disillusionment and fatalism. He considered not reenlisting because he felt he had proven that he had sufficiently done his duty. But he did reenlist, and he trained the new soldiers and even praised their development. Murphy identifies specific reasons for Taylor's expressions of disillusionment, such as Union defeats or the "cowards" at home who would not do their duty by enlisting. Taylor died from a wound in fall 1864.

235. TAYLOR, NELSON. *Saddle and Saber: Civil War Letters of Corporal Nelson Taylor, Ninth New York State Volunteer Cavalry to His Father Shubael Taylor and Sister Hannah, Clifton Park, New York, November 14, 1861–October 30, 1864.* Compilation, editing, and commentary by his grandson, Gray Nelson Taylor. Bowie, Md.: Heritage Books, 1993. 198 pp.

November 1, 1861–October 30, 1864. Letters. Corporal. Ninth New York Cavalry. Duty at the defenses of Washington, D.C.; the siege of Yorktown; Pope's Virginia campaign; Gettysburg and the pursuit of Lee, including Williamsport and Boonsboro; Kelly's Ford; duty along the Rappahannock; Spotsylvania; Todd's Tavern; Sheridan's Richmond raid; Sheridan's Trevilian raid; the Petersburg campaign, including demonstrations north of the James; Sheridan's Shenandoah Valley campaign, including Berryville and Shepherdstown; duty at Camp Remount, Maryland; and discharge in Baltimore. In his early letters Taylor predicted that his unit would be discharged because of an abundance of cavalrymen and the men's refusal to be transferred into the infantry or artillery. At various times Taylor said that he would not reenlist, but on other occasions he was equally determined to see the war to its conclusion. He never espoused causes, although he favored emancipation in the abstract. Because he believed that all Northerners should pitch in, he was upset at those who participated in the New York draft riots. Fighting and movement constituted most of Taylor's correspondence after Gettysburg. Among comments associated with soldier life, Taylor extolled the virtues of coffee: "if it was not for coffee I do not know what we would do it is half of a soldiers living" (p. 163). Care of the horses is another theme of these letters. The appendix includes several of Taylor's letters, one of which describes a Gettysburg reunion of 1893.

236. TENURE, CORNELIUS. *Civil War Letters of the Tenure Family, Rockland County, N.Y., 1862–1865.* Edited by Larry H. Whiteaker and W. Calvin Dickinson. New City, N.Y.: Historical Society of Rockland County, 1990. 98 pp.
September 8, 1862–May 26, 1865. Letters. Private. 135th New York Infantry, which became the Sixth New York Heavy Artillery. Duty at Fort McHenry (Baltimore) and Harpers Ferry; Rappahannock Station; the siege of Petersburg; and Cedar Creek. The Tenure family had long been hardworking, lower-middle-class subsistence farmers from Rockland County, New York. The eldest son, Cornelius, and his brother Irving were laborers and the sources of economic support. When they joined the army in August 1862, the family's livelihood became precarious. Only a mother, an elderly father, two younger brothers, and three younger sisters remained on the farm. The letters Cornelius wrote to his mother and several brothers are more important for what they reveal about the home front than as records of his military experiences. When the father died in October 1863, Cornelius wrote a letter to his brother John Henry that was fraught with distress. Cornelius received the impression (through the words of others) that his mother blamed him for failing to provide her with more money and refusing to accept a furlough to come home. Cornelius was frustrated with other members of the family. Irving would not send money to his mother on a regular basis and caused his family to worry about his welfare because he was negligent in communicating. (Irving was illiterate.) John Henry would not return to the farm because he chose to continue his apprenticeship elsewhere. The burden of running the farm fell on Edward, the youngest teenage brother. Cornelius did not want the farm to be sold and suggested it be put into pasture if crops could not be planted. Cornelius was wounded at The Wilderness and spent the last year of the war in hospitals in Washington and Philadelphia. During that time he disagreed with John Henry over political issues and perhaps personal matters. The editors add that after the war Cornelius never returned to the family farm. Irving became mentally unstable and lived out his life in a mental home, completely out of contact with the rest of the family. The editors pose the question about the degree to which the Civil War was to blame for the disintegration of what had formerly been a stable family (p. x).

237. THOMAS, JAMES B. *"I Never Again Want to Witness Such Sights": The Civil War Letters of First Lieutenant James B. Thomas, Adjutant, 107th Pennsylvania Volunteers.* Edited by Mary Warner Thomas and Richard A. Sauers. Baltimore, Md.: Butternut and Blue, 1995. 367 pp.
May 31, 1861–December 25, 1864. Letters. Twentieth Pennsylvania Infantry (three-month) and Lieutenant, 107th Pennsylvania Infantry. Defense of Washington until April 1862; guard duty along the Orange & Alexandria Railroad; Cedar Mountain; Pope's Virginia campaign, including Thoroughfare Gap and second Bull Run; South Mountain; Antietam (described); Fredericksburg; Burnside's "Mud March"; Chancellorsville; Gettysburg; the Petersburg campaign, including assaults on Petersburg, the battle of Globe Tavern, and the Weldon Railroad expedition to Hicksford. Thomas often appraised his superior officers. Banks and Fremont were "paper generals" (p. 58). Initially he believed that Pope would "straighten things out"; however, after second Bull Run he agreed with those who thought that Pope would make a better corps commander. In 1862 Thomas approved of Gen. John W. Geary's order

to burn houses in retribution for railroad line destruction by the Confederates. During the expedition to Hicksford in December 1864 several Union stragglers were bushwhacked, prompting the army to hang a guerrilla and burn plantations. Thomas again praised such retribution. Thomas was in awe of Stonewall Jackson and believed that Jackson's death was a great advantage to the Union army because he had heard the men speak of Jackson as if he could not have been whipped. In April 1863, while on the picket line, a corporal of a New Jersey regiment gave birth to a new recruit. Thomas wrote: "*he* flatly refuses to take a discharge, being determined to serve out *his* enlistment" (p. 159). He reported that along the Petersburg siege lines Confederate troops had retained a Union soldier as a prisoner while the opposing sides were fraternizing. The Union soldiers retaliated by inviting a Confederate major and a lieutenant over to their lines for coffee and a newspaper and then holding the Confederates captive. After second Bull Run, Thomas wrote that his brother Seal was returning to Philadelphia with "a little nigger for the girls." Thomas provided instructions for the young man's care and discipline, part of which included a "severe flogging" (p. 87). But in July 1864, when Thomas commended the black soldiers' work on a dirt fort before Petersburg, he employed a different term of reference: "American citizens of African decent" (p. 209). Although there are no letters written by Thomas after 1864, the editors have concluded this work with other accounts that follow the 107th Pennsylvania to the end of the war.

238. THOMAS, HORACE HOLMES. "'I Was an Ogre': Horace Holmes Thomas, Provost Marshal's Office, Knoxville, Tennessee." *Civil War: The Magazine of the Civil War Society* 47 (October 1994): 60–61.
August 1863–September 1864. Memoir. Lieutenant. Eighth Tennessee Infantry (U.S.). This work includes brief recollections of experiences in Union-occupied Knoxville.

239. THOMPSON, RICHARD S. *While My Country Is in Danger: The Life and Letters of Lieutenant Colonel Richard S. Thompson, Twelfth New Jersey Volunteers.* By Gerry Harder Poriss and Ralph G. Poriss. Hamilton, N.Y.: Edmonston Publishing, 1994. 229 pp.
April 7, 1862–February 21, 1865. Letters and diary. Lieutenant Colonel. Twelfth New Jersey Infantry. Provost duty at Ellicotts Mills, Maryland, and Falmouth, Virginia; Chancellorsville; Gettysburg, including pursuit of Lee; Bristoe Station; recruiting duty in Trenton, New Jersey, between December 1863 and May 1864; and the siege of Petersburg, including Reams' Station. The letters begin with Thompson's militia duty, followed by his recruitment of two companies that became part of the Twelfth New Jersey. At Chancellorsville, after the regiment saw its first fighting, Thompson was pleased at how well the unit had performed. At Gettysburg he wrote that the unit distinguished itself at the battle on Bliss farm and during Pickett's Charge. After being badly wounded at Reams' Station, Thompson was removed from the war. His remaining correspondence treats his recovery in hospitals in Philadelphia and Washington. Thompson's letters indicate that he was insightful and considerate. When he observed the enlisted men fraternizing with the "Rebs" at times when the men thought that the officers (such as himself) were not watching, he remained silent. Thompson described the forced march to Gettysburg vividly: "To see men fall from exhaustion, clothes wet, faces and teeth black with dust, lips parched, eyes sunken, feet blistered, and then driven on at the point of the bayonet. This is a forced march" (p. 64). Thompson was aware of his flaws. Once, after he had ranted about the "preposterous goals" of the Confederacy, Thompson begged his sister and brother to forgive him: "My pent up enthusiasm will at times boil over" (p. 41). Concluding this work are letters with news about the Twelfth New Jersey written by its members after Thompson was wounded and a biographical sketch of Thompson's marriage and postwar law practice.

240. TIDBALL, JOHN C. "Fort Pickens Relief Expedition of 1861: Lt. John C. Tidball's Journals." By Eugene C. Tidball. *Civil War History* 42 (December 1996): 322–39.

April 6–July 1861. Journal and memoir. Lieutenant. Second U.S. Light Artillery, Battery A. Fort Pickens, Pensacola Harbor, Florida. The author combines historical narrative and Lieutenant Tidball's writings to describe the relief of Fort Pickens. The article begins with the removal of all federal forces to Fort Pickens by Lt. Adam J. Slemmer (First U.S. Light Artillery, Company G) and continues by relating the secret relief mission, which reached Fort Pickens on April 18, 1861. The article also covers the improvement of the garrison's defenses, major events that occurred there during the next year, the strategic importance of the fort's retention to the North, and sketches of the subsequent careers of those who played principal roles in the defense of Fort Pickens.

241. TIPTON, WILLIAM. *Dearest Carrie: Civil War Letters Home.* Lawrenceville, Va.: Brunswick Publishing Corp., 1995. 150 pp.

January 19, 1862–August 11, 1865. Letters. Engineer aboard the USS *Circassian* and the USS *Sacramento*. The majority of these letters were written while William was at sea aboard the *Sacramento* in the North Atlantic during 1864 and 1865. While he occasionally mentioned European and South American ports of call, Confederate blockade runners, and conditions aboard ship, most of William's letters to his wife were about personal matters. He asked for news about their young son, sent money, and instructed Carrie on how to get part of his pay from "Navy agents." William begged Carrie to write him because he was concerned that she might forget him. When she became sick and died in early 1865, he was filled with remorse for having been away so long. Several letters between Carrie's sister, Jennie, and William reveal details about the marriage. On Carrie's deathbed she wished that her young son be raised by Jennie, and William agreed. Postwar letters from the Tipton family mention that William remarried and died in 1867. "Part Two" of this work contains letters pertaining to the captivity of Jennie's husband, Andrew Hopkins, who was chief engineer aboard the USS *Smith Briggs* when it was destroyed by Confederate forces on February 1, 1864. Jennie's letters express her emotional and financial plight and requests for Union officials to press for Andrew's release from Libby Prison.

242. TOBIE, EDWARD P. "Life in a U.S. Army Hospital, 1862: From the Diaries and Letters of Pvt. Tobie." By Thomas W. W. Atwood. *Army* 38 (January 1988): 52–57.

May–November 1862. Diary and letters. Private. First Maine Cavalry. U.S. Army General Hospital Episcopal Seminary (Alexandria, Virginia). Atwood paraphrases and quotes from the perceptive writings of a hospitalized soldier who was regaining his strength following a bout with dysentery. Assigned as a clerk, Tobie watched the facility grow from a pleasant convalescent camp into a crowded hospital flooded with wounded soldiers from the Peninsular campaign and second Bull Run. He characterized the surgeon in charge of medical and administrative aspects of the institution, Dr. H. A. Armstrong, as being tireless and competent but equally irascible. The manner in which the doctor meted out punishment to malcontents bordered on cruelty. For example, he assigned "hard cases" to beds for ten days or, kept them in "bomb proofs" for solitary confinement. Tobie observed the reactions of friends and relatives when they came to visit the patients. Sometimes the patients were already dead, and if they were not, the patients were often depressed after the visits, leaving them in worse condition than before. Among the other topics Tobie mentions are the weekly reports he was assigned to fill out; men who showed up at the hospital without their personnel records (called "descriptive lists"); incompetent or untrained "contract" doctors; and funerals. At the time of his writing, female nurses had not been assigned to the hospital yet, and Tobie considered the civilian volunteer male nurses cowards for not enlisting.

243. **TORKELSON, IVER.** "A Norwegian in Blue: Letters of Iver Torkelson, 15th Wisconsin." Edited by Anthony Torkelson. *Military Images* 9, no. 4 (1988): 6–13.

January 5, 1862–October 12, 1863. Letters. Sergeant. Fifteenth Wisconsin Infantry. Island No. 10 and duty in Tennessee, including Stones River. Torkelson was concerned when his family worried about his well-being. He also did not like them to have to pay the taxes on his property. He mentioned the enlistment of Norwegian friends, reported on the battle of Perryville, and described being detached from his regiment to operate a sawmill near Murfreesboro. He also served with the Invalid Corps (Veteran Reserve Corps) at Camp Dennison, Ohio, while he was recuperating from an illness.

244. **TROWBRIDGE, GEORGE MARTIN.** "Such Is Military: Dr. George Martin Trowbridge's Letters from Sherman's Army, 1863–1865." By Horace W. Davenport. *Bulletin of the New York Academy of Medicine* 63 (November 1987): 844–82.

1863–1865. Letters. Trowbridge was a recent graduate of the University of Michigan Medical School, and he accompanied Sherman on the Atlanta campaign and the March to the Sea. In Atlanta he established the Second Division, XIV Corps Hospital, where, according to Davenport, Trowbridge succeeded in virtually eliminating gangrene. Trowbridge described filling out his monthly reports and noted such interesting aspects of his treatment of patients as the fact that scurvy was reduced when the soldiers ate ripe wild berries. He also commented on the impact that Sherman's army was making on both the Southern soldiers and civilians. Davenport paraphrases and quotes from Trowbridge's correspondence.

245. **TUCKER, ELIJAH.** "'My Life Has Not Been a Blank': The Autobiography of Captain Elijah F. Tucker of Greensburg, Kentucky." By Bruce Curtis. *Filson Club History Quarterly* 64 (April 1996): 264–76.

1861–1864. Memoir. Captain. Thirteenth Kentucky Infantry. Duty in Tennessee and Kentucky. Curtis quotes from and paraphrases the Civil War section of Tucker's reflection on his complete life, which was written in 1923.

246. **TYLER, WILLIAM N.** *The Dispatch Carrier and Memoirs of Andersonville.* Bernalillo, N.M.: Joel Beer and Gwendy MacMaster, 1992. 59, 43 pp.

1861–1865. Memoir. Sergeant. Ninth Illinois Cavalry and Ninety-fifth Illinois Infantry. Duty in Missouri and Arkansas; Brice's Cross Roads; and Andersonville Prison. Serving around Jacksonport, Arkansas, in early 1862 Tyler was asked by Gen. Samuel R. Curtis to carry a message some 150 miles through enemy lines to the acting brigadier general at Little Rock. Tyler recounted his trek in adventuresome terms as he described the uncertain military situation and divided sectional loyalties. An illness forced his discharge from the Ninth Illinois Cavalry in September 1862. Tyler's second enlistment was with the Ninety-fifth Illinois Infantry. While the unit was participating in Sturgis's expedition to Guntown, Mississippi, he was captured at Brice's Cross Roads and taken to Andersonville Prison. Tyler blamed Henry Wirz for the prison conditions, and he penned many anecdotes about Wirz. One alleged that his wife threatened to poison her husband if Wirz did not do something for the relief of the Union prisoners (she once succeeded). Tyler remained a prisoner until the end of the war. At Vicksburg he and other Andersonville prisoners were placed on the first transport ship bound for Saint Louis. The second steamer, also filled with prisoners, was the ill-fated *Sultana*. These two booklets were published in Belvidere, Illinois (1887), and Rapids City, Illinois (1892). A descendant remembers them being sold as a part of "Grandpa Tyler's lecture tour."

247. **VAN LENTE, JOHANNES.** *The Civil War Letters of Johannes Van Lente.* Edited by Janice Van Lente Catlin. Okemos, Mich.: Yankee Girl Publications, 1992. 173 pp.

September 7, 1862–May 9, 1865. Letters. Private. Twenty-fifth Michigan Infantry. Induction at Kalamazoo; and duty in Kentucky (including battle of Tebb's Bend), Tennessee, and North Carolina. Van Lente wrote to his family and friends in the Dutch colony at Holland, Michigan. He described the strangeness of life outside the religious community and transmitted news of mutual acquaintances. He frequently requested his family to pray for him, as well as to give him information about their health. Several passages relate to Van Lente's acculturation. He once asked a child to write in Dutch so he could better understand what the boy was trying to say. Another time he referred to a comrade, who was being buried, as an "American" (p. 37). After Van Lente was taken ill in the Atlanta campaign, his letters became fewer. However, the letters he received from home while he was hospitalized reveal how the war was affecting the Dutch community. All letters are translated from the Dutch. Genealogical information is also included.

248. **VANDERHOEF, LORENZO.** *"I Am Now a Soldier": The Civil War Diaries of Lorenzo Vanderhoef.* Edited by Kenneth R. Martin and Ralph Linwood Snow. Bath, Maine: Patten Free Library, 1990. 148 pp.

April 27, 1861–July 3, 1863. Diary. Sergeant. Eighth Ohio Infantry. Organization of the unit and training at Camp Dennison (Ohio); duty in West Virginia at and near Romney (including battles of Hanging Rock Pass and Mill Creek Mills); and the battle of first Kernstown. Vanderhoef's diary for the period through first Kernstown is filled with interesting and humorous descriptions of camp incidents, marches, and battles. He related that one night he was nearly suffocated when he was squashed while sleeping between two tentmates. He told how a march across the rough terrain of West Virginia in the cold, wet weather of winter took its toll on men who had become used to camp duty. And he revealed that soldiers tipped over the wagons of sutlers because one was overcharging for his goods and the other was illegally selling whiskey. Vanderhoef often reflected on his situation. He wondered why the Confederates said that the war would be fought to its conclusion in the border states when there were so many Unionists in West Virginia. He also pondered the propensity of some officers to act as if they were better than enlisted men. Vanderhoef's diary entries written between April 9, 1862, and February 23, 1863, are missing; the editors believe they were probably lost at Antietam, where he was shot four times at the "Bloody Lane" and stripped of all his possessions. In his final entries, written after he returned home to Homerville, Ohio, he describes farming, having his teeth filled, and washing sheep.

249. **VEIL, CHARLES HENRY.** *The Memoirs of Charles Henry Veil: A Soldier's Recollections of the Civil War and the Arizona Territory.* Edited, with an introduction, by Herman J. Viola. New York: Orion Books, 1993. 194 pp.

Summer 1861–Spring 1865. Memoir. Private, Thirty-eighth Pennsylvania Infantry (Ninth Reserves); I Corps, Army of the Potomac; and Lieutenant, First U.S. Cavalry Regiment. Organization at Pittsburgh; duty around Washington, D.C.; the Seven Days' Battles; second Bull Run; Fredericksburg; Chancellorsville; Gettysburg; The Wilderness; the Spotsylvania campaign (including Todd's Tavern, Yellow Tavern, and Sheridan's Richmond raid); Cold Harbor; Sheridan's Shenandoah Valley campaign (including Fisher's Hill and Cedar Creek); the Appomattox campaign; the expedition to Danville; and the Grand Review. Veil was an orderly to Gen. John F. Reynolds and was present when Reynolds was mortally wounded at Gettysburg. Veil claimed that he prevented Reynolds's body from being carried away by Confederate soldiers. (The editor mentions Veil's different versions of this event.) Veil was also present on September 23, 1864, when several of Mosby's guerrillas were hanged in retribution for the alleged killing of Union scouts. Their bodies were left hanging in public view with a card pinned to each man's clothing that read: "Hung in retaliation for shooting and killing wounded officers and men after being wounded" (p. 48). One young boy ran away to avoid being hung but was pursued and shot by Union soldiers. Veil said that his mother was first relieved when she saw that the boy's body was not among those left hanging but became distraught when her dead boy was found lying in a field. Veil described the distribution of rations and the intermingling of both armies at the surrender at Appomattox. He observed that "To have seen us no one would have supposed that for four long years we had been involved in a deadly war" (p. 66). The first sixty-eight pages of this memoir pertain to the Civil War.

250. VINCENT, MARTIN LUTHER. *Dr. Michael Vincent, Born 1784, Columbia County, New York and His Descendants, Including the Civil War Letters of His Grandson, Corporal Martin Luther Vincent, 112th, Illinois Infantry.* Compiled by Sheridan E. Vincent. Rochester, N.Y.: N.pub., 1996. 191 pp.

July 2, 1863–June 4, 1865. Letters. Corporal. 112th Illinois Infantry. Duty in east Tennessee (including Saunders' raid in east Tennessee) and Kentucky; the Atlanta campaign; operations against Hood and Forest in north Georgia and north Alabama; the Franklin and Nashville campaign; and duty in North Carolina, including the Carolinas campaign. Vincent wrote to his mother with a spirit of exuberance. As late as August 17, 1864, he wrote that he was glad that he had been in a war, "for I always wanted to see the Southern States" (p. 136). Vincent's running tally of the military actions in which the regiment had been engaged totaled over one hundred skirmishes and sixty hard fights. While he was proud that he had missed only a few, he almost always made light of the fighting with such phrases as "a good many spats." During the last summer of 1864, after the heavy fighting of the Atlanta campaign and a series of incidents, his enthusiasm seems to have waned. He wished the sound of shelling would stop so they could rest for a while. Vincent and a friend were taking refuge behind a tree when the friend was shot through the heart and the same shell nicked his own throat. The death of his brother from his wounds at Kennesaw Mountain devastated him. Vincent attempted to console his mother, but it is clear that he was also grieving. The accumulation of these events prompted Vincent to wonder why he was still alive when so many others were dying. He concluded: "There must be something for me to do yet or else I think I wouldn't of been here yet" (p. 132). After the surrender Vincent prophesied that had Abraham Lincoln lived he would have proven to be the South's best friend in the postwar period, and he predicted that Andrew Johnson was going to be hard on the former Confederacy.

251. WAID, SETH, III. *The Civil War Diaries of Seth Waid III.* Edited by Robert Ilisevich and Jonathan Helmreich. Meadville, Pa.: Crawford County Historical Society, 1993. 141 pp.

September 2, 1861–September 1864. Diary. Eighty-third Pennsylvania Infantry. Defenses of Washington; Chancellorsville; Gettysburg, including pursuit of Lee; and duty along the Rappahannock and Rapidan Rivers. The thirty-six-year-old sensitive and religious Seth Waid struggled emotionally and physically to adapt to soldiering. As the regiments organized at Camp Erie, he found the men in "high spirits" and was hearing more swearing than he had ever before heard. He reported that diarrhea was rampant and that officers and sergeants did not know how to drill their charges. On one occasion Waid crawled out of his tent into a cornfield to escape the chaos of the camp. Alone in the quiet of the night, he yearned for the war to end so that he could "once more clasp the form of my loving wife in my arms" (p. 11). Waid later found a good friend, a young man with whom he developed a loving relationship that lasted throughout his service. Waid never complained about his plight, and he was apparently a good soldier, especially as a hospital nurse. After one sick spell he remained at a Philadelphia hospital for most of 1862 through the spring of 1863. In one entry he described sitting with a young soldier, attending the boy's wounds, and comforting his mother. When the boy died,

Waid washed and prepared the corpse and watched as the doctor removed the boy's shattered leg bones before burial. Waid described other operations in which he assisted. When he was sent back to his regiment, Waid was involved in the fighting at Chancellorsville and Gettysburg. At Little Round Top, after the battle, he thought it "was *affecting*" to see Union soldiers retrieve the wounded Confederates. During the months immediately after Gettysburg, Waid expressed his most patriotic statements. And, as he observed and described the execution of deserters, he supported the harsh penalty. In the fall of 1863 Ward became sick again. When he returned to duty in late December, many of the men who had reenlisted were home on furlough. As they returned from their veteran furloughs, he recorded their reactions. Some called the army's policy of reenlistment for a leave "35 days in heaven and then 3 years in hell" (p. 133). Others said they were not content at home and had returned to camp early (p. 133). Between April and September 1864 Waid was again in a Philadelphia hospital with a tumor on his chest, which, after a lengthy delay, he was able to have lanced. His last passages record a joyous trip back home to Meadville, Pennsylvania.

252. WAKEMAN, SARAH ROSETTA. *An Uncommon Soldier: The Civil War Letters of Sarah Rosetta Wakeman, Alias Private Lyons Wakeman, 153rd Regiment New York State Volunteers.* Edited by Lauren Cook Burgess, with a foreword by James M. McPherson. Pasadena, Md.: Minerva Center, 1994. 110 pp.

November 24, 1862–April 14, 1864. Letters. Private. 153rd New York Infantry. Duty at Alexandria, Virginia, and Washington, D.C., and Banks' second Red River campaign, including Mansfield and Pleasant Hill. Sarah left her home in Afton, New York, in August 1862; disguised herself as a man; and worked briefly as a coal handler on a canal barge. She joined the 153rd New York as Lyons Wakeman, and her true identity remained undetected by military authorities. Her letters to her parents are similar to those of every other soldier. Sarah said that she enjoyed drilling and was getting to be "the fattest fellow you ever see" (p 27). She requested boxes, wrote that she used a lot of tobacco ("it prevents disease"), griped about officers, and sent money home, directing the family to use it for themselves. While her letters contain no direct references to her disguise, her enlistment had obviously caused a rift in her relationship with her family. She attempted to make amends in her first letter. She pleaded with her father: "I want to drop all old affray and I want you to do the same and when I come home we will be good friends as ever" (p. 18). Later, on May 25, 1863, in a letter to her sister Sarah wrote that she forgave her for everything and that she wanted her sister to do the same for her. The next month she was more abrupt as she again attempted to explain her enlistment: "I can tell you what made me leave home. It was because I had got tired of staying in that neighborhood. I know I could help you more to leave home than to stay there with you. So I left. I am not sorry that I left you" (p. 31). Her father gave her typical parental advice, once cautioning her about lending money. She assured him that she was keeping good company, although once she wrote cryptically about succumbing to "temptations" (p. 53). It was important to Sarah that her parents know that she was becoming a good soldier, prepared to handle herself in battle with the enemy as well as with combative comrades. On one occasion she wrote: "Then Mr. Stephen Wiley pitched on me and I give him three or four pretty good cracks and he put downstairs with him Self" (p. 60). Sarah was unconcerned that relatives and friends at home knew that she was serving as a man. She even encouraged her father to join her company if he entered the army. Throughout her letters Sarah was ambivalent about coming home to live again. As late as December 28, 1863, she wrote: "I don't care about Coming home for I [am] aShamed to Come" and then praised army life and the good friends she had made. But in her last letter she reversed her intentions as she encouraged her father to work another farm. She assured him that when she came home she would help him. Sarah died on June 19, 1864, of chronic diarrhea and is buried in Chalmette National Cemetery (New Orleans) under the name of Lyons Wakeman.

253. WALDRON, CARROLL SCOTT. "'I preferred to take my chances': Memoirs of Carroll Scott Waldron, 17th and 146th New York." Edited by Edmund Cocks. *Military Images* 14 (March/April 1993): 22–30.

1861–1865. Memoir. Seventeenth and 146th New York Infantries. The Peninsular campaign; second Bull Run; and The Wilderness, where he was captured and sent to Andersonville and then Florence Prisons. Waldron's terse entries written during his confinement relate the prisoners' resourcefulness, such as digging wells to obtain clean water and building semipermanent dwellings. Waldron, who served on the prison police force, commented on the hanging of the Andersonville raiders. Although food was expensive, it was available at Andersonville. "With all the wretchedness and starvation there were stores of all kinds of eatables for sale in the camp" (p. 28). Waldron's escape attempt was unsuccessful, but he said that at least it provided him with a chance to eat well for a while. Paroled on February 26, 1865, in North Carolina, Waldron was shipped to Fortress Monroe, where he received his pay and was finally able to cleanse himself. Ironically, at Fortress Monroe, Waldron came down with what he described as "Itch." His mother arrived at the camp with a salt-filled coffin, expecting to transport her son's body home. Instead she nursed him back to health. However, the editor says that Waldron suffered from malaria the rest of his life.

254. WALLACE, ROBERT C. *A Few Memories of a Long Life.* New edition by John M. Carroll. Fairfield, Wash.: Ye Galleon Press, 1988. 137 pp.

1861–1865. Memoir. Corporal, First Michigan Infantry (three-month), and Lieutenant, Fifth Michigan Cavalry. This work relates events of first Bull Run, Gettysburg (including pursuit of Lee), Kilpatrick's raid on Richmond, Sheridan's Trevilian raid, The Wilderness, Cold Harbor, Sheridan's Shenandoah Valley campaign (including third Winchester), Five Forks, the surrender at Appomattox, and the Grand Review. Writing in 1915, Wallace recalled all of his wartime experiences with fondness. The Confederate soldiers he met when he was captured in 1862 were reputed to be of high intelligence. And he was proud to have served under Gen. George A. Custer. Wallace recounted in detail how Sheridan obtained information about enemy strength around Winchester from Union supporter Rebecca Wright and put it to good use in the battle of third Winchester. Wallace also related the guerrilla warfare in fall 1864 and the execution of Mosby's men at Front Royal. The first seventy-five pages of this work contain the author's reminiscences of the war.

255. WALTON, THOMAS BECK. *A Pennsylvanian in Blue: The Civil War Diary of Thomas Beck Walton.* Edited by Robert A. Taylor. Shippensburg, Pa.: Burd Street Press, 1995. 65 pp.

March 9, 1865–February 3, 1866. Diary. Private. 195th Pennsylvania Infantry. Duty in the northern Shenandoah Valley and in Washington, D.C. Walton was on picket duty to prevent Mosby's raiders from striking Union posts until the war ended. From August 1865 until February 1866 he was often on provost duty in the nation's capital, guarding government property and enforcing discipline. The editor points out that the army's policy against early discharges created morale problems and desertions, but Walton reveals no discontent.

256. WATROUS, JEROME A. "Reminiscences of War Time Service: Captured." *Milwaukee History* 14, no. 2 (1991): 63–66.

March 31, 1865. Memoir. Twenty-fourth Wisconsin Infantry. Battle of Gravelly Run. Watrous recalled the surprise of having his horse shot out from under him during the battle. He was quickly captured by a Confederate colonel and sent back to the enemy lines in the company of a Confederate sergeant. On their march the two men were shot at by skulkers and saved only because an unidentified Confederate general ordered the men to stop shooting. Watrous said that foremost in his mind all along the way to prison were the orders given by his brigade commander that morning which Watrous would be unable to carry out.

257. WEBSTER, FLETCHER. "Col. Fletcher Webster's Last Letter: 'I Shall Not Spare Myself.'" By Wiley Sword. *Blue & Gray Magazine* 13 (October 1995): 20–27.
July 29, 1862. Letter. Colonel. Twelfth Massachusetts Infantry. Second Bull Run.

258. WELCH, JOHN COLLINS. *An Escape from Prison during the Civil War—1864.* Fairfield, Wash.: Ye Galleon Press, 1995. 78 pp.
April–December 1864. Memoir. Lieutenant. Welch spent much of the period being moved from Libby Prison to Andersonville, then to prisons at Macon, Savannah, Charleston, and Columbia. However, he escaped, and during November and December he traveled fifty days and thirteen hundred miles through South Carolina, Georgia, North Carolina, and into eastern Tennessee. Welch relates numerous incidents of his escape: the food his party found to eat; the help they received from slaves; escape from pursuers in the Blue Ridge Mountains who were intent on hanging the Yankees; the Unionists they met in North Carolina; the weather; and the trek through the swamps and over mountainous terrain until they reached Chattanooga. He arrived at his home in Angelica, New York, the day before Christmas.

259. WESCHE, CHARLES E. "The Civil War Diary of Major Charles E. Wesche." Introduction by Jerry D. Thompson. *Password* 39 (Spring 1994): 37–47.
January 26–February 25, 1862. Diary. First New Mexico Militia. Battle of Socorro.

260. WESTLAKE, OSCAR. "Give My Love To All." By Joseph Bilby. *Civil War Times Illustrated* 28 (May 1989): 38–43.
1861–1864. Letters. Lieutenant. Third New Jersey Infantry. Westlake describes his enlistment and participation in first Bull Run, the Peninsular campaign, second Bull Run, Crampton's Gap, Antietam, Fredericksburg, Gettysburg, and the early part of the Virginia campaign. He was killed at Cold Harbor.

261. WHEELER, WILLARD WATSON. *Civil War Diary, August 1861–February 1862: Including Time Spent in Parish Prison, New Orleans, La.* Peoria, Ill.: Charity G. Monroe, 1995. 51 pp.
August 24, 1861–February 15, 1862. Diary. Seventh Ohio Infantry. Wheeler was captured while on picket duty shortly after being deployed to West Virginia. He spent a brief time in Richmond, but most of his captivity was in New Orleans. En route to New Orleans he noted the beauty of the Shenandoah Mountains and described Southern cities. At New Orleans Parish Prison the Union soldiers were confined in tight quarters with common convicts. Wheeler seldom complained about the poor food and living conditions, but sarcasm is apparent in his comment that their treatment "argues for a very moderate degree of civilization for the South" (p. 33). However, abuse of religion exceeded Wheeler's tolerance. Wheeler was a devout Congregationalist; thus, when an Episcopalian minister substituted the words "President of the Confed States for the President of the United States in their Prayer book," he and the men hissed and many left (p. 29). When another preacher came to the prison and prayed for Jefferson Davis, he was met with a similar reaction and never returned. Prayer meetings and scripture reading sustained Wheeler, but he also spent time making rings and crosses for friends back home; listening to war news; and awaiting parole, which came in February 1862.

262. WHITE, DANIEL B. *Dear Wife: The Civil War Letters of a Private Soldier.* Edited by Jack C. Davis. Louisville, Ky.: Sulgrave Press, 1991. 238 pp.

September 6, 1864–July 5, 1865. Letters. Private. 144th New York Infantry. Duty at Hilton Head, South Carolina. White's letters to his wife, Amanda, are primarily about camp events, health concerns of the unit, the Lincoln reelection campaign, the presence of "wenches," and his desire to return to everyday life on their farm in Delaware County, New York. White apparently joined the army at that late date for the bounty, but he called it "the dearest fought money I ever had in my life" (p. 136). White appreciated humor. He related how a man who had argued against the Lincoln administration was tricked into believing that such talk had nearly placed him in the guardhouse. Once White wrote a letter for another man. He said "the boys" put him up to adding a message, without the soldier's knowledge, in which the man allegedly swore that he would remain "virtuous for the coming year" if his wife would do the same. When the wife's return letter was filled with assurances, it contained "Dear Charley 40 times I guess." White remarked: "It was rather rough of me, I will admit, but soldiers will have their fun, cost what it may" (p. 64). White's letters to Amanda are also filled with his unique brand of humor. On one occasion he said that he wanted to be home to spark the girls again and added: "I get tired of sparking wenches" (p. 148). In another letter he apologized for teasing her, but he continued anyway. He announced that he had found the girl he was "looking for at last" and that he had "just made up my mind to marry her if she would have me" (p. 205). But despite White's inexplicable humor, he made certain that Amanda knew that he approved of the manner in which she ran the farm. He told her that the other soldiers thought she was the one who wore the "breeches" in the family. He also encouraged her to spend money on herself, vowed that their separation had only increased his love for her, and promised to teach her how to chew tobacco, a habit he had acquired. White's Company K guarded Confederate prisoners while the rest of the regiment was involved in heavy skirmishing. The Confederates were held in such poor conditions that he predicted: "Our Rebs are all going to die if they are kept here," and he feared a mass escape attempt (p. 126). Several letters from White's friends and one from Amanda are also included in this work.

263. WHITE, GEORGE R. *Letters Home from Geo. R. White, Private, Co. G, 19th Reg. Mass. Volunteers.* Wenonah, N.J.: Robert C. Bartz, 1991. 40 pp.

September 9, 1861–June 25, 1862. Letters. Private. Nineteenth Massachusetts Infantry. Duty around Washington, D.C., and the siege of Yorktown. White mentions camp matters; troop movements; the sights in Washington, D.C.; troop reviews by George McClellan; blacks loafing about; and the USS *Monitor* anticipating the arrival of the CSS *Virginia*. A final letter from another soldier describes how White was killed at the battle of White Oak Swamp on June 30, 1862.

264. WHITE, HENRY S. *Prison Life Among the Rebels: Recollections of a Union Chaplain.* Edited by Edward R Jervey. Kent, Ohio: Kent State University Press, 1990. 94 pp.

May 5–September 1864. Memoir. Chaplain. Fifth Rhode Island Heavy Artillery. White describes his capture near Croatan, North Carolina, on May 5, 1864; shipment to Andersonville (for one day); and then transport to Macon's Camp Oglethorpe until the end of July. White spent August and September in the Savannah stockade and at Charleston, where he was released. Written by an Old Testament Methodist, an abolitionist, and a staunch Unionist, White's criticism of the Confederacy and slavery is full of biblical overtones. In an early letter he wrote that there was an absence of unity between the Southern states and the Confederate government. From this he concluded: "The doctrine of States Rights has produced its legitimate fruit. The people of the South have little reverence for any general government, ours or Jeff's" (p. 3). White was aware that preachers in the military were generally held in low esteem by soldiers, but he admitted that in prison it was worse: "He is not wanted there" (p. 62). However, White became something of a hero to the soldiers at Macon when he delivered a patriotic sermon and criticized the Confederacy. Immediately a local Baptist church proceeded to whip him "with its ecclesiastical lash." The schism among Methodists was apparent when the local Methodist church failed to provide the humanitarian and religious materials White requested. He responded that the "Church South" was most "bitter and hard on the North" (p. 76). Because White was curious about the conditions in the South, he observed numerous details. He inspected the recently constructed Confederate ironclad *Neuse* and told (with satisfaction) how it ran aground. He explained the organization of Andersonville and Macon Prisons. He related the effect that Sherman's advance was having on Georgia. He also conveyed his feelings about being placed under Union bombardment at Charleston, a tactic that Confederate authorities employed to discourage federal shelling of the city. Between November 1864 and July 1865 White published his memoirs in eighteen letters to the *Zion's Herald,* a New England Methodist newspaper. Portions of this narrative were published in two journals: *Georgia Historical Quarterly* 70 (Winter 1986): 669–702 and *Civil War History* 34 (March 1988): 22–45.

265. **WHITE, JONATHAN.** *Diary of a Soldier, Jonathan White, 2nd Wisconsin Volunteers, Civil War, 1862.* Compiled by Frances Dugger Rowan. Bishop, Calif.: F. D. Rowan, 1996. 67 pp.

May 4–December 31, 1862. Diary. Second Wisconsin Infantry. Duty around Fredericksburg and the second Bull Run campaign. In entries written prior to the end of July, White expresses concern only with drills, the weather, and selling pens and maps he received from home. But on August 28, 1862, after several weeks of cannonading and skirmishing, he wrote: "Found the enemy near Gainsville . . . terrific! . . . I was wounded in the groins" (p. 26). The editor describes the wound: "The bullet that struck his body went through the left groin, cutting into the neck of the bladder. It went through the pelvic bone and lodged in the right hip" (p. 49). For the next few months White stoically recorded his recuperation. At first he was in a makeshift Confederate hospital. Then he was paroled and proceeded to walk to a crude hospital in Centreville. An ambulance eventually took him to the Episcopal Seminary Hospital (Alexandria), where he finally began to receive treatment. He recorded the condition of his injury with such graphic descriptions as: "The urine all discharges through the wound" (p. 31). Finally, on September 16 he could write: "I made water through my penis for the first time since the cath [catheter] was taken out—this makes me feel much better" (p. 35). But in entries recorded throughout mid November, White describes the slow process of healing, as well as the specific medications, the food, and treatments he received. His recovery suffered reversals; still, White remained optimistic and soon resumed his business of selling pens. On November 17, 1862, he was released from the hospital to travel to his grandparents' home in Massachusetts. White hints at being glad to be leaving the army; at least he somewhat cryptically wrote: "My wound was more than I would liked to have had it" (p. 46). The editor adds that the bullet was not removed until 1866. Then in 1883 a stone that had formed around a fragment of floating bone was removed from his bladder.

266. **WHITE, PLYMPTON A.** "A Newspaper Account of Life at Camp Wilkins, April 27–June 11, 1861." By James Wudarczyk. *Journal of Erie Studies* 17 (Spring 1988): 56–66.

May 10, 1861. Letter. Lieutenant. This article is primarily a history of Camp Wilkins (Pittsburgh, Pennsylvania) as reported by several of the city's newspapers. The single letter written by Lieutenant White (unit unidentified) relates the miserably cold, rainy conditions. However, he thought the people of Pittsburgh had treated the recruits well and reports that the men were content.

267. **WILLETT, ALFRED C.** *A Union Soldier Returns South: The Civil War Letters and Diary of Alfred C. Willett, 113th Ohio Volunteer Infantry.* Edited by Charles E. Willett. Johnson City, Tenn.: Overmountain Press, 1994. 118 pp.

October 23, 1862–February 16, 1865. Letters and diary. 113th Ohio Infantry. Organization and training at Camps Chase and Dennison; duty in Tennessee, including the Tullahoma campaign, the siege of Chattanooga, relief of Knoxville; Georgia, including the Atlanta campaign (especially Jonesboro) and operations against Hood in northern Georgia and Alabama; the March to the Sea; and the siege of Savannah. Letters written during the first eighteen months to Willett's future wife, Sophia Snider, pertain to camp routines, sleeping accommodations, rations, battles in which he was involved and those nearby, and his satisfaction that he had remained a good Christian man by avoiding such vices as playing cards. He longed to be back home, but he believed that it was his duty to help put down the "wicked rebellion." Beginning with the Atlanta campaign, Willett's diary entries replace his letters. Willett saw some locations on which battles had occurred the previous fall. At Chickamauga he saw human remains still lying above the ground. While at Lookout Mountain he reported that a commercial photographer had recently fallen to his death. Demonstrations of his affection for Sophia included sending her a rose that he collected as the fighting raged through the garden of a home and expressing pride that he had been able to retain her picture throughout the war. Willett's writings dwindled after he went into the hospital near Savannah in mid December 1864. The editor summarizes Willett's remaining service and the rest of his life. Willett and Sophia returned to the South, where they lived out their lives near Florence, Alabama.

268. **WILLISON, CHARLES A.** *Reminiscences of a Boy's Service with the 76th Ohio.* New edition with additional material. Huntington, W.Va.: Blue Acorn Press, 1995. 190 pp.

August 11, 1862–July 15, 1865. Memoir. Private. Seventy-sixth Ohio Infantry. Duty in Arkansas and Missouri; Chickasaw Bluffs; Arkansas Post; the Vicksburg campaign, including duty at Young's Point, Jackson, and the assault of May 22 (observed); the siege of Jackson; Lookout Mountain; Missionary Ridge; Ringgold; the Atlanta campaign; the March to the Sea; the siege of Savannah; the Carolinas campaign; and the Grand Review. More than forty years after the war Willison presented his experiences to boys and girls. In his introduction he says that he wanted them to know why the scores of old men, whom the children might have seen in their villages, valued the bronze buttons they wore close to their hearts more than they did money. Willison was sixteen years of age in 1862 and stood only five feet, four and a half inches tall. He claims not to remember hearing a single sermon during the war or seeing a burial that was accompanied by a religious service. He relates the failure of Grant's various canal projects during the gloomy winter of 1863. What he recalled in greatest detail after the siege of Vicksburg was the pleasure of being able to change his clothes and wash himself. While Willison claims that he "swipped" only once, he adds that all soldiers plundered and foraged, especially in South Carolina. Willison confesses that the soldiers in Canton, Mississippi, confiscated unsigned Confederate notes and affixed signatures. At the end of his work Willison tells his readers: "I never considered myself brave." However, he obviously was proud that he was able to say that he "always had enough strength of will and valued reputation my reputation too much, to shirk" (p. 126). He adds that "under fire, or when once in the turmoil and excitement of battle, I declare I was not conscious of fear" (p. 126). Originally published: Menasha, Wis.: George Banta Publishing Company, 1908.

269. **WILLSEY, BEREA M.** *The Civil War Diary of Berea M. Willsey: The Intimate Daily Observations of a Massachusetts Volunteer in the Union Army, 1862–1864.* Edited by Jessica H. DeMay. Bowie, Md.: Heritage Books, 1995. 196 pp.

March 10, 1862–June 24, 1864. Diary. Private. Tenth Massachusetts Infantry. The Peninsular campaign, including Seven Pines and Malvern Hill; Antietam; Fredericksburg; Burnside's "Mud March"; Chancellorsville; Brandy Station; Gettysburg; The Wilderness; Spotsylvania; North Anna; and Cold Harbor. Willsey's entries reflect the war from the view of a hospital nurse. His regular duties included setting up tents, tending the sick and wounded, and carrying knapsacks of medicines. While retrieving the wounded during Seven Pines, he recorded: "I had to creep on my hands & knees, as our cannon were firing as fast as they could" (p. 24). He described the difficulty of providing care for the wounded at Fredericksburg. Death became so commonplace that Willsey often mentioned those who had died, or were dying, with little emotion. His entries also contain the varied nonnursing duties required of the hospital corps: serving picket duty; digging rifle pits; building breastworks; foraging for food; and once hacking down a tall oak tree filled with wasps. He worshiped McClellan; exhibited an appreciation for black humor when he related a bizarre accident in which a man was run over by a horse. He observed an argument that contained "language that I shall always remember" (p. 58), and played "ball" and dominoes. Although Willsey was even-tempered, he admitted to having the "blues" during the winter of 1862–1863. He substantiated his mood of that period by lashing the military with uncharacteristic sarcasm. When the Virginia campaign began (and perhaps earlier at Gettysburg), he was a full-time infantryman.

270. **WILLSON, ANDREW.** "Captain Willson and the Shells: How He Hated the Artillery." Edited by William F. Howard. *Civil War Times Illustrated* 26 (December 1987): 22–27.

April 21–July 12, 1864. Letters. Seventeenth New York Infantry. Peninsular campaign. Although his description of combat displays a mixture of admiration and horror toward war, Willson reserved a special hatred for the Confederate artillery fire.

271. **WILSON, CHARLES HENRY.** "'I Miss the Cannon's Roar': Letters of a Pennsylvania Surgeon in the Second Bull Run Campaign, August–September 1862." *Lincoln Herald* 89 (Spring 1987): 3–8.

August 7–September 16, 1862. Letters. Assistant surgeon. 110th Pennsylvania Infantry. Second Bull Run campaign. In the brief period encompassed by these letters, Wilson experienced the extremes of a soldier's life. At second Bull Run he exclaimed: "Oh, this is terrible. I am sick of this terrible war, with its fearful havoc. I have witnessed so frightful wounds today-dreadful-dreadful" (p. 7). But when the intensity of battle had subsided, the monotony of camp life resumed and he became discontent. Then he wrote, "and besides I miss the cannons roar, which got to be quite musical to me" (p. 7). When the U.S. Sanitary Commission people came on the scene, Wilson interpreted their presence as an intrusion into the medical domain. In his last lines he again complained about the army's inactivity and again was frustrated because he could hear cannonading in the direction of Sharpsburg.

272. **WINTERS, JOSHUA.** *Civil War Letters and Diary of Joshua Winters: A Private in the Union Army, Company G, First Western Virginia Volunteer Infantry.* Edited, with an introduction, by Elizabeth Davis Swiger. Parsons, W.Va.: McClain Printing Company, 1991. 140 pp.

November 8, 1861–November 28, 1864. Letters and diary. Private. First West Virginia Infantry. Duty in West Virginia and Virginia, including first Kernstown, Jackson's Shenandoah Valley campaign, Cedar Mountain, second Bull Run, Siegel's expedition to New Market (including the battle of New Market), and Sheridan's Shenandoah Valley campaign (including second Kernstown, third Winchester, and Fisher's Hill). This work consists of comments about family and friends from Marshall County, West Virginia; information about troop movements; weather reports; and references to battles and skirmishes. Winters's letters from summer 1864 relate his recuperation from an accidental, self-inflicted wound. Winters's phonetically written and erratically spelled letters are generally devoid of emotion. However, his final entry is clearly written and exuberant: "I AM FREE ONCE MORE" (p. 122). Genealogical information is appended.

273. WOLCOTT, SAMUEL W. "A Connecticut Yankee in St. Augustine, 1863." By William McGuire. *Escribano* 28 (1991): 56–80.

May 14–June 25, 1863. Letters. Private. Seventh Connecticut Infantry. Garrison duty at Saint Augustine, Florida. In his position as clerk, the most eventful part of Wolcott's tour was administrating oaths of loyalty, taking the census, and arranging old Spanish documents. He commented about the lush vegetation, the heat, and the large fleas. Although Wolcott longed for a furlough, he knew it was unrealistic since he was not one of his commanding officer's favorites. Much of this article consists of research by McGuire. He relates Wolcott's previous and subsequent service, as well as family information, and includes other letters that pertain to him.

274. WOODCOCK, MARCUS. *A Southern Boy in Blue: The Memoir of Marcus Woodcock, 9th Kentucky Infantry (U.S.A.).* Edited by Kenneth W. Noe. Knoxville: University of Tennessee Press, 1996. 348 pp.

September 19, 1861–June 4, 1864. Memoir. Lieutenant. Ninth Kentucky Infantry. Enlistment and organization; duty at Camp Boyle; the siege of Corinth; pursuit of Bragg in Kentucky, including Perryville (in reserve); Stones River; Chickamauga; the siege of Chattanooga; Orchard Knob; Missionary Ridge (observed); march to the relief of Knoxville; and the Atlanta campaign, including Pickett's Mill, where he was wounded and sent home. Writing during the spring of 1865, Woodcock explained the reasons that he and others from Macon County, in middle Tennessee, joined the Union cause. Woodcock's military activities were first delayed by the measles. In November 1861 he was placed in a hospital room in Columbia, Kentucky, which was twenty square feet and filled with fifteen patients. The stench was overpowering, since new straw was simply piled on old spoiled hay and the walls were used as spittoons. During the siege of Corinth, as well as at Lookout Mountain and Stones River, Woodcock related that the men who anticipated going into battle left letters and personal items behind to be sent to loved ones if they did not return. Woodcock's first real taste of battle was at Stones River. He described the ebb and flow of the battle, emphasizing events that occurred within the fighting. About the soldiers he wrote: "Some were on one knee, others were nearly flat on the ground, while others were standing up . . . I could not see fear on a single face, some were looking calm as death . . . some were pleased apparently, and seemed to laugh as heartily at the occasional tumble of a rebel" (p. 133). A few days later he wrote: "The sun rose bright and clear this morning to spread his brilliant light over thousands of mangled human bodies" (p. 139). Woodcock's descriptions of how the Ninth Kentucky was overrun on both days of Chickamauga are detailed and dramatic. He was exhausted and demoralized and admitted that he had lost all taste for fighting even when Union reinforcements arrived. Following Chickamauga, Woodcock described how the bedraggled soldiers filled the road back to Chattanooga. Later he related the conditions the men endured during the Confederate siege of the city. In November 1863 Woodcock was sent home to recuperate from chronic diarrhea. He returned to duty at the start of the Atlanta campaign and was wounded at Pickett's Mill. The editor's epilogue sums up Woodcock's service.

275. WOOTON, DANIEL. "Civil War Letters of Daniel Wooton: The Metamorphosis of a Quaker Soldier." By Jacquelyn S. Nelson. *Indiana Magazine of History* 85 (March 1989): 50–57.

April 26, 1861–October 30, 1863. Letters. Lieutenant. Second Indiana Cavalry. Nelson points out that two themes emerge from Wooton's writings. The first is the usual soldier's depiction of camp life, duties, battles, etc. The second theme reveals the conflict of Wooton's antiwar beliefs inherent in his Quaker religion with his desire to put the rebellion down by force. By the end of these letters Wooton had reconciled this conflict. Proud of his accomplishments, he reenlisted with the Army of the Cumberland for an additional three years.

276. WREN, JAMES. *From New Bern to Fredericksburg: Captain James Wren's Diary, B Company, 48th Pennsylvania Volunteers, February 20, 1862–December 17, 1862.* Edited by John Michael Priest. Shippensburg, Pa.: White Mane Publishing Company, 1990. 140 pp.

February 20–December 17, 1862. Diary. Forty-eighth Pennsylvania Infantry. Burnside's expedition to North Carolina (including the battle of New Bern), Groveton, second Bull Run, South Mountain, Antietam, and Fredericksburg. Wren's comments about camp life, marches, and battles are upbeat, detailed, and graphic. While in North Carolina he recorded that a drunken band of soldiers broke into a building occupied by the contrabands "and abused them most shamefully, using bayonets and Knives"; he then continued on to describe the specific cuts (p. 8). In another entry he described the scene near the hospital after the battle of South Mountain. Wren picked up one "Beautiful, plump arm Laying there" and placed it near what he believed was the other arm from the same man (p. 69). Most of his depictions of men being shot in battle were recorded without emotion. However, Wren's remorse when Gen. Jesse Reno was mortally wounded at South Mountain was effusive. Also, he was adamant in his concurrence with the guilty verdict handed down by the "Coart Martial" that tried Gen. Fitz John Porter "for failing to come up" at the battle of second Bull Run (p. 60). Wren's description of the fighting at Burnside's Bridge is especially vivid, as is that of Fredericksburg. The editorial work was accomplished by Priest and his high school history students at South Hagerstown, Maryland.

277. ZYCHLINSKI, LUDWIK. *The Memoirs of Ludwik Zychlinski: Reminiscences of the American Civil War, Siberia, and Poland.* Translated by Eugene Podraza. Edited, with an introduction, by James S. Pula. New York: Columbia University Press, 1993. 111 pp.

1862–1863. Memoir. New York Independent Infantry Battalion "Enfant Perdus." Zychlinski immigrated to the United States in April 1862 after having served in Garibaldi's campaign in Sicily in 1860. He joined the Union army soon after arrival and spent four months guarding the defenses of Yorktown. Throughout this work the editor points to the inconsistencies between this memoir and military records. Zychlinski describes his enlistment in the New York Independent Battalion, a unit that was primarily composed of French and Germans. Zychlinski's criticism of Union military organization provides an interesting perspective on how the army was administered. For example, he criticizes the North's recruitment of "volunteers," which, he believed, was based on monetary considerations rather than such ideals as patriotism or freedom for the slaves. Furthermore, Zychlinski perceived the differences in the ways newspapers reported the reasons Americans were volunteering and what he believed to be reality. Zychlinski describes being a participant in the first battle of Williamsburg, but records do not confirm that his battalion was present. However, the unit was engaged in an action at Williamsburg on September 9, 1862. Nevertheless, Zychlinski goes on to describe the Peninsular campaign. Zychlinski also comments about the other Europeans serving in the Union army and especially how Americans regarded the Poles. The first part of this memoir was written in November 1862. The second part, which was written some twenty years later, includes an encounter with the Indians near Saint Louis, other skirmishes, and a review by President Lincoln. The editor says that Zychlinski confuses geography and chronology of events, especially in the second memoir. However, his pithy comments about the military and American society in general provide an interesting critique of the era. The concluding portion of Zychlinski's memoir pertains to his return to Poland in mid 1863 to participate in his country's uprising against Russian forces and his subsequent exile in Siberia.

B. North Civilian
Items 278–311

278. BAILEY FAMILY. *"I Seate Myself with Pen in Hand": Letters of the Bailey Family During the War Between the States.* Compiled by Max Duran. Fayetteville, N.C.: N. pub., 1991. 74 pp.

1862–1865. Letters. West Virginia and Virginia. The compiler describes this work as a "patch-work of letters between brothers and sisters, and parents and cousins" that provides glimpses of individuals (p. 1). Duran has written a synopsis of each letter and reproduced the original. Most of the letters are laments over being separated and well-wishes for the health and safety of the recipient. Both John H. and William Bailey are identified as members of the Tenth West Virginia Infantry, but details of their military activities are unclear.

279. BOWDITCH, CHARLES PICKERING. "'We had a very fine Day': Charles Bowditch Attends Lincoln's Inauguration." By Katherine W. Richardson. *Essex Institute Historical Collections* 124 (January 1988): 28–37.

March 3–4, 1861. Letters and memoir. Bowditch was a member of a prestigious Boston family and, at the time of these letters, was also a Harvard sophomore on suspension. Using his family's social connections, Bowditch managed to obtain an invitation to Lincoln's first inauguration. Bowditch was assigned to escort the Lincoln women from the Willard Hotel to the Supreme Court. He wrote that Mrs. Lincoln was "a very pleasant looking woman & is by no means coarse looking as has been said" (p. 33). He also commented on Lincoln, Chief Justice Roger B. Taney, Stephen Douglas, and other dignitaries. Unfortunately, the location of Bowditch's seat was so poor that he heard little of Lincoln's address. Following the inauguration Mrs. Ninian Edwards commented that Lincoln had received many threats, which caused the whole family to feel insecure. Brief quotations from Bowditch's memoirs provide greater detail to the letters quoted in this article.

280. BROADHEAD, SARAH M. *The Diary of a Lady of Gettysburg, Pennsylvania from June 15 to July 15, 1863.* Introduction by Walter L. Powell. Hershey, Pa.: Gary T. Hawbaker, 1990. 24 pp.

June 15–July 15, 1863. Diary. The impact of the battle on Gettysburg civilians is chronicled by this Gettysburg housewife. First there were rumors of the approaching Confederate army, followed by its appearance, then several tumultuous weeks. The battle raged about them; still the Broadheads refused to leave their home. Miraculously their house received only one unexploded shell. Gettysburg was ill-prepared to accommodate the flood of wounded, and every building soon overflowed with maimed soldiers. Mrs. Broadhead, together with others of the community, ministered to the wounded until the Sanitary Commission arrived. After the fighting subsided, the town was inundated by legions of curiosity seekers. Although Broadhead's literary style is not without descriptive passages, the sense of immediacy combined with the pace of her terse entries elevate the diary's dramatic impact. This work is a reprint of an unpublished transcript issued in 1864 to raise money for the Great Central Fair for the U.S. Sanitary Commission held in Philadelphia, June 7–28, 1864.

281. BUNTEN, SIRENE. "A Civil War Diary from French Creek: Selections from the Diary of Sirene Bunten." Edited by Stephen Cresswell. *West Virginia History* 48 (1989): 131–41.

January 4, 1863–April 5, 1901. Diary. Bunten was a teenage girl who recorded a personal view of life in Upshur County, West Virginia, an area of Unionist loyalties. Her diary reveals many personal conflicts. On one hand she wanted to know details of the war and worried about her three brothers in the Union army. But adolescent insecurity also caused her to be concerned about what life held in store for her. Sirene observed the passage of soldiers of both sides through the region. She pondered their missions, as well as the meaning of nearby battles. Before the war ended she mourned the deaths of two of her brothers. Successive entries from 1865 relate elation over the surrender of the Confederacy, followed by sorrow over Lincoln's assassination. Thirty-five years later Sirene reread her diary and entertained thoughts about the past. She reflected: "Now my bonnie brown curls are getting so gray. . . . Youth is far behind me and I begin the descent" (p. 140). Without romanticizing the earlier period, she remembered the war years as being stirring times: "I am glad I saw it" (p. 140). As she perused her old diary, Sirene thought she could smell the sweet perfume of the apple blossoms, and she recalled the apple trees that grew nearby the window where she had recorded her private thoughts many years earlier.

282. CHASE, SALMON P. *The Salmon P. Chase Papers.* Edited by John Niven et al. Kent, Ohio: Kent State University Press, 1993–1997.

————. Volume 1. *Journals, 1829–1872.*

————. Volume 2. *Correspondence, 1823–1857.*

————. Volume 3. *Correspondence, 1858–March 1863.*

————. Volume 4. *Correspondence, April 1863–1864.*

1861–1864. United States of America. Secretary of the Treasury. The Civil War portions of Chase's papers touch on practically all of the political issues that confronted the Lincoln administration, as well as Chase's role as a presidential adviser in military matters. The journals especially reveal Chase's personal interests and religious and moral convictions. Collectively, the works document such issues as his support for the Emancipation Proclamation and belief in free labor in the South, his various programs to finance the war, and his continuing attempt to gain Republican Party support for the presidency. Volume 4 includes Chase's failed effort to secure the Republican-Union nomination for the presidency in 1864 and his resignation from Lincoln's cabinet in June 1864, and it concludes with his appointment as chief justice of the Supreme Court. Each volume includes introductions, calendars of events, sources of documents, and footnotes to identify individuals and events.

283. CHESTER, THOMAS MORRIS. *Thomas Morris Chester, Black Civil War Correspondent: His Dispatches from the Virginia Front.* Edited, with a biographical essay and notes, by R. J. M. Blackett. Baton Rouge: Louisiana State University Press, 1989. 375 pp.

August 14, 1864–June 12, 1865. The siege of Petersburg, the first assault of Fort Fisher, and the capture and occupation of Richmond. Following a ninety-one-page biography of Chester's life are these dispatches that Chester wrote for a white newspaper, the *Philadelphia Press,* about the black soldiers deployed in the Army of the James. Chester depicted the black soldiers as stalwart fighters, obedient to orders, loyal to the Union cause, and willing to accept the 'black flag" mode of warfare. (Ironically, Chester reported that amicable relationships occasionally developed between black and Confederate troops along the Petersburg siege line.) Chester related several desertions by black troops and reported that a lieutenant had shot a North Carolina recruit "for alleged stubbornness, disobedience of orders, and manifesting a mutinous spirit" (p. 115). Chester speculated that these incidents were either the result of poor officers or perhaps "placing contrabands in a regiment of free colored men" (p. 119). Chester frequently mentioned distinctions between black soldiers from different regions, especially those who had been slaves and those who had been free. In response to the Confederate attempt to raise black regiments of its own, Chester admitted: "It must not be supposed that the blacks to a man are loyal to the old flag." However, he explained that the absence of loyalty existed because of "The hesitating policy of the Government at the outbreak of the war" (p. 249). Chester was alert to mistreatment and neglect of black soldiers. He complained that they had not received adequate recognition for their participation at the battle of New Market Heights. And he repeated the surgeons' concern that black soldiers were not being sent to the hospital quickly enough to obtain medical leaves or discharges. As Chester observed the prisoners who were released from the Confederate prison at Danville, he noted that only six of the original eighty-three black soldiers had survived their ordeal. The capture of Richmond and the first month of Union occupation fill the last eighty pages of his letters. Some of the organized looting by civilians was led by "a colored man who carried upon his shoulder an iron crow-bar, and as a mark of distinction had a red piece of goods around his waist which reached down to his knees" (p. 292). In his final dispatches from Richmond, Chester said that Confederate men could be seen still wearing their uniforms and some embittered women refused to walk under the flag of the United States of America.

284. CHINCOUPIN. "Reporting from an Enemy's Land: The Indiana Letters of 'Chincoupin,' 1861." *Missouri Historical Review* 90 (April 1996): 309–29.
June–November 1861. Missouri. An unidentified writer known only by his pen name kept citizens of Mishawaka, Indiana, informed of events in Pleasant Hill, Missouri, through a series of articles published in the *Mishawaka Daily Enterprise*. The information was valued by the Indianans because many had friends and relatives in Missouri. The editor characterizes the writer as articulate and committed to the preservation of the Union and the protection of federal supporters in Missouri. He wrote from the perspective of a nonprofessional correspondent who was sincerely concerned about the events. "Chincoupin" covered all the major issues in the months before the state's allegiance was settled.

285. COLTON FAMILY. *The Colton Letters: Civil War Period, 1861–1865.* Compiled and edited by Betsey Gates. Scottsdale, Ariz.: McLane Publications, 1993. 393 pp.
January 18, 1861–December 30, 1865. Contains the correspondence of the Colton family—a mother, father, four daughters, and two sons—who lived in Milan, Ohio. Letters from relatives and friends are also included. Comments about the Civil War are contained in the letters written through the middle of 1862. On May 13, 1861, son Sheldon requested his family's permission to enlist. He said that he wanted to do what he could for the country, but he also wanted to prove his bravery. "I would like to have a reputation for courage for the sake of influence, because then whatever I might say in favor of peace and love to all men could not be attributed to cowardice" (p. 38). Mrs. Colton agreed but felt that the other son, Carlos, should stay at home because he could not endure the hardships of being a soldier. Sheldon helped raise a company of the Sixty-seventh Ohio Infantry. He was wounded at first Kernstown and captured briefly. Sheldon served out the war in the office of the adjutant general of Ohio in Columbus. Brother Carlos served with the Eighth Ohio Infantry (three-month) in mid 1862. The majority of these writings concern domestic matters and everyday events that are unrelated to the war.

286. CUSTER, ELIZABETH BACON. *The Civil War Memories of Elizabeth Bacon Custer.* Reconstructed from her diaries and notes by Arlene Reynolds. Austin: University of Texas Press, 1994. 181 pp.

1861–1865. Memoir. Washington, D.C., and northern Virginia. Reynolds explains that Libbie Custer's "War Book" was a work in progress from the 1890s almost to the time of her death in 1933. In 1890, after she had completed her third book about life with George Armstrong Custer in the West, Libbie began jotting down notes about their experiences during the Civil War and collecting reminiscences about those years from others. Reynolds has arranged these and other documents chronologically and "attempted to retain the same narrative style that [Libbie] used in her other three books" (p. ix). Thus, they are "Libbie's free and unembarrassed expressions of the events as she saw, experienced, and remembered them" (p. xiv). The bulk of the work covers the fourteen months that she and "Autie" were married during the war. It contains a recitation of her childhood in Monroe, Michigan; events of George's life as a cadet; their courtship; and George's acclaim on the battlefield. Veneration of George's character is an integral part of the work, but Libbie's personal experiences are more informative. During the spring of 1864, as a young woman of twenty-two, Libbie was left alone in Washington, D.C. Such was the variety of inhabitants of the city that "Washington belonged to everyone and no people in particular" (p. 94). She recalled that "The city was taken possession of Sodom and Gomarrah by a class of lawless brazen women over whom the police apparently had no control" (p. 95). At first Libbie stayed at a boardinghouse, oblivious to the "undesirable character of the women who kept the house" (p. 96). Washington was filled with sick and wounded, and she visited the hospital that sheltered the Michigan Brigade. At her first meeting with Abraham Lincoln he exclaimed: "And so you are the wife of the man who goes into the cavalry charges with a whoop and a yell" (p. 86). Libbie spent the fall and winter of 1864 and 1865 in the camp with George. She returned to Washington for Lincoln's second inaugural ball and traveled to Richmond shortly after the surrender (she met Varina Davis and spent the night in Jefferson Davis's bed) before again returning to Washington. Accompanying Libbie on her travels was her black servant, Eliza, with whom she had a close relationship. In the "Epilogue," written in 1917, Libbie reflects on the differences in conditions during the "present war," World War I, and the Civil War.

287. DRAPER, LAURA, and ELIZA DRAPER. "'Dear Sister': Letters from War-Torn Missouri, 1864." By Arthur G. Draper. *Gateway Heritage* 13 (Spring 1993): 48–57.

1864. Letters. Northeastern Missouri. Draper begins this article by describing the guerrilla warfare in the region. He characterizes it as often involving feuding neighbors who were out to settle old animosities. As a result of Bill Anderson's massacre in Centralia on September 27, 1864, civilian fears were in a heightened state. Eliza's letters relate an incident at Clarksville on October 31. Although the encounter she describes was far less violent than the Centralia raid, her letters illustrate the degree of civilian apprehension that fall.

288. DUNN, SOPHIA CLARK. "The Civil War Homefront in Seneca County: Two Letters of Sophia Clark Dunn." Edited by Richard Manion. *Northwest Ohio Quarterly* 62 (Winter/Spring 1990): 11–16.

July 9–13, 1863. Letters. Hopewell Township, Ohio. Sophia expressed relief that her son Arlington (123rd Ohio Infantry) had been released following his capture at second Winchester. She also inquired about a neighbor's son, related yields of the harvest, thanked Arlington for his "likeness," commented on the shirt she sent him, and mentioned visits by neighbors.

289. FERREE, NEWTON. "Eyewitness to History: Newton Ferree, the Lincoln Assassination, and the Close of the Civil War in Washington." By John K. Lattimer and Terry Alford. *Lincoln Herald* 89 (Fall 1987): 95–98.

March 4–July 7, 1865. Diary. Government clerk at the Examining Office of the Paymaster General. During this period Ferree observed the concluding portion of Lincoln's second inauguration ceremony. He saw the wild celebration attendant to the surrender of Richmond and the public jubilation when Lee surrendered. Ferree was near Ford's Theater at the time Lincoln was shot. He witnessed the public confusion and rushed to the stage at the theater. Ferree watched as Lincoln was being carried from his box and retrieved Lincoln's bloodstained collar as it fell to the floor. (An affidavit by Ferree's daughter-in-law expands on these notations and mentions that Ferree and his friend William T. Kent went to the box and located Booth's derringer.) Ferree wrote that by noon of April 15 all of Washington appeared draped in mourning. His final entry is brief but conclusive: "Executions. Was a very hot and sultry day" (p. 97).

290. **FITCH, EDWARD, and SARAH FITCH.** "Letters of Edward and Sarah Fitch, Lawrence, Kansas, 1855–1863." Edited by John M. Peterson. (Part II) *Kansas History* 12 (Summer 1989): 78–100.
June 8, 1857–September 2, 1863. The final letter written by Sarah contains a graphic description of her husband's murder during Quantrill's Raid on Lawrence.

291. **FONDA, TEN EYCK HILTON.** "A Midnight Ride." *Civil War Times Illustrated* 33 (March 1994): 24, 69–70.
June 30, 1864. Memoir. Civilian telegrapher. Gettysburg campaign. Fonda delivered a message to Union headquarters on horseback because the telegraph lines to the front between Harrisburg and Terrytown had not been installed. The message was from Secretary of War Edwin Stanton, who was informing Gen. Meade that the Confederate forces of Jubal Early and Robert E. Lee were advancing as separate movements and that Meade should take the offensive.

292. **FRENCH, BENJAMIN BROWN.** *Witness to the Young Republic: A Yankee's Journal, 1828–1870.* Edited by Donald B. Cole and John J. McDonough. Hanover, N.H.: University Press of New England, 1989. 675 pp.
March 6, 1861–December 28, 1865. The editors characterize French as "an upper-class Northern public servant whose career spanned the Age of Jackson through the Civil War and Reconstruction." As a young politician from New Hampshire and later a quintessential "man-about-Washington," he associated with important people and held numerous political and civic posts (p. xi). During the Civil War years French was often near the president and Mrs. Lincoln. As chief marshall of Lincoln's inaugural parade, he was called to a meeting by Gen. Winfield Scott to develop a plan to prevent Lincoln's assassination by the "Southern Confederacy" (p. 343). Lincoln appointed French commissioner of public buildings, an office that included the long-awaited placement of the capitol dome. French also served as a prime functionary at receptions held by Mrs. Lincoln, whom he favorably referred to as "The Queen." Because of his official capacity, French was soon caught in a disagreement between the couple. Mrs. Lincoln had exceeded the amount appropriated for redecorating the White House, and the president refused to increase the allocation. Later, French described the couple alone beside the body of their son, Willie, mourning his death. French was with the president at the dedication of the Gettysburg battlefield and later was at Lincoln's funeral. The moods of Washington early in the war reflect those of French's personal life. During 1861 and 1862 he recorded that the city alternately reacted to Union defeats and victories with apprehension and elation. During that period French's wife became ill and died. He grieved and was "gloomy" for a while but regained his spirit after he remarried. As the war wore on, French continued to record his varied public and personal activities, as well as his views. He served on one committee to help families of war victims and another that established a school for the deaf; he labored with gas fitters to locate a leak that almost asphyxiated the president; and he suffered the losses of a pointer pup, a prize cow, and a grandson. By 1864 his Washington was no longer a "*civil* city"; rather, it had become a place of "Camps, corrals, and soldiers . . . a goodly number of whom are continually drunk!" (p. 457). French visited Richmond shortly after the surrender and played "Yankee Doodle" on Varina Davis's piano. For the rest of 1865 he worked with President Andrew Johnson on

such matters as acquiring furnishings for the White House. On July 14, 1865, he described the condition of the presidential home: "I do not see how the house could have [been] stripped so completely of its furniture. I knew much had disappeared, but had no idea how much!" (p. 484).

293. GREGG, SARAH GALLOP. "The Diary as Historical Evidence: The Case of Sarah Gallop Gregg." By Kathleen S. Hanson and M. Patricia Donahue. *Nursing History Review* 4 (1996): 169–86.
1863–1865. Nurse. Western Theater. The authors first explain the value of personal diaries as historical resources. Next they discuss the methodology required to identify the diarist and verify the authenticity of the events presented in the account. As a case study, they utilized the diary of Sarah G. Gregg, a milliner from Ottawa, Illinois, who served as a nurse in the Mississippi River region. Her diary exists as a typed manuscript in the Illinois State Historical Library. Methodology required in determining the creditability of a diary includes verification of the transcription. The copy must be compared with the original, when it can be located, and/or references to the diary's existence found in other sources. Another step in determining the creditability of the diary involves verifying the accuracy of the events the diarist mentioned. In this case study the authors applied these criteria to nurse Gregg's diary and conducted searches of genealogical and military records, as well as newspapers and other personal accounts. The authors conclude that the accumulation of evidence suggests that the diary "is probably an accurate, but not necessarily complete, transcription of the original diary" (p. 181).

294. HAWKS, ALICE. "The Civil War Home Front: Diary of a Young Girl, 1862–1863." Edited by Virginia Mayberry and Dawn E. Bakken. *Indiana Magazine of History* 87 (March 1991): 24–78.
January 1, 1862–June 8, 1862. Diary. Goshen, Indiana. The Civil War scarcely existed in the thoughts of this seventeen-year-old, middle-class girl. Alice occasionally mentions prevailing rumors about the war and such events as seeing the boys being sent off to war. But school, church, and social occasions; care of her home; and anticipation of her father's return from his frequent business trips constitute the majority of her entries. The editors make the point that many civilians were untouched by the war.

295. HOPKINS, ANDREW (FAMILY). "Prisoner of Circumstances." *Civil War Times Illustrated* 31 (November/December 1992): 28, 30, 32, 34, 36, 38, 84, 86–87.
February 2, 1863–May 20, 1865. Letters concerning the release of Andrew J. Hopkins, the chief engineer of the USS *Smith Briggs*. Hopkins was retained by Confederate authorities because they were convinced that he was a Confederate deserter. Hopkins was only a worker at the Portsmouth Navy Yard when the war began.

296. LEE, ELIZABETH (BLAIR). *Wartime Washington: The Civil War Letters of Elizabeth Blair Lee.* Foreword by Dudley T. Cornish. Edited by Virginia Jeans Laas. Urbana: University of Illinois Press, 1991. 552 pp.
December 5, 1860–April 25, 1865. Letters. "Lizzie" was in a unique position to record events in the nation's Capitol. Her father, Francis P. Blair, had been a member of Andrew Jackson's Kitchen Cabinet and was an adviser to Abraham Lincoln. Her brother, Montgomery Blair, was postmaster general. Another brother, Frank A. Blair, was a pro-Union congressman from Missouri and a general. And her husband, Rear Adm. Samuel Phillips Lee (North Atlantic Blockading Squadron and Mississippi Squadron), was Robert E. Lee's third cousin. Lizzie and their young son lived at Blair House, across the street from the White House, or on their farm in Maryland, only six miles from Washington. Writ-

ing in a stream-of-consciousness style, Lizzie's letters informed "Phil" about their son and other family matters, and she relayed news of events and people that she gleaned from her many social contacts and activities. For example, while she and her mother were in Congress in January 1861 to witness Kansas's admission to the union as a state, she reported the reaction when the senators from Alabama and Florida announced that their states were leaving the Union. Comments about prominent people or the war appear in every letter, often with an abrupt change of focus. After one of several negative comments about John C. Fremont ("it seems that Ft.— is an opium eater & really imbecile—"), Lizzie immediately followed with a passage about their son: "Blair slept well & is the most joyous little darling you ever saw" (p. 88). Lizzie blamed Robert E. Lee both for resigning from the Union army and for declining Abraham Lincoln's request that he accept command of the Union army. The request had been tendered through Lizzie's father. Lizzie reported Mary Lincoln's comment "that there was not a member of the Cabinet who did not stab her husband & the Country in the back except my brother" (p. 231). Lizzie visited Mrs. Lincoln several times just after the president's assassination and related her bereavement. The Blair family had originally been slave owners. While she strongly opposed secession, Lizzie retained her racial prejudices. She insisted that contact with "the African degenerates our white race" and favored colonization to Africa or Central America (p. 223). Scattered throughout these letters is mention of Lizzie's numerous domestic chores, including helping to maintain both her parents' and her own households; her work with the Washington City Orphan Asylum, of which she was appointed director in 1862; and her attempt to further her husband's career, even appealing directly to President Lincoln.

297. MCKELVY, DAVID. "Soldier Voting in 1864: The David McKelvy Diary." Edited by Margaret McKelvy Bird and Daniel W. Crofts. *Pennsylvania Magazine of History and Biography* 115 (July 1991): 371–413.

September 30–October 17, 1864. Diary. Virginia. McKelvy was a civilian commissioner assigned to obtain absentee votes from Pennsylvania soldiers (the Fifty-eighth and 188th Infantries and two companies of the First Pennsylvania Artillery) for the state election to be held in October 1864. Following a lengthy review of the importance of the soldier vote to Lincoln's reelection, the editors point out that McKelvy's diary is valuable because it sheds light on how the absentee voting process was carried out. Before leaving for Virginia he had interviews with several Washington dignitaries. McKelvy thought the president was homely, careworn, and not well. Benjamin Butler was ungainly, corpulent, very nearsighted, but a good conversationalist. McKelvy's first view of Virginia society was different than he expected, and he even admitted to a "reverence for the old families and their customs, in spite of their many prejudices" (p. 391). While he disparaged the institution of slavery, McKelvy referred to the slaves as being possessors of "Negro absurdity" whose antics would grace a "comic almanac." At the battle front McKelvy grasped some rudiments of the military situation. He was aware of the priority for vehicles to carry provisions and the need for soldiers to forage, and he understood the rules that opposing pickets had worked out to fraternize. McKelvy was enchanted by the night scenes. He wrote that the campfires, the silent marches of sentries, and sweet martial music of bands awakened in his breast "some feeling of sublimity, grandeur, and splendor" (p. 404). At the close of his brief experience McKelvy was convinced that he had seen the war up close and that he had "felt something of its hardships and enjoyments" (p. 412).

298. OLMSTED, FREDERICK LAW. *The Papers of Frederick Law Olmsted. Volume IV. Defending the Union: The Civil War and the U.S. Sanitary Commission, 1861–1863.* Edited by Jane Turner Censer. Baltimore, Md.: Johns Hopkins University Press, 1986.

June 1, 1861–September 1, 1863. Letters. Secretary. United States Sanitary Commission. In the spring of 1861 Olmsted took a leave of absence from the New York Central Park project to assist in the formation of the United States Sanitary Commission. The editor has organized Olmsted's letters chronologically by chapters—preceded by a 114-page introduction and biographical directory—which reveal Olmsted's ambitions, successes, and failures. During his first months Olmsted sought to establish a centralized system of paid inspectors and volunteers who would provide aid and comfort to the soldiers and report to his office in Washington, D.C. Olmsted wanted the Sanitary Commission to reign supreme over other volunteer relief agencies but act as a support agency for the U.S. Army's Medical Bureau. Soon after the defeat at first Bull Run, Olmsted conducted a lengthy survey (which is reproduced) to identify reasons why the soldiers reacted chaotically. He concluded that those units that were the best fed, clothed, and disciplined were less likely to panic. Thus, to Olmsted, discipline and respect for proper health and sanitary conditions were imperative for success on the battlefield. Olmsted was convinced that improvement of the Army Medical Bureau was necessary. He waged a lengthy political struggle that revitalized the Medical Bureau and replaced the head of the bureau with William A. Hammond as surgeon general. In early 1862 Olmsted sought to assist blacks in their transition from slavery to freedom in the Port Royal experiment, but he was not selected to head the project. In the spring of 1862 his agency was challenged by the care and transportation of the sick and wounded of the Peninsular campaign. In late summer 1862 he returned to Washington from Virginia to find that the executive committee of the Sanitary Commission had (he believed) usurped his authority. Also, other agencies, such as the Western Sanitary Committee and the U.S. Christian Commission, resisted his attempts to control all relief efforts. When movements arose that threatened the Northern aim to abolish slavery, Olmsted lent his support to the Union League, a patriotic group that promoted unity. Following a tour of the Western Theater, he returned to Washington in late summer of 1863. Overwhelmed by the accumulation of problems, Olmsted resigned. He was convinced he had accomplished little, but the editor disagrees. Censer points out that Olmsted developed a system of dedicated workers that was instrumental in the distribution of supplies to soldiers most in need. She wrote, "The Commission must be seen as one of the great voluntary, nationalistic, and bureaucratic achievements of the war" (p. 61).

299. PARKER, CHARLES CARROLL. "A Christian Commission Delegate at a White House Levee, 1864." Edited by Reidun D. Nuquest. *Vermont History* 61 (Fall 1993): 233–39.

March 29, 1864. Letter. Parker was a minister of the Waterbury, Vermont, Congregational Church and served as a chaplain for the United States Christian Commission at Brandy Station in early 1864. In this letter to his wife and daughter he relates a visit to Washington. After his work was completed at Soldiers' Rest, he attended one of the president's biweekly Tuesday receptions. Parker describes how the president and Mrs. Lincoln contrasted in appearance. President Lincoln was tall and homely and looked like a rail-splitter. He seldom smiled, except when telling a funny story or greeting a guest; then his face became radiant. Mrs. Lincoln "was round & soft as though she had been moulded out of the nicest dough" (pp. 235–36). He had "character"; she was "characterless" (p. 235). As the evening progressed, Parker returned to the Green Room to observe Lincoln again. He said that the president appeared jovial when meeting a stream of people, but when "there was a break in the current, he would lift up his eyes & look through the doorway to see what next was coming & his whole look would be as solemn as though it was never blest with a smile" (p. 236). Parker observed that near the end of the reception Lincoln sat down, and he received his remaining guests while seated.

300. SAUNDERS, SUSAN H. "The Letter He Never Received: 'My Dearest Courtie.'" By Henry V. Winkler. *North-South Trader's Civil War* 17, no. 6 (1990): 18–23.

September 15, 1862. Letter. The wife of Capt. Courtland V. Saunders (118th Pennsylvania Infantry) wrote this fretful letter from Philadelphia. However, the captain was killed at the battle of Shepherdstown, West Virginia, before receiving her letter. Winkler's research in identifying the individuals mentioned in Susan's letter adds an additional element of interest to this article.

301. STEWART, SALOME MYERS. *Ties of the Past: The Gettysburg Diaries of Salome Myers Stewart, 1854–1922.* By Sarah Sites Rodgers. Gettysburg, Pa.: Thomas Publications, 1996. 287 pp.

1860–1865. Diary. Gettysburg resident. This work is a composite of the life and writings of "Sallie" Myers. The entries for 1860 and 1862 are complete, as are those for June and July 1863. Entries for 1864 are relatively complete, but those for 1865 to 1868 are sparse. Interspersed with Sallie's writings (and later memoirs) are transcripts of those portions of her diaries that were later deemed historically important by her son but are no longer extant. Much of Sallie's diary describes social and religious functions, family matters, romantic involvements, and her duties as a schoolteacher. The editor points out that the diary served as a refuge for Sallie's private thoughts; thus, it reveals something of the independence that nineteenth-century women were beginning to feel about themselves. The war made its intrusion into Sallie's life slowly. First local men volunteered (she was concerned for her father's health until he was rejected for service), and news spread of rebel raids in such places as Chambersburg in October 1862. In June 1863 she noted that the rebels were approaching Gettysburg in great numbers, but she appears to have been unaffected. She did, however, pity the "poor darkies" who were fleeing the town. On June 21 her mood had changed: "This is the first time for more than 2 years I have been alarmed and excited" (p. 161). During the next week she briefly recorded her interactions with the Confederate cavalry, which had taken the town. Sallie wrote almost nothing about the battle itself; she was busy at work as a nurse at her home, in church hospitals, and at the United States General Hospital (Camp Letterman). The remainder of this book contains letters written by her future brother-in-law, who died at Gettysburg, and expressions of gratitude from several of those she nursed. The editor completes the biography of Sallie's life up to her death in 1922.

302. STOUFFER, AMOS. "'The Rebs are yet Thick About us': The Civil War Diary of Amos Stouffer of Chambersburg." Edited by William Garrett Piston. *Civil War History* 38 (September 1992): 210–31.

January 6–December 13, 1863. Diary. This farmer from the Chambersburg, Pennsylvania, area wrote daily entries throughout the year, but the presence of Confederate troops in Pennsylvania is most vividly recorded. Rumor of their approach quickly became reality. When they arrived, the Confederates seized livestock, grain, and blacks but were well behaved and paid for some civilian goods with script. Stouffer related the general anticipation that a battle would occur somewhere. Later he described the Gettysburg battlefield. He recorded that the fighting continued as Lee's retreat was hampered by the flooded Potomac. Following the Gettysburg entries Stouffer mentions Confederate actions that might have been threats to the region, war news from Virginia and other fronts, his farming activities, and the Pennsylvania state elections in which Copperheads were defeated. Stouffer noted Edward Everett's oration at the dedication of the Gettysburg battlefield but did not mention Lincoln's address.

303. TAYLOR, JAMES E. *The James E. Taylor Sketchbook: With Sheridan Up the Shenandoah Valley in 1864. Leaves from a Special Artists Sketch Book and Diary.* Transcribed by Florence Freeland. Footnotes by Dennis E. Frye, Martin F. Graham, and George F. Skoch. Dayton, Ohio: Morningside House, 1989. 631 pp.

August 8–December 17, 1864. Diary and sketches. Taylor first explains how, after two years of service with the Tenth New York Infantry, he undertook the assignment of sketching Sheridan's impeding Shenandoah Valley campaign for *Frank Leslie's Illustrated Newspaper*. During the 1890s he spent eight years compiling the manuscript published here for the first time. Writing in an adventurous style, and while on the move, Taylor blended the battles, vignettes of personalities, destruction and devastation of the Shenandoah Valley, awareness of Mosby's ever-present rangers, and anecdotes with events that had occurred previously. The battles that Taylor described in greatest detail are third Winchester, Fisher's Hill, Tom's Brook, and Cedar Creek. The over six hundred drawings are of physical structures in towns, cavalry officers, common soldiers, slaves, formal portraits of prominent and obscure individuals, landscapes, and occasionally maps and battle scenes. The editorial footnotes add considerably to an understanding of Taylor's work.

304. TUCKER, HILARY. "Race, Religion, and Rebellion: Hilary Tucker and the Civil War." By James Hitchcock. *Catholic Historical Review* 80 (July 1994): 497–517.

1862–1867. Diary. Catholic Priest. Tucker, a Missouri-born priest who was serving in the Diocese of Boston, considered fanatical Puritans to be at fault for the conflict. Hitchcock analyzes Tucker's diaries to reveal his hatred of the Union and sympathy for the Confederacy. Hitchcock points out that because Tucker viewed religion alone as being the cause of the war, he overlooked other important themes, such as positions taken by Catholics. After the war Tucker visited Missouri and observed the devastation caused by civilians and soldiers of both sides. He attributed the destruction to federal forces.

305. TYSON, CHARLES J. "A Refugee from Gettysburg." *Civil War Times Illustrated* 28 (November/December 1989): 16–17, 73–74.

June 26–July 4, 1863. Letter. A Gettysburg photographer describes events and conditions in the town during this period, with the exception of July 1–3, when he and many other residents left.

306. USHER, REBECCA. "Civil War Nurse, Civil War Nursing: Rebecca Usher of Maine." By Elizabeth D. Leonard. *Civil War History* 41 (September 1995): 190–207.

November 1862–1864. Letters. Nurse. Leonard utilizes Usher's correspondence to demonstrate that her experiences were within the realm of middle-class Victorian women who served as Civil War nurses. The forty-one-year-old, unmarried Usher left Hollis, Maine, in November 1862 to serve at the army's General Hospital at Chester, Pennsylvania. She served at Chester until the hospital was closed in April 1863. (She later worked as a soldier-relief worker at the Maine State Agency in City Point, Virginia, but that experience is not discussed in this article.) In her letters Usher describes the arrangement of the hospital facility and her duties as companion and surrogate "mother" (or "sister") to the soldiers, supervisor of the meals, and distributor of clothing in the ward that she oversaw. Her duties did not include providing medical assistance to the surgeons or the menial jobs of cleaning or laundry, which were performed by lower-class nursing employees. She described the relationship between the convalescent soldiers, who also served as nurses, and the other nurses. Leonard provides background detail on such issues as the stratification of hospital employees, the controversy between nonpaid volunteer nurses and paid nurses, societal expectations of middle-class Victorian women, and desirable age requirements for nurses. Leonard concludes that Usher was a typical middle-class volunteer nurse. She also suggests the long-term impact of these experiences on the social status of women in general. Unfortunately, the Usher papers provide no substantial clues as to whether Rebecca Usher ever reaped the benefits of her wartime contributions.

307. WARDWELL, ERNEST. "Military Waif: A Sidelight on the Baltimore Riot of 19 April 1861." Edited by Frank Towers. *Maryland Historical Magazine* 89 (Winter 1994): 427–46.

April 19, 1861. Memoir. Baltimore riot. As an adolescent Wardwell observed the bloody clash between Southern sympathizers and the Sixth Massachusetts Infantry en route to Washington, D.C. He wrote that the large crowd was filled with intense anti-Northern sentiment and heaped abuse on the Massachusetts troops. Wardwell also describes his service with the Sixth Massachusetts and his duty in Washington, New York, and Boston, where the three-month unit was mustered out.

308. WELLS, MELISSA. "Dearest Ben: Letters from a Civil War Soldier's Wife." By Albert Castel. *Michigan History* 71 (May/June 1987): 18–23.
December 20, 1863–August 14, 1864. Letters. Three Rivers, Michigan. These letters show a couple's problems remaining emotionally close because of some combination of their everyday routines, an inability to express their feelings, and inconsistent mail delivery. Misunderstandings and false impressions were created by the imprecise usage of the written word. Rifts existed over who did or did not write the other with the greatest degree of regularity. And the tedium of caring for children and being a farmer wore on Melissa. She also worried about Benjamin (Eleventh Michigan Infantry), who was frequently ill and serving near the battle fronts of Stones River, Chickamauga, and the Atlanta campaign. Benjamin's visits home were frustrating because they illuminated the couple's estrangement. In their letters they expressed longings for a time when they would be together permanently; they cherished moments of past joy. Melissa was the most realistic of the two. In a moment of clarity she admitted that the three years of separation had caused her to develop reservations about their future. She selected her words cautiously: "I guess you are the same Ben you always was . . . I cannot discover any change" (p. 23). In August 1864 Ben returned home, but the editor indicates that their subsequent life was not filled with the happiness they had desired.

309. WHITMAN, WALT. "'Here among Soldiers in Hospital': An Unpublished Letter from Walt Whitman to Lucia Jane Russell Briggs." *New England Quarterly* 59 (December 1986): 544–48.
April 26, 1864. Letter. In this letter of appreciation that Whitman wrote to Mrs. Briggs of Salem, Massachusetts, for the seventy-five dollars she collected to assist his work in the hospitals around Washington, D.C., Whitman also describes the appalling hospital scenes.

310. WOOLSEY, GEORGEANNA M. "Three Weeks at Gettysburg by George Anna M. Woolsey." Edited by Charles F. Johnson. *Gettysburg Magazine* 9 (July 1993): 116–21.
July 1863. Memoir. A member of the U.S. Sanitary Commission describes the care of the wounded following the battle of Gettysburg.

311. WOOLSEY, JANE STUART. *Hospital Days: Reminiscence of a Civil War Nurse.* With an introduction by Daniel John Hoisington. Roseville, Minn.: Edinborough Press, 1996. 139 pp.
Fall 1863–August 1865. Superintendent of Nurses, U.S. Army General Hospital (Alexandria, Virginia). Jane and her sister, Georgeanna, of New York City, went to the hospital located at the Virginia Episcopal Seminary to establish a system of administration for the nurses. As support for the doctors and patients, nurses were responsible for acquiring supplies and food, writing letters for the soldiers, and acting as intermediaries for families. The institution overcame problems and flourished because of Jane's administrative abilities and compatibility with the surgeon in charge, Dr. David Page Smith. The kitchen storeroom, which was kept under her ever-watchful eye, was stringently controlled. The nurses needed to be aware of the food patients should receive in order to aid in their recuperation and cater to their preferences, and she includes examples of menus. Jane denies that a formal system of nursing existed in part because of the irregular and unreliable recruitment of nurses. Volunteers were both paid and unpaid; soldiers' wives and friends helped out; state agencies sent delegates; and the general super-

intendent of nurses nominated assistants. Her chapters focus on such themes as gifts to soldiers, the role of the chaplain, mail call, celebrations of holidays, the influx of casualties, and the Negro camps which clustered about the hospital. Jane praises the clumsy but eager assistance of the Invalid Corps, even though they were ridiculed by the men they were trying to help. Her most notable complaint was the practice of hiring contract surgeons. Some of the undelivered letters that Jane retained are contained in this work. Also included are several letters written by her sister, Georgeanna, who left to serve in the Fredericksburg hospital in spring 1864, as well as correspondence from other women nurses located elsewhere. When the hospital was ordered to close in late July 1864, the administrators were given only one week to evacuate, make repairs, and pay rent to the owners of the facility. This work was originally privately published for family and friends: New York: D.Van Nostrand, 1870.

II. THE SOUTH

A. Confederate Military
Items 312–465

312. ALEXANDER, EDWARD PORTER. *Fighting for the Confederacy: The Personal Recollections of Edward Porter Alexander.* Edited by Gary W. Gallagher. Chapel Hill: University of North Carolina Press, 1989. 664 pp.

1861–1865. Memoir. Brigadier General. Chief of Artillery, First Corps, Army of Northern Virginia. First Bull Run; Seven Days' Battles; second Bull Run; Antietam; Fredericksburg; Chancellorsville; Gettysburg; Chickamauga; Chattanooga; siege of Knoxville; The Wilderness; Spotsylvania; Drewry's Bluff; Cold Harbor; the siege of Petersburg, including "the Crater"; and the Appomattox campaign. Alexander's account is filled with frank opinions of leaders. Robert E. Lee clearly is a hero but is not portrayed without flaws. Alexander criticizes Lee for engaging the Union army at Antietam, marching into Pennsylvania, and sending Jubal Early into the Shenandoah Valley rather than to the western theater. Recognizing some of Lee's salient qualities, Alexander wrote: "Under Lee his soldiers thought that some victories might be better than others, indeed, but all fights would be victorious" (p. 149). In the end, Alexander praises Lee's recognition that a dignified surrender was better for the country at large than prolonged guerrilla warfare. Stonewall Jackson's military accomplishments are acknowledged by Alexander, but he criticizes his slowness during the Seven Days' Battles, as well as aspects of Jackson's personality that affected his leadership. On the Union side, Alexander thought that Joseph Hooker's battle plan at Chancellorsville was a good one that might have succeeded had Hooker and his corps leaders not suffered from "the perfect collapse of moral courage" and had Grant been the Union leader (pp. 216–17). Alexander also recounts his own role in the fighting, especially his direction of the artillery at Gettysburg. Alexander often illustrated battles with hand-drawn maps and sketches. Throughout his writing Alexander interrupts himself to interject wisdom gained after the war. He evaluates the Confederate defeat in light of "Darwinian development" (p. 26). Alexander had come to believe that strict adherence to the concept of "states rights" would have stifled the technological changes of the late nineteenth century that had made the United States "what may almost be called a new planet" (p. 26). Thus, when writing these memoirs at the end of the century, Alexander concluded: "so we need not greatly regret defeat" (p. 26). The editor resurrected this work from the body of manuscripts that was long assumed to have been the source of Alexander's classic *Military Memoirs of a Confederate*, published in 1907 (reprinted, with introduction by Gary Gallagher, New York: Da Capo Press, 1993). Alexander first wrote *Fighting for the Confederacy* for family viewing, but after he had used sections for his more scholarly *Military Memoirs*, the manuscripts of the two works became interspersed. Gallagher's extensive footnotes and 51-page index explain references and present numerous themes of Alexander's narrative.

313. ALLEN FAMILY. *The Allen Family of Amherst County, Virginia Civil War Letters.* Edited by Charles W. Turner. Berryville, Va.: Rockbridge Publishing Company, 1995. 93 pp.

October 14, 1861–March 30, 1865. Letters. Thirteenth Virginia Infantry and Fifty-eighth Virginia Infantry. Battles of McDowell; Gaines' Mill; Malvern Hill; the Antietam campaign; Chancellorsville; The Wilderness; third Winchester; and the siege of Petersburg, including Fort Stedman. Contains letters written by six brothers to their widowed mother, sister, and each other. Information about troop movements, living conditions, and health predominates. In 1863 one brother recalled being detailed to serve in the mountains of Virginia to ferret out bands of ruffians made up of deserters and Unionists. Several letters describe the mortal wounding of two other brothers. The Allen family's closeness is evident in its concern for the welfare of each member.

314. **ALLEN, NATHANIEL S.** "For Lack of a Nail." By Max S. Lale. *East Texas Historical Journal* 30 (1992): 34–43.
March 7–April 19, 1864. Diary. Captain. Fourteenth Texas Cavalry. Battles of Mansfield and Pleasant Hill.

315. **ANDREWS, WILLIAM H.** *Footprints of a Regiment: A Recollection of the 1st Georgia Regulars, 1861–1865.* Annotated, with an introduction, by Richard M. McMurry. Atlanta, Ga.: Longstreet Press, 1992. 220 pp.
1861–May 17, 1865. Memoir. Sergeant. First Georgia Infantry. Duty in the Fort Pulaski–Tybee Island region; the Peninsular campaign; second Bull Run; the Antietam campaign; Fredericksburg; duty in Florida, including the battle of Olustee; expeditions to the Johns and James Islands; the siege of Savannah; the Carolinas campaign, including Bentonville; and travel home to Cuthbert, Georgia. Andrews first addressed himself to soldiers' behavior in battle at Malvern Hill. The Union artillery caused the men to run, "apparently demoralized, and apparently scared to death" (p. 50). He and a comrade were beyond that stage. He wrote: "To say that Wheeler and I were demoralized would be putting it mild. We were simply daft" (p. 51). Andrews thought that it was difficult to determine which men would make good soldiers until they had actually participated in battle. Men who were aggressive in camp might or might not be able to "face the music on the field" (p. 61). Andrews's opinion of soldiers' character was blunt: "As a rule, the soldiers are desperately wicked" (p. 98). While he offered the absence of religion in the military as one reason for the soldiers' wickedness, he was skeptical about the religious revivals of the spring of 1864. Andrews criticized the Confederate government as early as 1862 when it passed the conscription law. But he was even more critical of its inability to pay the men regularly because of the hardships it created on the home front. Soldiers were unable to send money to their families and deserted to go home to help out. Andrews reflected on the surrender and wrote, "don't think there is much regret for the loss of the Confederacy" (p. 186). During the course of the war Andrews lost his "best girl" to an "old widower." His response was "Hang the old widowers," and he suggested that they all be sent to the front (p. 117). But Andrews did recognize that because so many men of his own age were being killed, the women on the home front were forced to choose between older men and young boys. In his conclusion Andrews expresses pride in his service for the South but vows to become "as good a citizen for Uncle Sam as I was a soldier for the Confederacy" (p. 186). The editor provides a history of Andrews's narrative as it expanded from a wartime diary to a family memoir in 1891 and eventually to installments in the *Atlanta Journal* and the *Confederate Veteran.* A portion was published as "The 1st Georgia Regulars at Sharpsburg: Recollections of the Maryland Campaign, 1862" in *Civil War Regiments* 2, no. 2 (1992): 95–117.

316. **BAILEY, JOHN MERIMAN.** *Memoirs of Captain J. M. Bailey.* Edited by James Troy Massey. N.p.: James Troy Massey, 1994. 66 leaves.
1861–1865. Memoir. Captain. Sixteenth Arkansas Infantry. Wilson's Creek; Pea Ridge; Corinth; the siege of Port Hudson; duty in Arkansas, Louisiana, and Texas; and his journey home at the end of the war. Bailey describes how he escaped capture at Port Hudson. When he returned to Arkansas, both he and those who had been officially paroled suffered at the hands of the federal troops of occupation. Bailey frequently refers to the partisan warfare in Arkansas. He characterizes men of the Ozark region as preferring to serve in small irregular military units rather than perform the "irksome duties" of the Con-

federate army (p. 31). He reveals their unwritten law of handling captives: "prisoners were disposed of as their captors saw fit" (p. 41). On one occasion Bailey aided the escape of a captive because both were Freemasons. The winter of 1863–1864 was bitterly cold, and men lay close together to share body warmth. This effort to stay alive must have been a topic of jest, for Bailey remarks: "The boys called it spooning" (p. 28). In the spring of 1864 Bailey was reunited with the reorganized Sixteenth Arkansas Infantry.

317. BARBER, FLAVEL C. *Holding the Line: The Third Tennessee Infantry, 1861–1864.* Edited by Robert H. Ferrell. Kent, Ohio: Kent State University Press, 1994. 281 pp.

February 1862–May 12, 1864. Diary. Major. Third Tennessee Infantry. Fort Donelson; Camp Chase and Johnson's Island Prisons; the Vicksburg campaign, especially Chickasaw Bluffs and Raymond; duty at Port Hudson; the siege of Jackson; and duty in Georgia. Barber began his account with the defense and surrender of Fort Donelson. Barber reveals that despite their miserably cold and desperate situation, the night before the surrender the soldiers' morale remained high, and they were discussing how they could cut their way through Union lines. The next morning, as they watched one of Gen. Simon B. Buckner's aides ride by carrying the white flag, they were "thunderstruck." Barber fought the monotony of prison life with a disciplined daily routine that included writing this narrative. Later in the diary Barber describes Sherman's assault on Chickasaw Bluffs and portrays the surrealistic scene of the maimed Union soldiers lying on the battlefield during the rainy December night. On March 28, 1863, Barber wrote that the regimental chaplain preached that the war would never terminate "until we as a nation acknowledged our sins and humbled ourselves before the Creator." Barber agreed and added, "I think our national character will be much improved by this war" (p. 107). Writing during the last week of July 1863, Barber insists that, while Confederate troops were discouraged, they were not demoralized. He pleaded with God: "Chasten us, but do not entirely destroy us" (p. 141). Describing the last months covered in this narrative, which had become a journal, Barber relates duty in northern Georgia. Barber was mortally wounded at the battle of Resaca on May 14, 1864. The editor concludes this work with a revision of two regimental rosters compiled by Barber.

318. BARCLAY, TED. *Ted Barclay, Liberty Hall Volunteers: Letters from the Stonewall Brigade (1861–1864).* Edited by Charles W. Turner. Berryville, Va.: Rockbridge Publishing Company, 1992. 192 pp.

June 10, 1861–August 21, 1864. Letters. Lieutenant. Fourth Virginia Infantry. Barclay's initial letters relate the formation of the volunteer unit from Washington College's Liberty Hall. Subsequent letters describe duty in West Virginia, first Bull Run, Jackson's Romney campaign, first Kernstown, first Winchester, Chancellorsville, second Winchester, Gettysburg, and the Mine Run campaign. In his early letters from West Virginia, Barclay describes the devastation effected by Unionist civilians and Union soldiers, as well as the pervasive sectional divisiveness in the region. He was proud of his regiment's performance at the Stone Bridge at first Bull Run and scrounged the battlefield for souvenirs. As he read the letters taken from dead federal soldiers, the college-educated Barclay pronounced the Yankees ignorant because of their poor writing ability. During the Romney campaign the feud between Generals Jackson and William W. Loring erupted. Barclay related what he thought had transpired. While he approved of the Virginia legislature's decision to allow volunteers to reenlist after one year, he was not pleased to think that he would be forced to serve alongside draftees. During the retreat from Gettysburg, he reported that Confederate spirits remained high and that the Army of Northern Virginia was waiting for Union forces to contest their withdrawal. Barclay's faith in Christ and the eventual success of the Confederacy remained constant. He was captured at Spotsylvania, and his last three letters (June 7 to August 21, 1864) describe conditions and events at Fort Delaware Prison.

319. **BARRETT FAMILY.** *The Confederacy Is on Her Way up the Spout: Letters to South Carolina, 1861–1864.* Edited by J. Roderick Heller III and Carolynn Ayers Heller. Athens: University of Georgia Press, 1992. 157 pp.

June 7, 1861–October 11, 1864. This collection of letters was written by the three Barrett brothers and four other soldiers to a sister and brother-in-law of the Barretts. The family and their acquaintances lived in Pickens County in the northwestern region of South Carolina. Twenty of the thirty-three letters were written by Milton Barrett (Eighteenth Georgia Infantry) from places of duty in Virginia and Tennessee. The other two brothers served in Virginia and South Carolina. The complete collection of letters is integrated chronologically, each preceded by an editorial essay. Milton's succinct letters relate portions of the Peninsular campaign (especially Seven Pines), Lee's march into Maryland (but not the battles), Fredericksburg, and the Petersburg Mine Assault. Milton frequently commented on broad issues that affected the war, as well as the thoughts of an ordinary soldier. On April 14, 1863, Milton knew that many of the Northern soldiers' enlistments would be over but that their ranks were going to be enlarged with drafted men. He reflected that the Confederate soldiers did not have that option and wrote: "Tha is not as good feeling a mong the troops as mite be. tha all a giting tiard of this thing call war" (p. 93). While in Tennessee in April 1864, he related how dissatisfied the men were with the shortage of food. Using the justification that "Hungry will cose a man to do all most any thing," he reported that the soldiers pillaged civilian property and demanded that more food be issued or they would take the commissary by force. Milton wrote that the "genral" agreed to issue an extra day's rations "and got us all sorty pasafied" (pp. 115–16). On July 18, 1863, he wrote: "I say that the Confederacy is on her way up the spout. nothing more" (pp. 102–103). All of the brothers died during the war.

320. **BARRIER FAMILY.** *Dear Father: Confederate Letters Never Before Published.* Edited by Beverly Barrier Troxler and Billy Dawn Barrier. Margate, Fla., and North Billerica, Mass.: Auciello Publishers, 1989. 148 leaves.

July 9, 1861–February 25, 1865. This work contains letters written to Mathias Barrier of Mount Pleasant, North Carolina, by his sons, Rufus A. and William L., and his son-in-law, Daniel M. Moose. Rufus was a colonel with the Eighth North Carolina Infantry. Between July 9, 1861, and March 17, 1865, he related Burnside's Roanoke Island expedition, the bombardment of Charleston, and Grant's Virginia campaign. Rufus abhorred the "speculators and extortioners" who were depriving families of food in North Carolina (p. 20). In his letters he criticizes those Unionists in the South who hired substitutes. William served with the First North Carolina Cavalry and wrote between July 9, 1861, and May 8, 1864. Among the battles he describes (or refers to) are second Bull Run, Antietam, Brandy Station, Stuart's Gettysburg raid, and Williamsport. William was often concerned for the condition of the horses. He believed it was imperative to keep the animals fit and suggested shipping them back to North Carolina to improve their physical condition. Both brothers emphasize family concerns over details of battles. Son-in-law Daniel M. Moose, Fifth North Carolina Infantry, wrote between January 11, 1863, and February 25, 1863. He mentions battles at Fredericksburg and Gettysburg. Daniel provides interesting commentary about the Fifth North Carolina. He praises their performance at Gettysburg, where they had been decimated, but admits that low morale and a high desertion rate were epidemic. He estimates that by early 1865 one-third of the battalion was absent. Daniel expresses pessimism about Confederate victory and seems to have been equally fatalistic about his survival. He remained determined to fight to the end but seldom expresses patriotic rhetoric. While Daniel never wanted a furlough to visit home, in his final letter he relents because he was convinced the war would last forever.

321. **BARTON-JONES FAMILIES.** *Defend the Valley: A Shenandoah Family in the Civil War.* Edited and compiled by Margaretta Barton Colt. New York: Orion Books, 1994. 441 pp.

1861–1865. The editor utilizes the reminiscences of brothers Robert T. Barton (Private, Second Virginia Infantry) and Randolph (Captain, Thirty-third Virginia Infantry), as well as numerous other family accounts, to present the impact of the war on a Shenandoah Valley family. The relatives of David W. Barton and Fannie L. (Jones) Barton were important members of Winchester and Frederick Counties. Six of their sons, a brother-in-law, and a Jones cousin were soldiers. Four of the men were killed during the war. Robert wrote between March 1862 and the spring of 1863, as well as during later service with the Confederate Nitre and Mining Bureau. Randolph wrote of duty with the Stonewall Brigade from first Bull Run to Appomattox. (All of the soldiers' service records are included in the appendix.) The civilians focused on such themes as the family's worry for their kinfolks' safety, their morale, federal occupation, apprehension about impending battles, daily activities, and the deaths of loved ones. All of the writings are blended into chapters chronologically. The beginning prewar chapter is "The Valley at Peace: The Family" and the last chapter covering the postwar period is "The Devastated Valley at Peace: The Family Dispersed." The editor ties together myriad events with her own research and presents the significance of the documents and the identification of the writers. An extensive genealogical chart, together with maps of the region and photographs, further provides cohesion to the collection.

322. BEVENS, WILLIAM E. *Reminiscences of a Private: William E. Bevens of the First Arkansas Infantry, C.S.A.* Edited, with an introduction, by Daniel E. Sutherland. Fayetteville: University of Arkansas Press, 1992. 282 pp.

1861–1865. Memoir. First Arkansas Infantry. First Bull Run (his unit was not engaged); Shiloh; evacuation of Corinth; Bragg's invasion of Kentucky; Perryville; Stones River; Chickamauga; Lookout Mountain; the Atlanta campaign, including Rocky Face Ridge, Dallas, Atlanta, and Jonesboro; the Franklin and Nashville campaign; and the retreat to Tupelo. In December 1864 Bevens was furloughed and remained at home. Bevens begins his memoir by describing the atmosphere of war fever and comparing the economic vitality of Jacksonport, Arkansas, in 1861 to its dilapidated condition in 1914. He wrote that the "Jackson Guards" were formed to protect the South's "rights," but that the men had no real idea about war. They drove the captain "to distraction" with questions about how many suits and trunks they should bring along. Camp entertainment that first winter in Virginia included dances, with the smallest men dressed as girls; jumping contests; and drinking too much alcohol at Christmas. At Shiloh, Bevens was picked out of a lottery to serve in the infirmary corps. He wrote that during a retreat he walked backward so that if he were shot, it would not appear that he had run away. Bevens recalls several acts of humanity during battles. At Lookout Mountain two brothers from Kentucky fighting on opposite sides were given permission to spend the day together. And on June 27, 1864, as the burning dry leaves and brush at Kennesaw Mountain threatened the dead and wounded Union soldiers, a Confederate officer waved a white flag of temporary truce; both Union and Confederate soldiers worked to rescue the men. Bevens ends his account with details of his lengthy journey back to Arkansas. The editor also traces the publication of Bevens's account, *Reminiscences of a Private, Company "G," First Arkansas Infantry, May 1861 to 1865* (Newport, Ark.: N. pub., 1914).

323. BLACK, HARVEY. *The Civil War Letters of Dr. Harvey Black: A Surgeon with Stonewall Jackson.* Edited by Glenn L. McMullen. Baltimore, Md.: Butternut and Blue, 1995. 249 pp.

April 4, 1862–December 3, 1864. Letters. Surgeon in charge with the Fourth Virginia Infantry, the Stonewall Brigade, and the Second Corps Field Hospital. Jackson's Shenandoah Valley campaign; second Manassas; Fredericksburg; Chancellorsville; winter camp at Orange Court House; and Sheridan's Shenandoah Valley campaign. Thirty-three-year-old Harvey Black left his Blacksburg, Virginia, medical practice and his wife and four children for patriotic reasons. In his early letters to his wife, Mollie, he criticizes soldiers who attempted to obtain discharges for medical reasons. The editor notes that Black's letters written between August 31 and December 15, 1862, are darker in tone than the ones written during the earlier spring campaign. McMullen surmises that the hardships of running field hospitals and being overburdened with patients and paperwork, as well as continuously observing death, all combined to change Black's mood. Black was an assisting surgeon to Dr. Hunter McGuire when McGuire amputated Stonewall Jackson's arm. In one letter Black anticipates Jackson's death from pneumonia, which Black supposed Jackson contracted after he bathed in cold water. Black remarks in a letter written after Gettysburg about how his old regiment had been decimated. But in the same letter he encourages his wife not to give in to gloomy feelings about the fate of the Confederacy. Black wrote more about medical treatment, personalities, and military situations than he did about what went on inside the operating tent. Black believed it was general opinion that Stonewall Jackson had treated Richard Garnett unfairly at first Kernstown. He noted the improvement of the Union cavalry and, during the fall of 1863, was aware that they seemed to be "getting the advantage of our cavalry most of the time" (p. 61). In his final letter Black relates with pleasure how the usually dour Jacob Early was pleased when Gen. Thomas Rosser captured a large quantity of federal supplies at New Creek, West Virginia, in November 1864. In the editor's introduction McMullen describes the development of the Confederate hospital system and includes information about Black's postwar career and a profile of Blacksburg, Virginia, in 1860.

324. **BLACK, HARVEY, and JOHN S. APPERSON.** "Tending the Wounded: Two Virginians in the Confederate Medical Corps." By Glenn L. McMullen. *Virginia Cavalcade* 40 (Spring 1991): 172–83.

1861–1865. Letters and diary. McMullen blends the writings of Dr. Harvey Black and hospital steward John S. Apperson, who served together from Bull Run to Appomattox. Dr. Black made certain that Apperson was with him from the time Black became surgeon of the Fourth Virginia Infantry and after Black was assigned surgeon of the Second Corps Field Hospital. Throughout the war Dr. Black encouraged the younger Apperson's interest in medicine. However, McMullen points out that as the war progressed, the two men pursued divergent paths. Black became more concerned with the condition of his family, while Apperson grew increasingly interested in his medical career. On April 21, 1865, a brief entry by Apperson states that Black gave him "good advice." McMullen believes this implies that Black encouraged Apperson to pursue a medical career. After the war Black became a prominent Virginia physician and Apperson a country doctor.

325. **BLUE, JOHN.** *Hanging Rock Rebel: Lt. John Blue's War in West Virginia and the Shenandoah Valley.* Edited by Dan Oates. Shippensburg, Pa.: Burd Street Press, 1994. 324 pp.

May 18, 1861–May 1865. Memoir. Lieutenant. Eleventh Virginia Cavalry. Duty in West Virginia, including the battles of Hanging Rock Pass, the Union capture of Romney, Blue's Gap, and Jackson's Romney campaign. Other battles that Blue observed (or in which he participated) were second Bull Run, Cedar Mountain, Jones's and Imboden's West Virginia raid, Brandy Station, Gettysburg (including Pickett's Charge), and Lee's retreat. Blue was captured in October 1863 and spent the remainder of the war in Yankee prisons at Old Capitol, Johnson's Island, Point Lookout, and Fort Delaware. The memoir is chock-full of anecdotes, troop movements, captures, escapades as a courier, and references to famous officers. Blue's memoirs were originally published in numerous installments of the *Hampshire Review* between 1898 and 1901.

326. **BOSTICK FAMILY.** *Old Enough to Die.* By Ridley Wills II. Franklin, Tenn.: Hillsboro Press, 1996. 180 pp.

1861–1865. This is a collection of letters by the extended Bostick family and their friends, who resided near Nashville and in northern Mississippi. The author has woven a historical and genealogical narrative around the letters and experiences of the four Bostick brothers, their several sisters, and a cousin. The brothers' letters are highly literate; each was a college-educated professional man. In general, they wrote of news by and about each other, events that affected the family, and their concern for their widowed mother in Nashville. Abe (Seventh Tennessee Infantry) wrote the first long segment of letters from Virginia until he was killed at Seven Pines. Litton (Twentieth Tennessee Infantry) wrote from Tennessee and during the Atlanta campaign, especially Pickett's Mill. He was killed in July 1864. Tom (Seventh Tennessee Infantry) wrote a few letters from Virginia, and Joe (Thirty-fourth Tennessee Infantry) wrote even fewer of duty in Tennessee. The sisters' writings also concern their mother, the deaths of their brothers, and their own circumstances. Tom and Joe were paroled in North Carolina. The author's final chapter follows the family fortunes until the end of the century.

327. BOYD, DAVID FRENCH. *Reminiscences of the War in Virginia.* Edited by T. Michael Parrish. Baton Rouge: United States Civil War Center, Louisiana State University, 1994. 37 pp.

Spring 1862–Spring 1863. Memoir. Major. Ninth Louisiana Infantry; Jackson's Shenandoah Valley campaign; Seven Days' Battles; second Bull Run; Antietam; Fredericksburg; and Chancellorsville. This work is a composite of humorous anecdotes about Generals Stonewall Jackson, Jubal Early, Richard Ewell, and Richard Taylor, all of whom served together in Virginia during this period. Originally published in the *New Orleans Times-Democrat* on January 31 and February 7, 1897.

328. BUCKNER, SIMON BOLIVAR. "Major General Simon B. Buckner's Unpublished After-Action Report on the Battle of Perryville." Edited by Kenneth A. Hafendorfer. *Civil War Regiments* 4, no. 3 (1996): 50–64.

October 8, 1862. Report. Major General. Third Division, Left Wing, Army of Mississippi. Battle of Perryville. Buckner's report is not included in *The War of the Rebellion: The Official Records.* The editor admits that the report contains little new information but believes it deserves to be made public because it documents the role of Buckner and his division in the battle.

329. BURFORD, ELISHA SPRUILLE. "Elisha Spruille Burford, Soldier and Pastor, 1839–1894." *West Tennessee Historical Society Papers* 46 (1992): 103–7.

June 7–September 12, 1861. Diary. Fifth Louisiana Infantry. This work includes scattered entries that romanticize the "halcyon days before the war" (p. 103); document the regiment's movement from Louisiana to Virginia; and give the author's impression of Generals. A. P. Hill, John Magruder, and Stonewall Jackson. Burford concludes with comments about the inauguration of Jefferson Davis and the promise of the Confederacy.

330. BURGWYN, WILLIAM H. S. *A Captain's War: The Letters and Diaries of William H. S. Burgwyn, 1861–1865.* Edited by Herbert M. Schiller. Foreword by Richard J. Sommers. Shippensburg, Pa.: White Mane Publishing Company, 1994. 186 pp.

August 27, 1861–March 12, 1865. Letters and diaries. Lieutenant, Twenty-second North Carolina Infantry; then, Captain, Thirty-fifth North Carolina Infantry. Harpers Ferry; Antietam; Fredericksburg; siege of New Bern; Gum Swamp; Batchelder's Creek; the Bermuda Hundred campaign, including Drewry's Bluff; Cold Harbor; Fort Harrison; and Fort Delaware Prison. Burgwyn, son of a wealthy

North Carolina plantation family, entered the army at age fifteen and a half. His duties included training troops, constructing fortifications, and serving as staff officer (inspector general) to Brig. Gen. Thomas L. Clingman. Wounded at Cold Harbor, Burgwyn returned to duty in July, was captured at Fort Harrison on September 30, and spent most of the remaining months of the war at Fort Delaware Prison. Despite his privileged background and young age, Burgwyn easily adapted to the rigors of camp life and requirements of an officer. Burgwyn expressed his feelings about the future of slavery early when he wrote to his father: "I can't help think that slavery received its death blow in this war with the whole world against it" (p. 3). However, Burgwyn was not conceding defeat; he refers to the period "After our independence" (p. 4). Burgwyn points out that there was a large community of poor white men willing to work and that both he and his father knew that the white man could work in the hot sun as well as the "Negroes." Burgwyn appreciated the assistance provided by his manservant, Pompey, and trusted him to travel home on his own. Burgwyn was a loving son, and his writings contain frequent references to relatives and acquaintances. The series of diary entries and letters to his mother pertaining to the death of his brother, Henry, at Gettysburg, are especially poignant.

331. BYERS, JOHN ALEMETH. "'The Whole World Was Full of Smoke . . .': The Civil War Letters of Private John Alemeth Byers, 17th Mississippi Infantry." Edited by Hartman McIntosh. *Military Images* 9 (May/June 1988): 6–11.

July 29, 1861–October 24, 1864. Letters. Seventeenth Mississippi Infantry. Ball's Bluff; the siege of Petersburg; and Sheridan's Shenandoah Valley campaign. These letters predominately contain information about camp life and troop movements, requests for items from home, and mention of friends in common. Included is a letter of condolence informing Byers's family of his death at the battle of Cedar Creek.

332. CALLAN, CHRISTOPHER. "Civil War Letters of a Washington Rebel." By Kevin Conley Ruffner. *Washington History* 4 (Fall/Winter 1992/1993): 56–71.

July 4, 1861–February 24, 1864. Letters. Seventh Virginia Infantry and Twenty-fourth Battalion of Virginia Partisan Rangers (Scott's). Ruffner uses Callan's letters and other documents to try to unravel the military career of Christopher Callan. Callan was a Georgetown lawyer who joined a Confederate unit composed of residents of the District of Columbia and Maryland. He was discharged in November 1861 for medical reasons. Then he unsuccessfully sought employment with the Confederate government. Later his experience as a captain in the Partisan Rangers proved unsatisfactory. In January 1864 Callan allowed himself to be captured by the Union forces. However, in his research Ruffner found conflicting documentation that blurs details of Callan's actions and motives.

333. CAMMACK, JOHN HENRY. *Personal Recollections of Private John Henry Cammack: A Soldier of the Confederacy, 1861–1865 . . . To Which Is Added Press Notices and Other Papers Containing Final Tribute to His Memory.* Huntington, W.Va.: Marshall University Library Associates, 1991. 164 pp.

1861–1865. Memoir. Private. Thirty-first Virginia Infantry, Twentieth Virginia Cavalry, and Tenth Virginia Heavy Artillery. Operations in West Virginia, including Cheat Mountain and Camp Alleghany; Jackson's Shenandoah Valley campaign; Seven Days' Battles; and Grant's Virginia campaign, especially Chaffin's Farm. As Cammack wrote of events more than half a century later, he admitted that he was not writing a history but rather only those things he remembered. He remained honest to his intention. Cammack apologized for not remembering names; however, faces and humorous events, as well as mental horrors, all remained indelible. Thus, the memory of a quart of pus expressed from Cammack's abscessed neck was as vivid as incidents of battle and impressions of leaders. Cammack begins his narrative by describing the sectional strife in West Virginia. He continues by relating such events as seeing Jefferson Davis being turned away from Libby Prison by a guard; mentioning Dr. Mary Walker's detention at Castle Thunder in 1864 as a spy; describing the mass escape of Union officers from Libby Prison on February 9, 1864; telling of shots fired at the black soldiers across the picket lines because they broke the common soldiers' rules of conduct by taunting the Confederate troops; praising the loyal slaves who stayed with their families; and relating episodes of soldiers who took "French leaves" to be with their families. Original publication: Huntington, West Virginia: Paragon Ptg. and Pub., 1920.

334. CARR, WILLIAM DICKSON. *The Civil War Letters of W. D. Carr of Duplin County, North Carolina, with Additional Notes on His Family and the Campaigns in Which He Served.* Compiled and edited by Robert Aycock and Elsie J. Aycock. N.C.: R. and E. Aycock, 1995. 72 pp.

June 7, 1862–February 24, 1865. Letters. Forty-third North Carolina Infantry. Peninsular campaign; encampment at Drewry's Bluff; duty in North Carolina; and the siege of Petersburg. William Carr's letters to his family and friends contain news of acquaintances and relatives (at home and in camp), illnesses, desertions, and brief comments about specific battles. Carr also wrote several letters to the overseer of his farm instructing the man on the raising of crops and care of animals. He relates two camp accidents in a single letter. One incident involved a man who was chopping wood when the ax entered near the toe and "split his foot to the bottom skin nearly to the ankle"; Carr expressed his empathy by writing, "The Dr. dressed the wound and it seems to be healing well" (p. 39). The second accident occurred when a man was cleaning his gun with the load in it; when it fired, the ball and rammer went through his hand. Carr was separated from his regiment during much of its fighting because he was ill or detached to guard duty. In early 1865 at Petersburg, when the Yankee lines were close, William was on guard duty when six men of the Forty-fifth North Carolina deserted. Even when shot at by their comrades, they would not return. William was killed on April 2, 1865, during the evacuation of Richmond.

335. CAVE, ROBERT CATLETT. *Raw Pork and Hardtack: A Civil War Memoir from Manassas to Appomattox.* Shippensburg, Pa.: Burd Street Press, 1996. 87 pp.

1861–April 26, 1865. Memoir. Private. Thirteenth Virginia Infantry. Jackson's Shenandoah Valley campaign; Seven Days' Battles, especially White Oak Swamp; Cedar Mountain; second Bull Run; Chancellorsville; Gettysburg (described); the Mine Run campaign; the Virginia campaign, including The Wilderness and Cold Harbor; Lynchburg; Sheridan's Shenandoah Valley campaign, including third Winchester; and Waynesboro. Cave blended his own experiences with the postwar writings of others. He addresses several instances of Stonewall Jackson's leadership. He agreed with other soldiers who thought that Jackson's performance at White Oak Swamp was not equal to the quality of the spring Shenandoah Valley campaign. Cave credits Lee for planning the flank attack of May 2 at Chancellorsville and credits Jackson for executing it. He quotes those at Gettysburg, where Cave was not present, who blamed J. E. B. Stuart and James Longstreet for the Confederate "repulse" (not defeat). He admits that Jackson was a military genius, but when Cave wrote about Lee, it was with reverence: "The whole aspect of the man spoke of moral cleanness, spirited beauty, and knightly nobility" (p. 29). After second Bull Run, Cave recounted how a Confederate soldier was attempting to pull the leggings off a Union soldier whom he thought was dead. The man suddenly sat up and asked the Confederate to wait until he had actually expired before stripping him. Cave's humorous stories frequently involve misfortune. He understood that such humor might seem heartless to civilians, but he assures readers that making light of bad situations was just the soldiers' way of meeting misfortune. After Gettysburg, Cave was transferred to the signal corps, and he related his duties as a signaler during the Virginia campaign and in the Shenandoah Valley.

336. CHAMBERS, WILLIAM PITT. *Blood & Sacrifice: The Civil War Journal of a Confederate Soldier.* Edited by Richard A. Baumgartner. Huntingdon, W.Va.: Blue Acorn Press, 1994. 281 pp.

March 25, 1862–May 16, 1865. Diary. Sergeant. Forty-sixth Mississippi Infantry. The Vicksburg campaign, including the bombardment of Vicksburg, Chickasaw Bluffs, and the siege of Vicksburg; the Atlanta campaign, including Dallas, Kennesaw Mountain, and Allatoona; and the Mobile campaign, including the capture of Fort Blakely. From Vicksburg, Chambers recorded the passage of Union gunboats and construction of Vicksburg's defenses. When Jefferson Davis and Joseph Johnston reviewed the troops in December 1862, Chambers thought Davis was an "ugly man," but Johnston impressed him as being the perfect specimen of a soldier (p. 47). Chambers blamed the Confederate surrender of Vicksburg on Gen. John C. Pemberton. In his diary he commends the Yankees for never insulting Confederate courage by saying "We have taken Vicksburg" (p. 107). In July 1864 he related the soldiers' indignation when Gen. Johnston was replaced by Gen. Hood. He wrote that when President Davis and Gen. Hood reviewed the troops on September 26, 1864, the dignitaries were given a cool reception and his brigade raised "Three cheers for Gen. Joe Johnston" (p. 170). On October 5 Chambers was wounded at Allatoona and sent home until the end of 1864. His entries for 1865 record the activities of the remnant of the Army of Tennessee. Chambers knew of the probable fate of the Confederacy and how badly the South needed men, but he still did not approve of the unit of "galvanized Yankees" that he saw. His brigade debated, then approved, a proposal to arm the slaves; Chambers was convinced that "it is not right" (p. 203). Much earlier, Chambers had written that the war was not worth the "nominal freedom" of an "inferior race" (p. 119). After Appomattox, Chambers proclaimed: "The people of the South are *unworthy* of freedom" (p. 222). A short time later he denounced the whole nation: "As Americans, it seems to me that we are incapable of governing ourselves" (p. 225). Nevertheless, Chambers saw the hand of God in the outcome and believed that the consequences of the war were for the good of America.

337. CHANDLER, DAVID RUFFIN. "'Yours Truly Until Death': The Civil War Letters of Private David Ruffin Chandler." By Darrell Wayne Chandler. *Virginia Cavalcade* 44 (Summer 1994): 4–12.

August 12, 1862–October 8, 1862. Letters. Private. Fifteenth North Carolina Infantry. Duty in Virginia and the battle of Crampton's Gap. Chandler described to his wife in Person County, North Carolina, the battle at Crampton's Gap. He told her that he had lost all of his belongings and was wounded in his left leg. Later he begged her to raise enough money to come and take him home to convalesce. Chandler died after only three months of service. A final letter of condolence was written by a nurse.

338. CHAPMAN, CONRAD WISE. "Conrad Wise Chapman: Artist-Soldier of the Orphan Brigade." By Ben Bassham. *Southern Quarterly* 25 (Fall 1986): 40–56.

August 1861–July 1862. Memoir. Third Kentucky Infantry. Kentucky, Tennessee (including Shiloh), and Mississippi. Bassham paraphrases the memoir, which describes a previously unknown portion of Chapman's activities early in the war. Except for a description of Shiloh, the entries pertain to the several times Chapman was confined to hospitals for a head wound and various illnesses. Bassham examines the content and quality of Chapman's paintings from this period.

339. CLARK, REUBEN G. *Valley of the Shadow: The Memoir of Confederate Captain Reuben G. Clark, Company I, 59th Tennessee Mounted Infantry.* Edited, with commentary and regimental history, by Willene B. Clark. Knoxville: University of Tennessee Press, 1994. 163 pp.

1861–1865. Memoir. Lieutenant, Third Tennessee Infantry; then, Captain, Fifty-ninth Tennessee Infantry. First Bull Run (aftermath); the Vicksburg campaign; duty in Virginia, especially the battle of Piedmont and Sheridan's Shenandoah Valley campaign; and duty in Tennessee. Clark was captured at the battle of Morristown, Tennessee, on October 28, 1864. Following his capture, he was held at the Knoxville County jail. The eastern Tennessee Unionist William G. "Parson" Brownlow, editor of *The Knoxville Whig,* falsely accused Clark of murdering a Union officer and called for Clark's execution. He described his period of captivity in the cagelike building. In December 1865 Clark was acquitted of the crime, but because his life had been threatened, he made his home in Rome, Georgia. Throughout his memoir Clark mentions the harsh treatment of those who supported the Confederacy within Unionist eastern Tennessee. The editor's commentary corrects Clark's sometimes faulty memory of events and fills in the gaps of information that exist in Clark's overview.

340. COCKRELL, DANDRIDGE WILLIAM, and NAOMI BUSH COCKRELL. *Civil War Letters of Dandridge William and Naomi Bush Cockrell, 1862–1863.* Edited by Pauline Franklin and Mary V. Pruett. Lively, Va.: Brandyland Publishers, 1991. 38 pp.

April 13, 1863–November 22, 1863. Letters. Private. Ninth Virginia Cavalry. Dandridge makes few references to the fighting in northern Virginia—Stuart's first ride around McClellan is treated in greatest detail—and reveals only slightly more about his own circumstances. Collectively, however, both sets of letters indicate how a husband and wife sought to raise a family and run their farm in the midst of war. Dandridge gave plenty of advice, but Naomi's letters indicate that she was already a good manager of the cotton and sheep, five children, and a truculent slave named Buck. Buck later proved to be of great help to Naomi, perhaps because Dandridge had advised her to apply strong disciplinary measures to the slave. Naomi expressed more love and warmth than did Dandridge. The editor suggests that because Dandridge was illiterate, he may have been reluctant to reveal feelings of intimacy to those who wrote for him.

341. COLES, ROBERT T. *From Huntsville to Appomattox: R. T. Coles's History of the 4th Regiment, Alabama Volunteer Infantry, C.S.A., Army of Northern Virginia.* Edited by Jeffrey D. Stocker. Knoxville: University of Tennessee Press, 1996. 318 pp.

1861–1865. Memoir. Adjutant. Fourth Alabama Infantry. First Bull Run; the Peninsular campaign; second Bull Run; Antietam; Fredericksburg; the siege of Suffolk; Gettysburg; Chickamauga; the Knoxville campaign; The Wilderness; Spotsylvania; the siege of Petersburg; the Appomattox campaign; the surrender at Appomattox Court House; and Coles's return trip to northern Alabama. This regimental history is also a memoir. Writing in 1909 and 1910, Coles consulted other sources and surviving comrades but blended his own perspective as an eyewitness observer. Throughout the work his pride in the accomplishments of the Fourth Alabama is undeniable. Stocker says that, except for a day at second Bull Run and several months in late 1864 and early 1865, Coles was with the regiment during the whole war. The editor occasionally corrects Coles and adds additional or more recent information in his endnotes. The editor has also added the accounts of three other members of the Fourth Alabama as appendixes. They are: "Letter of Captain Edward D. Tracy Regarding the Battle of First Manassas Battlefield . . ."; "Incidents and Personal Experiences on the Battlefield at Gettysburg: [an] Address by Captain W. C. Ward . . ."; and "Battle of the Wilderness by P. D. Bowles. . . ."

342. COLSTON, RALEIGH EDWARD. "Conversation in Confidence." *Civil War Times Illustrated* 33 (January/February 1995): 20, 61–62.

July 1864. Memoir. Brigadier General. Atlanta campaign. A few days after Joseph Johnston's removal as commander of the Army of Tennessee, the general related to Colston his reasons for assuming a defensive strategy against Sherman's advance.

343. COPLEY, JOHN M. "Battle of Franklin with Reminiscences of Camp Douglas." *Journal of Confederate History* 2, no. 1 (1989): 26–54.

November 28–December 2, 1864. Memoir. Forty-ninth Tennessee Infantry. Battle of Franklin. Copley's company was captured at Franklin and marched to Nashville during the night, just managing to stay ahead of Hood's bombardment. In Nashville the Confederate troops were held in public view at Capitol Square, where they were chastised by Vice President Andrew Johnson. Copley's account of Camp Douglas is not included here.

344. COTTON, BURWELL THOMAS, and GEORGE JOB HUNTLEY. *The Cry Is War, War, War: The Civil War Correspondence of Lts. Burwell Thomas Cotton and George Job Huntley, 34th North Carolina Troops. . . .* Edited and annotated by Michael W. Taylor. Dayton, Ohio: Morningside House, 1994. 194 pp.

October 23, 1861–June 17, 1864. Letters. Lieutenants. Thirty-fourth North Carolina Infantry. Collectively these letters relate the organization of the unit, duty in North Carolina, the Peninsular campaign, Cedar Mountain, Chancellorsville, Gettysburg, Falling Waters, the Virginia campaign, and the siege of Petersburg. The editor points out several similar aspects of these writings. Both men were from remote regions of North Carolina; they were in their early twenties; both were schoolteachers; and their many letters to their sisters were written with a sense of freedom of expression. Huntley repeatedly advised his father not to volunteer but rather to stay home and grow crops that would exempt him from the draft. After Chancellorsville, Huntley fraternized with Union troops and observed the bones of half-buried soldiers protruding from the battlefield. Several times he confessed that he was ready for an honorable peace, one in which the Yankees would give the South back its rights. Huntley believed that the war was intended as a scourge upon America for its pride and wickedness and that it would not cease until "our country is thoroughly purged and cleansed" (p. 76). The camp was one example of wickedness; Huntley wrote: "men curse, swear, and play cards all night in a tent where there is a corpse. The death of a man here is nothing more than a death of a hog" (p. 77). Huntley was mortally wounded at Gettysburg on July 1, 1863. In February 1864 Cotton longed to go home but felt "there is no chance for peace and the cry is war war war" (p. 165). Cotton often wrote about desertion among North Carolina troops and how the deserters were punished by whipping and execution by firing squads. At the end of August 1863 he wrote: "If N. Carolina will abandon the idea of going back into the Union I think there will not be so much desertion in the army" (p. 154). He mentioned that during the Gettysburg campaign Confederate troops vandalized private property. Cotton described how the troops panicked at Falling Waters when the Army of Northern Virginia retreated back into Virginia. He said that he would have surrendered, but he was afraid of being shot by pursuing Union soldiers. Cotton was killed on June 22, 1864, near the Jerusalem Plank Road.

345. CRAIGHILL, EDWARD A. *Confederate Surgeon: The Personal Recollections of E. A. Craighill.* Edited by Peter W. Houck. Lynchburg, Va.: H. E. Howard, Inc., 1989. 106 pp.

March 1861–1865. Memoir. Major. The author rose from the rank of private in the Second Virginia Infantry to surgeon in charge of the General Hospital at Lynchburg. His duty with the Stonewall

Brigade began as it marched between Harpers Ferry and Martinsburg destroying the B & O Railroad. Craighill was detached from the ranks by Dr. Hunter McGuire to serve as a medical steward prior to first Bull Run, and he later served in a brigade hospital. Craighill recalled how little any of the doctors knew about treating battlefield wounds. In 1863 he served at the field hospital of Gordonsville and reported the illnesses that raged throughout the hospitals. Measles struck down one healthy-looking group of Georgia troops shortly after their arrival in Virginia. Body lice exacerbated all other ailments. Craighill wrote that he watched a man dig his own grave because the man was so certain he was doomed. Another man actually died of fright because he thought he was infected with smallpox. Craighill noted differences between commanders. Joseph Johnston was "a sleepy, stoop-shouldered indolent nobody," while Stonewall Jackson was "alert, quick-motioned, dressy and busy all the time" (p. 4). Craighill thought that both Jackson and Lee were admired as leaders. However, he believed Jackson to be callous about the number of lives that might be lost in an attempt to achieve victory, while he felt that Lee took into consideration the number of human lives a battle would cost. It was Craighill's opinion that Jackson died from a case of pneumonia he had contracted by sleeping on the bare ground the night before he was shot. Other anecdotes include Jackson's preference for remaining aloof from the soldiers and his having the fleshy part of his index finger shot away at first Bull Run. Craighill spent the last two years of the war at the Lynchburg General Hospital, and the battle of Lynchburg dominates this period of his memoirs. The editor includes several appendixes, which record locations of hospitals in Lynchburg and physicians who served there, in addition to other information about the hospital. Craighill wrote his memoirs in 1905.

346. CRAWFORD, WILLIAM A. "'. . . Our Noblest and Best Spirits Have Lain Down Their Lives . . .' The William Ayres Crawford Letters." *Civil War Regiments* 1, no. 2 (1991): 70–75.
December 20, 1861–May 26, 1865. Letters. Colonel. First Arkansas Cavalry (Crawford's). This work is made up of scattered comments Crawford wrote to his wife from Virginia, Arkansas, and Texas.

347. CROCKER, JAMES FRANCIS. *My Capture at Gettysburg and Prison Reminiscences: An Address before Stonewall Camp, Confederate Veterans Portsmouth, Virginia, February 2nd, 1904.* Suffolk, Va.: Robert Hardy Publications, 1986. 37 pp.
July 1863–April 1865. Memoir. Lieutenant. Ninth Virginia Infantry. Captured during Pickett's Charge, Crocker was allowed free run of the town of Gettysburg. Having graduated from Gettysburg's Pennsylvania College, Crocker retained friends there. He recalled after he was moved to David's Island Hospital (New Rochelle, New York) that the local ladies (who were from Virginia) treated the captured Confederates with kindness. Shortly after his transfer to Johnson's Island in September, Crocker was allowed a medical parole to go to Sandusky, Ohio, to have his wounded leg treated. He was allowed freedom to stroll the streets in his Confederate gray uniform. Among his remembered experiences of Johnson's Island was that rations remained good until news of the treatment of Union prisoners at Andersonville became widespread. Then the Union prison officials began cutting the prisoners' food in half. Exchanged in January 1865, Crocker traveled back to Virginia and North Carolina. While returning to Richmond to rejoin the war, Crocker learned from Confederate soldiers straggling home that Lee had surrendered.

348. CROW, WILLIAM HARRISON. *When I Think of Home: The Civil War Letters of William Harrison "Tip" Crow.* Researched and compiled by DeWayne R. Welborn. Decorah, Iowa: Anundsen Publishing Co., 1996. 77 pp.

131

April 4, 1861–July 22, 1862. Letters. Private. Twelfth Alabama Infantry. Virginia. As Crow addressed the issue of secession in his first letter, he wrote with reverence for the "old government . . . that our ancestors fought for" (p. 8). He was opposed to splitting the Union but recognized the problems between the sections over the issue of slavery. He wrote, "We cant bild an impassable gulf between us an the north" (p. 8). After he had enlisted he said that he was fighting to protect his family from the "grasp of the enemy" and that he would "fight til the last drop of blood seaces to flow" (pp. 54–55). He wrote from Richmond with a sense of wonderment. He saw thousands of unruly troops, "all kindes of wickedness," and was humbled by watching the Confederate congress meet in the same halls where great men, such as George Washington, had walked (p. 12). He also wrote of the battlefield after first Bull Run and sickness in the camp (he contracted measles), and he requested boxes of food and clothing. After a close friend died, he was quietly outraged at having to bid for the man's clothing. Other themes of Crow's letters include the Confederate Conscription Act of 1862, the army's refusal to allow furloughs, the Trent Affair, sickness during winter camp of 1861 and 1862, news of battles, and reorganization of the regiment. Crow was fatally wounded at Seven Pines. Letters of condolence describe his death.

349. **CURRY, WILMOT WALTER.** "To the Potomac with Sergeant Curry: A Southern Sergeant's View of the First Confederate March on Washington, D.C." Edited by Paula Mitchell Marks. *Civil War Times Illustrated* 28 (September/October 1989): 24–25, 59–65.

June 12–October 20, 1861. Diary. Hampton's Legion, South Carolina. Curry relates formation of his light artillery unit (Washington Mounted Battery), acceptance into Hampton's Legion, travel to Virginia, camp incidents, changes of commanders, and the battles of first Bull Run and Ball's Bluff.

350. **DAVIS, HARVEY A.** "Harvey Davis's Unpublished Civil War 'Diary' and the Story of Company D of the First North Carolina Cavalry." Edited by Francis B. Dedmond. *Appalachian Journal* 13 (Summer 1986): 368–407.

May 11, 1861–March 1863. Memoir. Private. First North Carolina Cavalry. Duty in northern Virginia; Malvern Hill; and the Antietam campaign, including Harpers Ferry and the battle of Antietam. Davis frequently mentions men with whom he served (especially those from Wautaga County, North Carolina) and the skirmishes and raids of Stuart's Cavalry Division. The editor, whose notes add considerably to the account, completes information on the remainder of Davis's service, as well as that of the regiment.

351. **DAVIS, SAMUEL H.** "Chronicle of a Mississippi Soldier: The Civil War Letters of Samuel H. Davis of Kemper County." By Henry E. Mattox. *Journal of Mississippi History* 52 (August 1990): 199–214.

December 21, 1861–September 25, 1862. Letters. Lieutenant. Thirty-fifth Mississippi Infantry. Following a narration of Davis's military activities in northern Mississippi, Mattox utilizes brief quotations from Davis's letters to indicate how he disliked being separated from his wife and children. Davis was killed at Corinth on October 3, 1862.

352. **DAVIS, WILBUR FISKE.** "An Excerpt from the Memoirs of Wilbur Fiske Davis, an Antebellum Student and Civil War Veteran, 1857–1862." Edited, with an introduction, by J. Harvey Bailey. *Magazine of Albemarle County History* 44 (1986): 22–40.

Summer 1857–Spring 1862. Memoir. Most of this article concerns Davis's life prior to the Civil War when he was a student at the University of Virginia. In February 1861 he attended the Virginia convention of secession, but he left when it became obvious that Virginia was not going to secede at that time. In March 1862 Davis joined the Charlottesville Artillery and served with Ewell's Division in the Shenandoah Valley. The editor adds that the Davis family were deeply religious members of the Methodist Episcopal Church (South), and Davis later became a minister. After the war Davis believed himself to be a failure, a feeling he traced back to not having entered the ministry while in college.

353. DAY, HENRY C. "A Confederate Aide-de-Camp's Letters from the Chattanooga Area, 1863." Edited by Charles A. Earp. *Journal of East Tennessee History* 67 (1995): 106–19.

November 20–December 1863. Letters. Volunteer aide to Gen. John C. Breckinridge. Second Corps, Army of Tennessee. Missionary Ridge. Although Day was unable to obtain a commission on Breckinridge's staff, he stayed on to serve as a volunteer. In these three letters he relates the later part of Missionary Ridge and "our great skedaddle" to Dalton (p. 112). In his last letter he summarizes the events of this period and criticizes "The confusion in the Administration," a remark directed at Braxton Bragg (p. 112).

354. DEAVENPORT, THOMAS HOPKINS. "The Wartime Diary of Reverend Thomas Hopkins Deavenport. Chaplain of Third Tennessee Regiment, CSA." *Journal of Confederate History* 1 (Summer 1988): 35–48.

September 5, 1861–Spring 1862. Diary. Chaplain. Third Tennessee Infantry. Duty in Kentucky; the battle of Fort Donelson; and incarceration at Camp Douglas Prison. Although intensely patriotic, the young minister of the Methodist Episcopal Church (South) wondered if he could stand up to the hardships of being a soldier. Also, he was concerned about whether he could restrain himself from vice and corruption. Following a lengthy prayer his peace of mind was restored, and the ninety-five-pound recruit was reluctantly accepted by the examining surgeon. Several long, hard marches in the vicinity of Bowling Green, Kentucky, proved his endurance. Deavenport described the fighting at Fort Donelson, his capture there, and the trip to Camp Douglas. He recalled how the train purposefully went beyond the prison, forcing the prisoners to march back in front of a jeering crowd who ridiculed them. From Camp Douglas he wrote that he was busy conducting prayer meetings.

355. ELLIS, VOLNEY. "'An Experience in Soldiers Life': The Civil War Letters of Volney Ellis, Adjutant, Twelfth Texas Infantry Walker's Texas Division, C.S.A." Edited by Thomas W. Cutrer. *Military History of the Southwest* 22 (Fall 1992): 109–72.

July 1, 1862–November 7, 1864. Letters. Captain. Twelfth Texas Infantry. Duty in Texas, Arkansas, and Louisiana, including battles of Mansfield and Pleasant Hill. Ellis's personal code of conduct was an essential element of his patriotism. He was proud to be a yeoman volunteer who had joined the army out of choice and set high standards for soldiers and society alike. He regretted the fact that the soldiers had become used to bloodshed because he feared it might render those men unfit for normal society. And he criticized the civilians on the Texas home front who sought to profit from the war. As he observed women in Louisiana associating with Union soldiers, Ellis expressed what he felt to be woman's elevated role. She should be the "chief cornerstone of the happiness, prosperity, and refinement of any people" (p. 163). Ellis was a lawyer and small farmer, and his wife Mary was a schoolteacher. The couple lived in Lavaca County, Texas. While Ellis was away Mary taught for at least one year. She reared two children, raised the garden, tended livestock, made a rug and clothes for children, dealt with a disobedient slave, and collected debts owed to his business practice. Ellis stressed to Mary that their daughter and son were different and, thus, must be treated differently. Throughout his absence he expressed pride in her accomplishments. In May 1864 he may have wondered if Mary was becoming too independent: "you have recently remained studiously silent upon the subject of your 'own prospects'" (p. 162). Numerous affectionate passages bear testament to his love, and he assured her of his freedom from vices, especially those involving women. During the last year of the war Mary apparently asked him to return home; after all, she saw many other Texas soldiers doing it. He explained that he could not leave the army for fear of being considered disloyal. Unlike many Trans-Mississippi soldiers, Ellis was willing to cross the Mississippi if it would end the fighting.

356. EVANS, CLEMENT ANSELM. *Intrepid Warrior: Clement Anselm Evans, Confederate General from Georgia; Life, Letters, and Diaries of the War Years.* Compiled and edited by Robert Grier Stephens Jr. Dayton, Ohio: Morningside House, Inc., 1992. 598 pp.

November 26, 1859–December 15, 1864. Letters and diary. Major, Thirty-first Georgia Infantry, to Brigadier General, Second Corps, Evans' Division, Army of Northern Virginia. The Peninsular campaign; Fredericksburg; Chancellorsville; the Gettysburg campaign (including Wrightsville, Gettysburg, and Lee's retreat); the Mine Run campaign; Morton's Ford; The Wilderness; Spotsylvania; Early's Washington raid (including Monocacy); Sheridan's Shenandoah Valley campaign (especially Cedar Creek); and the siege of Petersburg. This substantial collection of Clement's letters to his wife, Mary Allen (Allie), also includes a number of letters written by her. His initial letters address the coming of the war—he was a senator in the Georgia legislature—and a trip to Virginia as a civilian, just after first Bull Run. Clement wrote optimistically about troop movements and soldier life, often indicating the state of morale in the Confederate army. Early in June 1863 he could not conceal his excitement at the thought of marching into Pennsylvania: "that would indeed be glorious, if we could ravage that state making her desolate like Virginia" (p. 184). Writing in mid June, as he felt the spirit of adventure among the soldiers, he added, "and but for you I should enjoy an invasion very much (p. 205). Clement was wounded five times during the war, but he seldom expounded on the realistic aspects of battle. Clement praised the common soldiers and often remarked that their behavior was superior to that of the Yankees. He also praised Gen. John B. Gordon; however, for two years he held Jubal Early in low regard because of his profane manner and poor generalship. Evans interpreted Early's defeat at Cedar Creek as God's punishment. Allie's letters describe life in Lumpkin (Stewart County), Georgia. She moved between the homes of relatives in Virginia, North Carolina, and Georgia; reared their children; and managed the family properties. Because Clement was determined that the family be out of debt by the end of the war, Allie worked tirelessly to sell the house. Their marriage was obviously strong and their relationship affectionate, but seriocomic marital tiffs appear in several letters. On one occasion Clement sent home a trunk of "surplus baggage" which contained Allie's picture. Allie was piqued that he considered her picture "surplus baggage." Clement refused to apologize, and the two bantered the issue for several months. The couple's letters always included news about their two children. And they commented favorably on their few slaves, one of whom was Clement's trusted and patriotic manservant. The editor describes Clement's service between December 1864 and the surrender at Appomattox. After the war Clement became a minister with the Methodist Episcopal Church, fulfilling a vow he had made at Fredericksburg, and he edited the twelve-volume *Confederate Military History . . .* (Atlanta: Confederate Publishing Co., 1899).

357. FARRIS, JOHN KENNERLY, SR. "A Confederate Surgeon's View of Fort Donelson: The Diary of John Kennerly Farris." Edited by Jim Stanbery. *Civil War Regiments* 1, no. 3 (1991): 7–19.

February 13–16, 1862. Diary. Forty-first Tennessee Infantry. Battle of Fort Donelson. In addition to a description of the battle, evacuation, and surrender, Farris also related his treatment of the wounded.

358. **FIELDER, ALFRED TYLER.** *The Civil War Diaries of Capt. Alfred Tyler Fielder, 12th Tennessee Regiment Infantry, Company B, 1861–1865.* Compiled by Ann York Franklin. Louisville, Ky.: Ann York Franklin, 1996. 279 pp.

July 23, 1861–June 18, 1865. Diary. Captain. Twelfth Tennessee Infantry. Belmont; Shiloh; siege of Corinth; Smith's invasion of Kentucky, including the battle of Richmond; Perryville; Stones River; Chickamauga; siege of Chattanooga; Missionary Ridge; the Atlanta campaign, including Kennesaw Mountain, Peachtree Creek, and the battle of Atlanta; and duty in Mississippi, Georgia, and North Carolina. Persistent themes in the diary of this forty-seven-year-old (in 1861) farmer from Dyer County, Tennessee, are his unswerving devotion to God and constant defense of the Confederacy's unspecified rights. Fielder usually wrote without emotion, but he recorded Sunday prayer meetings (including the religious conversions during the summer of 1863) and battle experiences with intensity. At both Missionary Ridge and during the battle for Atlanta, Fielder was wounded and sent to North Carolina to recuperate. At a train station en route to North Carolina during his second period of recuperation, Fielder met an "old gentleman" named "Edward Ruffin" who "told me that he fired the first gun at the taking of Ft. Sumter from the federals" (p. 156). During his last six months of service Fielder moved between Mississippi, Georgia, and North Carolina. Paroled near Greensboro, North Carolina, on May 3, 1865, Fielder spent three weeks traveling home; then he immediately began cutting hay. Appended are lists of clothing (with prices) that Fielder distributed in his official capacity and genealogical charts.

359. **FIGURES, HENRY S.** "Henry S. Figures: Letters Relating to the Battle of Gettysburg." By Ralph G. Poriss. *Manuscripts* 43 (Summer 1991): 207–14.

June 21–July 18, 1863. Letters. Forty-eighth Alabama Infantry. Gettysburg campaign. These letters describe Lee's movement from Culpepper, Virginia, to Gettysburg; the foraging of the Confederate army; his regiment's attempt to take Little Round Top; a frightened group of women and children huddled in a house; and Lee's retreat into Virginia. Figures calls Little Round Top "the steepest place I ever saw in my life" (p. 211). He wrote that when the Confederate army moved back south to Downsville, Maryland, it built breastworks near the Potomac and awaited the Union attack. But when the Union army appeared, it also built fortifications and waited. While Figures did not enjoy the trip to Gettysburg "like some did," he was especially proud that he had not taken any civilian possessions (p. 212). Union troops had earlier mistreated his home in Huntsville, Alabama, and he did not want to feel guilty of the same actions.

360. **FLEET, CHARLES B.** "The Fredericksburg Artillery at Appomattox." Edited by Chris Calkins. *Civil War Regiments* 1, no. 1 (1990): 35–41.

Fall 1864–April 1865. Memoir. Sergeant. Appomattox Court House. Fredericksburg Battery, Virginia Light Artillery. Fleet wrote that his unit fired the last artillery shot of the war the morning of April 9. The editor views this statement as controversial and cites the claims of other Confederate units who believed that they had fired the last shot.

361. **FORD, RICHARD WATSON.** "'I Fear . . . We Must Go Up': With a Confederate Inside Port Hudson." Edited by Russell Surles. *Civil War Times Illustrated* 25 (February 1987): 30–39.

May 21–July 15, 1863. Diary. Lieutenant. Seventh Texas Infantry. Siege of Port Hudson. Ford noted the fraternization and kindness of the Yankee soldiers following the surrender and the fact that the enlisted men were paroled and allowed to return to Confederate lines. He characterized the Union assault on May 27, made by the black troops, as being so ineffectual that it was amusing.

362. FORSGARD, GUSTAV A. "The Gustav A. Forsgard Diaries." By Doris Glasser. *Houston Review* 14, no. 1 (1992): 2–65.
January 1, 1860–April 2, 1863. Diary. Hargrove's Company, Texas Cavalry. The entries of this Swedish immigrant's diary for 1860 concern social and business matters in Houston, as well as impressions of his travel in eastern and central Texas. The diary pages for 1861 are missing. Forsgard's military service began in May 1862. He joined Hargrove's Cavalry Company in the belief that he would be attached to the Fifth Texas Cavalry in Virginia. Forsgard chaffed when he was stationed in central Texas. In one diary entry he sarcastically describes the repetition of boring activities during a typical day of camp life. The Confederate problems with the Unionist German population of the region reached their peak in January and February 1863. Forsgard regarded one unspecified "Dutch hunt" to be a "black spot in the future of a free people" (p. 57). In March 1863, following his transfer to the signal corps and move to Galveston, it is clear that he became a much happier soldier. Forsgard's diary ends with a lament that the girl he thought loved him, alas, did not.

363. FOWLER, JOHN D. "Fowler the Soldier, Fowler the Marine." Edited by David M. Sullivan. *Civil War Times Illustrated* 26 (February 1988): 28–35, 44–45.
August 17, 1861–July 7, 1863. Private, Fourth Alabama Infantry; then, Second Lieutenant, Confederate States Marines. First Bull Run and duty at Gosport Navy Yard (Norfolk, Virginia).

364. FROST, GRIFFIN. *Camp and Prison Journal.* Introduction by W. Clark Kenton. Iowa City, Iowa: Camp Pope Bookshop, 1994. 315 pp.
1861–1865. Diary. Service with several unidentified Missouri Home Guard units. Battles of Lexington, Pea Ridge, and Helena; and recruiting duty in northern Arkansas, where he was captured twice. Frost spent his first captivity in Gratiot Street Prison in Saint Louis from December 1862 through April 1863, when he was paroled. He returned to Arkansas and was recruiting in Missouri when he was captured in October 1863. Frost spent the rest of the war alternately at Gratiot Street Prison, in Alton Prison, and finally again at Gratiot. During his imprisonment he wrote sections of a diary and smuggled them out with the help of his wife. The diary had evolved into a book by 1867. In his preface Frost says that he had hoped to counter Union charges of the atrocious conditions in Confederate prisons with his own experiences in Union prisons. To substantiate his case Frost appended accounts of the Union prisons at Camp Morton and Camp Douglas written by others. The editor says that Frost fell far short of his goal; in fact, Frost's experiences seemed luxurious compared to the worst Confederate prisons. Frost wrote in an entertaining manner, often exhibiting a sarcastic wit. However, he did document conditions within the two prisons. And his descriptions of rustic social conventions in Arkansas portray the people of the region. Originally published: Quincy, Ill.: Quincy Herald Book and Job Office, 1867. The editor adds that because of a fire at the print shop, 650 of the 700 copies printed were destroyed.

365. GAREY, JOSEPH. *A Keystone Rebel: The Civil War Diary of Joseph Garey Hudson's Battery, Mississippi Volunteers.* Edited by David A. Welker. Gettysburg, Pa.: Thomas Publications, 1996. 113 pp.
July 23, 1861–August 12, 1867. Diary. Private. Mississippi Light Artillery, Hudson's (Pettus') Flying Artillery Battery. Duty near New Madrid, Camp Beauregard, Bowling Green, and Nashville, and the battle of Shiloh, and the siege of Corinth. Nearly all of this diary was written between July 23, 1861, and June 18, 1862. Garey recorded the routine of camp life and repeated what he had heard about the battles of Belmont, Logan's Cross Roads, and Forts Henry and Donelson. He exclaimed his patriotic defiance and waited. The battery's first battle was at Shiloh. Although Garey's entries are brief, the editor says that they are valuable because no detailed record for Hudson's Battery at Shiloh exists in the

Official Records. Also, Garey's single-page entry on July 28, 1862, is the most complete record of the battery's movements between the evacuation of Corinth and the siege of Vicksburg. Garey was paroled at Vicksburg and returned home to Cockrum, Mississippi. When he attempted to rejoin the battery in January 1864, he found that it had been redeployed. He returned to his parents' home in Pennsylvania for the duration and later moved to Tennessee. Three letters written after the war bemoan the loss of the Confederacy and the unsettled conditions in Tennessee.

366. GARNETT, THEODORE SANFORD. *Riding with Stuart: Reminiscences of an Aide-de-Camp.* Edited by Robert J. Trout. Shippensburg, Pa.: White Mane Publishing Co., 1995. 124 pp.

October 1863–July 1864. Memoir. Captain. Stuart's Cavalry Corps, Army of Northern Virginia. The Mine Run campaign; winter encampment at Orange Court House; the Kilpatrick-Dahlgren raid on Richmond; The Wilderness; Spotsylvania; Sheridan's Richmond Raid; Yellow Tavern; and the Wilson-Kautz raid on Petersburg. Garnett had served eighteen months as a clerk in the office of the secretary of the navy when he was assigned to Stuart in May 1863. Garnett's memoir, often rewritten between 1871 and 1913, recounts anecdotes of battles, details of winter encampment at "The Wigwam," and his duties as Stuart's aide, and it comments about Stuart's personality. The editor emphasizes that the primary importance of Garnett's account lies in the fact that Stuart's other contemporaries neglected to write about this later period. Additional information about Stuart is contained in an address presented by Garnett in 1907 and in several official messages regarding Lee's instructions to Stuart prior to Gettysburg.

367. GILL, JOHN. *Courier for Lee and Jackson, 1861–1865: Memoirs.* Edited by Walbrook D. Swank. Shippensburg, Pa.: Burd Street Press, 1993. 78 pp.

April 1861–May 1865. Memoir. First Maryland Infantry and First Maryland Cavalry Battalion. First Bull Run, Jackson's Shenandoah Valley campaign; Stuart's Catlett's Station raid; second Bull Run; Gettysburg, including Lee's retreat; Grant's Virginia campaign; Yellow Tavern; Hawes' Shop, Trevilian Station; third Winchester (observed); and duty in the Shenandoah Valley with Mosby's raiders. Gill recounts his exploits as cavalryman and courier for Generals Stonewall Jackson and Fitzhugh Lee, and as bodyguard for Gen. Richard Ewell at Gettysburg. Sketchy details and brief but vivid incidents predominate. First published as *Reminiscences of Four Years as a Private Soldier in the Confederate Army, 1861–1865* (Baltimore, Md.: Sun Printing Office, 1904).

368. GORDON, JOHN B. "The Gordon-Barlow Story, with Sequel." Edited by John J. Pullen. *Gettysburg Magazine* 8 (January 1993): 5–7.

July 1–3, 1863. Brigadier General. Second Corps. Early's Division. Army of Northern Virginia. Battle of Gettysburg. This article is a reprinted portion of a lecture delivered by Gen. Gordon in Brooklyn, New York, on February 7, 1901. Gordon recounted his battlefield meeting with Union general Francis C. Barlow on the first day of Gettysburg. Assuming that Barlow was mortally wounded, Gordon gave him comfort and water. He also accepted a packet of letters written by Barlow's wife, which Gordon promised to return to her. Gordon said that during the night he aided her safe passage through Confederate lines to be with her husband. Barlow soon recuperated from his wound and believed that Gordon had later been killed. Some fifteen years later the two men—both believing the other to be dead—met accidentally at dinner with a mutual friend.

369. GOREE, THOMAS J. *Longstreet's Aide: The Civil War Letters of Major Thomas J. Goree.* Edited by Thomas W. Cutrer. Charlottesville: University Press of Virginia, 1995. 239 pp.

April 7, 1861–August 6, 1865. Letters. Major. Aide-de-camp to Gen. James Longstreet, First Corps, Army of Northern Virginia. Travel from Texas to Virginia in the company of Longstreet, Benjamin F. Terry, and others; Blackburn's Ford; first Bull Run; Dranesville (described); Seven Pines; Seven Days' Battles; the siege of Suffolk; Longstreet's eastern Tennessee campaign (described); duty around Richmond; and, after Appomattox, travel to Talledaga, Alabama, with Longstreet. Goree became one of Longstreet's aides just prior to first Bull Run and served in that position throughout the war. Goree's descriptions of the general in these letters are favorable. He describes Longstreet at Blackburn's Ford as riding among his men "Amid a perfect shower of balls . . . with his cigar in his mouth, rallying them" (p. 26). Goree wrote that Longstreet wanted to carry the Confederate victory at first Bull Run on to Washington but Jefferson Davis refused. Goree describes Longstreet as "low spirited" after he had lost three children to scarlet fever in February 1862. Goree remarks that while Longstreet was in Georgia recuperating from the wound he received during The Wilderness, everyone said that Lee needed Longstreet back in Virginia. He wrote: "Genl. Lee needs him not only to advise with, but Genl. Longstreet has a very suggestive mind and none of his other Lt. Genls. have this" (p. 126). When Longstreet returned to duty in late September 1864, Lee was pleased and the soldiers of the First Corps cheered. Goree remarks that Longstreet was grateful for the response, even though he knew he was "no favorite with the President & Bragg" (p. 137). Goree often criticizes Jefferson Davis, primarily for his favoritism, and other generals for battlefield losses. Goree wrote that when he returned to Richmond with Longstreet, morale was higher than he had been led to believe. Although Goree saw the much needed replacement soldiers arriving, he believed that the Confederacy should let the slaves fight: "We had better free the negroes to gain our independence than be subjugated and lose slaves, liberty, and all that makes life dear" (p. 137). Many of Goree's letters to his mother and sister in Texas contain information about friends and other relatives, and especially the health and well-being of his two brothers. Also included is postwar correspondence between Goree and Longstreet, E. Porter Alexander, and G. Moxley Sorrel. Some touch on aspects of battles not included in the wartime letters, such as on the third day at Gettysburg and Gen. Custer's demand that Longstreet surrender at Appomattox.

370. GORGAS, JOSIAH. *The Journals of Josiah Gorgas, 1857–1878.* Edited by Sarah Woolfolk Wiggins. Foreword by Frank E. Vandiver. Tuscaloosa: University of Alabama Press, 1995. 305 pp.

January 1, 1857–July 1, 1878. Journals. Brigadier General. Confederate States of America. Army. Chief of Ordnance. Gorgas, a career ordnance officer from Pennsylvania, married Amelia Gayle in 1853 while serving near Mobile, Alabama. When offered a commission in the Confederate army, he accepted, "being much urged by my own sympathies & likings, & importuned by my Southern friends" (p. 37), as he put it. While Gorgas's abilities to garner and distribute the meager Confederate supply of ordnance are widely acknowledged, unfortunately his journals provide few insights into those accomplishments. However, he does mention all types of materials, supplies, and manpower that were vital to the war effort. On April 8, 1864, he expressed pride in the Confederacy's progress toward achieving self-sufficiency in the production of ordnance. Gorgas also documented the importance of blockade-running when he wrote about the Bermuda to Wilmington run: "This is our chief source of supply for arms, and we get our steel, tin, zinc, & various other articles wholly in this way" (p. 77). Throughout the war Gorgas recorded the public mood of Richmond: the widespread apprehension whenever Yankee raids were thought to threaten the city; the "bread riots" (although he did not really think the populace was suffering); and in the end, how "Every body is dumbstruck at the proximate evacuation of Richmond" (p. 153). Gorgas was critical of all Confederate cabinet members. His comments about President Jefferson Davis vary. At no time did Gorgas think Davis was capable of devising campaigns. In June 1863 Gorgas noted: "Our President is no military genius" (p. 43). On January 6, 1865, Gorgas recorded what he said he had feared for two years: "There is no master at the helm? When I see the President trifle away precious hours & idle discussion & discursive comment, I feel as tho' he is not equal to his task. And yet where could we get a better or wiser man? Where, indeed!" (p. 148). During the spring of 1865 Gorgas portrayed Robert E. Lee as the bastion of hope for the defense of Richmond, but at other times he considered him "inactive." After the war, on April 9, 1867, Gorgas wrote, "How little we are disposed to criticize Gen. Lee," and he expressed his belief that "Gen. Lee fell short of his reputation" (p. 208). The welfare of Gorgas's wife and six children was always on his mind. When Richmond was evacuated, the family members were separated. Amelia moved to Maryland for safety, and Gorgas followed the trail of Jefferson Davis's retreat into North Carolina before heading westward to Alabama. In the years following the war Gorgas wrote that he was considered a "traitor," and he felt as though he were "walking in a dream" as he observed planters forced to ask the Freedmen's Bureau what they could or could not do with their former slaves. He also observed that uneducated blacks were allowed to vote. He wondered: "Is it possible that we were wrong?" (p. 186). For thirteen years after the war Gorgas continued to record his less-than-successful civilian life as a businessman and educator. The editor summarizes the final five years of his life. She also explores the mystery of defaced sections of the manuscripts and restored passages that were omitted in *The Civil War Diary of General Josiah Gorgas,* edited by Frank E. Vandiver (Tuscaloosa: University of Alabama Press, 1947).

371. GRAYSON, GEORGE WASHINGTON. *A Creek Warrior for the Confederacy: The Autobiography of Chief G. W. Grayson.* Edited, with an introduction, by W. David Baird. Norman: University of Oklahoma Press, 1988. 181 pp.
1862–1865. Memoir. Captain. Second Creek Indian Regiment (C.S.A.) Duty in Indian Territory, including Honey Springs, the capture of the steamer *J. R. Williams,* Flat Rock Creek, and Cabin Creek. Grayson covers his life from birth until around 1910, the time of his writing. The editor points out that this work must be read with an appreciation of Creek history, especially the animosity that existed between the full-blood and mixed-blood (métis) Creeks. The editor provides this information in his introduction. Grayson was a métis. Grayson, who had difficulty recalling dates and the correct sequence of events, claims that he joined the Second Creek Regiment about a year after the war began. (The editor believes it was in late 1862 or early 1863.) He initially wrote that he enlisted because "the pride of my manhood had been ruffled by the criticisms," but he later confessed that as a young man he enjoyed the action and excitement (p. 66). Battles and raids constitute the bulk of his memoirs, and he often included details about the performances of the Indian troops. He recalled a stirring speech by his colonel prior to the battle at Honey Creek but admitted to being disappointed when his company was held in reserve. After the battle, as the Confederate army retreated, he was able to follow his family, who, along with Cherokee civilians, were fleeing the Union army. After the Union steamer *J. R. Williams* was captured, he described how the Indian troops reveled in trading their plunder. The Confederate troops were ordered to evacuate their position, and the Indians were directed to protect the withdrawal. However, because Grayson was unable to convince his men to perform the rear-guard duty, he stood guard alone. Disappointed, he wrote: "I was sorry and ashamed of my Creek soldiers" (p. 85). At the battle of Flat Rock Creek, the raid on a Union haying camp resulted in the slaughter of federal colored troops. Grayson wrote that the bloodshed was sickening to him. He recalled that "the men were like wild beasts and I was powerless to stop them from this unnecessary butchery" (p. 96). But he did stop them from killing a white soldier and explained: "it was negroes that we were killing now, not white men" (p. 96). He related how the prisoners were stripped of their clothes after the successful raid on the Union supply wagon at Cabin Creek, and he explained how poorly clad the Confederates were late in the war. In February 1865 Grayson was stricken with smallpox; he was cared for by his mother during the last few months of the war. In the remainder of this work Grayson recounts his valuable contributions to Creek governmental affairs during the years following the war.

372. GRIFFIN, JAMES B. *"A Gentleman and an Officer": A Military and Social History of James B. Griffin's Civil War.* By Judith N. McArthur and Orville Vernon Burton. New York: Oxford University Press, 1996. 362 pp.

April 14, 1861–February 27, 1865. Letters. Major and Lieutenant Colonel, Hampton's South Carolina Legion; Lieutenant Colonel, Fifth South Carolina Reserves; and Colonel, First South Carolina State Troops. During the first year of the war Griffin was in Virginia with Hampton's Legion (cavalry and infantry) and fought during the Peninsular campaign, especially at Eltham's Landing and Seven Pines. During the fall and winter of 1862 and 1863 he served along the South Carolina coastal defenses. From the fall of 1864 through the end of the war he served at several places in South Carolina. In the eighty-one-page first chapter the editors indicate why their treatment of Griffin's eighty letters to his wife, Leila, constitutes a "military and social history." Griffin was one of the "large planters" (he owned sixty-one slaves) in South Carolina's Edgefield District, the state's leading cotton-producing district. In June 1861 he was thirty-five years old and had seven children, a pregnant wife, and many friends and acquaintances of the aristocratic class. Griffin's letters contain inferences of "changes and experiences in the lives of the people of Edgefield" and "frame the people that Griffin wrote about in the precise socio-economic structure of the Edgefield District" (p. 4). Also, Griffin's experiences and attitudes present a case study of the Southern male gentry. Griffin regarded his obligations and responsibilities—as planter, slave owner, local leader, husband and father, and defender of the Confederacy—all to be contributions to a unified community. Griffin's letters, most of which were written from Virginia, are filled with expressions of endearment for his children and wife, as well as practical advice on how she should run the plantation and manage the slaves. The patriarchal Griffin did not worry about the boys; he felt that they could take care of themselves. On the other hand, he wrote that "Females are very dependent" (p. 163). After Griffin's mansion burned to the ground in late 1864, he felt powerless to control his community of family and slaves because he was unable to leave the army. He wrote: "My darling I am almost crazy about your condition . . . but you are thrown upon your own resources and you must do the best you can" (pp. 281–82). While he was in Virginia, Griffin asked Leila to tell the slaves "Howdy" for him. When the shortage of meat necessitated that the slaves' rations of bacon be reduced, he advised her simply to explain the situation to them. "Talk to them reasonably in this way" and "Tell them remember what I am going through. And what the country is now suffering" (p. 187). While he expected them to understand, he added that he also expected them to "submit without a murmur." Later, as Sherman was thought to be headed for Edgefield, he advised Leila on the role the slaves should play in dispersing the valuables on the property. However, he knew some slaves would leave. He asked Leila to "Tell the negroes they can go if they choose, of course—but to remember they will always regret it" (p. 291). In mid June 1862 Griffin returned to South Carolina, where he drilled troops and served two tours of duty in state service. After the war the combination of the fire on his plantation, debts, and the loss of slave labor left Griffin without means of support. In the concluding chapter the editors reveal that within a year Griffin had migrated to Texas. He later became a successful brick maker and patriarch of a different kind of community. Thus, the editors conclude, Griffin "had removed himself from his old community of Edgefield both physically and psychologically" (p. 325). This interesting work is replete with documentation and evidence of the editors' prodigious research in social, economic, and military resources.

373. **GUERRANT, EDWARD O.** "Diary of Edward O. Guerrant Covering the June 1864 Kentucky Raid of General John Hunt Morgan." Edited by Edward O. Guerrant. *Register of the Kentucky Historical Society* 85 (Autumn 1987): 322–58.

May–June 1864. Diary. Captain. First Brigade, Morgan's Cavalry Division, Department of Southwestern Virginia. This work includes details of Morgan's raids on Lexington and Cynthiana, Kentucky.

374. **GULLEDGE, SAMUEL BLACKWELL.** *Letters to Lauretta, 1849–1863 from Darlington, SC and a Confederate Soldier's Camp.* Edited by W. Joseph Bray Jr. and Jerome J. Hale. Bowie, Md.: Heritage Books, 1993. 339 pp.

May 17, 1861–June 11, 1863. Letters. Thirteenth Mississippi Infantry. Organization of regiment; and duty in Union City, Tennessee, and in Virginia, including battles of Ball's Bluff, the Seven Days' Battles, second Bull Run, Fredericksburg, and Chancellorsville. Samuel initially intended to serve out his twelve months, go back home, and attend school. He assured his parents: "Now I don't want to trouble your minds for I have got my belly full of soldering" (p. 173). When Samuel was conscripted by the Confederate government, he initially objected, but he accepted the situation out of patriotism. Samuel included himself among those who "will spill the last drop of blood in their veins before they will Submit to the Federal Government" (p. 176). He continued with, "I would rather die the Death of a brave and truehearted Southern Soldier than to see my Country trodden down by the Northern invader" (p. 176). Samuel's letters to his mother are those of a dutiful son. He worried that something was wrong at home when her letters were delayed. He wanted her to know that he was attending the Methodist religious revivals, which by April 2, 1863, had extended to six weeks. He was filled with pride when he presented his mother with the reality that he was "a faithful soldier of Christ as well as of my country" (p. 199). Letters describing his death at Gettysburg are also included. This book consists of letters written to Lauretta (McBride) Gulledge of Jasper County, Mississippi, by her niece, Elizabeth (Blackwell) Pettigrew of Darlington, South Carolina, in addition to the Civil War letters by Lauretta's son, Samuel. Family group sheets and other genealogical materials, as well as several other letters, are included.

375. HAIRSTON, PETER W. "The Civil War Diary of Peter W. Hairston, Volunteer Aide to Major General Jubal A. Early, November 7–December 4, 1863." Edited by Everard H. Smith. *North Carolina Historical Review* 67 (January 1990): 59–86.

November 7–December 4, 1863. Diary. Civilian volunteer aide to Early's Division, Ewell's Second Corps, Army of Northern Virginia. Battles of Rappahannock Station and the Mine Run campaign. Among Hairston's entries are observations of his generals. Robert E. Lee had the ability to convince the North Carolina soldiers, without offending them, to obey his wishes. Richard S. Ewell suffered from physical and emotional deterioration during this period, and Jubal Early's personality amused Hairston. Hairston also noted opposition to war within North Carolina.

376. HALL, LUCIEN. "Prison Sketchbook: Written on Johnson's Island—Ohio 1865." (Part I) *Northern Neck of Virginia Historical Magazine* 42 (December 1992): 4834–50.

————. (Part II) *Northern Neck of Virginia Historical Magazine* 43 (December 1993): 4988–5006.

March–June 18, 1865. Memoir. Lieutenant. Ninth Virginia Cavalry. Appomattox campaign, including Five Forks and Sayler's Creek, where he was captured and sent to Washington's Old Capitol Prison and then Johnson's Island. In later writings from his "enlarged" diary, Hall describes battles and skirmishes that occurred during the few days preceding his capture. He also relates details of the hard march to City Point and shipment to Old Capitol Prison. Hall was among the prisoners being held in Washington when Lincoln was assassinated and whose lives were threatened by a vengeful mob. No description of life inside Johnson's Island is included.

377. HIRSCH, HERRMANN. "Herrmann Hirsch and the Siege of Jackson." By Michael B. Dougan. *Journal of Mississippi History* 53 (February 1991): 19–33.

Summer 1863. Letters. Private. Third Florida Infantry. These letters relate events of the period when Jackson, Mississippi, changed hands several times.

378. HOLLIS, ELISHA TOMPKIN. "The Diary of Captain Elisha Tompkin Hollis." Introduction by William W. Chester. *West Tennessee Historical Society Papers* 39 (1985): 83–118.

January 1, 1864–February 12, 1865. Diary. Captain. Twentieth Tennessee Cavalry. Okolona; Fort Anderson (Paducah, Ky.); Fort Pillow; Brice's Cross Roads; Tupelo; Memphis; and Athens, Alabama. Hollis's terse entries document Nathan Bedford Forrest's constant movement during this period.

379. HOLT, DAVID. *A Mississippi Rebel in the Army of Northern Virginia: The Civil War Memoirs of Private David Holt.* Edited by Thomas D. Cockrell and Michael B. Ballard. Baton Rouge: Louisiana State University Press, 1995. 354 pp.

1856–December 1864. Memoir. Private. Sixteenth Mississippi Infantry. Jackson's Shenandoah Valley campaign; the Seven Days' Battles; Fredericksburg; Chancellorsville; Gettysburg, including Lee's retreat; the Bristoe campaign; the Mine Run campaign; The Wilderness; Spotsylvania; North Anna River; Cold Harbor; and the Petersburg campaign, including Deep Bottom Run. Captured at Globe Tavern, Holt was sent to Point Lookout Prison and exchanged in December 1864. Holt, who wrote these memoirs around 1920, devotes the first fifty-eight pages of this work to his childhood life on a plantation in Wilkinson County, Mississippi. Early in his service Holt was initiated into the different ways soldiers reacted to adversity. A train wreck had damaged a bridge, forcing the men to get out, wade across a river, and march in mud while carrying their rain-soaked gear. Holt wrote: "Some bore the mishap with fortitude and silence; others cursed and did nothing to help us get on our way" (p. 68). Holt presents an incident at Chancellorsville as evidence of the Confederate soldiers' "grit, endurance, and wit." A soldier whose arm had been amputated was led away on the back of an ox. The soldiers cheered because the man was "playing 'old Stonewall'" (p. 167). Holt also related several ways soldiers reacted to fear. He remembered that at Fredericksburg, on night guard duty: "The baby feeling comes and some are tempted to cry, 'Oh, momma. I want my momma.' Some of our feelings never grow up" (p. 144). He wrote again later of night duty: "The silence was oppressive" (p. 147). And at Spotsylvania it was fear that caused a soldier to "lose heart" in the face of a Union charge. When the man raised a white flag, the other soldiers yelled "shoot him," and a comrade promptly complied. Holt understood the circumstances and wrote: "He was a good soldier, but allowed himself to be overcome by the horror of the situation" (p. 260). Several postwar themes that creep into Holt's memoirs are his opposition to Gen. James Longstreet, defense of the South's treatment of Union prisoners at Andersonville, and an absence of rancor toward Union soldiers.

380. HOLT, JOHN LEE. *I Wrote You Word: The Poignant Letters of Private Holt, John Lee Holt, 1829–1863.* Edited by James A. Mumper. Lynchburg, Va.: H. E. Howard, Inc., 1993. 158 pp.

July 19, 1861–June 30, 1863. Letters. Private. Fifty-sixth Virginia Infantry. Enlistment and organization in Richmond; Fort Donelson; duty in Abbington, Virginia, and Bowling Green, Kentucky; hospitalized in Atlanta; duty at Chaffin's Bluff; the Seven Days' Battles; the Antietam campaign; hospitalized in Winchester, Staunton, and Richmond (where he was deemed unfit for duty); Fredericksburg; duty in North Carolina; and the Gettysburg campaign. Holt was a tobacco grower and schoolmaster from Campbell County, Virginia, who felt that he had to leave his pregnant wife and one son because it was his duty to prevent invasion of his country by a ruthless and tyrannical foe who sought destruction and confiscation of the South. He called the Union government "vandals" and pleaded with Southerners to respond to "the great Patrick Henry in the days of ''76 & say give me Liberty or give me death" (p. 79). Despite his patriotism, nearly every letter is filled with heartrending expressions of his desire to be back home with his family. He longed for the time when "peace and tranquillity is restored to our beloved South" (p. 47). Holt told his wife about the locations where he was serving and the general conditions of the soldiers, but he always skimmed over the fighting. He related how his regiment was removed from Fort Donelson just before its surrender. He also described how he pulled his wounded brother to safety at Turner's Gap at the battle of South Mountain and then remained with him in a hospital at Winchester. Holt was killed in Pickett's Charge.

381. HOWARD, CHARLES MALONE. "A Letter from Fort Gaines." *Gulf Coast Historical Review* 2, no. 1 (1986): 71–78.
April 6, 1862. Letter. Fort Gaines, Alabama. A doctor serving a ninety-day enlistment related his adjustment to military life to his wife. He described the fort and requested food, lighter-weight clothing, and Nelson (a slave).

382. HOWELL, WILLIAM RANDOLPH. *Westward the Texans: The Civil War Journal of Private William Randolph Howell.* Edited, with an introduction, by Jerry D. Thompson. El Paso: Texas Western Press, 1990. 184 pp.
April 30, 1861–July 15, 1862. Journal. Private. Fifth Texas Cavalry. Sibley's New Mexico campaign, including Valverde and Glorieta Pass. Howell did not participate in either battle; he guarded a wagon train at Valverde and assisted a sick friend in Albuquerque during Glorieta. His brief entries are a record of the details of the march, especially the hardships Confederate soldiers endured during the retreat back to San Antonio. Howell kept a record of miles traveled, the topography and flora and fauna of the region, and the health of the troops. The editor's essays and notes provide an overview of Sibley's campaign, the historiography of campaign, and an overview of accounts written by other participants.

383. HUDGINS, ROBERT S., II. *Recollections of an Old Dominion Dragoon: The Civil War Experiences of Sgt. Robert S. Hudgins II, Company B, 3rd Virginia Cavalry.* Edited by Garland C. Hudgins and Richard B. Kleese. Orange, Va.: Publisher's Press, 1993. 127 pp.
1861–1870. Memoir. Sergeant. Third Virginia Cavalry. Big Bethel; Magruder's burning of Hampton, Virginia; the duel between the USS *Monitor* and the CSS *Virginia* (observed); Stuart's first ride around McClellan; the Seven Days' Battles; Malvern Hill; Kelly's Ford; Chancellorsville; Brandy Station; Aldie; Stuart's Gettysburg raid; Lee's retreat to Virginia; Yellow Tavern; the evacuation of Richmond; and the surrender. Except for mentioning several grand dances and balls, Hudgins's anecdotes pertain to military events. He recalls J. E. B. Stuart's popularity and wonderful singing voice. He praises other officers of Stuart's entourage, such as John Pelham and Heros von Borcke. Hudgins, who was nearby when Stonewall Jackson was shot, believed that the cause of Jackson's death was pneumonia contracted on the rainy night before Jackson was shot. A year later Hudgins observed J. E. B. Stuart's fatal wounding. Hudgins described the grand cavalry review at Brandy Station on June 6, 1863. After participating in Stuart's ride into Pennsylvania, Hudgins praised the appearance of the inhabitants of that state and wrote that he obeyed Lee's order not to pillage the region. At the end of the war Hudgins described the conditions in Richmond as it was being evacuated. In Hudgins's final chapter he relates his return to "Lambington" (near Hampton) and how he reclaimed his farm from scalawags and liberated slaves. The months of July 1862 to March 1863 and May 1864 to March 1865 are not covered in Hudgins's memoir, although he refers to events that occurred during those periods.

384. JACKMAN, JOHN S. *Diary of a Confederate Soldier: John S. Jackman of the Orphan Brigade.* Edited by William C. Davis. Columbia: University of South Carolina Press, 1990. 174 pp.

September 26, 1861–May 30, 1865. Diary. Fifth (then Ninth) Kentucky Infantry. Shiloh; the siege of Corinth; the bombardment of Vicksburg in 1862; duty in Louisiana and Mississippi; Stones River; the siege of Jackson; Chickamauga; Chattanooga; the Atlanta campaign, including Rocky Face Ridge, Resaca, and New Hope Church; and duty in Georgia during 1865. The editor explains in his introduction that Jackman was frequently ill and often served as brigade clerk. Jackman's entries about service with the "Orphan Brigade" are enhanced with anecdotes. At Shiloh, as "surgeon, pro tempore," he used his chloroform-soaked handkerchief to sedate the patients and became dizzy himself (p. 31). At Corinth he watched as the infirmary corps followed the regiments into battle, the corpsmen bearing white litters which, he predicted, would soon be stained with human gore. Jackman recounted how a group of men in a hospital listened intently until a dying man took his last breath. Then one soldier remarked with solemnity, "He never will draw another breath as long as he lives" (pp. 36–37), a dramatic utterance that caused the men to laugh. As Jackman observed the sun reflecting off thousands of polished guns, he likened the scene to "a tide of metal flowing on by the green fields" (p. 45). In September and October 1862 Jackman mentioned a mutiny within the brigade over whether the "C.S. Government" had the right to conscript them (p. 57). During winter camp at Dalton in 1864, Jackman described the snowball fight of March 22, 1864, as well as the numerous religious revivals. On June 14, 1864, the same Union battery that had killed Gen. Leonidas Polk also hit Jackman with a shell fragment. Jackman did not rejoin the brigade until December. At the end of the war Jackman was ordered to transport the brigade archives to Washington, Georgia, and was present in Washington when Jefferson Davis arrived. Jackman watched as Davis and the cabinet separated. He exclaimed with finality: "and the Confederate government ceased to exist" (p. 167). His last entries record his journey back to his home in Bardstown, Kentucky.

385. JOHNSTON, JOHN. "Reminiscences of the Battle of Nashville." Edited by Tim Burgess. *Journal of Confederate History* 1 (Summer 1988): 152–68.
December 15–16, 1864. Memoir. Private. Fourteenth Tennessee Cavalry. Battle of Nashville.

386. JONES, CHARLES COLCOCK, JR. "'I Am an Eyewitness': Evacuation Under Fire: Southerners Leave Fort Wagner." *Civil War Times Illustrated* 26 (January 1988): 38–40.
September 13, 1863. Major. Chatham Battery, Georgia Light Artillery. This article relates the evacuation of Battery Wagner (Morris Island), Charleston harbor.

387. JONES, WILLIAM. "Wounded & Captured at Gettysburg: Reminiscences by Sgt. William Jones, 50th Georgia Infantry." Edited by Keith Bohannon. *Military Images* 9 (May/June 1988): 14–15.
July–October 1863. Memoir. Sergeant. Gettysburg. Fiftieth Georgia Infantry. Jones left this explicit account of how he was cared for after being wounded at the Wheatfield. He lay on the field in the boiling sun until the night. After his foot was amputated, he was shipped by the Confederate ambulances as far as Williamsport, where he was left to be cared for by civilians. He was soon captured by Union troops, who transported him to a Union hospital at Chester, Pennsylvania, where Jones said he received good medical treatment. When the gangrene diminished, Jones was sent to Point Lookout Prison, and he was later paroled.

388. LAKE, LUTHER B. "I Kneeled Down and Kissed the Soil." Edited by Richard Andrew. *America's Civil War* 59 (December 1996): 66–70.
September 1863. Memoir. Eighth Virginia Infantry. Point Lookout Prison. Lake recounts his escape from the Maryland prison camp and the trek back into Virginia.

389. LANDERS, ELI PINSON. *Weep Not for Me Dear Mother.* Edited by Elizabeth Whitley Roberson. Washington, N.C.: Venture Press, 1991. 168 pp.

August 11, 1861–October 2, 1863. Letters. Sergeant. Sixteenth Georgia Infantry. The Peninsular campaign; Crampton's Gap; the Gettysburg campaign; and Chickamauga. Landers's first letters describe the regiment's travel from Augusta to Richmond and his reaction to the approximately thirteen thousand Confederate army troops encamped about the Confederate capital. Frequent drum rolls and fife music signaled training exercises by infantry and artillery units, and the many Union soldiers held prisoner added to the chaotic atmosphere. Landers often wrote of his devotion to "the Cause" and expressed a desire to show the world that the Confederacy was an "Independent Nation." He was also concerned about personal "honor." Landers had a keen eye for detecting differences in people. For example, he noted that the Union prisoners in Richmond were not the "Little people" the folks at home said they were, but rather "Big Devils." Most of his letters are to his widowed mother and his sister at home in Gwinnett County, Georgia. He shared with them details of camp life, the effects of sickness, and the results of battles, especially Malvern Hill. He continually worried about his mother and advised her how to handle affairs on the family farm. Her problems provide an indication of shortages on the Georgia home front. Another theme reveals that sick soldiers were sometimes placed in the homes of private citizens for recuperation, as Landers was during the fall of 1861. Landers briefly mentions the prostitution in Richmond, an activity in which he may have participated (p. 52). Landers died on October 27, 1863, in Rome, Georgia, from a "fever." Roberson's introduction relates the rescue of these letters from an Atlanta city dump to their eventual publication. The editor has published another version of these letters as *In Care of Yellow River: The Complete Civil War Letters of Pvt. Pinson Landers to His Mother* (Gretna, La.: Pelican Publishing Company, 1997).

390. LEUSCHNER, CHARLES A. *The Civil War Diary of Charles A. Leuschner.* Edited by Charles D. Spurlin. Austin, Tex.: Eakin Press, 1992. 120 pp.

May 8, 1864–June 15, 1865. Diary. Sergeant. Sixth Texas Infantry. Atlanta campaign and Franklin, where he was captured and imprisoned at Camp Douglas. Leuschner's terse entries written during the summer of 1864 describe the constant fighting. On April 15, 1865, he wrote one long paragraph about the wretched conditions at Camp Douglas and harsh treatment at the hands of the guards. One specific incident occurred when a prisoner cheered the news of Lincoln's assassination; the man was beaten and punished for two weeks. Leuschner wrote about his prison experiences with constrained bitterness: "I can never forget what I seen there" (p. 52). Released on May 1, 1865, he traveled back to Victoria, Texas. He concluded his diary with a lengthy entry full of anguish as he attempted to accept the reality of the Confederate defeat.

391. LIVAUDAIS, EDMOND ENOUL. *The Shiloh Diary of Edmond Enoul Livaudais.* Translated by Stanley J. Guerin. Edited by Earl C. Woods. New Orleans: Archdiocese of New Orleans, 1992. 59 pp.

March 18–April 29, 1862. Diary. Louisiana Infantry, Orleans Guards Battalion. Shiloh. This twenty-year-old Creole from New Orleans recorded his battalion's movement from New Orleans to Grand Junction, Tennessee, and then to Corinth. While encamped at Corinth, Livaudais related an incident of soldier humor. Common soldiers, dressed up as officers and priests, conducted a sham graveside ceremony with great solemnity. When the white sheet was pulled back, the "corpse" was revealed to be a pile of rotten, stinking beef. Livaudais wrote that on the first day Shiloh his unit was anxious to get into battle. While the men were devouring food the Union soldiers had abandoned, they were fired upon by Tennesseans. The Orleans Guards wore blue uniforms, and the Tennesseans mistook them for Yankees. Livaudais said that the next day they wore their jackets inside out. Throughout the account he mentions friends who were killed and describes the battlefield strewn with dead and wounded of both sides. On the second day of the battle he was nearby when Gen. Alfred Mouton was wounded. When the Confederates retreated to Corinth, Livaudais said that every house was filled with casualties. After five days of marching and fighting, he removed his shoes for the first time and found his feet so swollen that he was forced to go barefoot for the next eight days. In mid April the exhausted Livaudais became ill and was granted a medical leave to go home to New Orleans. After several delays he reached New Orleans just as it was being surrendered. A consistent theme of Livaudais's diary is his sense of comradeship with other Creoles, and especially their pride in Creole leaders such as Gen. Pierre G. T. Beauregard.

392. **LOUIS, DEOPOLD DANIEL.** "'Our Separation is Like Years': The Civil War Letters of Deopold Daniel Louis." Edited by Jason H. Silverman and Susan R. Murphy. *South Carolina Historical Magazine* 87 (July 1986): 141–47.

December 2, 1862–February 4, 1863. Letters. Eleventh South Carolina Infantry (Reserves). Duty at Pocotaligo, South Carolina. In this brief sequence of letters the forty-three-year-old Louis, a family man who owned a prosperous general store, seems to have been more concerned about affairs at home than his military responsibilities.

393. **MAGILL, ROBERT M.** *Personal Reminiscences of a Confederate Soldier Boy: Robert M. Magill, Co. F. 39th GA Reg. Inf.* Edited by Brenda D. Phillips. Milledgeville, Ga.: Boyd Publishing Co., 1993. 69 pp.

April 24, 1862–February 5, 1865. Memoir. Thirty-ninth Georgia Infantry. The Vicksburg campaign and siege (including Champion Hill); Lookout Mountain; Missionary Ridge; the Atlanta campaign (including the battles of Atlanta and Jonesboro); and Franklin and Nashville. Magill's entries are primarily a record of troop movements and reports of news about the war. In early 1864 he related the fun the men were having in winter quarters in northern Georgia. He told of the debating societies, singing groups, and a regimental snowball fight. He witnessed two executions during that same period. One man faced the firing squad for "leaving Company G of our regiment and joining Home Guards" (p. 46). During the same period he saw fourteen men of the Fifty-eighth North Carolina executed for desertion. He contemplated this extreme punishment with doubt: "Will this army prosper after such as this?" (p. 47). On September 26, 1864, he wrote of a visit by Jefferson Davis: "Jeff came at 11 a.m. Each regiment cheered him as he passed their colors. Pretty weak cheering. Some shouting Johnston. Give us Johnston again" (p. 56). On October 16 Magill met with a civilian friend who told him that "Hood's raid would ruin his army, and advised me to leave it" (p. 57). On January 1, 1865, Magill characterized morale after Hood's defeats in Tennessee: "Reported Jeff Davis dead. Great many glad to hear it. . . . Worst demoralized army it is possible to see. About two-thirds of them declare they are going home" (p. 64). Magill's final entries relate the march home through Alabama and Mississippi by his and other regiments.

394. **MCCLELEN, BAILEY GEORGE.** *I Saw the Elephant: The Civil War Experiences of Bailey George McClelen, Company D, 10th Alabama Infantry Regiment.* Edited by Norman E. Rourke. Shippensburg, Pa.: White Mane Publishers, 1995. 50 pp.

1861–1864. Memoir. Tenth Alabama Infantry. Enlistment, organization of the regiment, and shipment to Virginia; first Bull Run (aftermath); Dranesville; the Seven Days' Battles; second Bull Run (including aftermath); Antietam; Chancellorsville; and Gettysburg. McClelen recalled only episodes of his wartime experiences. En route to first Bull Run, his unit was prevented from reaching the battle by a conductor who purposely caused a collision. The man was arrested and tried, and he met with "summary punishment for the crime" (p. 16). Early on, McClelen and many others were stricken by measles, and when the army moved to Bristoe Station, the illnesses reoccurred. McClelen wrote: "Measles and brain fever were two uncompromising maladies. Our camp became a general field hospital" (p. 17). Then, during the winter of 1861–1862 pneumonia swept through the camps. At second Bull Run, McClelen received one of his two wartime wounds. He remembered that he and the other wounded were instructed to march back to Staunton, Virginia, a distance of ninety miles. On the second day of Gettysburg he was hit again and captured; he was paroled in September 1863. Throughout the memoir McClelen provided the names of men of the Tenth Alabama who were sick, injured, or killed.

395. MCKINNEY, WILLIAM FORTUNATUS. "The Camp Ford Diary of Captain William Fortunatus McKinney." Preface by Howard O. Pollan. Introduction and footnotes by Randal B. Gilbert. *Smith County Historical Society* 25 (Summer 1986): 15–25.
April 8–November 20, 1864. Diary. Captain. Nineteenth Kentucky Infantry. Camp Ford Prison. McKinney recorded his capture at the battle of Mansfield, the trek to Camp Ford Prison amid throngs of curious Texans, and events within the open stockade. During the period that McKinney was at Camp Ford, the population reached its peak number of inmates, some forty-six hundred, and most of the recent arrivals had already been robbed. The many rumors were favorable to the Confederacy but were usually false. The general food rations were poor, although molasses, sugar, and tobacco were available from the Confederates at exorbitant prices. McKinney's entries relate cold-blooded murders by prison guards and such punishments as standing on a stump (or a block) in the hot sun. Attempts to escape were frequent. One popular method involved concealment in the carts that carried the refuse and fecal matter from the camp. McKinney wrote that the Confederate guards were among those who ran away. The kindness of the wife of the commandant, Mrs. R. T. P. Allen, was appreciated by the prisoners. Paroled on October 23, 1863, McKinney embarked on an arduous trip back to Alexandria and freedom.

396. MCPHEETERS, WILLIAM MARCELLUS. "'I Acted from Principle': William Marcellus McPheeters, Confederate Surgeon." By Cynthia Dehaven Pitcock and Bill J. Gurley. *Missouri Historical Review* 89 (July 1995): 384–405.
June 1, 1863–July 16, 1865. Diary. Surgeon and Medical Director of the Confederate District of Arkansas. Missouri and Arkansas. The editors first summarize the persecution of this prominent pro-Confederate Saint Louis physician and then relate the specific reasons why the doctor left his family to serve with the Confederate army. McPheeters's entries include his preparation of medical facilities in anticipation of the battle of Helena; pleasure when he heard that Gen. Theophilus Holmes had been removed as commander of the Military District; participation in an organization of surgeons that met to discuss common problems and treatments; the battle of Jenkins' Ferry, including care and treatment of the wounded; and Price's Missouri raid, especially Mine Creek. By the end of 1864 McPheeters had become pessimistic about the success of the Confederacy. In February 1865, when he learned that his family had been banished from Saint Louis to exile in Arkansas, McPheeters left the army to join his wife and children. His final entries indicate continued belief in the correctness of the Confederate cause, but an equally persistent resolve to put the past behind him.

397. MARYE, JOHN L. "The First Gun at Gettysburg: 'With the Advance Guard.'" *Civil War Regiments* 1, no. 1 (1988): 26–34.
June–July 3, 1863. Memoir. Lieutenant. Fredericksburg Battery, Virginia Light Artillery. Battle of Gettysburg. This article first appeared in *The American Historical Register* 2 (1895): 1225–32.

398. MERRICK, MORGAN WOLFE. *From Desert to Bayou: The Civil War Journal and Sketches of Morgan Wolfe Merrick.* Introduction and notes by Jerry D. Thompson. El Paso: Texas Western Press, 1991. 135 pp.

February 1861–July 1863. Journal. Second and Third Texas Cavalries. Merrick describes the surrender of the federal forces of the Department of Texas at San Antonio while he was a member of the Knights of the Golden Circle. He served with the First Texas Cavalry and participated in Baylor's occupation of the Mesilla Valley during the spring and summer of 1861. The Confederate troops marched 435 miles along the San Antonio–El Paso Road to occupy Fort Davis. A later march from Fort Davis to Fort Bliss included the battles of Mesilla and San Augustin Pass and the occupation of Fort Fillmore. Writing in an anecdotal style, Merrick related soldier high jinks, accidents alongside the road, and observations of Indian rock paintings and the vegetation and wildlife. At Fort Davis he met Mescalero chiefs and recorded Indian customs. At Fort Fillmore he was appointed hospital steward. Between late 1861 and the spring of 1863 he saw duty in Louisiana. Thompson admits that many of the events Merrick depicted during June and July 1863 are "confused and chronologically incorrect" (p. 116). He suggests that later portions of Merrick's writings were from his original manuscript, whereas the more polished earlier portion about the Southwest had been rewritten. Approximately one-half of his forty-four pen-and-ink sketches illustrate structures, places, events, and people in the Southwest, including a portrait of the Mescalero chief Espejo. The Louisiana sketches are of battles and camp life.

399. MOORE, WILLIAM H. "Writing Home to Talladega." *Civil War Times Illustrated* 29 (November/December 1990): 56, 71–74, 76–78.

September 29, 1863–August 1, 1864. Letters. Lieutenant. Twenty-fifth Alabama Infantry. Chickamauga and Missionary Ridge. Moore related battle scenes and camp experiences to his lady friend. He commented that the men felt disappointment when they returned home on leave only to find that they had been forgotten by those they believed they had been defending. When Moore returned to Alabama on leave, he personally experienced this phenomenon. His old friends and acquaintances "seemed most indifferent to me" (p. 84). He blamed his own vanity for expecting too much from them.

400. MOSES, RAPHAEL JACOB. *Last Order of the Last Cause: The Civil War Memoirs of a Jewish Family from the "Old South."* Compiled, edited, and expanded by Mel Young. Lanham, Md.: University Press of America, 1995. 352 pp.

1861–1865. Memoir. Major. Chief Commissary Officer, First Corps, Army of Northern Virginia, and Commissary General, State of Georgia. The Civil War portion of this work consists of excerpts from Moses's memoirs and official reports and brief diaries of other family members. They are integrated with historical narrative by the editor. In writings from the 1890s Moses recounts how his duties with the commissary contributed to military actions. He informs readers that the purpose for Longstreet's siege of Suffolk was to provide a shield for the commissary so that it might gather supplies for the soldiers fighting at Chancellorsville. Moses explains that Lee's army slowed its approach to Gettysburg by one vital day because it needed to wait near Cashtown for Gen. Ewell's supply train to pass. Moses reveals that during Longstreet's East Tennessee campaign, only about one-half of the supply trains that left Virginia actually reached Longstreet's corps in Tennessee. Although Tennessee was poor of forage, Moses managed to thresh the available wheat. He also ordered the sheep that wandered the hills to be caught. Mutton was not considered fit to eat, but he traded the sheep to the local Tennesseans, who needed the wool, for caches of bacon they had secreted from the soldiers. In the spring of 1864 Moses was sent to Georgia to persuade the farmers to sell their crops to replenish food supplies for the Army of Northern Virginia. As commissary general of Georgia, Moses wrote reports that document the difficulties of the office during and after Sherman's March to the Sea. Moses was present at the final meeting of the Confederate staff, on May 5, 1865, in Washington (Wilkes County), Georgia. The "Last order of the Lost Cause" instructed Moses to transport ten thousand dollars in gold bullion from Washington to Augusta; this money was needed to purchase rations for the Confederate troops and provide funds for the hospital. Moses relates the perilous trip and the surrender of the bullion to a "Mass. Provost Marshal" (p. 256). A few letters and a brief journal of two sons are among the family writings included. This work also includes prewar and postwar memoirs and genealogical information about this Jewish family.

401. MULLIGAN, ALFRED BIRMINGHAM. *"My Dear Mother & Sisters":* *Civil War Letters of Capt. A. B. Mulligan, Co. B, 5th South Carolina Cavalry-Butler's Division-Hampton's Corps, 1861–1865.* Edited by Olin Fulmer Hutchinson Jr. Spartanburg, S.C.: Reprint Company, 1992. 201 pp.

January 1, 1861–January 12, 1865. Letters. Captain. Fifth South Carolina Cavalry. Duty in the Charleston area and in North Carolina from the end of 1861 through early May 1864; then duty in Virginia, including Sheridan's Trevilian raid, Reams' Station, and first Hatcher's Run. Mulligan wrote to his family in Spartanburg, South Carolina, of his own inactivity around Charleston. While he mentioned the Yankee presence on the harbor islands, Mulligan thought that the failures of Adm. Du Pont's attack on Charleston and the Union assaults on Battery Wagner were proof that the city was invincible. His regiment was thrown into action immediately after it was shipped to Virginia. During those first days of May 1864 Mulligan wrote that he did not think it possible for men to endure such exposure. But a month later he praised his regiment's performance: "Our boys fight like Trojans. The Yankees fear the fire eaters from South Carolina as they call us" (p. 127). Writing in early July, he boasted that the cavalry brigades had saved the country. In the summer and fall of 1864, as the Confederate soldiers were busily building entrenchments, he wrote that many officers who had once considered digging trenches to be "rather cowardly" now thought it was a sensible act. For most of October 1864 he was acting major in charge of a group of dismounted cavalry in defense of a bridge at Burgess' Mill. Mulligan was wounded at first Hatcher's Run and removed from duty for the remainder of the war. The editor included an essay on the Mulligan family written by Mulligan's daughter and several accounts of battles written by Mulligan's contemporaries.

402. NEESE, GEORGE M. *Three Years in the Confederate Horse Artillery.* New introduction, notes, and index by Lee A. Wallace Jr. Dayton, Ohio: Morningside, 1988. 396 pp.

December 11, 1861–July 4, 1865. Memoir and diary. Sergeant. Virginia Light Artillery, Chew's Battery. Enlistment with Chew's Battery; Jackson's Romney campaign; Jackson's Shenandoah Valley campaign, including first Kernstown, Front Royal, first Winchester, Cross Keys, and Port Republic; Stuart's Catlett's Station raid; the Antietam campaign, including Crampton's Gap; Brandy Station; Stuart's Gettysburg raid, including Fairfield and Lee's retreat into Virginia; Bristoe Station; the Mine Run campaign; Charlottesville; The Wilderness; Spotsylvania; Trevilian Station; the siege of Petersburg; and Sheridan's Shenandoah Valley campaign. Neese was captured at Tom's Brook and placed in Point Lookout Prison for the remainder of the war. Most of Neese's memoirs and anecdotes are devoted to the frequent movements and the numerous battles and skirmishes in which Chew's Battery was engaged. Neese admits experiencing fear when shots were fired around him soon after he joined Chew's Battery at Dam No. 5 along the Potomac River. In May 1862, after he was appointed first corporal, he confessed, "this gunnery business is new to me"; he added, "If any Yanks get hurt by my first attempts at gunning it will be their faults not mine" (p. 54). After the Catlett's Station raid he wrote: "Raiding with General Stuart is poor fun and a hard business . . . our battery looks as if the whole business had passed through a shower of yellow mud last night" (p. 102). During one of Stuart's June 1863 reviews at Brandy Station, Neese was ordered off the field by Stuart because his mule's ears twitched. Neese frequently notes how the cavalry was utilized, as well as the problems involved in transporting the artillery, keeping it in good repair, and retaining serviceable horses. The editor relates Neese's travails in getting his memoirs published; they were first published in 1911 (New York: Neale Publishing Company).

403. NELSON, GEORGE WASHINGTON, JR., and MARY SCOLLAY. "Letters from the Heart." Edited by Chris Fordney. *Civil War Times Illustrated* 34 (September/October 1995): 28, 73–82.

July 6, 1863–May 14, 1865. Letters between a Confederate Captain (Hanover Light Artillery) and his fiancée, "Molly," of Middleway, Virginia. Nelson was captured near Winchester, and his letters describe incarceration at Johnson's Island, Point Lookout, Fort Delaware, and Fort Pulaski. After Lee had surrendered, Nelson wrote that the officers held at Fort Delaware debated the nature of their obligation to the fallen Confederacy. An overwhelming majority voted to take the oath of allegiance and return to their loved ones. Molly wrote of everyday life in Middleway. In both sets of letters the couple express their love for each other, as well as hope that Nelson would soon be exchanged.

404. NORRELL, WILLIAM O. "Memo Book: William O. Norrell—Co. B 63rd Ga. Regt. Vols. Mercer's Brigade, Walker's Division, Hardee's Corps, Army of Tennessee." *Journal of Confederate History* 1 (Summer 1988): 49–82.

May 12–July 10, 1864. Diary. Sixty-third Georgia Infantry. Atlanta campaign. This forty-one-year-old Augusta merchant struggled with the rigors of soldiering. Sleeping on the ground made him stiff. He wrote that climbing the hills "would almost break my legs" and caused him to straggle (p. 59). Norrell was forced to see the regimental doctor for his problems with his bowels and was given opium. Norrell held the workers at the division infirmary in contempt because of their indifference to the sick and wounded. Furthermore, they stole from boxes that had been sent to the patients by relatives and friends. Norrell was certain that in the future he would not be able to "think of a Confederate Army surgeon without coupling him with a robber of the sick" (p. 66). Norrell said that while fraternization with the enemy was frequent, the soldiers did not always keep their promise to hold their fire. Pickets often shot at each other, which he considered "beneath the dignity of civilized warfare" (p. 61). Norrell's description of being shelled at night is surrealistic.

405. NUNNALLY, MATTHEW. "Captain Matthew Nunnally: Letters From the 11th Georgia Infantry." By Keith Bohannon. *Military Images* 10 (September/October 1988): 14–15.

1861–1863. Letters. Captain. Eleventh Georgia Infantry. First Bull Run (aftermath); Peninsular campaign; and the siege of Suffolk. Bohannon relates Nunnally's service utilizing snippets of his diary and references to Nunnally made by others.

406. OLD, JAMES W. "The Civil War Letters of James W. Old." By Murray L. Brown. *Manuscripts* 42 (Spring 1990): 129–42.

May 18, 1861–February 24, 1862. Letters. Corporal. Eleventh Virginia Infantry. Duty in Virginia, including battle of Dranesville. Most entries are about soldier life and camp routines, picket duty, clothing allotments, and the extremely bitter winter in northern Virginia. This work was heavily edited with information added about the Eleventh Virginia. Old died of "illness" at Lynchburg, Virginia, in July 1862.

407. OWEN, URBAN GRAMMAR. *Letters to Laura: A Confederate Surgeon's Impression of Four Years of War.* Edited by Sadye Tune Wilson, Nancy Tune Fitzgerald, and Richard Warwick. Nashville, Tenn.: Tunstede Press, 1996. 304 pp.

June 20, 1861–April 1, 1865. Letters. Surgeon. Twentieth Tennessee Infantry and Fourth Tennessee Infantry. Duty in eastern Tennessee (especially the Cumberland Gap); Stones River; duty in Chattanooga and field hospitals at Dalton and other places during the Atlanta campaign; and in Alabama, South Carolina, and North Carolina. News of acquaintances from their home in Williamson County, Tennessee, fills Owen's letters to his wife. During the spring and summer of 1864 Laura fled to her grandmother's home in North Carolina, and it was left to Urban to keep her informed of news of home that he heard from other men. Urban repeatedly assured Laura that he was safe because doctors did not have to go near the battlefield. He described the surgeon's work at Stones River in detail, and at Dallas he wrote that the wounded were "rolling in." As he observed Atlantans scurrying to get out of the city, Urban remarked that Tennesseans had little sympathy for the Georgians: "they have been turning up their noses at poor Tenn refugees. All Tenn want Atlanta to go up Spout for it is the swindling hole of the South" (p. 172). On November 5, 1864, Urban wrote that the soldiers' morale was high and that they anticipated a severe fight soon. In his next letter, of February 23, 1865, he addressed the Confederacy's prospects: "I think Gen'l Lee, Jeff Davis & Squad had better look for a hole to get out." He also mentioned punishments. At the start of the Atlanta campaign, sixteen deserters were shot at one time and Rev. James Findlay (Chaplain, Fifty-third Alabama) was hung for "trying to get the soldiers to mutiny & giving news to the Yankees about our army (bully for the preachers)" (p. 153). This work contains other materials about the Owen family, including a supplementary "Genealogic Chart," edited by Sadye Tune Wilson.

408. PACA, EDWARD TILGHMAN, JR. "'Tim's Black Book': The Civil War Diary of Edward Tilghman Paca, Jr., C.S.A." Edited by Edmund C. Paca. *Maryland Historical Magazine* 89 (Winter 1994): 453–66.

September 1862–March 1863. Diary. First Maryland Cavalry Battalion (C.S.A.). Paca recorded his journey through Union lines from Maryland to Richmond, where he waited with others to join the Confederate army. He became a member of Winder's Cavalry Company in January 1863. Paca described such incidents as scrounging for food, observing Marylanders fleeing the North to avoid the draft, being assigned to capture conscripts from their homes in Henrico County, watching two deserters executed, and helping to bury a comrade. Paca did not mind taking the conscripts from their homes because "the men of that region are the worst kind of men." But Paca wrote that when their pretty women began to cry and scold the soldiers, "generally, you begin to feel infernally cheap" (p. 462). The two executions were performed within days of each other. He said that at the first, the click of the rifle made the observers' hearts run cold. He wrote that at the second execution: "I am getting so I don't care in the least about seeing such a scene" (p. 463). When Paca acted as a pallbearer at a burial, he felt that it was a comforting feeling to assist in laying a fellow soldier to rest, one he would never forget if he got out of the war alive. The editor relates Paca's subsequent military career, during which he was captured shortly after his last entry and once again later.

409. PAXTON, WILLIAM EDWARDS. "A Report on the Battle of Shiloh." Edited by Ken Durham. *Louisiana History* 35 (Winter 1994): 85–87.

April 6–7, 1862. Letter. Nineteenth Louisiana Infantry. Shiloh. On the night before the attack, this regimental quartermaster was in the rear bringing up forage and provisions. During the two days of fighting he delivered ammunition and a message from Gen. Beauregard to Gen. Bragg and dodged exploding shells before the Confederate troops retreated to Corinth. Paxton's earlier letters to his wife were published in *Louisiana History* 20 (Spring 1979): 169–96.

410. PEEL, WILLIAM. "The Gettysburg Diary of Lieutenant William Peel." By Terrence Winschel. *Gettysburg Magazine* 9 (July 1993): 98–107.

June 25–July 3, 1863. Diary. Lieutenant. Eleventh Mississippi Infantry. Gettysburg campaign and battle.

411. PEGRAM, WILLIAM RANSOM JOHNSON. "'The Boy Artillerist': Letters of Colonel William Pegram, C.S.A." Edited by James I. Robertson Jr. *Virginia Magazine of History and Biography* 98 (April 1990): 221–60.

August 14, 1862–March 14, 1865. Letters. Pegram's Battalion, Artillery Brigade, Third Corps, Army of Northern Virginia. Cedar Mountain; second Bull Run; the Antietam campaign; Chancellorsville; and the siege of Petersburg (including the Petersburg Mine Assault, Peebles' Farm, and first Hatcher's Run). In these seven letters to his sister, Pegram reveals the activities that contributed to his rapid rise from a lieutenancy in Purcell's Battery to battalion commander. He describes battles, comments on the war in general, and exhibits concern for his family. Pegram was disappointed that Marylanders did not greet Lee's army more warmly during the Antietam campaign, but he attributed the cool reception to having made the crossing into two Unionist counties. When he relates the soldiers' gloom over Jackson's death, Pegram assures his sister that the troops would continue to fight well under any leader. Pegram describes the battle at "the Crater" in detail, including the Confederate fury in repelling the black troops. He wrote that the assault had a "splendid effect on our men" (p. 244). In a letter written in October 1864 he reflects on the length of the Virginia campaign. Although he considered the defenses around Petersburg still strong, and morale continued to be high, he believed that the defenders' vigor had been drained: "Nearly every man & officer feel the want of physical strength" (p. 248). In February 1865 he mourned the death of his brother, killed at second Hatcher's Run. In March he continued to write letters that were meant to instill confidence in the progress of the war. Pegram was killed at Five Forks.

412. PERRY, WILLIAM F. "A Forgotten Account of Chickamauga." Edited by Curt Johnson. *Civil War Times Illustrated* 32 (September/October 1993): 52–56.

September 18–20, 1863. Memoir. Colonel. Forty-fourth Alabama Infantry. Chickamauga. Perry states unequivocally that he assumed command of Law's Brigade on September 20, after Col. James L. Sheffield (Law's replacement) was wounded, and led the brigade to victory. Thus, the credit that has usually been attributed to "Sheffield's Brigade" belongs to Perry.

413. POWELL, ROBERT M. *Recollections of a Texas Colonel at Gettysburg.* Edited by Gregory A. Coco. Gettysburg, Pa.: Thomas Publications, 1990. 62 pp.

May 28–July 1863. Memoir. Fifth Texas Infantry. Gettysburg campaign, including the battle. Powell was wounded and taken captive during the assault on Little Round Top. He described the attack and what he saw of Pickett's Charge the following day and related incidents of his hospitalization at Gettysburg's Lutheran Theological Seminary. This was originally published in the *Weekly Times* (Philadelphia) on December 13, 1884.

414. PRATHER, BENJAMIN FRANKLIN. "Lee and Lincoln in Burkittsville: The Prather Letter Reexamined." By Timothy J. Reese. *Maryland Historical Magazine* 82 (Summer 1987): 159–64.

September 21, 1862. Letter. Burkittsville, Maryland. Reese probes the authenticity of a recently (1976) discovered letter that supposedly had been written by a mortally wounded Confederate soldier. The letter indicates that Lee and Lincoln were present in Burkittsville during the Maryland campaign. Reese concludes that the Prather letter is "fiction created for unknown motives" (p. 163).

415. PRESTON, WILLIAM. "'At the Moment of Victory . . .': The Battle of Shiloh and General A. S. Johnston's Death as Recounted in William Preston's Diary." Edited by Peter J. Sehlinger. *Filson Club Historical Quarterly* 61 (July 1987): 315–45.
April 4–7, 1862. Diary. Colonel. Aide-de-camp to Gen. Albert Sidney Johnston, Army of Mississippi. Shiloh. This work contains hour-by-hour entries of this period and intimate details of Johnston's death on April 6, 1862.

416. PRICE, HENRY M. "Alternative to Appomattox: A Virginian's Vision of an Anglo-Confederate Colony on the Amazon, May 1865." Edited by Frank J. Merli. *Virginia Magazine of History and Biography* 94 (April 1986): 210–19.
May 24, 1865. Letter. Forty-fourth Virginia Infantry. This is a letter to the British minister in Washington, Sir Frederick Bruce, which was intended to induce English support for a Confederate enclave abroad. The editor considers the letter in the context of its era, which included British and Confederate social similarities, Victorian society, and a unique class of Southerners. Merli also speculates on Price's exact identity. There is no official record of response.

417. RABB, JOHN WESLEY. "'We Are Stern and Resolved': The Civil War Letters of John Wesley Rabb, Terry's Texas Rangers." Edited by Thomas W. Cutrer. *Southwestern Historical Quarterly* 91 (October 1987): 185–225.
September 19, 1861–January 11, 1865. Letters. Corporal. Eighth Texas Cavalry. Kentucky (including battles of Woodsonville, Bardstown, and Perryville); Tennessee (including Stones River and the Chattanooga campaign); Georgia (including the Atlanta campaign and Wheeler's raid on Rome); and duty in South Carolina. Rabb's letters relate incidents rather than chronicle his regiment's battles. He wrote nothing about the death of Col. Benjamin Franklin Terry in the unit's first fight. Perryville was described almost as an afterthought. He told of being shot at by "Linkonite" bushwhackers in Kentucky, mourning the loss of his three horses, and burying the Confederate dead at Stones River. At Stones River the Union soldiers were not so fortunate; Rabb wrote: "the hogs get a hold of some of the Yankey dead before the fight was over" (p. 210). Rabb wrote a great deal about his family in Fayette County, Texas, including his mother, sister, and brother Virgil (Sixteenth Texas Infantry). While he feared a Yankee invasion of Texas and expressed concern about the destruction that might be caused by Union soldiers, Rabb seemed to feel that the family could take care of itself. He advised his mother to consider sending the slaves to the mountains to prevent their being stolen. His last letter, written from South Carolina, was filled with bitterness about the actions of Confederate troops from the west. "We lost Atlanta & Savannah because the troops on the West side of the Mississippi River refused to come over here & help us out. . . . Things look rather dark over here at this time" (p. 223). The editor completes the unit's history after January 11, 1865.

418. RABB, VIRGIL SULLIVAN. "'Bully for Flournoy's Regiment, We Are Some Pumkins, You'll Bet': The Civil War Letters of Virgil Sullivan Rabb, Captain, Company I Sixteenth Texas Infantry, C.S.A." Edited by Thomas W. Cutrer. (Part I) *Military History of the Southwest* 19 (Fall 1989): 161–90.
———. (Part II) *Military History of the Southwest* 20 (Spring 1990): 61–90.

June 7, 1862–May 3, 1865. Letters. Captain. Sixteenth Texas Infantry. Texas; Arkansas; and Louisiana, including Milliken's Bend and Banks's Red River campaign of 1864. Although Rabb missed most of the battles in which Walker's Division was engaged, his letters chronicle the rapid marches of "Walker's Greyhounds." Much of the correspondence to his mother and sister in Fayette County, Texas, involves details on how he was faring, specific troop movements (especially during the second Red River campaign), and matters of family interest. On several occasions he laments the devastation of Louisiana plantations and farmland caused by armies of both sides. Typical of Rabb's avoidance of war news is an oblique reference to his participation at Milliken's Bend: "I have been in some tolerable close places since I got back to the Army, but thus far I have come out right-side up with care" (Part I, p. 179). His sister apparently once asked him to come home and help with the farm. He replied that he would stay in the army because the wages were good: it would "bring me out even at the end of the war" (Part I, p. 177). He provided some advice on how to run the farm, but he apparently felt confident in the family's abilities. Rabb was concerned about a possible Yankee invasion of Texas. He advised the family that if that happened, they should hide the slaves. Another matter involving the slaves included selling them for profit because they were bringing high prices late in the war. Rabb was more than willing to cross the Mississippi River to fight, and he chastised those who were unwilling to go. He wrote optimistically about the war and conveyed many positive, but unfounded, rumors. Beginning in 1865, however, his mood had changed. He tersely told his family that he had no war news. He never mentioned Lee's surrender. In the last letters, which were written after Johnston's surrender, Rabb wrote that he was persevering in his attempt to obtain a leave.

419. **RANDAL, HORACE, and JOSEPH L. BRENT.** "Two 'Lost' Battle Reports: Horace Randal's and Joseph L. Brent's Reports of the Battles of Mansfield and Pleasant Hill, 8 and 9 April 1864." Edited by Jane Harris Johansson and David H. Johansson. *Military History of the West* 23 (Fall 1993): 169–80.

April 8–9, 1863. The editors first discuss reasons for the scarcity of Confederate reports in the *Official Records*. Then they identify the importance of these two missing reports from the *OR*. The report by Randal (Colonel, Randal's Brigade, Walker's Division, District of West Louisiana, Trans-Mississippi Department) "documents the brigade's casualties at both Mansfield and Pleasant Hill, discusses the independent operations of the Randal's Brigade at Mansfield, and provides an overview of both of those battles" (p. 170). The account by Brent (Colonel, Chief of Artillery and Ordnance, District of West Louisiana, Trans-Mississippi Department) "is the only battle report known that directly discusses the activities and casualties of Confederate artillery at Mansfield and Pleasant Hill" (p. 171).

420. **RAWLINGS, BENJAMIN CASON.** *Benjamin Cason Rawlings: First Virginia Volunteer for the South.* By Byrd Barnette Tribble. Baltimore, Md.: Butternut and Blue, 1995. 155 pp.

December 1860–April 1865. Memoir. Private, First South Carolina Infantry (Provisional Army), and Captain, Thirtieth Virginia Infantry. In 1904 Rawlings dictated this anecdotal record of his Civil War experiences to his son. Rawlings's service began in December 1860, when, as a sixteen-year-old boy, he traveled from his Spotsylvania County, Virginia, home to Charleston to join the First South Carolina Provisional Infantry. Stationed on James Island, he was on duty when Fort Sumter was shelled and watched as Edmund Ruffin was knocked down by a salvo from the fort. When Rawlings returned home, he found he had become a celebrity because of his youth and his experiences. In May 1861 he joined the Thirtieth Virginia and spent the rest of the year on duty in northern Virginia. He briefly related events of the Peninsular campaign, the capture of Harpers Ferry, Antietam (described in detail), Fredericksburg, the winter 1863 encampment (including a great snowball fight), the siege of Suffolk, duty in East Tennessee, and his capture during the Mine Run campaign while he was home on leave. Rawlings spent the next eleven months in captivity at Old Capitol Prison, Fort McHenry, Point Lookout (he was critical of the Union colored troops who served as guards), and Fort Delaware, and he was exchanged in October 1864. Rawlings briefly related his regiment's activities along the Petersburg siege lines and in the Appomattox campaign and his return to his family. The editor has included several letters written by and about Rawlings, as well as newspaper articles about his service.

421. RICE, ZACHARIAH A. "An Atlantan Goes to War: The Civil War Letters of Maj. Zachariah A. Rice, C.S.A." Edited by Stephen Davis and William A. Richards. *Atlanta History* 36 (Spring 1992): 20–39.

August 17, 1861–July 8, 1862. Letters. Major. Cobb's Georgia Legion, Cavalry Battalion. Rice describes the legion's organization, its duty at and near Yorktown, details of the first winter, Burnside's expedition to North Carolina, and the Peninsular campaign. Rice relates a portion of the sermon he had attended at Second Presbyterian Church in Richmond in which the minister equated religion, the Confederacy, and victory. During the Peninsular campaign Cobb's Cavalry was often on picket and reconnaissance duties. A friendly episode of fraternization with Union officers allowed Rice the opportunity to lecture them about the "real" origin of the war. Cobb's Cavalry, which served in Stuart's Cavalry Corps, was wearied from hard riding by late June of 1862, but Rice was satisfied that Jackson and Stuart had driven McClellan away from Richmond.

422. RILEY, AMOS CAMDEN. "Confederate Col. A. C. Riley, His Reports and Letters." Edited by H. Riley Bock. (Part I) *Missouri Historical Review* 85 (January 1991): 158–81.

———. (Part II) *Missouri Historical Review* 85 (April 1991): 264–87.

July 4, 1861–March 4, 1864. Letters and reports. Colonel. First Missouri Infantry; then, First and Fourth Missouri (Consolidated). Shiloh; battle of Corinth; Champion Hill; and the siege of Vicksburg. Riley's letters to his parents blend war news with camp life and reports on the health of the men from the New Madrid area. He occasionally offered such advice as protecting the slaves by sending them farther south. He asked for and received one slave to serve him. Riley's official battle reports are detailed descriptions of the battles. The editor's extensive narrative and copious notes include the fact that Riley was killed at the battle of Dallas on May 30, 1864.

423. RILEY, FRANKLIN LAFAYETTE. *Grandfather's Journal: Company B, Sixteenth Mississippi Infantry Volunteers, Harris' Brigade, Mahone's Division, Hill's Corps, A.N.V. May 27, 1861–July 15, 1865.* Edited by Austin V. Dobbins. Dayton, Ohio: Morningside House, 1988. 304 pp.

May 27, 1861–July 15, 1865. Diary. Private. Sixteenth Mississippi Infantry. First Bull Run (aftermath); Jackson's Shenandoah Valley campaign (including first Winchester and Cross Keys); Gaines' Mill; second Manassas; Antietam; Chancellorsville; the Gettysburg campaign (including battle and retreat); The Wilderness; Spotsylvania; the siege of Petersburg (including the Weldon Railroad operations, the Petersburg Mine Assault, Reams' Station, and first Hatcher's Run); and the battle for Fort Gregg, where he was captured and sent to Point Lookout Prison. Riley's compassion for the enemy is often in evidence. He pitied the wounded Yankees caught in burning undergrowth at Chancellorsville and again a year later at The Wilderness. But Riley was equally compassionate toward the cold, desperate Confederates who were driven to desert the trenches of Petersburg. Riley appreciated humor. Before Petersburg both sides tried unsuccessfully to discard a piece of wormy hardtack. The hardtack was repeatedly hurled away, landing in the enemy's trench, only to be promptly tossed back. Riley became realistic about the possibility of the Confederacy's demise as early as Antietam. The debate over putting the slaves in uniform reached its peak in February 1865 when soldiers were asked to express their opinions.

Riley's brigade, which voted in favor of the action, felt that "if the blacks are willing to fight for their freedom, as we are, then they should be given the opportunity to earn it" (p. 232). While at Petersburg, Riley mentioned in his diary the presence of one "Bird" Davidson, an inventor who attempted to solicit money to build balloons to drop bombs on the enemy but ended up in jail for "trying to humbug the soldiers" (p. 232). A recurring theme of Riley's account is the Confederate dependence on being able to capture Yankee food, clothing, and weapons, i.e., "Gen. Pope is the best Commissary officer our army ever had" (p. 102). Cultural differences came to Riley's attention on several occasions. Shortly after he arrived in Virginia he observed differences between Mississippians (like himself) and Virginians. And writing during the march through Chambersburg in 1863, he commented that the Pennsylvanians seemed even less like "us" than the Marylanders. He wrote: "The women here are so insolent and ugly. Apparently this is the place they get the comic pictures they put in the almanacs" (p. 148). Riley's teasing friendship with Bal (Balsorah) back in Mississippi grew into love, then marriage. At Point Lookout Prison he busied himself selling rings and broaches, which he had carved out of bones. Even when he was in prison and ill, he refused to become disconsolate. As he wrote Bal, "Life has too much in store for us" (p. 252).

424. ROBERTSON, FRANK S. "Reminiscence of the Years 1861–1865." Edited by L. C. Angle Jr. and Edwin T. Hardison. *Historical Society of Washington County, Virginia Bulletin* 23 (1986): 6–39.

1861–1865. Memoir. Captain. Forty-eighth Virginia Infantry. Battles of Germanna Ford, Chancellorsville, Brandy Station, Gettysburg (including Williamsport); and the Appomattox campaign. In the middle of writing his recollections Robertson paused: "I shall simply continue this ramshackled narrative as I recall the salient points of my personal experience" (p. 22). When the war began, Robertson was a student at the University of Virginia. Soon his company of students was sent to Harpers Ferry; afterward he served with the Forty-eighth Virginia in western Virginia, but he developed heart trouble, which kept him out of action for an undefined period of time. At Fredericksburg he was appointed to J. E. B. Stuart's staff as "Second Lieutenant Engineers" and served with the "mounted pioneers," rising to engineer officer of the division. Robertson recalled the Gettysburg campaign in greatest detail: Stuart's movements prior to the battle, the cavalry action on July 3, and the Confederate retreat back into Virginia. He insisted that Gettysburg was not a defeat and "that the pursuit of the victorious army of Mead" was scarcely noticeable (p. 28). Robertson's recollection of the actions during the last weeks of the war, the collapse of the Confederate forces, and his return home are fragmented.

425. ROBINSON, GEORGE, and JAMES F. ROBINSON. *Remember Me: The Civil War Letters of Lt. George Robinson and His Son Sgt. James F. Robinson of "The Glenn," Hamburg, South Carolina, 1861–1862.* Edited by Richard L. Beach. Bowie, Md.: Heritage Books, 1991. 94 pp.

January 9, 1861–August 17, 1862. Letters. First South Carolina Infantry (Gregg's) and Seventh South Carolina Infantry. The letters of George (January 9–April 26, 1861) and James (January 10, 1861–August 17, 1862) describe service in Charleston working to fortify the city's harbor defenses. They relate the assembling of troops, the excitement and tension of the weeks prior to the firing on the *Star of the West,* and the bombardment of Fort Sumter. When Fort Sumter surrendered, George wrote, "we *can* and *will* make them respect us" (p. 31). George returned home when the company disbanded. James joined the Seventh South Carolina Infantry and wrote of first Bull Run. A letter from a third party relates James's death and attests to his sterling personality.

426. ROLSTON, JESSE, JR. *". . . Until Separated by Death": Lives and Civil War Letters of Jesse Rolston, Jr. & Mary Catharine Cromer.* Edited by Joyce DeBolt Miller. Bridgewater, Va.: Good Printers, 1994. 208 pp.

October 16, 1861–November 24, 1864. Letters. Fifty-second Virginia Infantry. Jackson's Shenandoah Valley campaign (especially Front Royal and Port Republic); Chancellorsville; the Mine Run campaign; and Point Lookout Prison. For over two years the thirty-seven-year-old Jesse provided his wife, Mary, with a steady stream of advice about the family farm. But on December 13, 1863, he admitted feelings of helplessness: "I do not no sometimes what to think much less what to rite. you rit of seling the sow and pigs. i leave that for you too attend to" (p. 57). For Jesse the opposition seemed to be the war in general because it kept him away from his farm near Mount Solon, Virginia. Jesse desired peace but not surrender, and he remained confident of the Confederacy's ability to defend itself against Yankee subjugation. Jesse and Mary often thought of his returning home. In one letter Mary suggests that he hire a substitute and later mentions that he might obtain a discharge because as a farmer he was needed to raise food for the Confederacy. However, Jesse knew that leaving camp without permission was risky; he had already observed the harsh punishment one man received for leaving camp. Mary must have wanted to know more about the situation because in a subsequent letter Jesse explains why punishment for "flank a fight" (to leave during battle) was treated with greater severity than to "flank a picket" (to leave during peaceful times). Jesse never espoused patriotic causes nor demeaned the North. As he fraternized with Union soldiers on the picket line, Jessie found "their is some nise men among that we talk with" and that they wanted "pease as bad as we do" (p. 47). Jesse's letters constitute most of the Civil War correspondence.

427. ROSS, LAWRENCE SULLIVAN. *Personal Civil War Letters of General Lawrence Sullivan Ross with Other Letters.* Transcribed and compiled by Perry Wayne Shelton. Introduction by T. Michael Parrish. Edited, with additional notes and index, by Shelly Morrison. Austin, Tex.: S. and R. Morrison, 1994. 106 pp.

September 1, 1861–January 12, 1865. Letters. Major, Sixth Texas Cavalry to Brigadier General, Ross's Brigade, Jackson's Division, Forrest's Cavalry Corps, Department of Alabama, Mississippi, and East Louisiana. Organization of regiment in Camp Bartow, Texas; raids into Missouri; duty in Arkansas, including Pea Ridge; siege and evacuation of Corinth; Iuka; the Vicksburg campaign; Wheeler's raid into northern Georgia and eastern Tennessee; the Meridian campaign; the Atlanta campaign; and the aftermath of Hood's Franklin-Nashville campaign. Ross's letters consist primarily of descriptions of battles and the condition of his men and horses. In early 1863 he wrote: "Never a week and scarcely a day passes but we have a fight" (p. x). During the Atlanta campaign "his command fought eighty-six separate engagements that would span more than one hundred days" (p. x). Several topics in Ross's letters concern the internal conflict between the Creek Indians in Indian Territory in 1861, the divided loyalties of Missourians, the animosity that existed between Gens. Ben McCullough and Sterling Price, and his own series of promotions. Shortly after he left home he assured Lizzie, his wife of a few months, that he would be back home soon. In the meantime Ross encouraged her to enjoy herself and "not become old and wrinkled with care. . . . There are better days coming" (p. 7). On September 7, 1861, he wrote that "Prominence does not suit my inclination. I prefer, on the contrary, seclusion, since I have a Wife to bless me with her cherished presence." At the end of 1862 he went home for a leave and was restless. After he returned to the army he apologized and explained that he was preoccupied by the call of duty. His emotions were in turmoil; he confessed to having a feeling he had not had in a long time, "homesickness" (p. 48). Similar expressions of sentiment for the remainder of the war are rare. In a letter of November 29, 1863, he offers condolence to Lizzie upon the death of their child, but the words are stiff. Others from home had provided him with "the intelligence of the death of our child. I am sorry I could not be at Home with you, but feel fully resigned to the great affliction, although I had anticipated much happiness in finding a little stranger to welcome my return" (p. 57). Affairs of the heart again return in his letters to Lizzie written following the war, as he was achieving the prominence he had once eschewed (he eventually became governor of Texas).

428. RUSH, JOHN WESLEY. "The Lots of War." By John Sledge. *Blue & Gray Magazine* 2 (August/September 1984): 55–58.
1861–1863. Letters. Fourth Infantry, C.S.A. The evacuation of Fort Pillow; surrender of Island No. 10; and imprisonment at Camp Chase.

429. SAFFELL, RICHARD. "'A Brave Officer': The Letters of Richard Saffell, 26th Tennessee, C.S.A." By Mike Miner. *Military Images* 12 (September/October 1990): 16–18.
June 1861–1864. Letters. Captain. Twenty-sixth Tennessee Infantry. Fort Donelson (where he was captured and imprisoned at Johnson's Island); Chickamauga; and Missionary Ridge. Saffell believed that he was expressing all Tennessee soldiers' appraisal of the residents of Kentucky when he wrote: "The women are the ugliest I ever saw." He continued, "Our boys hate the people around here and say if they had known that they were going to be sent to defend such, they would have stayed home" (p. 17). Other disparaging remarks were directed toward officers. Criticism of Gen. William Hardee was surpassed by that about Gideon Pillow's leadership at Fort Donelson: "Gen. Pillow is a damned white livered coward. He sold us to save his own carcass and ran on the battlefield behind a big poplar tree" (p. 17). After the battles around Chattanooga, Saffell wrote that the "boys are now well over their scare," and he confidently predicted that "Old Jo Johnston is the man to win the next fight" (p. 18).

430. SANDERS, JARED YOUNG, II. *Diary in Gray: Civil War Letters and Diary of Jared Young Sanders II.* Edited and annotated by Mary Elizabeth Sanders. Baton Rouge: Louisiana Genealogical & Historical Society, 1994. 113 pp.
March 12, 1862–May 18, 1865. Letters and diary. Twenty-sixth Louisiana Infantry. Includes the surrender of New Orleans and march to Camp Moore, Louisiana; the Vicksburg campaign, including Chickasaw Bluffs, the siege of Vicksburg, Grant's bayou expeditions (February–April 1863), assaults of May 19 and 22; and parole camp at Demopolis, Alabama. Following Vicksburg, Sanders's account became an odyssey. He traveled to Richmond via Charleston on a furlough; went behind Union-occupied lines to his home in Saint Mary's Parish, Louisiana, to retrieve the regiment's paroled men; traveled to east Texas with his brother; and escaped from the watchful eyes of federal authorities to rejoin his regiment near Alexandria, Louisiana. In Louisiana, Sanders wrote of the destruction to property in the Bayou Teche region, as well as the general conditions within the Union-occupied portion of the state. He was especially interested in the plantation owners and the manner in which the federal troops utilized the blacks as paid (or forced) laborers. Sanders's father, who was ill, refused to leave his sugar plantation near Brashear City and died after being pressured by the federal authorities. Sanders wrote contemptuously of Union soldiers. In an excerpt of a letter to Bessie Wofford (the lady he would eventually marry), Sanders pleads that she not allow herself to be "humiliated by their presence, never be insulted by that cowardly race, but flee them as you would a hideous pestilence" (p. 7). His sensibilities were shaken by Southern women using tobacco. Near Enterprise, Mississippi, he watched a young woman smoking. On still another occasion he had been served a fine dinner when the wife "shocked me by commencing to smoke"; then she complained because the blockade had kept snuff out of the country (p. 39). On his travels in Louisiana, Sanders suffered from "flux." A doctor gave him a "compound consisting of 1 grs. opium, 2 grs. sugar of lead, ´ grs. camphor-per pill" (p. 39). On April 27, 1865, he learned of both Lee's surrender and Lincoln's assassination. He responded with: "The former is the greatest of calamities—the latter the greatest of blessings."

431. SCHARF, JONATHAN THOMAS. *The Personal Memoirs of Jonathan Thomas Scharf of the First Maryland Artillery.* Edited by Tom Kelley. Baltimore, Md.: Butternut and Blue, 1992. 81 pp.

August 1861–1863. Memoir. First Maryland Light Artillery Battery and CSS *Chicora*. Williamsburg; Seven Pines; Mechanicsville; Gaines' Mill; Malvern Hill; Cedar Mountain; second Bull Run; Chantilly; Antietam; Shepherdstown; Fredericksburg; Kelly's Ford; and Chancellorsville. Scharf was adamant about his reasons for leaving his family in Baltimore to join the Confederacy: "I did not like the white negroes, The North, The Yankee, etc., etc. I can not express my hate for them" (p. 2). Because of his feelings, a rift developed within his family that had not been resolved at the time he penned these memoirs. Scharf described his travels to Richmond, where he joined a group of Marylanders in an artillery company. Nearly all of this memoir is a recounting of the military actions of the First Battery of Maryland Artillery. After being wounded at Chancellorsville, Scharf left the army and became a midshipman. His account ends with mention that he was serving in Charleston harbor. Appended is Scharf's summary of why the South seceded.

432. SEARCY, JAMES T., and REUBEN M. SEARCY. "'When Shall Our Cup Be Full?': The Correspondence of Confederate Soldiers James T. and Reuben M. Searcy." By Maxwell Elebash. *Alabama Heritage* 31 (Winter 1994): 28–39.
1861–January 1864. Letters. Lumsden's Battery, Alabama Light Artillery and Thirty-fourth Alabama Infantry. The editor employs historical narrative and quotations from the Searcy correspondence to reveal one family's wartime experiences. James, who was a member of Lumsden's Battery, attempted to convince his younger brother, Reuben, to stay in school at the University of Alabama, both to obtain an education and for the sake of his parents. But by May 1862 Reuben had joined the 34th Alabama. In December 1862 he was promoted to lieutenant. Reuben's letters sent home informed his parents of a review by Jefferson Davis, of his presence at several executions, and how Christmas was observed in camp. He assured them how well he was getting on. Both brothers were at Stones River when the battle began. After dark on December 31, 1862, Reuben was mortally wounded when a shell fragment tore away his right thigh. James and a friend stayed in Murfreesboro, caring for Reuben after Confederate troops withdrew. On January 7, 1863, Reuben died. In a letter to his mother James tenderly recounted Reuben's last moments. Dr. Searcy, the boy's father, had rushed from Tuscaloosa, Alabama, to be with his son but was turned back by the Union army only twenty-five miles from Murfreesboro. The editor adds that James and the friend stayed in the Murfreesboro hospital caring for others before they were sent to the Camp Morton Prison and exchanged in June 1863.

433. SEDINGER, JAMES D. "War-Time Reminiscences of James D. Sedinger, Company E, 8th Virginia Cavalry (Border Rangers)." Edited by Steven E. Woodworth. *West Virginia History* 51 (1992): 55–78.
December 10, 1861–April 1865. Memoir. Eighth Virginia Cavalry. Duty in the Kanawha Valley of western Virginia, Tennessee, Virginia, and Pennsylvania. Battles of Scarey Creek; Carnifax Ferry; the siege of Knoxville; Hunter's Shenandoah Valley campaign; second Kernstown; the burning of Chambersburg; Fisher's Hill; and the Appomattox campaign. This work is a personal history of the unit, with running anecdotes. The editor adds that although the memoir reads as though Sedinger were an eyewitness to the entire war, he was in fact captured at Fisher's Hill.

434. SEMMES, RAPHAEL. "'Home is the Sailor, Home from the Sea': Semmes Returns to the South, November 1864." Edited by William J. Brinker. *Journal of Confederate History* 4 (1989): 56–60.
November 11, 1864. Letter. Brownsville, Texas. Writing to the friend with whom he stayed after the CSS *Alabama* was captured, Admiral Semmes described his travels from England back to Texas. He wrote to Louisa Tremlett that he had returned to Texas via Saint Thomas and Havana. He admitted some trepidation about traveling in Texas, which he called "This chivalrous warm-hearted state" (p. 59).

435. SEMMES, RAPHAEL. "'I Told Him I Should Burn His Ship': Captain Raphael Semmes, Commanding the CSS *Sumter* in the Strait of Gibraltar." Edited by William J. Miller. *Civil War: Magazine of the Civil War Society* 49 (February 1995): 73–76.
January 18, 1862. Memoir. CSS *Sumter.* En route from Cadiz to Gibraltar, Semmes captured and burned the *Neapolitan* out of Kingston, Massachusetts.

436. SEYMOUR, WILLIAM J. *The Civil War Memoirs of Captain William J. Seymour: Reminiscences of a Louisiana Tiger.* Edited, with an introduction, by Terry L. Jones. Baton Rouge: Louisiana State University Press, 1991. 162 pp.
March 1862–October 1864. Memoir. Aide-de-camp to Gen. Johnson K. Duncan, commander of the coastal defenses of New Orleans; then, Captain and aide-de-camp to Gen. Harry T. Hayes, First Louisiana Brigade, Second Corps, Army of Northern Virginia. Defense and surrender of Fort Jackson and New Orleans; Chancellorsville; Brandy Station; second Winchester; Gettysburg, including Lee's retreat; the Bristoe campaign; Rappahannock Station; the Mine Run campaign; The Wilderness; Spotsylvania; Cold Harbor; and Sheridan's Shenandoah Valley campaign, including third Winchester, Fisher's Hill, and Cedar Creek. Seymour, a New Orleans newspaper editor (the *Commercial Bulletin*), begins his memoir with a thirty-six-page account of the month-long naval bombardment of Fort Jackson and the capture of New Orleans. Following his parole Seymour returned to his newspaper, but in July 1862 he violated the censorship decree of Gen. Benjamin Butler by printing a patriotic eulogy in memory of his father, who had been killed at Gaines' Mill. Seymour was incarcerated at Fort Jackson for the next two and a half months. In April 1863 he volunteered to serve as aide to Gen. Hayes. The remainder of the memoir—from Chancellorsville to Cedar Creek—is an account of military actions, amended by Seymour's highly partisan sentiments and vignettes of officers. At The Wilderness, Seymour contrasted Lee and his "calm, collected and dignified" demeanor with "Gen. Ewell," who, "greatly excited and in a towering passion, hurled a terrible volley of oaths at the stragglers at the front" (p. 125). Seymour also related instances of bravery by Confederate soldiers, hardships created by insufficient clothing, and the execution of a deserter, which Seymour had to officiate. Seymour's memoir concludes at the start of Cedar Creek. In his introduction the editor says that Seymour's account is the only known narrative of the siege of Fort Jackson, outside of the *Official Records,* as well as the only published narrative of an officer of the First Louisiana Brigade. In a footnote he comments on how Seymour's memoir contributes knowledge of the First Louisiana Brigade during The Wilderness.

437. SIMPSON, RICHARD WRIGHT, and TALIAFERRO N. SIMPSON. *Far, Far from Home: The Wartime Letters of Dick and Tally Simpson, Third South Carolina Volunteers.* Edited by Guy R. Everson and Edward W. Simpson Jr. New York: Oxford University Press, 1994. 316 pp.
April 14, 1861–September 4, 1863. Letters. Private and Corporal. Third South Carolina Infantry. First Bull Run; Seven Pines; second Bull Run; Antietam; Fredericksburg; Chancellorsville; and Gettysburg, including Lee's retreat. In April 1861 these two brothers left their home in Pendleton, South Carolina, and their studies at Wofford College to perform their patriotic duty. Both men wrote informative letters to their family about camp conditions, the poor quality of food, battles, and homesickness. They often expressed Southern nationalism and cultural superiority. On the first anniversary of South Carolina's secession, Tally said that event would be remembered by future generations as the day their "revered State struck a blow which severed her from a detestable Union" (p. 100). Dick assured his family that enlisting was "no rash act, but my feeling of duty urges me to do it" (p. 4). When he read a collection of Yankee letters written in the summer of 1861, Dick discerned that it "showed plainly that those by

whom they were written were of the lowest set in the world" (p. 65). Dick wrote fewer letters than Tally because he was discharged for medical reasons in the summer of 1862. Included in Tally's usually light-hearted letters is a "romance" with a girl from Pendleton whom he never may have actually seen. Tally wrote little about battles. During the Gettysburg campaign he penned a glowing impression of the Pennsylvania landscape with its bountiful crops but a negative appraisal of its population. He wrote, "They have the fastest horses and the ugliest women I ever saw" (p. 263). He conceded that the people were neat and industrious. Tally, who opposed the Confederate pillage of civilian property in Pennsylvania, said that he was present when Gen. Lee watched it happen, but the general did not stop his soldiers. Many of Dick's letters contain greetings from his menservants to their families and friends, for example, "Zion says tell Hester to remember him to Col. Pickens' black folks, and if she stands of need of any thing, he will try to assist her" (p. 85). In the summer of 1863 Tally's change of mood is evident. He wrote a summary of the Confederacy's bleak future but then attempted to reassure his sister of his morale: "You are mistaken if you think I am blue and even in a state of despair" (p. 267). Tally was killed at Chickamauga. Seven letters of condolence are appended by the editors.

438. **SMITH, ARCHIBALD (FAMILY).** *The Death of a Confederate: Selections from the Letters of the Archibald Smith Family of Roswell, Georgia, 1864–1956.* Edited by Arthur N. Skinner and James L. Skinner. Athens: University of Georgia Press, 1996. 296 pp.

January 1, 1864–February 14, 1867. Letters. The Atlanta campaign; the March to the Sea; and the Carolinas campaign. These letters focus on a family's circumstances as it moved from its plantation in Roswell to a refugee home in Valdosta, Georgia. Many of the letters were written by and to the mother, Anne, and concern anticipation of Sherman's troops in northwestern Georgia and the welfare of the sons, Willie and Archie. Letters to and from Archie pertain to his military duties. As members of the Georgia Military Institute, Archie and other cadets aided in the defense of Milledgeville and Savannah, and in January 1865 Archie was sent back to Valdosta to recover from an illness. Willie was a member of the Eighteenth Georgia Infantry Battalion throughout the war, but he served on detached duty with the signal corps at locations around Savannah. He accompanied the Confederate evacuation of Savannah. Letters to and from Willie contain comments on war issues (including Gov. Joe Brown's resistance to the Confederate government), collection of plant life to be sent to Valdosta (in response to a request from his sister Lizzie), requests for and advice to his brother Archie, the defense of Savannah, and the Carolinas campaign. In March 1865 Willie became ill and was admitted to a hospital in Raleigh. He was cared for by a family in its home in Raleigh, but he died on July 7. The letters written between September 1865 and February 1867 are devoted to Willie's death and preparations for placing a stone to mark his grave in Raleigh. A chapter of family-related correspondence written between 1948 and 1956 concludes the work.

439. **SNAKENBERG, WILLIAM P.** "A Confederate Foreign Legion: Louisiana 'Wildcats' in the Army of Northern Virginia." By Lawrence L. Hewitt. *Journal of Confederate History* 6 (1990): 53–75.

1861–1864. Memoir. Private. Fourteenth Louisiana Infantry. Seven Days' Battles (at White Oak Swamp the regiment suffered devastating casualties); second Bull Run; Antietam; Chancellorsville; Gettysburg; The Wilderness; and Spotsylvania. This article makes it obvious why the unit earned its nickname and that its first colonel (Valery Sulakowski) left his personal mark on the unit. The foreign-born members further added an interesting flavor to the regiment. Hewitt bases the "story" on Snakenberg's memoirs, utilizing his quotations. Hewitt's own research identifies names and events. Also, Hewitt adds a list of changes in commanders and brigades and summarizes desertion rates. Contrary to popular assumption, he found that the highest rate of desertion was among the native-born, not the foreigners. Hewitt concludes with tables of desertion based on occupation.

440. SPEARS, EDWARD FORD. "'I consider the Regiment My Home': The Orphan Brigade; Life and Letters of Capt. Edward Ford Spears, 1861–1865." Edited by Samuel R. Flora. *Register of the Kentucky Historical Society* 94 (Spring 1996): 134–73.

August 23, 1861–January 2, 1865. Letters. Captain. Second Kentucky Infantry. Duty in Kentucky; Camp Chase and Johnson's Island Prisons (he was captured at Fort Donelson); winter camps at Manchester, Tennessee and Dalton, Georgia (his unit covered Bragg's retreat from Chattanooga); and the Atlanta campaign, especially Dallas. Written after he was wounded at Jonesboro, Spear's remaining letters mention his hospitalization and recuperation. Consistent themes of these nine letters to his sisters back home in Bourbon County, Kentucky, are Spear's high morale and devotion to his regiment and family. He was not ashamed of having been captured at Fort Donelson. He denied that Confederates were defeated at Stones River. After the battle he reflected on life in the military. He commented that "soldiering is truly a strange life," then contemplated the "peculiar charm in the excitement of moving about so much that I cannot help feeling better after the march is over" (p. 155). He was torn between desire for another hard fight, one that would make up for the Confederates that the Yankees had killed, and never again seeing another battle. But if there were to be another big fight, he was certain that he wanted to be with his regiment. He admitted that he looked forward to the day when he could tell "as big a story as any of our revolutionary fathers ever did" (p. 155). In fact, Spears's objection to soldiering was his inability to "communicate" with those at home. In all his letters remarks about the men from home and his longing to be back with his sisters prevail over the fighting. The editor's comments about the Orphan Brigade and Spears constitute much of the article.

441. STEPHENSON, PHILLIP DAINGERFIELD. *The Civil War Memoir of Phillip Daingerfield Stephenson, D.D.* Edited by Nathaniel Cheairs Hughes Jr. Conway, Ark.: UCA Press, 1995. 411 pp.

April 10, 1861–1865. Memoir. Thirteenth Arkansas Infantry and Fifth Battery, Washington Artillery of New Orleans. Camp Jackson affair; Belmont; siege and evacuation of Corinth; Missionary Ridge; the Atlanta campaign; the Franklin and Nashville campaign; and Spanish Fort. Throughout his memoirs Stephenson mixes the events that occurred during the war years with events of the subsequent three decades. As a sixteen-year-old boy, Stephenson observed the Camp Jackson affair in Saint Louis. Later that year he joined the Confederate army in Memphis. In his memoir he says that as a young soldier naïveté prevented him from grasping the reason that the old man who came to camp ostensibly to sell eggs always brought along his daughter. Some thirty-five years later he reflected: "I was as innocent and modest as a girl" (p. 19). He noticed that soldiers could be bullies in the safety of the camp but lack courage to face the enemy, and he cited fear as the reason an Irish bully ran from picket duty. Stephenson offers many favorable sketches of generals but especially of Joe Johnston for the way he instilled pride on the Army of Tennessee following its defeats at Franklin and Nashville. In his final chapter Stephenson describes the surrender of Mobile, his travel back to Saint Louis, and the harassment of civilians with pro-Southern sentiments. During the period after Lincoln's assassination Stephenson's family home was ransacked. Stephenson had great difficulty adjusting to everyday life. He felt cynicism, skepticism, and a loss of faith in God. He wrote, "Restlessness, restlessness, restlessness would come, intense to fierce" (p. 387). Eventually his relief came through religion, and he became a Presbyterian minister. Stephenson continued to believe that the United States would have been better off in every respect, including race relations, had the South won the war. He denounced emancipation as "an experiment, the results of which are still becoming more and more appalling" (p. 375). Chapter 1 was also published as "Like Sheep in a Slaughter Pen: A St. Louisan Remembers the Camp Jackson Massacre, May 10, 1861," edited by William C. Winter, in *Gateway Heritage* 15 (Spring 1995): 56–71.

442. **STIRMAN, ERASMUS I.** *"In Fine Spirits": The Civil War Letters of Ras Stirman.* Historical comments by Pat Carr. Fayetteville, Ark.: Washington County Historical County, 1986. 83 pp.

March 19, 1860–April 14, 1864. Letters. Colonel. First (Stirman's) Arkansas Cavalry Battalion. "Ras" Stirman describes the organization of the unit in Washington County, Arkansas, and early service on the Arkansas border, including the battles of Carthage and Wilson's Creek. He also relates events of the siege and battle of Corinth, Pea Ridge, Iuka, and Marks' Mill. Stirman's generally light-hearted letters kept his sister apprised of his flirtations (approximately five) and offered her advice on how she should handle would-be suitors. Ras was exhilarated by his first cavalry charge at Pea Ridge and was proud that his brigade was a crack sharpshooting unit. He seems to have been genuinely amazed that he rose so quickly from private to colonel. To Ras, the war was worth fighting because the Confederacy was "an oppressed Nation," and the South would be victorious because God would help "regain our liberties" and "whip the world combined against us" (pp. 35–36). Although Stirman admitted that he was in the minority, he strongly supported Jefferson Davis's decision to implement a conscription act in 1862. Additional documents supplied by Carr cover some details of the maneuvering of Stirman's Battalion in southeastern Arkansas during the last year of the war.

443. **STOKES, WILLIAM A.** *Saddle Soldiers: The Civil War Correspondence of General William Stokes of the 4th South Carolina Cavalry.* Edited by Lloyd Halliburton. Orangeburg, S.C.: Sandlapper Publishing Co., 1993. 265 pp.

September 5, 1861–April 2, 1865. Letters. General. Fourth South Carolina Cavalry. Stokes's letters to his wife relate the organization of his unit, light duties in defense of the South Carolina coast, the battle of Pocotaligo, Confederate reaction to Union probes on the mainland, and what he knew of the bombardment of Charleston and fighting on the harbor islands. From Virginia he described the battles of Haw's Shop, Cold Harbor, Sheridan's Trevilian raid (including the battle of Trevilian Station), Wilson's and Kautz's Petersburg raid, Reams' Station, and first Hatcher's Run. Stokes's letters indicate the toll that Grant's Virginia campaign had taken on the men and horses of the Confederate cavalry. On September 2 and 6, 1864, after reviewing the reduced number of effectives, he wrote, "so you can see how near our regiment is played out" and "The cavalry is not what it used to be" (p. 168). But conditions became even more desperate. On November 29, 1864, after he counted only sixty-three privates and about thirty noncommissioned and commissioned officers with serviceable mounts, he exclaimed: "A Regiment in name only" (p. 183). Stokes was given a three-week leave on December 23. Because he remained on leave three weeks longer, he was placed under arrest until March 29, 1865, and rejoined his regiment in South Carolina.

444. **STONE, JOHN H.** "The 'Diary' of John H. Stone, First Lieutenant, Company B, 2d Maryland Infantry, C.S.A." Edited by Thomas G. Clemens. *Maryland Historical Magazine* 85 (Summer 1990): 109–43.

June 15, 1862–July 1863. Diary. Lieutenant. Second Maryland Infantry. Duty in Virginia (including second Winchester) and the Gettysburg campaign (including the battle and Lee's retreat to Virginia). The diary, written in the form of letters, contains many details of Stone's daily activities. The editor explains the significance of this work and includes a biographical sketch of Stone.

445. **STUART, J. E. B.** "Letters to Laura." *Civil War Times Illustrated* 31 (July/August 1992): 12, 58, 60–61.

December 25, 1861–March 17, 1862. Stuart's Cavalry Corps, Army of Northern Virginia. This work consists of Stuart's letters to a lady friend, Laura Ratcliffe, who lived near Centerville, Virginia.

163

446. STUART, J. E. B. (STAFF) *With Pen and Saber: The Letters and Diaries of J. E. B. Stuart's Staff Officers.* Edited by Robert J. Trout. Mechanicsburg, Pa.: Stackpole Books, 1995. 350 pp.

May 9, 1861–May 17, 1864. Letters and diaries. Stuart's Cavalry Corps, Army of Northern Virginia. The editor states that these ten officers were among the thirty-nine who served on Stuart's cavalry staff at various times. Trout has arranged the writings chronologically and provided biographical sketches and editorial footnotes, maps, and photographs. The five letter writers are Peter Wilson Hairston (May 9 to October 11, 1861), Philip Henry Powers (July 1861 to May 1864), Chriswell Dabney (December 1861 to June 1863), Richard Channing Price (September 1862 to April 16, 1863), and Francis "Frank" Smith Robertson (March to June 1863). The four diarists are John Esten Cooke (June and July 1862 and January to April 1864), James Hardeman Stuart (July 1 to August 24, 1862), Thomas Randolph Price Jr. (1863), and Alexander Robinson Boteler (May 1864). A selection of poems by William Willis Blackford is included in the appendix.

447. TALIAFERRO, WILLIAM BOOTH. "Personal Reminiscences of 'Stonewall' Jackson." *Civil War Times Illustrated* 34 (May/June 1995): 18, 20, 22, 60–65.

1846–1863. Memoir. Major General. In this postwar speech delivered to the United Confederate Veterans in Richmond, Taliaferro lionizes Jackson. Taliaferro said that he "does not imply any discussion of his character or any critical review of his military performances" and, therefore, did not pursue the animosity that existed between the two men.

448. TAYLOR, WALTER HERRON. *Lee's Adjutant: The Wartime Letters of Walter Herron Taylor, 1862–1865.* Edited by R. Lockwood Towner, with John S. Belmont. Columbia: University of South Carolina Press, 1995. 343 pp.

May 15, 1862–March 27, 1865. Letters. Lieutenant Colonel. Aide and Assistant Adjutant General on the headquarters staff of the Army of Northern Virginia. Second Bull Run; Antietam; Chancellorsville; Brandy Station; Gettysburg; Bristoe Station; Kelly's Ford; and the Virginia campaign, including The Wilderness, the siege of Petersburg, and "the Crater." Taylor wrote to various members of his family and his fiancée, Elizabeth "Bettie" Seldon Saunders. Throughout the war Taylor remained optimistic. For example, he considered Antietam to be a stalemate from which the Confederate army had learned valuable lessons. While at Gettysburg he wrote that Pickett's Charge was a success and that Meade left the field before the Confederate army. During the course of the war Taylor's role on Lee's small personal staff increased dramatically. Because Lee treated paperwork with disdain, Taylor was forced to place priorities on correspondence, sign official documents, and make important decisions when Lee was away from headquarters. The youthful Taylor (twenty-two years of age in 1861) often felt overwhelmed by the responsibilities. During December 1863 he jested with Bettie about being "commanding general," but he quickly added, "I only hope the General will get back before I forget some serious matter or make any unfortunate blunders" (p. 97). In June 1864 Taylor became so fatigued that he feared he could not think rationally. He confessed: "The responsibility resting upon me frightens me at times" (p. 164). Lee's dependence on Taylor occasionally annoyed the aide. Taylor complained that he could not even dine out without being aroused by the words "General Lee wishes to see Col. Taylor" (p. 182). And he was disappointed that he could not leave camp with Lee because the general preferred that Taylor remain at headquarters when Lee was away. Despite the valuable services that Taylor rendered to Lee, he felt unappreciated. On one occasion, when Taylor faced a mountain of paperwork with a serious countenance, Taylor recounted that Lee "laughed heartily at me, facetiously tendered me some words of encouragement and altogether he made fun of my situation" (p. 192). He also believed that the general was slow in promoting him. Another time, after the men had argued, Taylor vented his anger on paper: "he is so unreasonable and provoking at times. I might serve him ten years to come and couldn't love him at the end of that period" (p. 182). While he acknowledged Lee's great moral influence, Taylor also wrote: "My chief is first rate in his sphere—that of a commanding general. . . . He is capable of planning a campaign . . . but not quick enough for such little affairs . . ." (p. 131). Taylor concluded the analysis with, "Oh, for a Jackson" (p. 131). As the war lengthened, Taylor altered his reference to Lee from "My chief" to "My old chief." During the last months of the Confederacy, Taylor's letters were frenetic. He had an urgent desire to be married before Richmond fell. The editor says that on the day Richmond was evacuated, Lee granted Taylor permission to return to Richmond to be married and explains that, in the postwar period, Taylor's appreciation for Lee increased. The editor utilizes other sources to expand on Taylor's experiences.

449. TRAWEEK, WASHINGTON F. "Break Out!" *Civil War Times Illustrated* 30 (November/December 1991): 26, 52–54, 56, 59–61.
Summer 1864. Memoir. Jeff Davis Battery, Alabama Light Artillery. The author recounts a successful escape from Elmira Prison through a tunnel.

450. TRUEHEART, CHARLES WILLIAM, and HENRY MARTYN TRUEHEART. *Rebel Brothers: The Civil War Letters of the Truehearts.* Edited by Edward B. Williams. College Station.: Texas A&M Press, 1995. 276 pp.
1861–1865. Letters. The two Trueheart brothers wrote to their parents at home in Galveston and to each other. Charles's letters (January 14, 1861–March 27, 1865) describe service with the Rockbridge Light Artillery and as an assistant surgeon with the Eighth Alabama Infantry and First Confederate Engineer Regiment. While he was studying medicine at the University of Virginia his student unit, the "Southern Guards," accompanied Virginia state troops to occupy Harpers Ferry. He joined the Rockbridge Artillery during the fall of 1861 and saw action during the Romney campaign, Jackson's Shenandoah Valley campaign, and the Seven Days' Battles. Following an attack of scurvy and a stint as a hospital steward at a Lynchburg hospital, Charles completed his medical training. He then served with the First Alabama Infantry. He was with the First Confederate Engineers during the Virginia campaign and the siege of Petersburg. Henry's letters (May 17, 1862–January 18, 1865) mention his role in the Confederate capture of Galveston (see item 451). He became a member of the Seventh Virginia Cavalry in June 1863 and later joined McNeill's Rangers. In his letters he mentions incidents of battles and raids in the Shenandoah Valley and northwestern Virginia, such as Early's Washington raid, Rosser's raid on New Creek, and McNeill's raid on Cumberland, Maryland, in which Union generals George Crook and Benjamin Kelly were taken captive. Charles encouraged Henry to leave McNeill's Partisan Rangers and join a regular army unit; however, Henry refused and expressed pride in the accomplishments of McNeill's Rangers. In January 1865 Henry visited Charles at Petersburg and described the siege lines and fraternization. As he observed how near the opposing forces were to each other, he contrasted it with the kind of fighting to which he was accustomed. "In my field of operations we never get that close to each other without shooting" (p. 213). Henry's final letter, written just after the fall of Fort Fisher, reflects the popular mood around Petersburg: "People are *blue, blue*" (p. 214).

451. TRUEHEART, HENRY MARTYN. "A 'Spirited Account' of the Battle of Galveston, January 1, 1863." Edited by Edward B. Williams. *Southwestern Historical Quarterly* 99 (October 1995): 200–215.
January 1, 1863. Letter. Battle of Galveston. Prior to his enlistment (see item 450) Trueheart was a Galveston businessman. Here he describes his role in the battle as an observer of the placement of

Union troops and ships in the harbor. He also assisted in the evacuation of residents of the city and carried messages for the Confederate army. Trueheart relates the capture of the USS *Harriet Lane* and the Forty-second Massachusetts Infantry.

452. **VENABLE, RICHARD M.** "A Different View on the War: The Civil War Diary of Richard M. Venable." By Michael E. Pilgrim. *Prologue* 28 (Winter 1996): 263–69.

November 3, 1863–November 28, 1864. Diary. Shreveport, Louisiana. Captain. Chief of the Topographical Bureau, District of West Louisiana and Arkansas, Trans-Mississippi Department. In his "diary" Venable wrote nothing about the war, soldiering, or the grand cause of the Confederacy. He wrote only of "discussions of the role of man and his relationships to the world around him" (p. 263). Themes include monotheism, happiness, truth, and the creation of one's character. Venable also composed a list of original maxims. Pilgrim presents this work simply as "a brief glimpse of the inner feelings of one Confederate" and "a fascinating view of Civil War era values and interests" (p. 268).

453. **WARD, WILLIAM W.** *"For the Sake of My Country": The Diary of Col. W. W. Ward, 9th Tennessee Cavalry, Morgan's Brigade, C.S.A.* Edited by R. B. Rosenburg. Murfreesboro, Tenn.: Southern Heritage Press, 1992. 164 pp.

March 30, 1864–April 6, 1865. Diary. Colonel. Ninth (Ward's) Tennessee Cavalry and First Kentucky Special Cavalry Battalion. After being captured on July 19, 1863, during Morgan's Kentucky, Ohio, and Indiana raid, Ward spent eight months at the Ohio State Penitentiary before being shipped to Fort Delaware Prison on March 28, 1864. In these entries, which cover his last three months of incarceration at Fort Delaware, Ward indicates that he received good treatment and had a cordial relationship with the prison commandant. But between June 28 and August 4, 1864, he was among the prisoners held in Charleston harbor aboard a Union ship under the guns of the blockading warships. These Confederate prisoners, "The Immortal Six Hundred," were used as hostages to discourage the Confederate batteries. This was done in retaliation for the holding of Union officers in Charleston in areas that were vulnerable to Union siege guns. During his six weeks on the ship Ward was often sick. He complained about the rancid food, oppressive July heat, confined movement, and his fellow prisoners. Writing on August 1, 1864, he attempted to be philosophical about his experience as a prisoner by summing up what he had learned about "human nature." Instead, he criticized his fellow prisoners' propensity to be vain and egotistical. After his release he traveled from Charleston to Abbington, Virginia, and then to Richmond. Along the way he described the conditions of travel and appearance of the cities, the people, and the landscape. In September 1864 he assumed command of the First Kentucky Cavalry Battalion. Writing from eastern Tennessee, Ward related the social conditions, scarcity of food, and military actions after Gen. Basil Duke assumed command of Morgan's Brigade. Ward mentions the deaths of the Union colored troops at Saltville, Virginia; a ride into the countryside to seek deserters and suspected members of the Unionist "Heroes of America"; and the battle of Bull's Gap, Tennessee, where he was wounded. Although he had not fully recuperated, Ward fought at Saltville, Virginia, in mid December, when the Union army disrupted the important Confederate saltworks. Following a trip to Richmond, Ward spent the remainder of the winter in a cold encampment near Wytheville, Virginia, but wrote little in his diary.

454. **WARING, THOMAS SMITH.** "Confederate Surgeon: The Letters of Thomas Smith Waring, A South Carolina Planter-Physician at War." Edited by W. Curtis Worthington Jr. *Journal of Confederate History* 2, no. 1 (1989): 44–92.

1861–October 25, 1862. Letters. Assistant surgeon. Seventeenth South Carolina Infantry. Duty at the Charleston harbor islands (including the battle of Secessionville); second Bull Run; and Antietam. Worthington paraphrases and quotes from these letters to reveal Waring's attitudes toward the war. In South Carolina, Waring assessed the Confederate ability to defend the coastlines. His responsibilities included the medical care of some six hundred men spread among four different camps. Writing in Virginia, he commented on the value to the soldiers' morale of grouping men from the same state together. At second Bull Run he wrote of constantly being called on by the wounded despite being wounded himself. Eager to help, he was admonished after the fighting subsided because he had moved his medical station too close to the combat. As he plundered the captured Union stores at second Bull Run, he retrieved "a beautiful amputating case and a very pretty Set of tooth extracting instruments" (p. 73). The editor says that some of Waring's descriptions of the fighting at Antietam may have been hearsay since Waring had been dispatched to the Shepherdstown hospital after the battle of South Mountain. Waring commented frequently about the strategy of battles and the Emancipation Proclamation, but (the editor says) Waring did not have a good record for accuracy. By the fall of 1862 Waring exhibited some ambivalence about his role in the war. Because of unspecified medical problems he resigned in December 1862. Worthington summarizes Waring's later writings and continues his attempt to analyze the surgeon's personality.

455. WATSON, GEORGE WILLIAM. *The Last Survivor: The Memoirs of George William Watson, a Horse Soldier in the 12th Virginia Cavalry (Confederate States Army).* By Brian Stuart Kesterson. Washington, W.Va.: Night Hawk Press, 1993. 68 pp.

March 1862–1865. Memoir. Sergeant. Fifth Virginia Infantry and Twelfth Virginia Cavalry. Jackson's Shenandoah Valley campaign (including first Kernstown, McDowell, and first Winchester); second Bull Run; Cedar Mountain; Jackson's capture of Harpers Ferry; Brandy Station; Fredericksburg; The Wilderness; Cold Harbor; Trevilian Station; the Hampton-Rosser cattle raid; Sheridan's Shenandoah Valley campaign; and Watson's capture during October 1864 and imprisonment at Point Lookout Prison. Watson wrote these reminiscences of his military activities and his subsequent life in 1923.

456. WATSON, ROBERT. "War Comes to Tampa Bay: The Civil War Diary of Robert Watson." Edited by Ronald N. Prouty. *Tampa Bay History* 10 (Fall/Winter 1988): 36–65.

December 13, 1861–June 27, 1862. Diary. Florida Volunteer Coast Guard, Mulrennan's Company. This diary describes routines performed by Gov. Milton's Coast Guard. The men drilled, built huts and batteries, chased Yankee ships, fought off mosquitoes and fleas, and hunted for food. The company became Seventh Florida Infantry Regiment, Company K.

457. WHITEHORNE, JAMES E. *Diary of J. E. Whitehorne, 1st Sergt., Co. "F," 12th Va. Infantry, A.P. Hill's 3rd Corps, Army of Northern Va.* Compiled by Fletcher L. Elmore Jr. Utica, Ky.: McDowell Publications, 1995. 114 pp.

June 9, 1861–June 3, 1862 and June 1, 1863–April 16, 1865. Diary and letters. Sergeant. Twelfth Virginia Infantry. Duty at Norfolk; the CSS *Virginia*'s attack on Union ships off Hampton Roads (observed); Seven Pines; Chancellorsville; the Gettysburg campaign, including battle and Lee's retreat; the siege of Petersburg; the Appomattox campaign; and his march back home to Greensville County, Virginia, after the surrender. During the Gettysburg campaign Whitehorne noted that the Confederate presence in Maryland was met with little enthusiasm. In Pennsylvania he observed that the soldiers had plenty of food, which they assured him they had paid for. As his unit approached Gettysburg on the night of July 1, Whitehorne commented on how the musketry and seeing the wounded being carried to the rear all affected him: "it takes all the moral courage that I possess to face the music" (p. 26). After being wounded on the second day, Whitehorne wrote about his trip to the hospital in Richmond. He rejoined the Twelfth Virginia the next year and was wounded during the charge into "the Crater." In March 1865 he observed: "Our prospects are gloomy in the extreme" (p. 59). Near the end of the war Whitehorne listed the corps he believed to be the most demoralized. He said that when news of Lee's surrender reached his unit, he did not cry like some others. Nevertheless, he thought it was sad that, after four years of suffering, the Confederacy had been forced to succumb to the overwhelming numbers of the Union. Whitehorne said that at Appomattox Court House, as the Confederates surrendered their arms, the Union soldiers were not offensive but, rather, "Conducted themselves with the utmost decorum" (p. 76). In his final entries he relates episodes of the soldiers walking back to their homes.

458. WHITEHORNE, JAMES E., and JAMES ELDRED PHILLIPS. "Final March to Appomattox: The 12th Virginia Infantry, April 2–12, 1865, An Eyewitness Account." Edited by Chris M. Calkins. *Civil War Regiments* 2, no. 3 (1992): 236–51.

April 2–12, 1865. Journal and diary. Twelfth Virginia Infantry. Sergeants. Appomattox campaign. The editor compares the writings of both men and the manner in which they expressed their experiences.

459. WIATT, WILLIAM EDWARD. *Confederate Chaplain William Edward Wiatt: An Annotated Diary.* Edited by Alex L. Wiatt. Lynchburg, Va.: H. E. Howard, 1994. 255 pp.

October 1, 1862–April 22, 1865. Diary. Chaplain. Twenty-sixth Virginia Infantry. Duty in northern Virginia; around Charleston (including the battle of Legareville) and in Florida; and then again in Virginia, including the battle of Nottoway Bridge, Butler's Bermuda Hundred campaign, the assaults on Petersburg, the siege of Petersburg, the Appomattox campaign, and the surrender at Appomattox Court House. Wiatt, a Baptist pastor from Gloucester County, Virginia, had served eighteen months with the Twenty-sixth Virginia as a private and a chaplain before he began this diary. In each entry he recorded his activities, as well as information about specific individuals. He tirelessly distributed tracts and testaments; preached everywhere, from large tents to guard houses and in the trenches; held private conversations about religion; aided the sick and wounded in the hospitals; wrote letters for those who were unable; buried many; and married others. He solicited money to aid the people of Fredericksburg, build a chapel, and purchase religious materials. He kept track of men's names, often noting whether they were prospective converts or "backsliders," or had been killed, wounded, or were ill. And he attended Masonic meetings and helped to found a Christian Association. After a long period of inactivity, the regiment was shipped to South Carolina in September 1863. For the remainder of the war Wiatt continued his religious activities, but he included more about the fighting and his personal life in his diary. He participated in an attempt to establish a battery near Legareville, South Carolina (on the Stono River), to ambush Union ships. The battery missed with some three hundred shots at the USS *Marblehead,* which made the usually low-keyed Wiatt mad. The ship turned her guns on the Confederate batteries and drove the men from their placement, forcing them to leave behind two howitzers. Wiatt wrote angrily that "it was a miserable and disgraceful failure" (p. 128). In 1862 Wiatt moved his family from their Gloucester County farm to Montgomery, Alabama. During late 1863 and early 1864 his wife suffered a series of hemorrhages and died. With sadness Wiatt distributed his four children among friends and relatives. After each of these personal tragedies Wiatt became even more attached to his unit. He first wrote: "I am broken up and have no home but with the 26th Virginia Regiment" (p. 44). After the death of his wife he wrote, "I feel like being in my right place" (p. 154). He recorded how depleted the original regiment became during the siege of Petersburg. On September 26, 1864, he wrote that only 175 officers and men from his regiment were on duty. After the surrender Wiatt wondered, "*has God forsaken us? is our Confederacy ruined* I, for one, can't believe it; God has humbled us to exalt us" (p. 237). A few days later he was even more adamant when he wrote: "will God, can God forget his people? *Impossible! Impossible!*" (p. 242).

460. WILLIAMS, HIRAM SMITH. *This War So Horrible: The Civil War Diary of Hiram Smith Williams.* Edited by Lewis N. Wynne and Robert A. Taylor. Tuscaloosa: University of Alabama Press, 1993. 176 pp.

February 16, 1864–June 6, 1865. Diary. Fortieth Alabama Infantry. Williams enlisted in the Fortieth Alabama in 1862. However, his civilian skills as a carriage maker were utilized in the shipyards of Mobile until the Atlanta campaign, when he was transferred to Gen. Alexander P. Stewart's pioneer corps (First Corps, Army of Tennessee). Soon after his transfer from Mobile to Dalton in February 1864, he described the Union shelling at Rocky Face Ridge. He learned to distinguish the sound of a shell bursting overhead from the shrill hiss of an approaching minié ball. He initially pretended to be unafraid of enemy fire but soon followed the older veterans to shelter. During the Atlanta campaign the pioneers built bridges, dams, breastworks, and roads for all units of the army. In May he described seeing hundreds of ambulances along the road all mingled up in "entangled confusion" (p. 70). At night he listened to the cries of the wounded who were having their limbs amputated. In the morning he helped dig holes for the dismembered arms and legs. In several vivid descriptions of burials, he betrays his personal fear of being laid to rest so far from home in an unmarked grave. Williams expresses his abhorrence of war in such phrases as "Another day of blood and strife. Enough to make the angels weep over the fallen natures of mankind" (p. 60). He called the war "so unholy . . . so useless as to results, so absurd as to the establishment of any great and vital principle . . ." (p. 33). Williams eventually joined the Fortieth Alabama in Mobile in January 1865, and the unit was soon shipped to the Carolinas. At Bentonville, when it was obvious to him that victory was not possible, he simply lay down and allowed himself to be captured. His diary entries from Point Lookout Prison are filled with satire about the wild rumors and several lengthy poems. All the while Williams longed to be back with his friends in Mobile and their theater group.

461. WILLIAMS, J. R. "An Account of Fredericksburg, 1863: Written by J. R. Williams." By Joe M. Rice. *Journal of the North Louisiana Historical Association* 17 (Winter 1986): 39–42.

May 14, 1863. Letter. Private. Ninth Louisiana Infantry. Battle of Chancellorsville.

462. WINGFIELD, JOHN T. "Wilderness to Petersburg: Unpublished Reports of the 11th Battalion, Georgia Light Artillery." *Civil War Regiments* 3, no. 2 (1993): 61–69.

May 5–November 5, 1864. Report. Lieutenant. Georgia Light Artillery, Eleventh Battalion. Virginia campaign and siege of Petersburg.

463. WOOD, HENRY B. "From Montgomery to Gettysburg: War Letters from Alabama Soldier Henry B. Wood." By Wayne Wood. *Alabama Heritage* 15 (Winter 1990): 26–41.

July 2, 1861–June 6, 1863. Letters. Twelfth Alabama Infantry. First Bull Run (aftermath); Seven Pines; and Chancellorsville. En route to Bull Run the engineer of the train (a Union supporter) purposefully delayed the train, preventing Wood's regiment from reaching the battlefield. Wood wrote that the man was condemned to death. The emphasis of these soulful letters is Wood's disenchantment with the war, or perhaps more accurately, Wood's longing to be home. He wrote to his wife: "please dont beg me so hard to come home. . . . It makes me study so much a bout home that it renders me unhappy" (p. 33). He mentions anticipation of battles, some details of the fighting, the high price of food in Richmond, and his struggle with an illness. He related his physical deterioration when he wrote that his manservant had told him "I looked like I had bin run threw a hacking mashine" (p. 40).

464. **WRIGHT, HENRY CLAY.** "A Johnny Reb in Sibley's New Mexico Campaign: Reminiscences of Pvt. Henry C. Wright, 1861–1862." Edited by Michael L. Tate. (Part I) *East Texas Historical Journal* 25, no. 2 (1987): 20–33.

———. (Part II) *East Texas Historical Journal* 26, no. 1 (1988): 23–35.
———. (Part III) *East Texas Historical Journal* 26, no. 1 (1988): 48–60.

1861–1862. Memoir. Fourth Texas Cavalry. Sibley's New Mexico campaign, including Valverde. Wright recalls the high spirits at the beginning of the march and how the Confederate soldiers antagonized the friendly Mexicans near El Paso. Wright relates the fighting at the battle of Valverde and explains why the Confederates did not follow the victory with the capture of Fort Craig. When they lost their supply base after the battle of Glorieta Pass, the Confederates were forced to retreat. Wright chose to stay in Santa Fe to care for the wounded. The Union army moved into Santa Fe and captured the wounded. Wright paid great respect to Gen. Edward Canby's wife and the ladies of Santa Fe for their care of the Confederate sick and wounded. The last part of this memoir describes being placed in prison under false charges. When Wright was eventually released, he was made to make the difficult trek across the west Texas desert. He arrived home in Moscow, Texas, in June 1862.

465. **ZACHRY, ALFRED.** "Fighting with the 3d Georgia." (Part I) *Civil War Times Illustrated* 33 (September/October 1994): 26, 66–77.

———. (Part II) *Civil War Times Illustrated* 33 (November/December 1994): 32, 100–112.

1861–1865. Memoir. Lieutenant. Third Georgia Infantry. Duty on Roanoke Island; the Peninsular campaign; Fredericksburg; the Gettysburg campaign; and the Virginia campaign.

B. South Civilian
Items 466–544

466. ABERNATHY, MARTHA STOCKARD. *The Civil War Diary of Martha Abernathy, Wife of Dr. Charles C. Abernathy of Pulaski, Tennessee.* Edited by Elizabeth Paisley Dargan. Beltsville, Md.: Professional Printing, 1994. 128 pp.
May 7, 1861–August 23, 1862. Diary. Pulaski, Tennessee. Early in this selection of entries Martha argues for the validity of Southern secession. Nevertheless, she expresses concern about her ability to bear her husband's absence after his call to service as surgeon with the Eighteenth (and later the Third) Tennessee Infantry in the fall of 1861. Martha assures Charles that she will care for their children; she also included a list of moral virtues. After John Hunt Morgan entered Pulaski on May 1, 1862, and captured 268 Union troops, everyday life for the civilians changed. When Morgan departed, the federals returned, and Pulaski became a military camp. Destruction of private property by soldiers and civilians was an everyday occurrence. The severest incident of social unrest was a fire that consumed many homes. Martha blamed restive slaves for the incident. In her later entries she seems to have acknowledged the permanence of occupation, but she was no less opposed to it. This work includes several letters from her husband, as well as letters, documents, prayers, and poems from other periods.

467. ADDISON-DARNEILLE, HENRIETTA STOCKTON. "For Better or for Worse." *Civil War Times Illustrated* 31 (May/June 1992): 32–35, 73.
July 1861. Memoir. This work documents Henrietta's perilous journey through Union lines from Baltimore to Richmond in the company of her father and husband, Benjamin. It includes comments about the war in general.

468. AGNEW, SAMUEL A. "A Civilian at Brice's Crossroads." Edited by Mark Grimsley. *Civil War Times Illustrated* 32 (January/February 1994): 39–40, 73.
June 5–June 14, 1864. Diary. Brice's Cross Roads. Reverend Agnew, a pastor of the Associated Reformed Church of Bethany, recorded rumors of the Union raid, the battle, and the aftermath.

469. ANDERSON, CARTER S. *Train Running for the Confederacy, 1861–1865.* Edited by Walbrook D. Swank. Shippensburg, Pa.: Burd Street Press, 1992. 74 pp.
1861–1865. Memoir. Conductor. Virginia Central Railroad. This work includes unedited anecdotes of railroading in Virginia during the war. Anderson relates transporting troops (especially during the spring and summer of 1862); near accidents; railroad men who occasionally drank too much; relationships (good and bad) between military and railroad authorities; the condition of the bridges, rails, tracks, and rolling stock; and Union raids on railroads in 1863 and 1864 (especially the Kilpatrick-Dahlgren raid on Richmond). The preface states that Anderson wrote his memoirs as a "series of stories" between 1892 and 1894.

470. ANDERSON, JAMES, and MARY ANDERSON. "The Approach of the Civil War as Seen in the Letters of James and Mary Anderson of Rockville." Edited by George M. Anderson. *Maryland Historical Magazine* 88 (Summer 1993): 189–202.

November 15, 1860–May 29, 1861. Letters. Washington, D.C., and Rockville, Maryland. Provides a glimpse of the politically charged atmosphere in the federal capital just prior to the war, especially the pro-Southern feelings that existed in Montgomery County, Maryland. James was employed as a clerk in the Treasury Department while Mary remained on their Rockville farm. The family's concern over its financial future deepened in May 1861. James lost his clerkship when he refused to sign the oath of loyalty to the federal government.

471. BACOT, ADA W. *The Confederate Nurse: The Diary of Ada W. Bacot, 1860–1863.* Edited by Jean V. Berlin. Columbia: University of South Carolina Press, 1994. 199 pp.

September 11, 1860–January 18, 1863. Diary. Charlottesville, Virginia. This twenty-seven-year-old widow from a plantation in the Darlington District of South Carolina began work at the Monticello Hospital in Charlottesville in January 1862. As a matron she dressed wounds, prepared medical supplies, wrote letters for the soldiers, and talked with them about religion. Throughout her diary Bacot expresses her strong sense of nationalism for her "beloved country." While she pitied the hospitalized Yankee soldiers, she wrote that she cared for them because "it is my duty" (p. 125). Bacot recorded many aspects of hospital life: the condition of those hospitalized; the sudden arrival of the recently wounded; shortages of supplies; and the activities of other helpers at the hospital. Much of her diary is devoted to her personal feelings and occurrences outside the facility. She obviously enjoyed the camaraderie of the staff, who boarded together in the city. She also describes such events as visits to Jefferson's Monticello and the passage of Jackson's army through the city on its way to the Virginia Peninsula. Although personally fulfilled by her experiences, Bacot struggled with homesickness and worry about her family in South Carolina. She became ill in late 1862 and returned to her plantation for a short time. The diary ends inconclusively. The editor adds that Bacot was back home again by the fall of 1863. Berlin suggests reasons why Bacot's service in Charlottesville ended and completes a biographical sketch of her subsequent life. Excerpts were published as "A Civil War Nurse in Charlottesville," *Magazine of Albemarle County History* 52 (1994): 125–46.

472. BECTON, SUSAN. "Disillusioned with Paradise: A Southern Woman's Impression of the Rural North in 1862." By John A. Hall. *Southern Studies* 25 (Summer 1986): 203–7.

December 14, 1862. Letter. This teacher from North Carolina observed the Northern women of Paradise, Pennsylvania (Lancaster County), performing the drudgery of household chores. She confessed that she preferred that slaves do such work.

473. BELL, MARY. "Coping in Confederate Appalachia: Portrait of a Mountain Woman and Her Community at War." By John C. Inscoe. *North Carolina Historical Review* 69 (October 1992): 388–413.

November 1861–February 1865. Letters. Franklin (Macon County), North Carolina. Mary Bell's husband, Alfred (Captain, Thirty-ninth North Carolina Infantry), left home in November 1861. Except for 1863, when Alfred was at home, Mary assumed management of their farm until Alfred returned permanently in February 1865. The couple lived in the village of Franklin, where Alfred had a thriving dental practice. Mary's letters to Alfred reveal how her competence and self-assurance increased in his absence. The author divides Mary's reaction to her experience into two periods. From late 1861 through 1862 Mary asked Alfred many questions, and he offered a great deal of advice. But during 1864 through early 1865 her self-confidence had increased to the point that Alfred asked Mary questions about the crops and business arrangements. In this later period Mary used the first person "I" more frequently and transacted the purchase of a three-member slave family. Throughout the article the author utilizes lengthy quotations from the letters to demonstrate not only Mary's transformation but also her individuality and the uniqueness of Macon County, which is located in southwestern North Carolina. Mary does not fit the pattern of those Southern women who praised the "Cause" in the beginning but later undermined the Confederacy by complaining about their hardships. Mary believed that since her husband was in the army, all eligible men should serve; however, her support of the Confederacy was mild. Often she was somewhat cynical and "thumbed her nose at the patriotism of other Franklin women" (p. 410). Mary's reaction to the war was personal; "from beginning to end, her own family's well-being were her only priorities" (p. 410). The author points out that one reason Mary was able to survive so independently was the help she received from community interdependency. Because Macon County did not experience the degree of divisiveness that ravaged other North Carolina counties, Mary did not suffer from the problems that plagued other women of the southern highland. The author's extensive footnotes contain important gender studies, as well as studies that treat the Appalachian region during the Civil War.

474. **BELL, NIMROD J.** *Southern Railroad Man: Conductor N. J. Bell's Recollections of the Civil War Era.* Edited by James A. Ward. DeKalb: Northern Illinois University Press, 1994. 194 pp.

1861–1865. Memoir. Until 1862 Bell was employed by the Western & Atlantic Railroad, which operated between Chattanooga and Atlanta. In 1862 he joined the East Tennessee and Georgia Railroad, which operated between Knoxville and Dalton. During 1864 and 1865 he worked for several lines in North and South Carolina. Writing in a highly anecdotal style, Bell relates some of his many duties as a conductor. His trains transported soldiers (he especially remembered the Louisiana Tigers) and freight (primarily corn in the West and cotton in the East). He touches on the condition of rails and bridges; cutting fence rails for fuel; the schedules of trains; and the manner in which conductors communicated with each other while the trains were in passage. He frequently mentions accidents involving trains, usually providing graphic portrayals of the results. Bell was exempted from the military because of his vital service on the Confederate railroads. At first his sympathies and prayers had been for the success of the Confederacy. "But toward the last I prayed for the close of the war any way—just so as to stop it, and that we might have peace once more in our country" (p. 33). The Civil War period of Bell's career is covered on pages 9 through 35. This is a new edition of Bell's *Railroad Recollections for Over Thirty-Eight Years,* published in 1896 in a limited edition.

475. **BIRD, EDGEWORTH, and SALLIE BIRD.** *The Granite Farm Letters: The Civil War Correspondence of Edgeworth & Sallie Bird.* Foreword by Theodore Rosengarten. Edited by John Rozier. Athens: University of Georgia Press, 1988. 330 pp.

April 22, 1861–May 21, 1865; February 5, 1866–January 29, 1867. "Granite Farm," Hancock County, Georgia. The majority of these letters were written by Edgeworth to his wife, Sallie, and their children, Sallie (Saida) and Wilson (Bud). Edgeworth and Sallie wrote many letters to their daughter, and Saida frequently wrote to her father. Some letters from Wilson and other family and friends complete this collection. Edgeworth (Fifteenth Georgia Infantry) served in Virginia and Tennessee. Edgeworth's letters about war news and personal matters usually ring with optimism. For example, during the Atlanta campaign Edgeworth wrote of a meeting in Richmond between Robert E. Lee and Jefferson Davis. He assures Sallie that the two leaders had devised a plan: "It is all arranged to gobble up Sherman" (p. 185). Domestic, not military, matters constitute the substance of this correspondence. Sallie assumed the responsibilities of managing the farm, paying debts, and raising the children. Edgeworth provided a torrent of practical advice about the farm and family, as well as lavish expressions of sentiment. Edgeworth wrote loving letters to Saida and implored his daughter to develop "a vigorous and cultivated mind," to rise above "stormy times" and make progress "due to your own industry and perseverance"

(p. 184). The slaves of "Granite Farm" were a constant worry for Sallie. While the Birds were apparently humane and paternalistic toward their slaves, in 1863 Edgeworth directed Sallie to sell several disobedient slaves. During the fall of 1863 Sallie perhaps doubted the future of slavery; Edgeworth wrote: "Your conclusions about slavery are not a sure thing. I think that it is entirely dependent on the results of the rebellion. If we come out with flying colours, it is established for centuries" (p. 145). The letters written during the fall of 1864 and the first half of 1865 indicate that "Granite Farm" suffered little from Sherman's march. In the final months of the war domestic matters seem to have been more important than defeat. The letters of 1866 and 1867 were to Saida, who was attending Georgetown College in Baltimore. While Sallie hardly mentioned hardships the former slaves were causing, in January 1867 she wrote that they would not work and were holding out for better contracts. Later that month she wrote that Edgeworth had obtained the assistance of his white neighbors to help him slaughter hogs. But in another letter written that cold January, Sallie informs Saida that her father had died of pneumonia.

476. **BLACK, NARCISSA L. ERWIN.** "Two Lives Intertwined on a Tennessee Plantation: Textile Production as Recorded in the Diary of Narcissa L. Erwin Black." By Mary Lohrenz. *Southern Quarterly* 27 (Fall 1988): 72–93.
January 1, 1861–February 26, 1886. Diary. McNairy County, Tennessee. Mrs. Black was forced to assume management of the family plantation because of her husband's lengthy illness. Lohrenz emphasizes that the war interrupted, but did not stop, plantation operations. Mrs. Black recorded processing practices (how the cotton was spun, dyed, etc.), purposes for which the finished product was used (barter, as well as outright sale), types of finished yard goods (usually quilting materials), and changes in the textile industry after the war. In addition, the diary reveals that the relationship between Mrs. Black and her slave weaver, Chany Scot Black, existed on both employer-employee and emotional levels. Lohrenz followed this relationship until 1872, when Chany left the plantation, but she was unable to trace the former slave's subsequent life. While marauding Yankees and local disturbances are mentioned in the diary, the central themes are the continuity of the plantation textile industry and the relationship between the two women. Lohrenz paraphrases and quotes from the complete diary, in addition to providing relevant genealogical and economic information.

477. **BREVARD, KEZIAH GOODWYN HOPKINS.** *A Plantation Mistress on the Eve of the Civil War: The Diary of Keziah Goodwyn Hopkins Brevard, 1860–1861.* Edited by John Hammond Moore. Columbia: University of South Carolina Press, 1993. 137 pp.
July 22, 1860–April 15, 1861. Diary. "Sand Hills," near Columbia, South Carolina. Brevard was a fifty-seven-year-old widow who managed an estate that included several hundred slaves, three plantations, a gristmill, and a town house in Columbia. Her diary is a record of occurrences on the estate and her own personal feelings about God, slavery, and secession. Brevard's escalating anxiety is apparent in her recitation of daily activities between July and October 1860, and she seems to have been in a state of near panic when Lincoln was elected in November. By contrast, her diary entries indicate that she accepted secession and the firing on Fort Sumter as an inevitable progression of events. Secession, the burden of slave holding, and the Northern insistence that the slaves be freed presented an inseparable conundrum to Brevard. While she did not want national unity to be broken, neither did she want the North to interfere with the South's rights. If the abolitionists were to prevail and the slaves were let loose into society, havoc would ensue. Brevard repeatedly wrote that she wished she did not have to take care of the slaves. At the same time, because she recognized that slaves had been contributors to her family wealth, she felt responsible for their descendants. Brevard continued to dissect her personal quandary: "we are attached to our slaves—they are as our own family & would to this day have been a happy people if Northern fanaticism had not warred against us" (p. 70). But as disobedience among her own slaves increased, she pondered the true nature of the relationship. She wondered if the slaves liked her. Other

slave owners felt that their slaves would stand by them if a war should occur, but she was more pessimistic. Brevard continually pleaded with God for deliverance from, or a solution to, the problems facing the nation. Variations of her lament "God save our country" are found on nearly every page. In a comment that reveals more personal desperation than a realistic solution to the crisis of slavery, disunion, and war, she suggests that the slaves be removed to a separate place together with the Northern abolitionists. When Fort Sumter fell, Brevard decided to end her diary.

478. **BROWDER, GEORGE RICHARD.** *The Heavens Are Weeping: The Diaries of George Richard Browder, 1852–1886.* Edited by Richard L. Troutman. Grand Rapids, Mich.: Zonervan Publishing House, 1987. 575 pp.

May 10, 1862–December 4, 1865. Diary. Kentucky. Browder was a circuit rider for the Methodist Church (South) and slaveholding farmer in south-central Kentucky. Browder willingly admitted the shortcomings of mortals and submitted to God's right to punish mankind. However, he was enraged by the federal government's violation of civil liberties, especially the imprisonment of those who refused to take the oath of allegiance (including his father) and the emancipation of the slaves. Browder wrote that the outcome of the war would ultimately prove whether "we of the South were wrong in our belief that God designed them for bondsmen forever. . . . If the war resulted in the liberation and improvement of the slaves condition my heart & tongue will say 'Amen'" (p. 142). Slavery and the condition of blacks are recurring themes throughout his diary. In one entry made early in the war he mentions the slaves' fear of becoming too familiar with the Yankees since "Forrest had hung quite a number" (p. 125). Browder also addresses the general restiveness of the black population. On April 20, 1864, after Fort Pillow, Browder noted the newspaper reports of "Forrests capturing & killing negro troops" and wrote, "There is a decided lull in negro enlistments. They *seem* more contented" (p. 176). Then, to him, the unimaginable occurred: "I was *drafted*! DRAFTED! Into the federal Army. Shocking, crushing, horrifying intelligence" (p. 185). Browder reasoned that because he was a man of peace, he could legitimately hire a substitute. A physical examination soon revealed that he was unfit for duty. Throughout these years Browder continued to preach to white and black congregations and attend revivals and church conferences. He often mentions his love for his wife and children, as well as prices and details of the management of his farm. When the war ended, he was true to his word in that he accepted the outcome as "providential settlement of the great slavery question" (p. 196). But forgiveness of his enemies was another matter. Browder expected God to scourge the North "for unnecessary cruelties & oppression to the Southern people" (p. 196).

479. **BROWN, JOSEPH E.** "Joe Brown vs. the Confederacy: The Governor Fights the Government." Edited by William Harris Bragg. *Civil War Times Illustrated* 26 (November 1987): 40–43.

September 27–October 3, 1864. Series of telegrams between Georgia governor Joseph E. Brown and Confederate officials. The governor contested the Confederate army's desire to send one thousand of the Georgia militia's rifles to the Confederate army of Gen. Hood. Brown initially opposed the transfer, but he eventually relented.

480. **BRUSH, SEBA BOGART.** "Business Travel Out of Texas during the Civil War: The Travel Diary of S. B. Brush, Pioneer Austin Merchant." Edited by Peyton O. Abbott. *Southwestern Historical Quarterly* 96 (October 1992): 259–71.

December 28, 1863–February 13, 1864. Diary. Written between Matamoros, Mexico, and Havana, Cuba. Brush was en route to New York City to sell cotton and purchase goods for his retail store in Texas when he wrote these diary entries. One entry anticipates a battle between rival Mexican political factions in Matamoros. While Brush relates his physical ailments caused by the stormy Gulf of Mexico, he never mentions fear of federal blockaders.

481. CALDWELL, SUSAN. *"My Heart Is So Rebellious": The Caldwell Letters, 1861–1865.* Edited by J. Michael Welton. Introduction by T. Triplett. Annotations by John K. Gott and John E. Divine. Warrenton, Va.: Bell Gale Chevigny, 1991. 295 pp.

June 23, 1861–March 26, 1865. Warrenton (Fauquier County), Virginia. Susan Caldwell wrote the majority of these letters to her husband, Lycurgus, who was employed as a government clerk in Richmond. Several were written by Lycurgus, others by additional family members. The Caldwells were a middle-class family with a small number of slaves. Susan was thirty-four years old in 1861, and Lycurgus was a few years older. In 1862 the couple had their fourth child. Susan stayed in Warrenton for the duration; thus, her letters record how the town fared during the war. Warrenton was occupied by both sides and was frequently subjected to raids. Susan mentions the physical appearance of the town and the departure of both white residents and slaves, as well as inflation, the stability of currency, and the scarcity of goods and commodities. During the first half of the war Susan faced the conflict and the Yankees with confidence. Her letters are filled with advice for Lycurgus about the kind of clothing he should wear. Every letter conveys news of the children's antics and reports on their health. Susan and the children had sufficient material possessions, but she often asked Lycurgus to send her cloth. Susan was adamant that Lycurgus not become a soldier. Her reasons ranged from his advanced age and how it would affect his health to the impact his enlistment would have on his family, which could not live on his army pay of eleven dollars a month. When the clerks and factory workers of Richmond were recruited into a local defense organization in July 1863, the news hit Susan like a "thunderbolt." She insisted on knowing the circumstances. She wrote: "I had buoyed myself up with the firm belief that you would never be *compelled* to leave your *desk* and don a uniform. Now tell me candidly, are you compelled. . . . Please tell me if you could not have avoided this trial to me" (p. 193). Susan continued her objections in subsequent letters. Lycurgus, who wrote several letters during 1863 and 1864, was patriotic and even excited. While serving with the Third Virginia Infantry Regiment (Local Defense) during the Kilpatrick-Dahlgren raid on Richmond, he remarked: "I know I did my whole duty as a soldier" (p. 213). During 1863 to the end of these letters, Susan's confidence seems to have declined. Not only was her husband in harm's way, but his mother had died earlier in 1863 leaving a "loneliness" in the house. In February 1864 she asked him to write her mother in Charleston because she was too busy with the housework, specifically washing clothes. Then, in September 1864 her two-year-old daughter died of scarlet fever, and the couple mourned their loss for months. Finally, in early February 1865, after going through this whole period unscathed by marauders, her house was plundered. Susan interpreted these events as God's punishment for her own religious shortcomings, i.e., her "rebellious heart" (pp. 241 and 255). But through her last letter Susan retained her politically rebellious heart. Writing on March 26, 1865, as her "heart ached" for her deceased baby, she continued to insist: "I want *Independence* and nothing else. I could not consent to go back with a people that has been bent upon exterminating us" (p. 262).

482. CARTER, ISABEL. "Praying for Southern Victory." *Civil War Times Illustrated* 30 (March/April 1991): 12–14, 50, 52–56, 58, 60–69.

April 17, 1861–August 1862. Diary. Written from "Carter's Green," near the Bull Run battlefield. Carter's first entry justifies Virginia's participation in the Confederacy and predicts that the war would be of short duration. Her immediate plans were to become a homemaker and improve the family residence. However, her dreams of domestic tranquillity were quickly shattered when her husband, Josiah T. Carter, enlisted. During Bull Run she was forced to leave her home on two occasions. Other topics in her journal reveal worry about her husband, concern over being a good mother, rumors of all varieties, depredations by Yankees and local thieves, and Confederate soldiers who needed to be fed. Her final entries record the beginning of the Antietam campaign.

483. DANIEL, HARRIET B. B. *A Remembrance of Eden: Harriet Bailey Bullock Daniel's Memories of a Frontier Plantation in Arkansas, 1849–1872.* Edited, with an introduction, by Margaret Jones Bolsterli. Fayetteville: University of Arkansas Press, 1993. 157 pp.

1861–1865. Memoir. "Sylvan Home," Dallas County, Arkansas. "Bailey" was eighty years old when she wrote this narrative of her childhood. She relates her family's migration from North Carolina to Tennessee and then to southwestern Arkansas between 1835 and 1848, where her father established a successful cotton plantation. She recalled that when she first heard the words *states' rights* and *secession,* she thought "there was something terrible the matter, and it was about my friends, the colored people" (p. 81). From Bailey's description of the war years, the family's properties seem to have avoided destruction. Her father continued to grow cotton (against Confederate regulations), concealing it from both sides, and he sold it at the end of the war for a high price. The plantation evidently prospered in other ways as well, since Bailey wrote that other families came for assistance. The only battle she mentions is Poison Springs. Generals Jo Shelby and John Marmaduke and their troops camped on the Bullock plantation. Mr. Bullock, anticipating that the plantation system would soon become a thing of the past, placed the house servants in the fields before the end of the war, forcing the Bullock girls to learn how to perform household chores. She recalled that after the war her father had problems with the new labor system. Once her father hit a farmhand with a hoe after the man "spoke impertinently" to him. After the worker won a court case, Bailey concluded: "Pa had another lesson in the treatment of freedmen" (p. 112). Two poignant letters recalling those earlier years were written to Bailey in 1917 by "old Slave Gal" (Eliza Bullock). They confirm that an extended family relationship existed between the Bullocks and their slaves.

484. DARNELL, SION. "Memoirs of a Partisan War: Sion Darnell Remembers North Georgia, 1861 1865." By Robert S. Davis Jr. *Georgia Historical Quarterly* 80 (Spring 1996): 93–116.

1861–1865. Memoir. This Georgia Unionist details the evolution of the antisecessionist sentiment and activities in northern Georgia and the mountainous regions of contiguous states. The Unionists supported the federal military both as active troops and spies. Darnell served as a sergeant with the Fifth Tennessee Mounted Infantry (U.S.) but does not specify his role in the events. The editor credits Darnell's speech before the Georgia Department of the Grand Army of the Republic in 1901 as being one of the few documentary sources of northern Georgia opposition to the Confederacy.

485. DAVIS, JEFFERSON F. "Mr. Davis Bids Adieu." Introduction by William J. Miller. *Civil War: Magazine of the Civil War Society* 49 (February 1995): 18–22, 24.

January 21, 1861. Preceding the text of Davis's speech, Miller describes the background of the Mississippi senator's departure from the United States Congress.

486. DAVIS, JEFFERSON F. *The Papers of Jefferson Davis.* Edited by Lynda Lasswell Crist, Mary Seaton Dix, and Kenneth H. Williams. Baton Rouge: Louisiana State University Press, 1992–1997. Volumes 7–9 (In progress).

1861–September 1863. President. Confederate States of America. Volume 7 (1992) covers 1861; volume 8 (1995) covers 1862; and volume 9 (1997) covers January through September 1863. Volumes 1 through 6 cover the prewar years and were also published by Louisiana State University Press between 1971 and 1989. This compilation of Jefferson Davis's papers includes seven categories of documents, which contain personal and political correspondence from and to Davis, his speeches, and a variety of documents relating to foreign affairs, tactics, troop movements, fiscal matters, and administrative matters. Some documents are printed in full text, with annotations, but many more are calendared, with substantial summaries. Each volume contains a chronology of events and activities for the period covered. The sources are identified for all the manuscripts and published documents. Taken as a whole, the documents illuminate the problems the president faced as the Confederacy established a system of government and waged war. Letters address such civilian concerns as desire for protection, subsistence, and exemption from service. Military concerns include the acquisition of arms and munitions, the selection of capable superior officers, and Davis's disagreements with generals over strategy. Conflicts with state governors about hegemony over manpower and resources in the South and attempts to obtain foreign recognition of the Confederate States of America are also presented. As the detailed indexes reveal, every conceivable issue that confronted the Confederacy, as well as Davis's personal physical and family problems, are included in these papers.

487. DAWSON, SARAH (MORGAN). *The Civil War Diary of Sarah Morgan.* Edited by Charles East. Athens: University of Georgia Press, 1991. 626 pp.
January 10, 1862–June 15, 1865. Diary. Sarah Morgan's wartime experiences include the Union occupation of Baton Rouge, fleeing the city and spending the winter and spring of 1862–1863 at a plantation near Clinton and on the north shore of Lake Pontchartrain, and then residing with a brother in New Orleans for the remainder of the war. The first version of Dawson's diary, edited by her son Warrington Dawson, was published as *A Confederate Girl's Diary* (Boston: Houghton Mifflin, 1913). In his introduction Dawson explains that he had taken no "liberties" nor made any alterations, "merely omitting here and there passages which deal with matters too personal to merit the interest of the public" (p. ix). In the introduction to this work the editor points out that the first edition contained only approximately one-half of Sarah's manuscript. In this expanded edition Sarah's descriptions of her family's travails and their everyday life are more detailed, and her attitudes on the roles of women in society and in marriage are more fully expressed. Although she was initially ambivalent about the war, Sarah's support of the Confederacy increased as the war dragged on. Her personal spirit of independence seems to have been particularly great during the weeks following Appomattox. She ridicules the citizens of New Orleans whose homes and places of business were heavily draped in mourning for the assassinated Abraham Lincoln. She especially mocks those who "hated" Lincoln but nevertheless participated in the ritual. As the South faced an uncertain future, she lamented the loss of the Confederacy but was unwavering in her belief of what it had stood for. On June 15, 1865, she wrote: "I only pray never to be otherwise than what I am at this instant—a Rebel in heart and soul. . . . It is incomprehensible, this change" (p. 611). In his introduction East summarizes Sarah's life after the war, which included marriage to Charleston newspaper editor Frank Dawson and a career as a writer. East also suggests aspects of Sarah's writings which indicate that she was both a typical Southern woman and a rebel within her own well-to-do level of society. *A Confederate Girl's Diary* was reissued in 1960 by Indiana University Press, edited, with foreword, by James I. Robertson Jr.

488. DULANY FAMILY. *The Dulanys of Welbourne: A Family in Mosby's Confederacy.* Edited by Margaret Ann Vogtsberger. Berryville, Va.: Rockbridge Publishing Company, 1995. 316 pp.
May 31, 1861–July 13, 1865. "Welbourne," Loudoun County, Virginia. Letters written by Col. Richard H. Dulany (Seventh Virginia Cavalry); his father, John Peyton Dulany; Richard's daughters; and various members of the extended Dulany family. Richard describes raising a cavalry company and participating in the fighting, especially at Strasburg, with Rosser's Brigade during late 1863 and January 1864,

and at Reams' Station. Throughout the war he advised his father about the farm and expressed his love to his daughters. John Dulany's letters, as well as scattered letters from the daughters, provide a mosaic of life in Loudoun County. The seventy-three-year-old patriarch was responsible for three farms, five grandchildren, and others who lived at "Welbourne." John's letters contain information on matters that affected the maintenance of the farm, general comments about the war, and news about the family. Yankee raids were frequent. On July 22, 1863, John wrote a letter to Gen. Marsena R. Patrick (provost marshal, Army of the Potomac) requesting a pass to allow him to replenish supplies that had been seized by the Union troops. By winter 1864/1865 the Union plundering had taken its toll on the land, as well as the spirit of the elder Dulany. The old man wrote to his son that he felt helpless at being unable to take better care of the family. Mosby's raiders are mentioned by various family members. When John first mentioned Mosby in a letter of June 1863, he thought that a Mosby raid was a mixed blessing because it generally resulted in Union reprisals on civilians. In October 1864 Richard was wounded for the third time, and he spent the remainder of the war recuperating. The editor concludes with reasons why the Dulanys' economic interests did not suffer after the war, as well as a summary of the family's history up to the time of Richard's death in 1906.

489. DUVAL, THOMAS H. "The Diary of Thomas H. DuVal: The Civil War in Austin, Texas, February 26 to October 9, 1863." Edited by James Marten. *Southwestern Historical Quarterly* 94 (January 1991): 434–57.
February 26–October 9, 1863. Diary. This United States District Court judge refused to resign his federal judgeship and remained in Austin until late 1864. DuVal comments about war news in general, the activities of other Unionists in Texas, and family matters.

490. DUVAL, THOMAS H. "On the Road with Thomas H. DuVal: A Texas Unionist's Travel Diary, 1863." By James Marten. *Journal of Confederate History* 6 (1990): 76–93.
October 10–November 14; December 3–December 24, 1863. Diary. The judge wrote of his uncomfortable and occasionally dangerous travel from Austin to Washington, D.C., and back to New Orleans. He traveled by wagon and on foot from Austin to Vicksburg; by boat to Cairo; and by rail to Washington. In the nation's capital he collected sixty-eight hundred dollars in back pay. Following a visit with the president he felt assured that he had convinced Lincoln to allow the Texas Unionists to form a state government based on the principal of gradual emancipation. DuVal was present when the "Statue of Freedom" was placed on the White House dome.

491. DUVAL, THOMAS H. "'Dancing Attendance in the Anti-chambers of the Great': A Texas Unionist Goes to Washington." By James Marten. *Lincoln Herald* 90 (Fall 1988): 84–86.
November 14–21, 1863. Diary. As the title of the article indicates, Judge DuVal was shuffled from one department to another as he attempted to obtain appointments with government officials.

492. DUVAL, THOMAS H. "A Texan Witnesses the First Thanksgiving: Adventures in War-Time Washington." By James Marten. *Lincoln Herald* 91 (Fall 1989): 110–13.
November 25–December 2, 1863. Diary. During the week covered by this diary the judge continued his goal of making contact with government officials. One successful meeting was with Secretary of State William H. Seward, who impressed DuVal as being "a philosopher & Statesman of the first order" (p. 111). During the Union's first Thanksgiving Day (November 26) the city of Washington was in a joy-

ous mood. However, DuVal attributed the widespread drinking to neither the holiday nor the recent victory at Chattanooga; he wrote, "I think they were in for a frolic on general principles" (p. 111). DuVal remained determined to obtain a second meeting with President Lincoln before returning to his family in Texas.

493. **DUVAL, THOMAS H.** "A Glimpse at Occupied New Orleans: The Diary of Thomas H. DuVal of Texas, 1863–1865." By James Marten. *Louisiana History* 30 (Summer 1989): 303–16.
December 25–26, 1863; February 3–May 31, 1865. Diary. These writings provide impressions of the city and indicate the general attitudes of the citizens of New Orleans toward those who opposed secession. The editor says that the diary reads like a "who's who" of Texas Unionists in exile.

494. **DUVAL, THOMAS H.** "The Civil War on the Western Gulf: The Diary of Thomas H. DuVal of Texas." Edited by James Marten. *Gulf Coast Historical Review* 6, no. 1 (1990): 38–55.
December 27, 1863–March 5, 1864. Diary. Following his return to New Orleans from Washington, D.C., DuVal sailed to Brownsville on the rough waters of the Gulf of Mexico. He describes the weather in Brownsville and the local military situation.

495. **EDMONDSON, BELLE.** *A Lost Heroine of the Confederacy: The Diaries and Letters of Belle Edmondson.* Edited by William and Loretta Gailbraith. Jackson: University of Mississippi Press, 1990. 239 pp.
1861–1864. Diary and letters. Western Tennessee, primarily Memphis area. During the years Union troops occupied western Tennessee, this young woman utilized her adventurous nature, attractive appearance, and feminine wiles to spy for the Confederacy. Although few activities are described in any detail, she smuggled boots, medicine, and mail through Union picket lines and provided Confederate scouts with information about the location and movement of Union troops. In mid 1864 Union authorities issued a warrant for her arrest, and she fled to Mississippi to live with relatives for the remainder of the war. Edmondson's diary entries, most of which are from 1864, reveal her personal feelings. The letters, which were written to Edmondson, contain primarily news about the family and social and economic information regarding the region. The editors' considerable genealogical research includes a "Who's Who in the Documents."

496. **ELLEN.** "My Darling Charlie." By Monte Akers. *North-South Trader's Civil War* 18 (1991): 18–25.
May 23–June 20, 1865. Letters. Gainesville, Mississippi. Akers pursues the identity of a young woman who is identified in her love letters to Pvt. Charles B. Hamilton (Seventeenth Mississippi Infantry and the Thirty-ninth Virginia Cavalry Battalion) only by her Christian name, Ellen. Akers employed professional genealogist Marie Melchiori to search official records and census records. Melchiori found that the two correspondents never married, but she was unable to solve the mystery of Ellen's full identity.

497. **ERWIN, EDWARD JONES.** "Fatherly Advice on Secession: Edward Jones Erwin to His Son at Davidson College, 1860–61." By John C. Inscoe. *American Presbyterians* 69 (Summer 1991): 97–109.
October 7, 1860–May 28, 1861. Letters. At first this Morganton, North Carolina, banker did not believe there would be war. He felt the North would soon submit to Southern demands and that then, with the

"Negro question" silenced, the country would again be happy and united. Nevertheless, Edward, who equated his Southern Presbyterianism with Southern liberty, was certain that his Scotch-Irish Presbyterian heritage would compel him to fight if necessary. Edward was a Breckenridge man and was disappointed that his son, George, supported the moderate John Bell in the 1860 election. In his early letters Edward advises George to continue his education. However, he soon relented and advised his son to obtain a lieutenancy through the influence of a friend.

498. FIELDING FAMILY. *"To Lochaber Na Mair"*: *Southerners View the Civil War.* Diaries edited, with notes and index, by Faye Acton Axford. Athens, Ala.: Athens Publishing Company, 1986. 246 pp.
June 6, 1861–July 25, 1867. Virginia and Athens, Alabama. This work contains the diaries of Pvt. William Eppa Fielding (June 6, 1861–February 5, 1865) and sisters Mary (April 25, 1862–November 12, 1865) and Eliza (January 1, 1866–July 25, 1867), as well as those of Capt. Hubbard Hobbs (February 12–June 25, 1862). The soldiers' accounts (Ninth Alabama Infantry) relate shipment to and service in Virginia, including first Bull Run (aftermath), the Peninsular campaign (where Hobbs was killed in the Seven Days' Battles), and the siege of Petersburg (including the Petersburg Mine Assault); and Fielding's furlough back home in Athens in 1864. Mary's entries describe Union general Basil Turchin's sack of Athens, Abel Streight's raid in northern Alabama, the period just following Hood's Nashville campaign, and several months after the war. Mary describes civilian activities and reactions to the Union presence in northern Alabama. Eliza Jane's postwar diary provides details of how life on the family farm continued for nearly two years after the war without the help of slaves. The quotation in the title is from William Eppa Fielding, who, when he revisited the desolate farm in 1895, wondered: "when shall I see it again? perhaps never" (p. xi).

499. FOX, RICHARD ANDREW. "'If Subjugation Ever Should Be Our Sad Lot': A Sermon by Richard Andrew Fox." Edited by Nelson D. Lankford. *Virginia Baptist Register* 26 (1987): 1304–11.
March 10, 1865. Mount Horeb Baptist Church, King William County, Virginia. This sermon was delivered in response to the Confederate government's call for a day of prayer and fasting. Fox stressed how Southern statesmen had recently attempted to put an end to the conflict. (This was in reference to the Hampton Roads Peace Conference of February 3, 1865.) Fox reiterated the importance of continued faith in God: "If subjugation be our sad lot . . . it will be because we fail to Trust, honour, and implore the aid of Jesus" (p. 1308).

500. FOX, TRYPHENA BLANCHE HOLDER. *A Northern Woman in the Plantation South: Letters of Tryphena Blanche Holder Fox, 1856–1876.* Edited by Wilma King. Columbia: University of South Carolina Press, 1993. 280 pp.
June 6, 1856–January 2, 1876. Letters. Tryphena moved from Massachusetts in 1852 to accept the position of tutor for the children of a Mississippi plantation owner. In 1856 she married a physician and the couple settled into a rustic life in Plaquemine Parish, Louisiana. A constant theme of Tryphena's letters is her determination to send money back to her widowed mother in Pittsfield, Massachusetts. As 1861 evolved, Tryphena noted the military units that were organizing. In a letter written later she mentions that companies of men were forming in the event of a slave insurrection. The ladies were preparing a flag for the local soldiers, but Tryphena seems to have been unconcerned. In letters written following first Manassas, however, her loyalties become clear. For example, she wrote, "The Southerners can never be conquered; they may be killed, but conquered, *never*" (p. 130). The eight letters written between January 1862 and December 1864 serve as glimpses into the family's travails. They subsisted

on little money, lived in rented houses which Tryphena attempted to make comfortable, and lost a daughter to scarlet fever. On July 3, 1863, while the family was living at the plantation of her in-laws, she wrote about the devastation of their properties during the fighting for Vicksburg. At that time Tryphena assumed that her own home, Hygiene, had been destroyed. In 1864 she wrote of her family's circumstances from DeKalb and Aberdeen, Mississippi, where Dr. Fox had a position examining conscripts. When the Confederacy surrendered, she called it "our great humiliation" but resolutely set about refurbishing Hygiene. Tryphena hounded federal officials for the return of her confiscated furnishings. She directed and accompanied the police to the homes of locals who had plundered her house. In addition, she sent money to her mother to purchase cloth. Although Hygiene accidentally burned to the ground in February 1866, the family quickly rebuilt. In correspondence of July 22, 1866, Tryphena proudly announces: "We have moved into our new house" (p. 191). The remainder of the letters describe domestic matters (she was glad that she no longer had to manage slaves) and relate news about the children and her husband. The editor emphasizes the value of this work as a social record of a middle-class Southern family. The epilogue summarizes Tryphena's life after 1876.

501. **FRENCH, LUCY VIRGINIA SMITH.** *The Beersheba Springs Diaries of L. Virginia French, 1863–1864.* Edited, with an introduction, by Herschel Gower. Beersheba Springs, Tenn.: Beersheba Springs Historical Society, 1986. 64 pp.

May 11, 1863–August 9, 1863. Diary. Tennessee. In spring 1863 the French family moved from its home in McMinnville to Beersheba Springs (Grundy County) in an attempt to find conditions more conducive to Lucy's health and literary aspirations. But because the war also shifted to the Beersheba Springs region, Lucy's goals were thwarted. Her most vivid diary entries concern a raid on July 26, 1863, when bushwhackers ransacked their mountain community. Lucy describes the chaos as furniture and other private possessions were stolen. The ransacking activities, which were encouraged by federal authorities, eventually abated, but civilian fear that guerrillas might again visit the town remained a constant theme. Most other entries are less dramatic and concern such issues as war news (and rumors), daily activities, the presence of Yankees, and the ebbs and flows of Lucy's emotions. In her final entry Lucy recorded the family's return to Forrest Home and their attempt to make the abused farm habitable. The editor concludes with a lengthy essay titled "Beersheba Springs and L. Virginia French: The Novelist as Historian."

502. **FROBEL, ANN S.** *The Civil War Diary of Ann S. Frobel.* Introduction and appendixes by Mary H. Lancaster and Dallas M. Lancaster. McLean, Va.: EPM Publications, 1992. 320 pp.

May 1861–December 1865. Diary. Wilton Hill, near Alexandria, Virginia. Before, during, and after the Civil War two middle-aged sisters, Ann and Lizzie, occupied the farm which had long been owned by the family. Successive waves of Yankee soldiers occupied and plundered their farm. With few exceptions, Ann hated the Yankee soldiers and composed anecdotes to illustrate their "detestable" and "vile nature." The sisters hid the silverware and secluded themselves in one portion of the house, and Ann recorded the indignities. Blacks are an important theme in Ann's diary. Mammy, who had helped to raise the women, and twenty-one-year-old Charles were constant sources of support. Mammy possessed commonsense wisdom, and Ann believed that the slave was as proud of the farm's heritage as were the two sisters. In one entry Ann comments on how aware the blacks were of what was occurring and that they communicated with each other nonverbally. But not all slaves are portrayed favorably. One slave, Milly, spied on the two sisters as they took their evening walks. And Caesar, a slave whom Lizzie had kicked off the farm earlier, returned in June 1865 to assert that he had as much right to be there as the women. Ann's comments about Lincoln's assassination and burial are unsympathetic. She wrote that they had been "dragging him about for exhibition for the last three or four weeks" and criticizes the lavish expenditure of public money on "that miserable old carcass" (p. 224). The final entry summarizes the immediate postwar period. Living conditions were as poor as they had been during the war; everyone was afraid that former slaves would attempt to take "the whole country"; and the slaves were acting in a "sullen and insolent manner" on the streets of Alexandria (pp. 247–48). In "The Silent Prisoner" Virginia Walcott Beauchamp compares Ann's prisoner-like status during the war with the constraints imposed on all women of the period (*Women's Studies Quarterly* 17, nos. 3–4 [1989]: 34–44).

503. GARCIA, CÉLINE FRÉMAUX. *Céline: Remembering Louisiana, 1850–1871.* Edited by Patrick J. Geary. Foreword by Bertram Wyatt-Brown. Athens, Ga.: University of Georgia Press, 1987. 277 pp.

1861–1865. Memoir. Louisiana. Céline Frémaux was a member of a first-generation French immigrant family that did not own slaves and were not wealthy but were staunch Confederates. Céline, who wrote these memoirs about the first twenty years of her life sometime in the 1890s, focuses on such matters as her running feud with her high-strung mother, the civilian side of the war, and her family's acculturation as it was forced to move between French and American societies. Céline's father was an engineer for the Confederate army who worked on fortifications at Port Hudson and Mobile. After the fall of Baton Rouge the family moved to Port Hudson for the winter of 1862. They spent the remainder of the war in Jackson, Louisiana. Among Céline's recollections are how her family scrambled to save their books and other possessions as Yankees approached Baton Rouge; the activities of blacks (including retribution against them); the destruction of homes and her school by Union soldiers; assaults on two women by Union soldiers; everyday shortages (Céline was assigned to make soap from bones); and skirmishes and raids, especially around Port Hudson and Jackson. Céline recalled that during the turmoil of these war years her mother insisted that she and her sister continue their educations. Her mother refused to take the oath of allegiance or trade cotton with federal authorities, even when these actions would have improved their economic situation. Céline's memoir describes the family's reunion at the end of the war, the Reconstruction years spent in New Orleans and the years preceding her marriage.

504. GARRETT-ASBELL FAMILY. "'Plain Folk' Coping in the Confederacy: The Garrett Asbell Letters." Edited by Lewis N. Wynne and Guy Porcher Harrison. *Georgia Historical Quarterly* 72 (Spring 1988): 102–18.

November 11, 1862–November 19, 1863. Letters between William Asbell and his in-laws, the Garrett family. Asbell served with a militia unit (Cobb's Rangers). Several of these letters describe Camp Lamar Cobb (Decatur County, Georgia), but more clearly they reveal how yeoman farmers coped with the rough life brought on by a war they were forced to endure.

505. GORDON, ELEANOR KINZIE. "Northern Rebel: The Journal of Nellie Kinzie Gordon, Savannah, 1862." Edited by Mary D. Robertson. *Georgia Historical Quarterly* 70 (Fall 1986): 477–517.

January 16–November 3, 1862. Diary. Savannah, Athens, and Madison Springs, Georgia, as well as various locations in Virginia. A member of a prominent Chicago family, Eleanor Kinzie married equally prominent William W. Gordon II of Savannah in 1854. The segment of her journal written during this time reveals her adherence to the Southern cause. She feared for her husband's safety with the "Georgia Hussars," in the Jeff Davis Legion (Mississippi Cavalry), as well as for the well-being of her Northern relatives serving in the Union army.

506. GREEN, ANN FORREST. "Diary of Ann Forrest Green of 'Rosedale.'" Edited by Elizabeth Lowell Ryland. *Northern Neck of Virginia Historical Magazine* 43 (December 1993): 4971–87.

January 2–December 18, 1861. Diary. Rosedale Plantation, Virginia. When sixty-four-year-old Mrs. Green first picked up her pen, she simply intended to record the year's events for her daughter. But as early as her second entry the sectional conflict intruded as she expressed hope for the "restoration of peace and good feelings among our United States" (p. 4972). In her last entry for the year she reflects on the previous January: "I little had thought of the startling events it was destined to record" (p. 4987). From her plantation in the Washington-Georgetown area she observed the coming of the war, the divided sentiment of the populace, the influx of federal troops, arrests for speaking in favor of secession, the secretive arrival of President Lincoln in Washington, the funeral of Col. Elmer Ellsworth, Bull Run, and Union soldiers foraging at nearby farms. Others were excited by the events, but the war made Mrs. Green feel old and tired. In one entry she describes her walk through her former home. She thought of her childhood and young womanhood and the beloved "silent tenants" of the graveyard. Through the year's events Mrs. Green tried to maintain a calm farm life. While she did not openly reveal her own sectional sentiments, she did write in admiration of the Confederate army at Bull Run. And on November 15 she commented: "What folly to continue to force a Union that can never more exist" (p. 4986).

507. HANSFORD, MOLLIE, and VICTORIA HANSFORD. *Civil War Memoirs of Two Rebel Sisters.* Edited by William D. Wintz. Charleston, W.Va.: Pictorial Histories Pub. Co., 1989. 84 pp.

1861–1865. Memoirs. Mollie recorded her experiences of the war in the Shenandoah Valley, and Victoria recorded hers from the Kanawha Valley. The two accounts are blended and editorial comments inserted. Photographs and maps are included, as are letters from other family members and documents about the era.

508. HARRIS, DAVID G. *Piedmont Farmer: The Journals of David Golightly Harris, 1855–1870.* Edited, with an introduction, by Philip N. Racine. Knoxville: University of Tennessee Press, 1990. 597 pp.

January 1, 1855–March 5, 1870. Journal. Spartanburg County, South Carolina. David Harris was a small slaveholder who, together with his wife, Emily, and their seven children, lived in a three-room house. The journal, primarily an agricultural record, shows David to have been educated and innovative and enthusiastically dedicated to improving his farm. Because he and Emily utilized the journal to record their personal thoughts, the work is also a chronicle of their hopes and despairs. David supported the war, but he did not rush to volunteer. Between 1862 and 1865 he served three stints of military service in the state militia on the South Carolina coast. Emily also recorded farm activities in David's absence, but her comments about her feelings are more memorable. One long entry written during December 1862 is a catalog of her burdens. She wrote that she had had too much company, several slaves and children were sick, the weather was rainy, the cows had lain outside overnight, and she was weaning an infant. She added, "worst of all I know my husband is somewhere miserably cold, wet, and comfortless" (p. 270). In later remarks she desires the return of her "guide and protector," fears that she is growing old and ugly, and confesses that she can foresee no pleasure in life (p. 309). During the fifteen-year period that David maintained his journal, he wrote about the slaves, then freedmen, in various ways. In 1866 he understood that they did not trust the white man and were afraid of losing their freedom. David's lack of enthusiasm for both "journalizing" and farming parallel each other. In January 1868 he wrote: "This journal, I keep as much for the benefit of my children as for my own benefit & gratification." He called it a "looking glass" and admitted: "The task of journalizing is becoming irksome to me. . . . There is so little pleasant to record" (p. 454). His final journal entry, made in March 1870, epitomizes his despair: "Taxes come up again & as usual, little or no money" (p. 496). Emily's writings are brought into sharper focus in Philip N. Racine's article "Emily Lyles Harris: A Piedmont Farmer during the Civil War," *South Atlantic Quarterly* 79 (Autumn 1980): 386–97.

509. HARRIS, GEORGE W. "The View from Across the River." *Blue & Gray Magazine* 1 (February/March 1984): 45–46.

May 7, 1861. Letter. An uncle from Upperville, Virginia, responded to his Northern nephew's criticism of secession with an impassioned defense of the South's right to secede.

510. HAWES, MARIA JANE SOUTHGATE. *Reminiscences of Maria Jane Southgate Hawes Written in 1882 and Published in 1986 by Mary Hawes Wood, Her Granddaughter.* N.p.: N. pub., 1986. 32 pp.

1861–1865. Memoir. Maria first recounted her upbringing in Cincinnati and New York. After her marriage to army officer James M. Hawes in 1858, the couple were constantly on the move. They were posted in Washington, D.C., and Forts Riley and Leavenworth. Hawes resigned from the United States Army in 1861 to join the Confederacy. For the next four years Maria recorded the efforts of a military wife trying to maintain contact with her husband in the midst of war. She moved from Kentucky to Alabama; then to a plantation near Shreveport, Louisiana; next to Arkansas; on to Galveston; and finally to San Antonio. She lodged with friends, relatives, and occasionally her husband. (She gave birth to three children during this period.) Her odyssey ended only when the war was over and the family returned to Paris, Kentucky. While friends and prominent people populate her narrative, Maria's relationship with her servant Emoline is portrayed as especially close. On one occasion Maria stayed with her servant to assist in the birth of Emoline's child while the rest of the party moved on. Maria refers to military events only casually, and she never provides any sense of her husband's importance to the Confederacy.

511. HEYWARD, PAULINE DECARADEUC. *A Confederate Lady Comes of Age: The Journal of Pauline DeCaradeuc Heyward, 1863–1888.* Edited by Mary D. Robertson. Columbia: University of South Carolina Press, 1992. 160 pp.

June 2, 1863–March 5, 1888. Journal. Nineteen-year-old Pauline began the Civil War portion of her journal from Montmorenci, her father's plantation near Aiken, South Carolina. During a few hectic months of the winter and spring of 1865 Pauline wrote a lot about the war. She had lost two brothers to camp illnesses prior to 1863 and worried about other soldiers. She remained aware of the ebb and flow of military events and was especially concerned as the Union bombarded Charleston during the summer of 1863. But she denied being afraid as Yankee soldiers marched across South Carolina in 1865. In February 1865 Kilpatrick's cavalry plundered their home several times. While her account is terrifying, Pauline remained unruffled. She was proud of a slave who refused to reveal where family valuables were buried. Later, however, she reacted differently toward the black soldiers of the Union army: "I felt every imaginable emotion upon seeing them, they, who two or three months ago were our respectful slaves, were there as impertinent as possible, pushing & jostling us about (p. 79). The final Yankee raid on her home, which occurred in late June 1865, prompted Pauline to go to Augusta and plead with federal authorities for guards. She also wrote about the unruly Confederate stragglers, who in late April plundered Augusta. Most of Pauline's journal is about her French-Catholic family (sometimes there were as many as eighteen people living at Montmorenci) and herself. She wrote that during social occasions she was usually the center of attention or sought after by some would-be suitor, which she professed to be a burden. Pauline revealed how she felt about war and marriage; continued to study French and read Shakespeare; and made frequent trips to Augusta, Charleston, and Savannah throughout the war. However, after she met Guerard Heyward on August 12, 1865, she no longer presented the war as a theme in her journal; it had been replaced by love and courtship. There are no journal entries for the period between March 28, 1867, and April 14, 1875. The sporadic entries for the final thirteen years describe her life as a mother. After her husband suddenly died, she concluded her journal with "Finis" (p. 141). The editor summarizes Pauline's final years.

512. HILDEBRAND, JACOB R. *A Mennonite Journal, 1862–1865: A Father's Account of the Civil War in the Shenandoah Valley.* Edited by John R. Hildebrand. Shippensburg, Pa.: Burd Street Press, 1996. 100 pp.

March 6, 1862–May 13, 1865. Journal. Hildebrand's entries blend war news, farming matters, descriptions of travels to the camps of his three sons, and expressions of his religion. Because Hildebrand's two farms were located in Augusta and Rockingham Counties, his strategic location, together with access to newspapers and the telegraph, provided him with an informed view of the war in the Shenandoah Valley. Among the battles he mentions are Jackson's Shenandoah Valley campaign and the Valley campaigns of Union generals David Hunter and Philip Sheridan. Throughout his entries Hildebrand recorded the crops he planted and harvested, the prices of goods, and the impact of the war on civilians of the Staunton-Rockingham area. His adherence to the pacifist beliefs traditionally held by the Mennonites seems to have lessened, for he openly supported the Confederacy, was concerned about political matters, and observed the days of prayer and humility proclaimed by Jefferson Davis. The journal entries for the period of June 1862 through July 1863 are missing.

513. HOUSE, ELLEN RENSHAW. *A Very Violent Rebel: The Civil War Diary of Ellen Renshaw House.* Edited by Donald E. Sutherland. Knoxville: University of Tennessee Press, 1996. 285 pp.

January 1, 1863–December 31, 1865. Diary. Knoxville, Tennessee, and Augusta, Georgia. Ellen was nineteen when she first started making occasional "journal" entries. But on September 1, 1863, when federal troops occupied Knoxville, she began to write in great detail. She continued until April 10, 1864, when she was expelled from the city. Between April and August 1864 she kept notations in a pocket diary while she was a refugee in Virginia and Augusta, Georgia. Throughout 1865, from Augusta and back home in Knoxville, she again wrote in detail. Ellen was a member of a Confederate eastern Tennessee family who hated anything associated with the United States, whether it be a neighbor, such as William G. "Parson" Brownlow, or the blue uniform. Ellen followed the battles of Burnside's east Tennessee campaign closely. When Longstreet reached eastern Tennessee, she was certain Knoxville would be liberated. During the siege she described the fighting (especially the assault on Fort Sanders), the destruction of properties, and the shortage of food and supplies within the city, and she worked to ease the sufferings of Confederates held in the local jail. Eventually Longstreet withdrew and she was forced to acknowledge that "the Yankees have completely over run Tennessee(p. 79). Between January and April 1864 she recorded events of her "gloomy" life and federal activities. A Confederate soldier (David S. Dodd) was executed as a spy. Her dog Leo was shot by a Union soldier. She loathed the presence of "the miserable wretches" or "vile creatures." After she had insulted a Union officer, Ellen was "asked" by the federal authorities to leave Knoxville. By early 1865 she was again "gloomy" and her life in Augusta seemed without purpose. Although the Confederacy was obviously crumbling, Ellen accepted news of Union victories with skepticism. She was somewhat comforted by news that Lincoln's assassin had escaped. After she returned to Knoxville in July, she wrote about the six murders that occurred during the next few months. One death was that of her beloved brother. As she reflected on the civil violence of the region Ellen declared: "The Devil seems to be walking at large in East Tennessee" (p. 195).

514. JACKSON, FANNIE OSLIN. *On Both Sides of the Line, by Fannie (Oslin) Jackson, 1835–1925: Her Early Years in Georgia and Civil War Service as a Union Army Nurse.* Edited by Joan F. Curran and Rudena K. Mallory. Baltimore, Md.: Gateway Press, 1989. 136 pp.

1861–1865. Memoir. Northern Georgia and Chattanooga. Fannie first recounts her childhood and early years of marriage and then follows with her life as a farm wife while her husband, Zach (Eighth Georgia Infantry Battalion), was on duty. Neither Fannie nor Zach favored secession, and both opposed slavery. During the Atlanta campaign her farm at Snake Creek Gap (near Resaca, Georgia) was utilized as the XVI Corps field hospital for the Union army. Fannie became a nurse, and she and her three children followed the hospital along Sherman's march to Atlanta. Fannie wrote more about the movement of the hospitals and her interaction with army personnel than nursing procedures. She does mention the organization of several hospitals and occasionally such details as washing and reusing bandages. Her memoir traces the improvement of one amputee from the time he was placed in her care until he was well enough to be discharged. By the time the hospital had reached Vining's Station, Georgia, Fannie had attained the position of matron. In Atlanta she was reunited with her husband. He was being held with other Confederates who had been wounded and captured at Kennesaw Mountain. When Sherman evacuated Atlanta, the hospital was removed to Chattanooga. She continued to be employed as a nurse, and Zach was allowed to work in Chattanooga for the military construction corps. Fannie related the family's move to Iowa and then Kansas after the war. She concluded with reflections on what she had previously written and provided recent information about her former coworkers.

515. JONES, MARTHA BUFORD. *Peach Leather and Rebel Gray: Bluegrass Life and the War, 1860–1865. Diary and Letters of a Confederate Wife.* Edited by Mary E. Wharton and Ellen F. Williams. Lexington, Ky.: Helicon Company, 1986. 189 pp.

January 9, 1860–September 11, 1864. Diary and letters. Edgewood Farm, Woodford County, Kentucky. Consists of Martha's diary entries for 1860, part of 1862, 1863, and part of 1864. Several letters to her husband, Willis (major, Field's Division, First Corps, Army of Northern Virginia), are included, as are a few letters from Willis to Martha and his mother. Information from local histories and newspaper accounts is also appended. These accounts, together with the editors' narrative, reveal the impact of the war on a south-central Kentucky family. The entries for 1860 describe a normal life filled with personal matters and management of a farm that specialized in raising horses and growing hemp. Martha's writings after 1862 reflect her despair over the war. A child died and her husband enlisted at about the same time. In mid 1864 she sought exile in Canada rather than face arrest by federal authorities for being the wife of a Confederate officer. Although she was able to return later in 1864, indebtedness forced the family to sell the farm. Willis was killed in October 1864 in Virginia. The editors add that in 1866 Martha died, the final auction of the farm was held, and Willis's body was returned from Virginia and reburied in Lexington.

516. LEE, FLORIDE (CLEMSON). *A Rebel Came Home: The Diary and Letters of Floride Clemson, 1863–1866.* Revised edition. Edited by Charles M. McGee Jr. and Ernest M. Lander Jr. Columbia: University of South Carolina Press, 1989. 189 pp.

January 1, 1863–October 24, 1866. Diary and letters. From her home near Bladensburg, Maryland, the young daughter of a pro-Confederate family reported news of the Gettysburg campaign and observed Early's Washington raid. In December 1864 she received a pass to Pendleton, South Carolina, where she remained for the duration. In South Carolina she recorded prices of food; despondency among the people; collection of goods for the victims of the Columbia fire; fear of Yankee raiders and insurrection by the freed blacks, whom everyone was turning away to starve or plunder; the flight of the formerly wealthy; and such rumors as plans to divide abandoned plantations among the freedmen. The letters written during 1866 concern primarily social and family matters. This work was first published as *A Rebel Came Home: The Diary of Floride Clemson* (Columbia: University of South Carolina Press, 1961). This edition includes an updated prologue and the addition of "Floride Clemson's Northern Trip, July–October, 1863," letters written to her mother during a trip from Maryland to Pennsylvania and New York.

517. LOGAN, ANNA CLAYTON. "Recollections of My Life." *Goochland County Historical Society Magazine* 21 (1989): 15–30.

1861–1868. Memoir. Goochland County, Virginia. Writing in 1917, Anna apologized in the middle of her story for an absence of clarity about her past: "All of these home scenes are like pictures in my mind. I see the faces. My life then is like a dream. I have much that I could tell of the home life, but I haven't time. It makes me tired" (p. 23). A sense of sadness pervades the memoir as Anna recalls the cause of the war and the coming and going of family and acquaintances. She remembered how her family and the slaves survived their ordeal; the Yankee soldiers who ransacked the farm (she said that family slaves were trustworthy guardians of valuables); and the use of the home, Dungeness, as a hospital. After the slaves were set free, the future was bleak for her family. Anna's father only knew how to be a planter. Because the family was without a livelihood and had incurred indebtedness prior to the war, the family was forced to abandon Dungeness in 1868.

518. MCCULLOH, WILLIAM J. "From Baton Rouge to Opelousas: An Eye-witness Account of the Wartime Removal of the State Capital." Edited by Shane K. Bernard. *Louisiana History* 36 (Fall 1995): 475–80.

May 6, 1862. This letter from the Louisiana State surveyor general contains little-known details of the evacuation of the state capital to Opelousas. The move had been ordered by Gov. Thomas Moore because of the Union threat to Baton Rouge after New Orleans fell.

519. MCDONALD, CORNELIA PEAKE. *A Woman's Civil War: Diary, with Reminiscences of the War, from March 1862.* Edited, with an introduction, by Minrose C. Gwin. Madison: University of Wisconsin Press, 1992. 303 pp.

1861–1865. Diary and memoir. Winchester and Lexington, Virginia. Cornelia maintained her diary between March 1862 and June 1863. The periods before and after she left Winchester are covered by postwar memoirs. As Winchester frequently changed hands, Cornelia and her eight children accommodated themselves to Confederates and Yankee intrusions. But fear of plunder by both sides, providing shelter for troops, and an effort to maintain a modicum of normalcy took their toll on Cornelia's nerves. Out of despair she confided to her diary: "I am growing thin and emaciated"; she wondered how long she could continue the struggle (p. 150). She recorded that the physical appearance of Winchester changed as a result of the war, rumors of local troop movements, and news about the progress of war in general. Cornelia bartered with Union soldiers for food and cared for the Confederate wounded of the battles of first Kernstown and second Winchester. When the family became refugees in Lexington, their existence became even more tenuous. They lived in rented rooms, depended on strangers for charity, ate bread and beans, and made clothing from tablecloths and curtains. During this ordeal her daughter, a stepson, and her husband (who served with the Confederate army and government) all died. While in Winchester, Cornelia emphasized the plight of slaves who were torn between occupying armies. She especially exhibited pity for one servant, Lethea, who had to be sold, and the servant's young son, who was separated from his mother. However, Cornelia was less understanding when the former slaves dressed in fine ladies' clothing and forced white women off the sidewalks to walk in the gutters. This work was first published and edited by Cornelia's son, Hunter McDonald as: *A Diary with Reminiscences of the War and Refugee Life in the Shenandoah Valley, 1860–1865* (Nashville: Cullom & Ghertner, 1935). In the introduction to this edition Gwin categorizes McDonald's diary as work of feminist autobiography, rather than a historical document. Thus, she says that she "streamlined" the notes to those "having implications for women's history and women's writing generally" (p. 5).

520. MOORE, DOSIA WILLIAMS. *War, Reconstruction and Redemption on Red River: The Memoirs of Dosia Williams Moore.* Edited by Carol Wells. Ruston: Department of History, Louisiana Tech University, 1990. 135 pp.
1862–1865. Memoir. Rapides and Natchitoches Parishes, Louisiana. While Dosia's youthful recollections of the war seem lighthearted, they also reflect the prevailing apprehension of the expected federal invasion. Contrary to her expectations, the Yankees that Dosia met proved not to be demons but, instead, were friendly and even protective of her family. She recalled the manner in which civilians handled an outbreak of smallpox in 1863. Dosia explains that a young cow was vaccinated with real smallpox to produce scabs. From the cow's scabs both civilians and soldiers were vaccinated. She also mentions the resourcefulness of Southern women, who made coffee from parched cornmeal, spun cloth, and concocted dye from a mixture of walnuts and sassafras. She remembered that some slaves became restive when the Yankees arrived but that those owned by her family remained faithful. Dosia also recalled several of the secret activities of her father, who was a scout with the Second Louisiana Cavalry. The battle of Yellow Bayou is the only fighting Dosia describes in detail.

521. MORGAN, JOHN ABELL. "The Civil War Diary of John Abell Morgan, S.J.: A Jesuit Scholastic of the Maryland Province." By George M. Anderson. *Records of the American Catholic Historical Society of Philadelphia* 101, nos. 3–4 (1990): 33–54.
June 4, 1862–March 19, 1867. Diary. This account reveals the passing of the war through the eyes of a pro-Confederate Catholic priest in Baltimore. The diary mentions such events as the welcome Marylanders gave Lee in the Antietam campaign, the arrest of a student for singing "Dixie," and applause during a performance of *Richard III* when the colors red and white (the colors of the Confederacy) were spoken of in the script. Morgan interpreted Lincoln's Emancipation Proclamation as an act of "judicial blindness." He did not react to Lincoln's assassination with an expression of sorrow but, rather, with apprehension over the possibility of mob retaliation on pro-Confederate citizens. However, Lincoln assassination conspirator, Mary Surratt, received Morgan's sympathy. The editor points to Morgan's favorable change in attitude toward blacks between 1862 and 1865. This possibly occurred because of Morgan's friendship with another Jesuit priest who was responsible for teaching and ministering to the needs of Baltimore blacks. The editor adds that Morgan had made his own contact with a group of intelligent black women.

522. NORMAN-DEAN FAMILIES. *Southern Life and Letters in the Mid 1800's.* By Susan Lott Clark. Waycross, Ga.: Susan Lott Clark, 1993. 471 pp.
October 15, 1861–March 21, 1865. This work is a compilation of letters, biographical sketches, genealogical materials, and illustrations concerning the Norman and Dean families, who lived primarily in Georgia and Alabama. The Civil War portion (pages 105–280) contains some seventy-three letters written by James T. Norman (lieutenant, Twenty-third Alabama Infantry) and approximately twenty-nine by his wife, Mary Elizabeth (Dean) Norman. Letters from other family members are also included. James related his duty around Montgomery and Mobile, Alabama; in Tennessee, especially the Cumberland Mountains; and during the Vicksburg campaign, where he was captured on May 1, 1863, at Port Gibson. He was imprisoned briefly at Alton, Illinois, then sent to Johnson's Island Prison until his release on February 25, 1865. James's letters include passages of love and devotion for his family and requests for food and clothing (he desperately needed shoes after marching through the Cumberland Mountains). While at Johnson's Island he wrote to several cousins who lived near Cleveland asking them for boxes of supplies. They complied but also used the occasion to blame him and the

South for the war. Mary's letters include family news and her financial needs, which necessitated her move to live with her father in Orion, Alabama. An interesting addition to this work is an essay by a present-day writer, Roger Long, "Adjutant James T. Norman on Johnson's Island" (pp. 214–23).

523. PATTERSON, E. B. (MRS.). "Memoirs of Mrs. E. B. Patterson: A Perspective on Danville during the Civil War." Edited by Christen Ashby Cheek. *Register of the Kentucky Historical Society* 92 (Autumn 1994): 347–99.

June 1862–1863. Memoir. The wife of a college president recalled events in wartime Danville, Kentucky. Mrs. Patterson assumed that the details of the battles and biographies of leaders had already "inundated" readers, and she observed that previous accounts had been written by participants and historians of "the stronger sex." Thus, she thought that she might add something for readers interested in "a woman's homely experiences and observations" (p. 349). Among the events Mrs. Patterson describes is civilian apprehension over a rumored raid by John Hunt Morgan in June 1862. A defense was hastily thrown together by the Home Guard to which her husband belonged. On September 3 Morgan did occupy Danville, and he arrested her husband. Robert reluctantly took an oath not to bear arms against the Confederacy rather than be sent to prison. Later, when he was threatened with conscription, Robert fled Danville and hid in the countryside. The battle of Perryville was fought during that period, but Mrs. Patterson refused to leave her home. For a short period the town became a hospital for both sides. When an epidemic of typhoid fever struck the soldiers, she helped nurse the convalescents. Although the town was within Union lines during 1863, civilians continually feared raids. Early in 1864 the couple left Danville when Robert accepted a position in the Pittsburgh, Pennsylvania, area. This memoir was first published in 1886 as an eight-part series in the weekly journal the *Herald and Presbyter* (Cincinnati and Saint Louis). The editor adds that one part was unavailable for reproduction here.

524. PEEK, MARIA SMITH. *Refugees in Richmond: Civil War Letters of a Virginia Family.* Edited by Henry C. Blackiston. Princeton, N.J.: Princeton University Press, 1989. 105 pp.

March 1859–November 4, 1873. Letters. The majority of these letters were written by sixteen-year-old (in 1862) Maria from Richmond to her future husband, Lt. Daniel G. Marrow. Several letters to and from her brothers are also included. The editor informs readers that Maria was living in Richmond because her country town of Hampton had been burned by Gen. Magruder, who razed the town rather than let Gen. Butler quarter his troops and runaway slaves there. Most of her letters pertain to the months between May 1864 and the end of 1865. In addition to providing encouragement to Marrow, Maria relates events involving family and friends, living conditions in Richmond, the excitement that Grant's Virginia campaign was creating in Richmond, and news of the battles around Richmond throughout 1864. On May 9, 1865, she wrote that she realized she was in "Yankeedom." She was confused by her feelings. She liked the former enemy, but she wanted to maintain "the spirit of revenge" (p. 61). Letters following the surrender pertain to family and social matters.

525. QUIGLEY, ANN E. "The Diary of Ann Quigley." By Russell E. Belous. *Gulf Coast Historical Review* 4, no. 2 (1989): 89–99.

January 1, 1861–September 12, 1884. Diary. Mobile, Alabama. Quigley was principal of a secondary school in wartime Mobile. During the war she recorded the rising prices of everyday commodities and lamented the impact of the war on civilians, especially the flood of refugees from New Orleans and Vicksburg. After the war Quigley treated the appearance of federal soldiers in Mobile on April 12, 1865, with disdain. She could accept the Confederate defeat only as being the result of the overwhelming numbers of men. Quigley viewed the liberated slaves without pity, calling them "half savage, ungrateful slaves" (p. 99). When an editor of *Frank Leslie's Illustrated Newspaper* compared Lincoln to Jesus, because they were both redeemers, Quigley labeled such a comparison "blasphemous" (p. 99). In 1871 she reflected on the postwar course of events: "Six years ago! What changes since! Am I the same or do I dream? The world seems to have lost its beauty & brightness. Hope, like our own 'Confederate flag' seems to have gone down in darkness & gloom" (p. 99).

526. RUFFIN, EDMUND. *The Diary of Edmund Ruffin. Volume III: A Dream Shattered, June 1863–June 1865.* Edited, with an introduction and notes, by William Kauffman Scarborough. Baton Rouge: Louisiana State University Press, 1989. 896 pp.

June 5, 1863–June 18, 1865. In the final volume of this ardent secessionist's diary, his personal decline and death parallel the demise of the Confederacy. By April 1863 Ruffin was confined by age and infirmities to his native Virginia, except for a lengthy visit to Charleston in fall 1863. During this period his sources of information were primarily newspaper accounts. Ruffin hoped for success until the very end. Even as late as April 1865 he had confidence that the Confederacy could be maintained in Texas. But a close look at his earlier entries reveals that he contemplated defeat. In January 1865, without altering his views on racial superiority, he approved of using slaves as Confederate soldiers. To Ruffin, it was better to forfeit the institution of slavery than return to the Union. Ruffin wrote about both the home front and the battles. He noted widespread shortages; destruction to private property (including his own) by Yankees, as well as by Southern civilians; and sagging public morale. Ruffin criticized everyone, including Confederate leaders in the field and Richmond, but he continued to castigate the North most of all. Near the end of his life Ruffin's passions were inflamed by the public veneration that "ennobled & glorified" the assassinated "vulgar buffoon," Abraham Lincoln. The old man's frustrations included the death of his son, Julian, at Drewry's Bluff. Ruffin frequently remarked that he had lived too long, and he often consulted the Bible's view of suicide. Eventually the ignominy of social and political change was too much for him to endure. Nine weeks after Appomattox he wrote his next-to-last sentence: "I here repeat, & would willingly proclaim, my unmitigated hatred to Yankee rule—to all political, social, & business connection with Yankees, & to the perfidious, malignant, & vile Yankee race" (p. 949). The editor recounts the details of how and when Ruffin shot himself. Earlier volumes of Ruffin's *Diary* were *Volume I: Toward Independence, October 1856–April 1861* and *Volume II: The Years of Hope, April 1861–June 1863.* They were also edited by William Kaufman Scarborough and were published by Louisiana State University Press in 1971 and 1976.

527. SEABURY, CAROLINE. *The Diary of Caroline Seabury, 1854–1863.* Edited, with an introduction, by Suzanne L. Bunkers. Madison: University of Wisconsin Press, 1991. 148 pp.

October 1854–July 1863. Diary. Twenty-seven-year-old Caroline Seabury left Brooklyn in 1854 to assume the position of teacher of French at Columbus Female Institute at Columbus, Mississippi. She maintained that position until July 1862, when she was released by the school because she was not a native-born Southerner. She spent her final year in Mississippi as a governess on Waverly Plantation. Prior to going to Mississippi, Caroline had lost seven of her nine brothers and sisters, her mother, and her father to consumption. Martha, her remaining sister, joined Caroline at Columbus in 1854, but she died of consumption in January 1858. Perhaps because of these deaths and the fact that she was an unmarried Northern woman living in an unfamiliar culture, an atmosphere of loneliness and isolation pervades Caroline's diary. Caroline opposed slavery but felt powerless because of her dependency on others. In the first months after her arrival in Mississippi she overheard a house servant being beaten for a crime she did not commit. Later Caroline was invited to observe a "hiring out" of slaves, the process of hiring out as servants those individuals who were held in guardianship. Caroline also describes the oddity of two men fighting a duel that was instigated because a woman had related to a mutual friend "that she did not consider the man to be a gentleman" (p. 50). Caroline seems to have felt the warmth of Southern hospitality in the greatest degree when the town presented her with cake and a silver set for nursing a boy back to health. Caroline's most descriptive passages are about her travels to and from the South; her attendance at a "Hard Shelled Baptist sermon," a convocation of "piney woods . . . foot-washers" (p. 71–72); and "a country barbecue & wedding" presided over by the slaves (p. 77). Caroline liked the Southern climate and vegetation and was sympathetic to the Southerners in many ways. She was ambivalent about Northern justification for the war. She watched how citizens anxiously awaited announcement of soldiers killed at first Bull Run, and after Shiloh she helped treat the wounded. She related local reaction to battles and such Northern political events as the Emancipation Proclamation in an objective manner. In the summer of 1863 she returned to the North. After a month of traveling through war-devastated Mississippi en route to her uncle's home, she arrived in Brooklyn, only to find that he was not there. As she sat alone in the house, she reflected on her experiences and contemplated her future. She mused: "I seem to have been living in another world—and slowly traveled back to this—For what—" (p. 116). The editor completes Caroline's life story and places this diary in the context of women's diaries.

528. SEDDON, ELVIRA BRUCE. "Goochland in the Civil War: The Diary of Elvira Bruce Seddon." *Goochland County Historical Society Magazine* 21 (1989): 6–14.
March 13–April 5, 1865. Diary. Goochland County, Virginia. The teenage daughter of James Alexander Seddon (Confederate States of America secretary of war) recorded rumors of Yankee forces in the region of the family's country estate, Sabot Hill. The last two entries, written in early April, reveal her desperate hope for rejuvenation of Lee's army and expectation of the calamities that would befall them if the Yankees appeared.

529. SHAKERS. *The Pleasant Hill Shakers in the Civil War, 1861–1865.* By F. W. Kephart. N.p.: N. pub., 1988. 41 pp.
August 1861–April 31, 1865. Diary. Pleasant Hill, Kentucky. This journal was kept sporadically by an unidentified woman of the Shaker Village of Pleasant Hill near Lexington, Kentucky. The entries written during the first year express the Shakers' dismay that the North and South would engage in war. The concept of armed conflict seemed incongruous to the writer. Although she was concerned for the disruption of Pleasant Hill and the other Shaker communities, the Shakers were treated with respect by both sides. The goods taken were necessary to sustain the military and often paid for with Confederate script. Only random acts of thievery occurred. The most harrowing period the writer experienced while writing the journal was before and after the fighting at Perryville. She wrote that thousands of bedraggled Confederate troops appeared at Shaker farms seeking food and water. She credited the soldiers' good behavior to the example set by General John Hunt Morgan. Several journal references reflect the dispute with Union authorities over the draft and the consequences of the Shakers' unwillingness to be conscripted or to pay a commutation fee. Entries written near the end of the journal indicate that the Shakers' lament over Lincoln's assassination cast a pall over Union victory and the end of the war.

530. SKINKER, THOMAS JULIAN, II. "The War Time Reminiscences of Thomas Julian Skinker II." Edited by Alexander Niven. *Journal of Confederate History* 7 (1991): 19–31.
1861–1865. Memoir. These are the hazy recollections of an eighty-two-year-old man about Union soldiers occupying and ransacking his northern Virginia farm when he was a teenager.

531. SMITH, MARIA MCGREGOR CAMPBELL. "Narrative of My Blockade Running." Edited by Evelyn M. Cherpak. *Southern Studies,* n.s. 3 (Fall
1992): 211–20.
November 1864. Memoir. The Northern-born wife of the Confederate assistant surgeon general
recounted her travel from Richmond to Cooperstown, New York, to visit her father, who was supposedly ill. The editor remarks that the account not only reveals the perils of wartime travel in enemy territory, but also indicates attitudes of an upper-class woman toward lower classes and blacks, as well as
Southerners' anxiety about their future.

532. SOLOMON, CLARA. *The Civil War Diary of Clara Solomon: Growing
Up in New Orleans, 1861–1862.* Edited, with an introduction, by Elliott
Ashkenazi. Baton Rouge: Louisiana State University Press, 1995. 458 pp.
June 15, 1861–July 11, 1862. Diary. Clara was a sixteen-year-old Sephardic Jewish girl whose father
was in the mercantile trade. Well educated and observant, Clara recorded her intimate thoughts and
family activities in detail. Until April 1862 the war existed primarily in the background of her life. She
did mention that "our regiment" had left for Virginia, the effect of the blockade, the appearance of Confederate money, and her father's sutler trade. But beginning with those written around the battle of
Shiloh, her entries focus on the war. After New Orleans capitulated she felt unable to write for over a
week, but she then described the details of the surrender and the presence of Union troops in New
Orleans. Clara actually felt relieved: "We have feared so much from the enemies in our midst but . . .
none have been found" (p. 350). Then, after she saw Yankee guards playing with the children, she
admitted: "I do not feel so vindictive toward the poor privates, but their wretched leaders are the ones
for whom the gallows are waiting" (p. 356). Ladies of New Orleans showed their defiance to the Yankees by wearing black crepe bows, but Clara opposed the gesture. She reasoned: "our cause is not *dead,
it is only sick.* The Yankees are only here for a *visit*" (p. 354). Clara also considered the wearing of Confederate flags by women to be unnecessary, "for they are well aware of the feelings & sentiments of
Southern women" (p 354). Nevertheless, the Yankees were a "loathsome" sight to her. While riding the
trolley cars "spying" on the Union soldiers, she wrote with indignation: "One tore my dress. A live
Yankee stepped on it" (p. 355). The remainder of the diary is a mixture of Clara's thoughts about the
events following the capture of New Orleans; Union regulations and restrictions; reasons Jefferson
Davis was to blame for allowing New Orleans to fall into Union hands; war news from Virginia; daily
activities; and worry about "Pa," who was a sutler in Virginia. The diary ends abruptly. The editor's
foreword places the role of Jews in New Orleans society, and the afterword traces the family's fortunes
following the war.

533. SPENCE, JOHN C. *A Diary of the Civil War.* Murfreesboro, Tenn.:
Rutherford County Historical Society, 1993. 164 pp.
1861–July 1865. Diary. Merchant. Murfreesboro, Tennessee. The Civil War as viewed from Murfreesboro is the focus of this diary, but Spence also recorded the impact of the war on Tennessee and the
complete Western Theater. The "diary" is a chronicle written later from notes made at the time of the
events. Historical narrative, sketches of personalities, anecdotes, and the author's personal views are all
blended together. The persistent themes are the activities of federal soldiers and authorities and the
activities of representatives of the U.S. Christian Commission and preachers from the North. Spence
also notes the actions of blacks, both the soldiers and those held in contraband camps. Among the battles he describes in greatest detail are Stones River, Fort Pillow, and Forrest's raid during Hood's
Nashville campaign. Spence portrays conditions during the first few months of peace, when refugees
returned, as did the soldiers who had fought for both sides. As Spence contrasted the appearance of

returning Tennessee soldiers, he noticed that those who had served the Union were laden with booty, while the Confederate soldiers were empty-handed. Spence concluded his account by relating the raising of the "Stars and Strips," describing the destruction of property in and around Murfreesboro, and reburying the Confederate dead.

534. SPENCER, EDWARD. "Dearest Braddie: Love and War in Maryland, 1860–61." Edited by Anna Bradford and Sidney Hovey Wanzer. (Part I) *Maryland Historical Magazine* 88 (Spring 1993): 73–88.

———. (Part II) *Maryland Historical Magazine* 88 (Fall 1993): 337–58.

December 13, 1860–August 15, 1861. Letters. Both love and war are represented in Spencer's correspondence with his future wife, Anna Catherine Bradford Harrison. Writing from near Randallstown (Baltimore County) to "Braddie" in Mount Pleasant (Talbot County), Spencer chronicled the escalation of political tensions that divided Marylanders as secession and then war became realities. Spencer welcomed the successes of the Confederacy and decried the Republican Party's abuse of civil liberties. He was observant of the scope of the war, possibly because he had relatives living in Missouri. Spencer often mentioned the strife in Baltimore, especially when the Union troops under Benjamin Butler arrived. Spencer's discussion of first Bull Run seems to indicate that he understood Confederate military strategy in northern Virginia. According to the last of these letters Spencer feared the destruction that federal forces might leave in their wake if they were driven through Maryland by the Confederate soldiers. Because Anna's family were Unionists, Spencer felt uncomfortable (and perhaps unwelcome) in her home. While he was disconsolate over his conflict with Anna's family, his situation was made more difficult because being the head of his own household compromised his freedom of movement. The editors add that the couple married and resided at Spencer's home.

535. STORY, ELLIOTT LEMUEL, and DANIEL WILLIAM COBB. "Southampton County Diarists in the Civil War Era: Elliott L. Story and Daniel W. Cobb." Edited by Daniel W. Crofts. *Virginia Magazine of History and Biography* 98 (October 1990): 537–612.

1830s–1870s. Diaries. While relatively little space is devoted to the Civil War, the writings of these two men who lived twelve miles apart in Southampton County show how differently two Virginians viewed the conflict. For example, Cobb was a Southern Whig who placed a high value on sectional accommodations. He thought that secession would be a mistake for Virginia and the South. Story feared abolitionists, resented the North, and saw little difference between the North and the Republican Party. He welcomed the war. The editor compares and contrasts the lives of these two men before, during, and following the war.

536. TAYLOR, SUSIE KING. *A Black Woman's Civil War Memoirs*. Edited by Patricia W. Romero, with a new introduction by Willie Lee Rose. New York: Markus Wiener Publishing, 1988. 154 pp.

1862–1865. Memoir. Charleston harbor and South Carolina–Georgia Sea Islands. Susie first recounted her childhood and life in Savannah (from 1848 through 1862) with her grandmother, who taught her to read and write. When she was fourteen, Susie was taken aboard a federal gunboat during the Union attack on Fort Pulaski. For the remainder of the war she was married to a sergeant of the First South Carolina Colored Infantry. Although vague about details, Susie wrote that she taught black soldiers (and others) to read, served the regiment as an unpaid nurse and laundress, and accompanied the soldiers on expeditions and raids. She notes the expressions of appreciation she received from people she had helped and mentions the prominent individuals she met. She held Col. Thomas W. Higginson, Gen. David Hunter, and Clara Barton, with whom she worked for eight months in the Sea Island hospitals, in high regard. Her memoirs conclude with a plea for recognition of the veteran black soldiers; a summary of her postwar life as a schoolteacher in Savannah; the death of her husband; her migration to Boston, where she remarried; and her participation in the organization of a segment of the Women's Relief Corps of the Grand Army of the Republic in Boston. Taylor's last two chapters, written in the 1890s, reflect her disappointment that race relations had not progressed as she had hoped. Originally published: *Reminiscences of My Life in Camp with the 33d United States Colored Troops, Late 1st South Carolina Volunteers*. Boston: The author, 1902.

537. THOMAS, ELLA GERTRUDE CLANTON. *The Secret Eye: The Journal of Ella Gertrude Clanton Thomas, 1848–1889.* Introduction by Nell Irvin Painter. Edited by Virginia Ingraham Burr. Chapel Hill: University of North Carolina Press, 1990. 469 pp.

July 13, 1861–October 12, 1866. Diary. This was written by a plantation owner who lived in Burke County, Georgia, near Augusta. Gertrude was in her late twenties when she began the Civil War portion of her diary (pp. 183–288). In 1861 she was euphoric that the men and women of the South were following in the footsteps of their revolutionary forefathers. She was elated that her husband, Jefferson, was a lieutenant with a local unit, the "Richmond Hussars" (Company A, Cavalry, Cobb's Georgia Legion). Gertrude's naïveté about the scope of the war is evident in an entry written when Port Royal was seized in November 1861 by Union troops: "I have never fully realized that we are engaged in a war that threatens to desolate our firesides" (p. 195). When she heard a rumor that the Union army had one thousand armed slaves with it, she wrote: "This attempt to arouse the vindictive passions of an inferior race so fills my soul with horror" (pp. 195–96). Gertrude never understood the North's determination to free the slaves, especially at the cost of so many lives. The institution of slavery is a continuous thread throughout her diary. She often mentions its "evils." In one entry she refers to slavery's "terribly demoralizing influence on our men and boys" (p. 236) .Still, she was convinced that "the Negro as a race is better off with us as he has been than if he were made free" (p. 236).On May 8, 1865, she wrote that she disliked losing so much slave property but that, at the same time, she felt relieved she no longer bore the responsibility of its management. On October 8, 1865, she explored the religious aspect of slavery. In the Bible, God justified slavery, yet he had allowed slavery to be taken away from the South. For a short period her faith was shaken. Gertrude wrote thoughtfully about a variety of other topics: why the South lagged behind the North in literary production; her belief in the necessity of education for women; and slave customs. When her father died she was bitterly disappointed that her husband had already borrowed great amounts against her inheritance. Part of her husband's "safe" investment was in Confederate bonds. She also wrote of domestic matters, such as giving birth. For one child she needed chloroform for the first time. For another she found it necessary to utilize a servant as a wet nurse. When the Yankees arrived, there were disruptions. After the war she wrote of problems involved with hiring servants at all, either black or white. In entries written by the end of 1866 Gertrude exhibits obdurate pride. She had matured as a woman, and she hated the Yankees as strongly as ever. On September 20, 1866, she wrote of an incident in which she denied food to a man wearing blue pants: "It reads like a little thing, but it is a part of the religion I have taught our children to dislike the Yankees" (p. 286).

538. THOMPSON, HENRIETTA. "An 'Unbroken Stallion' Comes Home from the Civil War." By Joan E. Cashin. *Manuscripts* 44 (Fall 1992): 307–14.

1863–1865. Letters. DeSoto County, Mississippi. Cashin paraphrases and quotes from the writings of the mistress of the plantation Forest Home. Mrs. Thompson became head of the household after her husband was killed at Chickamauga. Cashin focuses on the unwillingness of the eldest son, Fleming, to accept responsibility for either family matters or the changed economic and social conditions during and immediately following the war. He lived life as he might have done had the war never occurred; irresponsibly and oblivious to his family's sinking fortunes. Furthermore, he had become violently racist toward the former slaves. Mrs. Thompson was consumed by disappointment and dismay but retained her motherly love. She admitted that Fleming was unfit by nature for work, writing, "I might as reasonably expect an unbroken stallion to patiently bend his energies to the plow" (p. 310). She wrote that Fleming was like his father, who had never learned to direct "his noble energies" (p. 310). But she also knew that Fleming was not unique: "The country is full of just this description of young men" (p. 313). The letters end with the news that Mrs. Thompson had begun taking in boarders to stave off starvation. Cashin suggests that the example of Fleming might be used by social historians to probe the number of Confederate veterans who could not adjust to the new South.

539. **TILLMAN, SAMUEL E.** "Impressment, Occupation, War's End, and Emancipation: Samuel E. Tillman's Account of Seesaw Tennessee." Edited by Dwight L. Smith. *Tennessee Historical Quarterly* 49 (Fall 1990): 177–87.
1863–1865. Memoir. Tillman relates his brief impressment into Confederate service as a wagon driver. He also recalled the mixed reaction of slaves and freedmen to the Emancipation Proclamation and their freedom.

540. **TILLMAN, SAMUEL E.** "Secession, Armies, and a Federal Spy: Samuel E. Tillman's Account of Seesaw Middle Tennessee." Edited by Dwight L. Smith. *Tennessee Historical Quarterly* 49 (Summer 1990): 103–11.
1861–1863. Memoir. Bedford County, Tennessee. This is an autobiographical account by a teenager on the family plantation. It includes references to nearby battles, troop movements, and the visit of a Union spy.

541. **VAN LEW, ELIZABETH L.** *A Yankee Spy in Richmond: The Civil War Diary of "Crazy Bet" Van Lew.* Edited by David D. Ryan. Mechanicsburg, Pa.: Stackpole Books, 1996. 166 pp.
1861–April 2, 1865. Diary. Van Lew was a wealthy, middle-aged resident of Richmond who aided Union prisoners and spied for the North. Because she concealed her actions with erratic behavior, Van Lew was nicknamed "Crazy Bet." In February 1864 she arranged safe houses for the Union prisoners who escaped from Libby Prison. At about the same time she convinced Gen. Ben Butler (communicating in code) of the need to free the enlisted men held on Belle Isle. The effort culminated in the unsuccessful Kilpatrick-Dahlgren raid on Richmond. After Col. Ulrich Dahlgren was killed and buried outside a Richmond cemetery, Van Lew devised a plan to secretly transfer his body past Confederate guards and rebury it on the farm of another Union spy. Later in the spring of 1864 she passed information about Richmond's defenses to Gens. Grant and Meade. While she recorded some of these events in her diary, Van Lew was often vague about her specific activities, as well as the real names of other spies. However, the diary provides descriptions of Richmond as war approached (she especially blamed women for fanning the flames of secession), food shortages, the presence of other Unionists in Richmond, her narrow escapes from being revealed to Confederate agents, and the chaotic conditions as Confederate officials evacuated Richmond. In 1866 Van Lew requested that her messages to the War Department be returned. She destroyed the documents, fearing recriminations from the Southern people. Van Lew spent most of her personal inheritance on espionage, such as bribing workers in government offices for information and arsenal workers to sabotage munitions. After the war she sought compensation from the United States Congress. In 1869 Ulysses S. Grant appointed her postmaster of Richmond until 1875. Later she received a stipend from friends in Massachusetts. The letters included in the "Appendix," written by her and others, support the value of her espionage activities to the Union cause.

542. VANCE, ZEBULON BAIRD. *The Papers of Zebulon Baird Vance. Volume 2: 1863.* Edited by Joe A. Mobley. Raleigh: Division of Archives and History, North Carolina Department of Cultural Resources, 1995. 436 pp.
January 1–December 31, 1863. Papers. Governor. North Carolina. This selection of 406 letters and official documents (203 were written by Vance) indicates the obstacles faced by the recently elected governor. Some of these problems were common to all governors of Confederate states, while others were unique to North Carolina. In the editor's introduction he writes that "conscription, wholesale desertion from the Confederate ranks, the Emancipation Proclamation which would incite slaves to insurrection, shortages, speculation, illegal distilling, a tax in kind, battlefield losses and Federal raids all contributed to a decline in the will of North Carolinians to wage civil war" (p. xv). The difficulties between the governments of the state of North Carolina and the Confederate States of America may be found within the numerous letters from Vance to Secretary of War James A. Seddon and Jefferson Davis. Also included is a lengthy calendar of Vance correspondence for the year 1863 that is not published in this volume. Volume 1 of the Vance papers (1843 to 1862) was edited by Frontis W. Johnston and published in 1963 by the North Carolina State Department of Archives and History.

543. WATKINS FAMILY. *Letters from Forest Place: A Plantation Family's Correspondence, 1846–1881.* Edited by E. Grey Dimond and Herman Hattaway. Jackson: University Press of Mississippi, 1993. 512 pp.
May 4, 1846–December 30, 1881. Letters. Forest Place, Carroll County, Mississippi. These letters, which were written primarily by and to Sarah Watkins and her two daughters, Lettie and Mary, focus on concerns of the plantation and family affairs. Sarah's husband, Dr. Thomas Watkins, had abandoned his medical practice in Alabama in 1843 to become a prominent cotton planter (fifteen hundred acres) in north-central Mississippi. Before the war Lettie had married against his wishes, and Dr. Watkins denied his family communication with the daughter. Sarah acted as a buffer between family members and eventually attained a tenuous reconciliation. Such domestic matters as births, deaths, Dr. Watkins's activities, Sarah's personal feelings, and advice to her daughters constitute the routine topics of this correspondence. Opinions about the Civil War, which is covered on pages 215 through 333, intensified from "I hope it is all talk" to reality. The writers noted that military units were being organized in Mississippi and Texas (Lettie lived in Austin) and that shortages in Mississippi appeared early. Sarah wrote of the ladies' sewing societies for military needs; news of the battles of Shiloh, Corinth, and around Vicksburg; information about friends and relatives affected by the fighting; and Dr. Watkins's money problems. She also mentioned fear of slave insurrection and that one slave had been whipped to death (p. 233). But when Dr. Watkins found it necessary to hire out some of his slaves to the railroad, Sarah described the personal distress felt by "Pa" as he was forced to split up families. While their own slaves remained respectful in the face of Yankee invasion, slaves on other plantations were said to be determined to leave. Other slaves were seized by the federal troops. Letters from mid 1863 through early 1865 are sparse, although Sarah kept Lettie informed about the conditions in Mississippi. In March of 1865 Sarah suddenly became ill and died from an undisclosed cause. Lettie was especially distressed. Lettie's letters to Sarah, Mary, and her father throughout the war touched on such topics as the need to educate slaves in the ways of religion, the Texas troops' capture of Fort Fillmore, gratitude that her father had "buried the hatchet," comments about shipments of cotton through Texas, her husband, and remorse over her mother's death. In October 1861 Lettie received two cordial letters from her former servants back in Mississippi. She responded in detail, expressing her fond regards for their welfare. The family letters written during the postwar years reveal that the plantation did not recover. Within a few years Dr. Watkins was forced to sell the estate and move to Texas to live with the daughter he had once banished from his home.

544. **WILSON, ARABELLA LANKTREE.** "Arabella Lanktree Wilson's Civil War Letter." Edited by James W. Leslie. *Arkansas Historical Quarterly* 47 (Autumn 1988): 257–72.

November 2, 1863. Letter. A mother from Pine Bluff, Arkansas, wrote her son about the occupation of Pine Bluff by federal troops, the battle of Pine Bluff, and relations between civilians and Union soldiers.

III. ANTHOLOGIES, STUDIES, AND FOREIGN TRAVELERS

A. General
Items 545–564

545. AMERICAN WRITERS. *The Real War Will Never Get in the Books: Selections from Writers During the Civil War.* Edited by Louis P. Masur. New York: Oxford University Press, 1993. 301 pp.

1861–1865. Masur has selected the writings of fourteen literary figures who wrote and published during the Civil War to explore Walt Whitman's prophesy that "the real war will never get in the books." All fourteen, well known at the time, range alphabetically from Henry Adams to Walt Whitman. Each interpreted the war's impact on his creative spirit differently, and all struggled to convey their experiences in written words. Recent literary critics agree that although writing in general flourished during the period, belles lettres did not. However, as these writers addressed the issues of the day, they composed some of their finest writings in letters, diary entries, and essays for periodicals. Furthermore, "These wartime writings expose the connections between the political, and personal, and the creative" (p. ix). In the fourteen chapters Masur explores each writer's perspectives and wartime experiences.

546. ATLANTA. *Echoes of Battle: The Atlanta Campaign: An Illustrated Collection of Union and Confederate Narratives.* Edited by Larry M. Strayer and Richard A. Baumgartner. Huntington, W.Va.: Blue Acorn Press, 1991. 361 pp.

1864. Atlanta campaign. The editors have selected more than 260 narratives from Union and Confederate eyewitnesses that were written in first-person style. The accounts were taken from such sources as published and private letters, diaries, and journals; battle reports in the *Official Records;* regimental histories; and veterans' periodicals. Also included are 280 images. The accounts are divided into eleven chapters, which are preceded by editorial material. The sources are acknowledged; the index includes individuals, places, and units; and the extensive bibliography is divided into types of materials.

547. ATLANTA CAMPAIGN AND MARCH TO THE SEA. *Marching Through Georgia: The Story of Soldiers & Civilians During Sherman's Campaign.* By Lee Kennett. New York: HarperCollins Publishers, 1995. 418 pp.

1864. The Atlanta campaign and March to the Sea. Kennett informs the reader that this is not a classical campaign history that "places its readers at the general's elbow" (p. xi). Rather, it is written from the perspective of the men who participated in the war and the civilians whose homes lay in the path of the fighting. While Kennett keeps readers aware of decisions made by such ranking officials as Gen. William T. Sherman and Georgia governor Joe Brown, as well as drawing some of his own conclusions, for the most part he lets the participants tell the story. Recurring themes of the work are the character of Sherman and the Union soldiers and Union destruction. For example, Kennett addresses the issue of whether the Union soldiers' behavior had markedly deteriorated by the middle of 1864. From his reading of the narratives Kennett concludes: "there is precious little here to indicate that the war was degenerating into something more cruel and frightful" (p. 277). But he admits that during the March to the Sea the Union army had more opportunities for transgressions. When wanton destruction did occur, however, Kennett believes that Sherman was less to blame than individual groups of soldiers who, acting on their own, "really fixed the parameters of desolation" (p. 287). He also emphasizes that Confederate soldiers and civilians frequently plundered their own society. Among other themes treated are the troops' reaction to battle, the welcoming of federal soldiers by Unionists and slaves, and the apprehension of Georgia women as Union soldiers filed into their state. In his final chapter Kennett touches on how Sherman's campaign had already become legendary by the late nineteenth century and then how it was reconsidered in the twentieth century to exemplify the military construct of "total war."

548. CHATTANOOGA. *Echoes of Battle: The Struggle for Chattanooga: An Illustrated Collection of Union and Confederate Narratives.* Edited by Richard A. Baumgartner and Larry M. Strayer. Huntington, W.Va.: Blue Acorn Press, 1996. 483 pp.

1863. Tullahoma, Chickamauga, and Chattanooga campaigns. The editors selected more than 450 narratives from Union and Confederate eyewitnesses that were written in first-person style. The accounts were taken from such sources as published and private letters, diaries, and journals; battle reports in the *Official Records;* regimental histories; and veterans' periodicals. Also included are 465 images. The accounts are divided into ten chapters, which are preceded by editorial material. The sources are acknowledged; the index includes individuals, places, and units; and the extensive bibliography is divided into types of materials.

549. CHRISTMAS. *We Were Marching on Christmas Day: A History and Chronicle of Christmas During the Civil War.* By Kevin Rawlings. Baltimore, Md.: Toomey Press, 1995. 169 pp.

1861–1865. In the first chapter, "Christmas Comes to America," the author indicates that by 1860 most of today's Christmas traditions were in place. The final chapter, "Peace of Reunion, Goodwill Towards Former Foes," offers reflections on the recently concluded conflict. The chapters between contain annual summations of the progress of the war and descriptions of holiday celebrations at home and in the field. The author utilizes numerous eyewitness accounts from both published and manuscript sources to re-create the holiday. Homesickness and joy, determination and despair were pervasive emotions of both sides. The author provides overviews of the war, identifies the writers, and embellishes the work with illustrations from *Harper's Weekly.*

550. CIVIL WAR, NORTH AND SOUTH. *Civil War Eyewitnesses: An Annotated Bibliography of Books and Articles, 1955–1986.* By Garold L. Cole. Foreword by James I. Robertson Jr. Columbia: University of South Carolina Press, 1988. 351 pp.

1861–1865. This is a compilation of 1,395 personal narratives written by soldiers, civilians, and foreign travelers that were published as books and articles between 1955 and 1986. While diaries, letters, and memoirs constitute the majority of these items, this work also includes special studies that have utilized Civil War accounts as a unique resource to explore themes of the era. Entries are annotated with the date and type of document; the soldier's rank and military engagements or places of duty; and for civilians and foreign travelers, their occupations or nationalities and places from which their narratives were written. The entries also include comments that reveal the individuals' activities and responses to the war on the battlefield or at home, usually with pertinent quotations by the writers. The index includes all names, battles and places, military units, and subjects about which they wrote.

551. **CIVIL WAR, NORTH AND SOUTH.** *The Private Civil War: Popular Thought During the Sectional Conflict.* By Randall C. Jimerson. Baton Rouge: Louisiana State University Press, 1988. 270 pp.

1861–1865. Jimerson probes the "contours of Americans' sectional consciousness" by examining those soldiers and civilians who fought the war and endured its hardships. "Popular thought," as interpreted here, is gleaned from the writings of the common soldiers and plain folk of both sections. The sources of their perceptions about the war and each other are published and unpublished letters and diaries. Jimerson states that he attempted to achieve a balance between regions. He admits to subjective methodology, eschewing the capability of statisticians to quantify "idealism, courage . . . or anything else that makes us human." (p. 6) Jimerson explains why individuals within a nation of homogeneous values and a shared history decided to wage war on each other. Northerners fought for liberty, freedom, and to preserve the Union. Southerners also fought for liberty and freedom, but their concept of freedom specified exemption from Northern interference. Racial attitudes influenced the thinking of both sections. Northerners grew to accept emancipation as a wartime necessity (but without social equality), while Southerners became more entrenched in the need to control their slaves. Another theme Jimerson explores is the extreme notions that each section held about each other. Northerners saw Southerners as backward and ignorant, or arrogant aristocrats. Southerners regarded Northerners as plunderers or social inferiors. Jimerson also narrows his study to illuminate internal problems within each section. State and local loyalties created difficulties in the armies of both sides. Social classes clashed, as did common soldiers and enlisted men. And as the war dragged on, both sides experienced a marked decline in patriotism and morale. Jimerson's "Epilogue" is a brief summary of the impact of the war throughout the remainder of the nineteenth century.

552. **CIVIL WAR, NORTH AND SOUTH.** *Unfurl the Flags: Remembrances of the American Civil War.* Edited by William E. Edmonston Jr. Hamilton, N.Y.: Edmonston Publishing, 1989. 90 pp.

1861–1865. This work contains a series of "impressions" that the editor feels reflect "the realities of war, of civil war" (preface). The lengthy excerpted quotations by both soldiers and civilians are not specifically credited, but a general bibliography of the authors of the chapters is appended.

553. **CIVIL WAR, NORTH AND SOUTH.** *Voices from the House Divided: The United States Civil War as Personal Experience.* Compiled by Glenn M. Linden and Thomas J. Pressley. New York: McGraw-Hill, 1995. 276 pp.

1861–1865. This contains lengthy excerpts from the published writings of twenty individuals from all segments of society. The work is arranged chronologically by military event and linked by editorial passages. Extensive biographical information on the writers is included so that readers will be better able to "experience the past vicariously through their writings" (p. xv). Biographical sketches of the writers' lives after the war conclude this compilation.

554. **CIVIL WAR, NORTH AND SOUTH.** *Voices of the Civil War.* New York: Time-Life Books, 1995–In progress.

1861–1865. This series is devoted to individual battles, campaigns, and specific aspects of the Civil War. Each book contains brief excerpted writings of soldiers and civilians of both sides, as well as photographs of individuals, artifacts, maps, and battlefield scenes. While brief biographical sketches are included, the editorial narrative is kept to a minimum. The bibliographies in each work contain the books, periodicals, and manuscripts from which the participants' writings are taken. Volumes published to date are: *Gettysburg* (1995); *Second Manassas* (1995); *Atlanta* (1996); *Chancellorsville* (1996); *Sol-*

dier Life (1996); *Antietam* (1996); *Shiloh* (1996); *Fredericksburg* (1997); *Charleston* (1997); *Chicka-mauga* (1997); *Shenandoah, 1862* (1997); and *First Manassas* (1997).

555. CONFEDERATE AND UNION SOLDIERS. *Civil War Soldiers: Their Expectations and Their Experiences.* By Reid Mitchell. New York: Viking Penguin, Inc., 1988. 274 pp.

1861–1865. Mitchell begins his study by stating that if we can determine what the war meant to the Civil War generation, it will help Americans of today decide what it means to us. From the letters and diaries written by soldiers from both sides, he searched for the reasons they fought, what they thought of their American enemies, what they said it was like to face death and cope with fear, how they rationalized violence and destruction, and how they felt about slavery and race relations. Mitchell demonstrates why similarities between Americans, who shared a common heritage, did not translate into a common ideology. Men from both sides rushed to enlist, but they sought to fight for their own interpretations of the Constitution, those which protected their different ways of life. Nevertheless, civilian-soldiers of both sides rebelled against military discipline and saw in the conflict the hand of God meting out punishment for human sins. Both sides regarded the enemy as uncivilized and ignorant, often calling them "savages," and this lack of familiarity encouraged destructive excesses. In chapter 4 Mitchell follows Union soldiers into the South and describes their unfavorable depiction of the region. Although Mitchell says most Union soldiers were well behaved, others believed that destruction of Southern properties was justified. Because of their "cultural contempt," some Union soldiers perceived the struggle as a war against the Southern way of life and sought to remake the South in the North's image. While the Confederacy never occupied the North, Mitchell writes: "The Gettysburg campaign reveals that had they had the chance, Confederates would have rivaled Yankees in the work of destruction" (p. 157). When the soldiers met face-to-face, however, their biases often diminished. Mitchell addresses numerous other topics confronted by both sides: desertion, morale, reaction to combat, alienation toward those on the home front who were not supporting the war, and blacks. In his concluding chapter Mitchell notes that at the end of the war both sides turned away from the responsibility that accompanied victory and the reality of defeat. The North rejected black equality, and the South embraced the consoling myth of the "Lost Cause."

556. CONFEDERATE AND UNION SOLDIERS. *Embattled Courage: The Experience of Combat in the American Civil War.* By Gerald L. Linderman. New York: Free Press, 1987. 357 pp.

1861–1865. Linderman characterizes Civil War soldiers of both sides as marching off to war inspired by a romanticized notion of battle in which the concept of courage was "the cement of the armies" (p. 34). He describes the soldiers' psychological response to the drudgery of camp life and the dark side of battle and demonstrates that courage was not sufficient to sustain their morale. As they endured the hardships of soldiering and came to recognize that brutality toward enemy soldiers and civilians was a prerequisite to victory, the soldiers' initial mind-set about war was dramatically altered. Eventually both sides became isolated from civilians on the home front. Linderman believes that, as a result, America was waging two civil wars: the romantic one that the home front perceived; and the realistic war that soldiers saw firsthand. The longer the war lasted, the greater the men's disillusionment. Eventually survival supplanted courage as the soldiers' primary motivation. Linderman's final chapter about the postwar period, which he admits is more tentative than the earlier portions, is a reflection on how the soldiers later regarded their wartime experiences. Immediately following the war they were reluctant to talk about their service because of physical problems and psychological and social disorientation. When they did begin to relate their experiences, they failed to describe the realities of the war they had come to know. Instead, they reverted to their original romanticized concept of war, which emphasized manliness, virtue, and courage. As a result of stressing a concept of war which they had tested and found wanting, their accounts served to perpetuate the old myths. Consequently, American soldiers carried outmoded motivations into the Spanish-American War and into twentieth-century conflicts. Linderman's study is primarily based on the published memoirs of fifty-odd soldiers "who arrived early and tried to fight the war to its end" (p. 2). He presents biographical sketches in his "Dramatis Personae" (pp. 298–314). Linderman summarized the results of his study in "The Burden of Civil War Combat," *Northwest Ohio Quarterly* 62 (Winter/Spring 1990): 3–10.

557. CONFEDERATE AND UNION SOLDIERS. *Soldiers Blue and Gray.* By James I. Robertson Jr. Columbia: University of South Carolina Press, 1988. 278 pp.

1861–1865. "This is a work that could be written a dozen times without repetition." (p. vii). With this understatement Robertson informs readers that his study is intended to supplement the two seminal studies of the common soldier written by Bell I. Wiley, *The Life of Johnny Reb* (1943) and *The Life of Billy Yank* (1952). Like Wiley, Robertson follows a topical arrangement to explain who the Confederate and Union soldiers were, comparing and contrasting why they were willing to fight and describing the activities that constituted their daily experiences. Wiley relied more on manuscripts, while Robertson has gleaned the abundance of printed memoirs, diaries, and letters that have emerged since the Civil War centennial. Robertson has divided *Soldiers Blue and Gray* into eleven chapters. Chapter 1, "Rally 'round the Flag," explains why men of both sides were eager to enlist; chapter 11, "Beyond the Call of Duty," concludes with the finalities of battle. Chapters in between explain how men of diverse origins were blended into cohesive units and how the initial "novelties" of camp life soon wore off. He explains how some soldiers combated often appalling living conditions, irregular quality of rations, and a constant longing to be back home with doses of irreverence and vice. Still other soldiers were sustained by revivals and religious conversion. The fates of those who exceeded military regulations and received punishment are discussed in the chapter on "Problems of Discipline." The two most sobering chapters are "The Grimmest Reaper" and "In the Prison Cell I Sit," which discuss medical treatment and prison life. Robertson blends the abundance of source material in several ways. He allows the soldiers to tell their own stories with a judicious selection of quotations. Then he binds essays together with meaningful transitional statements and conclusions. At the end of the study Robertson points out the contributions that these men made to the United States of the future. Their legacy lies in the lasting realization that "when the great challenges come, this nation's common people can and will show that they value some ideals more than they value their lives." As a result of Civil War soldiers' sacrifices, "America matured into one, indivisible nation" (p. 228).

558. CONFEDERATE AND UNION SOLDIERS. *What They Fought For, 1861–1865.* By James M. McPherson. Baton Rouge: Louisiana State University Press, 1994. 88 pp.

1861–1865. McPherson believes that the Civil War soldiers' motivation for fighting was not to display personal courage or maintain primary group cohesion. Neither did they fight without a specific cause. McPherson asserts that soldiers of both sides fought for patriotism and that Confederate and Union soldiers alike derived their motivation from the American Revolution and the Constitution. At the core of their inspiration lay liberty and republicanism. However, the Constitution held different meanings for the two regions. "Confederates fought for liberty and independence from what they regarded as a tyrannical government; Unionists fought to preserve the nation from dismemberment and destruction" (p. 7). In chapters 1 and 2 McPherson treats these interpretations separately. In chapter 3 he compares and contrasts both sides' attitudes toward the issues of slavery and equality for blacks. McPherson demonstrates how in the South slaveholders defended their right to hold slaves, nonslaveholders fought to preserve the slave system, and still others sought racial supremacy. Southerners seldom wrote about slavery because within the section there existed a general consensus in favor of the institution. More frequently they expressed dedication to the protection of their homeland from the Northern invaders. In the writings of Northerners, especially after the first year of the war when emancipation became a war aim, the issue of slavery was often debated and created divisiveness within the ranks. In conclusion, McPherson insists that the initial convictions held by both sides persisted and provided each with motivation to persevere until the very end. Unfortunately, during the postwar years national reconciliation was accompanied by a romanticization of the war, and the welfare of former slaves was neglected. McPherson's study included some 25,000 letters and 100 diaries written by 374 Confederate and 562 Union soldiers. Throughout this work he identifies sections of his sample by region, rank, and often socio-economic status. He confesses to weaknesses in his sample when they exist. These themes are incorporated into McPherson's more comprehensive *For Cause and Comrades: Why Men Fought in the Civil War* (New York: Oxford University Press, 1997).

559. DOCTORS AND NURSES. *In Hospital and Camp: The Civil War Through the Eyes of Its Doctors and Nurses.* Compiled by Harold Elk Straubing. Harrisburg, Pa.: Stackpole Books, 1993. 166 pp.

1861–1865. This work contains excerpts of previously published accounts written by Northern and Southern doctors and nurses. Each account includes a brief preface.

560. FORT PICKENS–PENSACOLA, FLORIDA. "Life on the Front as Reflected in Soldiers' Letters." By Dean DeBolt. *Gulf Coast Historical Review* 4 (Spring 1989): 26–37.

1861–1862. This consists of quotations from letters written by both Union and Confederate soldiers stationed in the Fort Pickens–Pensacola area. Themes expressed in the letters include assessments of the composition of the opponents, illnesses and battles with insects, monotony of uneventful camp life, quality of living quarters, and the permanent occupation of the region by Union forces. Debolt summarizes events of this period.

561. GETTYSBURG (PICKETT'S CHARGE). *Pickett's Charge: Eyewitness Accounts.* Edited by Richard Rollins. Redondo Beach, Calif.: Rank and File Publications, 1994. 376 pp.

July 1–3, 1863. Rollins compiled 176 of the most pertinent published and unpublished accounts and reports of soldiers of all levels beginning immediately after the battle to the end of the century. The compilation points out the "overall conception of the operation and the elements that actually came into play" and includes the roles of the Confederate artillery and cavalry and the Union artillery in the repulse (p. xvi). The drama unfolds in nine chapters: "Planning the Charge"; "Preparing for the Charge"; "The Cannonade"; "The Charge of Pickett's Division"; "The Federal Left"; "The Charge of Pettigrew's and Trimble's Divisions"; The Federal Right"; "The Angle"; and "Afterwords." Each account is prefaced by an identification of the individual, his proximity to the battle, and the source of the document. The order of battle and maps of Pickett's Charge, which illustrate the locations of the units and the individual writers, are also included.

562. RUSSELL, WILLIAM HOWARD. *My Diary North and South.* Edited by Eugene H. Berwanger. Philadelphia, Pa.: Temple University Press, 1988. 336 pp.

March 3, 1861–April 14, 1862. Diary. As a war correspondent for *The Times* of London, Russell's earlier assignments had taken him to the Crimean War in 1854 and the Sepoy Mutiny of 1857–1858. As a result of his experiences, when he arrived in America to cover the impending crisis he was already respected in both the North and the South. While the editor believes that Russell attempted to achieve balance in his reportage, passions in America were so inflamed that he angered both sides. Russell first arrived in Washington, where he secured introductions to prominent individuals. Then he hurried to the South. Between mid April and early July 1861 he visited Confederate politicians and generals in Charleston, Savannah, Montgomery, Mobile, Fort Pickens, and New Orleans before returning to Washington via the Mississippi River, Chicago, and Niagara Falls. The aristocratic Russell revealed an affinity for the manners and lifestyle of upper-class Southerners but viewed middle and lower classes as crude. He was morally opposed to slavery, but he regarded blacks as backward. Russell perceived that the South's hatred for the North was so strong that it would be difficult for the North to coerce the South back into the Union. In the North, Russell observed a lack of consensus for pursuit of the war. Then, following his unfavorable report of the Union rout at first Bull Run, as well as the pro-Confederate stance taken by *The Times,* Russell's unpopularity reached its height during the fall of 1861. In early 1862 both the War Department and President Lincoln denied Russell a pass to travel with the army on the Peninsular campaign. Because he was unable to cover the war from the front lines, Russell felt compelled to return home. In 1863 he published his experiences in a two-volume work, *My Diary North and South* (London: Bradbury and Evans), which the editor has abridged for this edition. The editor's introduction indicates that Russell's work was not fully accepted at the time it was published, nor is it today. However, he praises Russell's "broad compelling interest in America as a whole," his descriptions of the landscape and culture, and his willingness to critique American values at the middle of the nineteenth century (p. 14).

563. RUSSELL, WILLIAM HOWARD. *William Howard Russell's Civil War: Private Diary and Letters, 1861–1862.* Edited by Martin Crawford. Athens: University of Georgia Press, 1992. 252 pp.

March 4, 1861–April 4, 1862. Diary and letters. British war correspondent for *The Times* of London. In his lengthy introduction the editor summarizes Russell's earlier career and the circumstances that conspired to make his assignment to cover the American Civil War unpleasant. Crawford points to differences between Russell's experiences published as *My Diary North and South* and those in this compilation, his unpublished diary (March 4–December 31, 1861) and a selection of letters. Russell's published work was a "narrative reconstruction based upon the correspondent's notebooks and reports" (p. vii). Because Russell had not ruled out a return to America, the language in his published account is relatively moderate and sympathetic. However, Russell's private diary and the letters to his publisher and friends are written with few inhibitions. And because he usually wrote terse, stream-of-consciousness entries or letters that addressed pressing issues of the moment, his writings evoke a sense of immediacy. His portrayals of leaders and personalities are more caustic. He opined that the South had less chance to win if the Union blockade were prolonged. He wondered why the North was taking so long to make war on slavery, criticized American newspapers as being irresponsible, and judged the American system of government unsuited to rule its populace. Russell's private writings also reveal sensitive aspects of his personality. He was hurt by the North's hostile reaction to his Bull Run report in *The Times.* He wrote that his unpopularity was so great that "They take me as the exponent of Englishmen England & The Times & would like to avenge themselves upon me" (p. 129). And in early 1862 he was disappointed by the lack of respect evinced by Union officials which prevented him from traveling to Virginia and accomplishing his mission as a war correspondent. Through much of this period he was worried about the health of his wife. Read with *My Diary North and South,* Russell's diary and letters indicate that he was a perceptive viewer of the first year of the war. Russell ran afoul of Anglo-American diplomacy, Northern reaction to his reportage of Bull Run, and support of the South by *The Times.*

564. SHILOH. *"Seeing the Elephant": Raw Recruits at the Battle of Shiloh.* By Joseph Allan Frank and George A. Reaves. Westport, Conn.: Greenwood Press, 1989. 215 pp.

April 6–7, 1862. Shiloh. This is a study of combat motivation and morale as exhibited by 381 raw Confederate and Union volunteers who experienced battle for the first time at Shiloh. The authors analyzed the letters, diaries, and memoirs of these men who, in their writings, addressed at least ten questions from a seventy-six-item questionnaire that the authors compiled from "works in military sociology and combat psychology written after World War II" (p. 5). The men under scrutiny were common soldiers and company and field grade officers. The questions, which are not reproduced here, examine such factors as "tactical preparation, political attitudes, logistics, and leadership, as well as esprit de corps, comradeship, and officer competence" (p. 2). Their six chapters cover the soldiers from their mobilization through the battle ("Seeing the Elephant"), and they conclude with the soldiers' appraisals after the fighting. Throughout the study the authors present results of their research in the text and endnotes. In the final chapter they review the soldiers' reactions to their first major battle. Both sides thought they had fought well, although their motivations varied. Shiloh was not "a wrenching experience" that was destined to transform the raw soldiers forever, and the men fought on in subsequent battles. The authors believe that the men were "essentially the same citizen-soldiers as they were before" (p. 181). In conclusion, the authors point to differences and similarities between the Civil War soldiers in this study and modern American soldiers. Briefly, Civil War soldiers were fighting in cohesive units in a "struggle for two mutually exclusive national alternatives: union or secession" (p. 181). Today's soldiers are placed "in large amorphous units in foreign wars for a vague national interest. . . . Patriotism is only invoked when the soldier sees a clear and present danger to his country," which wars far away over geopolitical interests do not merit (p. 181). However, the authors believe that if today's soldier were to feel that national survival was at stake, he would fight for reasons similar to those exhibited by the raw recruits at Shiloh. The bibliography of this work— which is comprised of manuscripts and other unpublished materials, newspaper accounts, periodical articles, and books—constitutes extensive coverage of the battle of Shiloh, as well as the broad topic of combat motivation.

B. The North
Items 565–588

565. BLACK SOLDIERS. *A Grand Army of Black Men: Letters from African-American Soldiers in the Union Army, 1861–1865.* Edited by Edwin S. Redkey. New York: Cambridge University Press, 1992. 302 pp.

1861–1865. These 129 letters were written by black soldiers to the editors of such black and abolitionist newspapers as the *Christian Recorder* (Philadelphia), the *Weekly Anglo-African* (New York), and *Pine and Palm* (Boston). The letters fall into two categories, events of army life and issues addressed. Chapter 1 contains letters written by black soldiers who served with white units early in the war. Chapters 2 through 4 are arranged by the geographic region from which they were written. Chapter 5 is devoted to troops on occupation duty. Chapters 6 through 8 deal with such issues as civil rights, equal pay, and racism. Chapter 9 contains letters from men who served with the United States Navy. The letters in chapter 10 are from veterans. Redkey says that "By the end of 1865, the newspapers carried no more letters from black soldiers" (p. xv). Redkey has written lengthy introductions to the chapters and shorter introductions to each letter.

566. **GETTYSBURG.** *The Bachelder Papers: Gettysburg in Their Own Words.* Transcribed, edited, and annotated by David L. Ladd and Audrey J. Ladd. Publisher's consultant, Dr. Richard Allen Sauers. Dayton, Ohio: Morningside House, 1994. 3 vols. 2,081 pp.

July 1–3, 1863. These interviews, published here for the first time, were conducted by artist and amateur historian John Badger Bachelder immediately after Gettysburg and during the Army of the Potomac's winter camp in the fall and winter of 1863. Bachelder claimed to have spoken with the commanders of every regiment and battery in the army. In fall 1863 he published an isometric map of the battlefield. Over the years his correspondence with Union and Confederate veterans about Gettysburg increased. By the time of his death in 1894 Bachelder had amassed a huge quantity of correspondence and notes with men of all ranks. In Dr. Sauers's preface he explains more about Bachelder's activities and publishing and points out that this primary resource lay untouched until the 1960s, when it was uncovered in the New Hampshire Historical Society by Professor Edwin Coddington. The editors provide explanatory footnotes and extensive indexes.

567. **GETTYSBURG.** *War Stories: A Collection of 150 Little Known Human Interest Accounts of the Campaign and Battle of Gettysburg.* Compiled by Gregory A. Coco. Gettysburg, Pa.: Thomas Publications, 1992. 72 pp.

June–July 1863. Coco compiled these accounts to illustrate that the story of Gettysburg should not be limited to strategy and tactics but must also include the range of events experienced by soldiers and civilians. The accounts are divided into chronological sections and prefaced by Coco's commentary.

568. **GETTYSBURG, UNION SOLDIERS.** *Killed in Action: Eyewitness Accounts of the Last Moments of 100 Union Soldiers Who Died at Gettysburg.* By Gregory A. Coco. Gettysburg, Pa.: Thomas Publications, 1992. 128 pp.

June 30–July 3, 1863. These descriptions of how one hundred Union soldiers died were culled from published and unpublished sources. Coco has divided the work into three parts—June 30 and July 1, 1863; July 2, 1863; and July 3, 1863—and introduces each account with information or reflections about the circumstances of the deaths. Photographs are also included.

569. **ILLINOIS SOLDIERS.** "Civil War Accounts as Literature: Illinois Letters, Diaries, and Personal Narratives." By John Hallwas. *Western Illinois Regional Studies* 13 (Spring 1990): 46–60.

1861–1865. Hallwas introduces his study by emphasizing that Civil War accounts have been evaluated almost exclusively for their historical content, rather than as literary artifacts or documents of self-expression. Such consideration is an oversight, for, as with other nonfictional writings, Civil War soldiers' accounts often transcend an understanding of the war to the level of literary art and revelation of the human experience. Hallwas examines the Civil War accounts of Illinois soldiers to demonstrate his assertion and encourage unpublished accounts to come to light. He begins with criteria that accounts must possess to have literary value. "In brief, it is prose that displays a fine blend of content, form, and style; that both analyzes personal experience and synthesizes it into a new unity, and that reveals a firm commitment to contemporary or historical factuality" (p. 47). Hallwas finds that few letters written by Illinois soldiers possess value as literary art and that their diaries vary in quality. He explains and utilizes often lengthy quotations to demonstrate why specific accounts do or do not meet the established criteria. Hallwas believes that the real value of the soldiers' accounts written in fine literary style is that they help us comprehend our own humanity.

570. ILLINOIS SOLDIERS. *117th Illinois Infantry Volunteers (The McK-endree Regiment), 1862–1865.* By Edwin G. Gerling. Highland, Ill.: Highland Printers, 1992. 222 pp.

September 19, 1862–August 5, 1865. 117th Illinois Infantry. Duty at Fort Pickering, Tenn.; the Meridian campaign; the second Red River campaign; Tupelo; Price's Missouri raid; Nashville; and the siege of Mobile. On pages 31 through 109 Gerling presents a composite journal made up "from the five diaries and many letters written by men in all companies of the regiment" (p. 25). The remainder of the work is primarily a modern-day regimental history made up of essays on leaders and campaigns, statistics about the regiment, genealogical information, photographs, and reunions.

571. IOWA SOLDIERS. *Iowa Valor: A Compilation of Civil War Combat Experiences from Soldiers of the State Distinguished as Most Patriotic of the Patriotic.* By Steve Meyer. Garrison, Iowa: Meyer Publishing Company, 1994. 505 pp.

1861–1865. This work is a compilation of more than two hundred accounts written by and about the military accomplishments of soldiers from Iowa. It includes original manuscripts, letters to newspaper editors, official reports, and previously published accounts. Although Meyer admits he could have included more items, he considers these two hundred to be highlights. The work is arranged by year, then by battle or campaign. Iowa units fought primarily in the Western Theater. His own research—aside from the selection of worthy accounts—involved providing background information on the eyewitness accounts. He provides full citations of the accounts, includes many photographs, and arranges appropriate indexes and other tables of military actions.

572. KANSAS SOLDIERS. *Kansans at Wilson's Creek: Soldiers' Letters from the Campaign for Southwest Missouri.* Edited by Richard W. Hatcher III and William Garrett Piston. Springfield, Mo.: Wilson's Creek National Battlefield Foundation, 1993. 105 pp.

June–September 1861. First and Second Kansas Infantries. This book consists of letters submitted to the *Leavenworth Daily Times* between June and September 1861. The Kansas troops, with the U.S. Regulars, moved from Fort Leavenworth to Kansas City and then south to link up with Gen. Nathaniel Lyon. The editors identify the authors of letters and their places of residence and add socio-economic information whenever possible. They also provide extensive footnotes that identify references to people mentioned, as well as explanations for the soldiers' attitudes. (See also the editors' "Kansans Go to War: The Wilson's Creek Campaign as Reported by the *Leavenworth Daily Times*," *Kansas History,* Parts I and II, 16, nos. 3–4, 1993.)

573. LINCOLN, ABRAHAM. *We Saw Lincoln Shot: One Hundred Eyewitness Accounts.* Edited by Timothy S. Good. Jackson: University Press of Mississippi, 1995. 215 pp.

April 14, 1865. "The accounts range from personal letters and diary entries to sworn legal testimony and also include many newspaper and magazines articles" (p. vii). The editor selected these one hundred accounts because he considered them the most informative. The work is divided into four chapters: "The First Accounts, April–May 1865"; "The Conspiracy Trial Accounts, May 1865"; "The Transition, 1877–1908"; and "The Last Accounts, 1909." Each chapter is preceded by a general introduction, and each individual account identifies the eyewitness, his proximity to the assassination, the source of the account, and the specific date it was given or appeared in print. An overview of these accounts precedes this compilation, and a complete bibliography and index of names mentioned concludes the work.

574. **MAINE SOLDIERS.** "Blending Loyalties: Maine Soldiers Respond to the Civil War." By Andy DeRoche. *Maine History* 35, nos. 3–4 (1996): 124–39.
1861–1865. DeRoche assessed Mainers' views on why the war was being fought and how families shaped their thoughts. He used a representative sample of thirty-seven letters and diaries written by common soldiers from all parts of the state who served in eighteen different regiments. Preservation of the Union was their primary motivation for fighting, but he discovered that loyalty to their families compromised their dedication. For example, Maine soldiers favored conscription, but not if it included other members of their own families. They believed that each family should do its share and that the "slackers" back home should be called to serve. Economic considerations were a factor in how long a volunteer chose to serve. If an enlisted man or officer was not paid enough to support his family, this encouraged him to enlist in a nine-month unit. Because officers earned much more than enlisted men, they might stay in the army longer. The author adds that a vote for Lincoln in 1864 meant rejection of the peace Democrats and demonstrated a blend of loyalty and devotion to those who had suffered for the Union.

575. **MANITOWOC, WISCONSIN.** *Fire Within: A Civil War Narrative from Wisconsin.* By Kerry A. Trask. Kent, Ohio: Kent State University Press, 1995. 279 pp.
1861–1865. *Fire Within* chronicles the Civil War experience of a Lake Michigan community in Manitowoc, Wisconsin. By blending personal narratives, newspaper accounts, and local history in a narrative writing style, Trask reveals how the war affected soldiers and civilians of the community, as well as the fabric of the town itself. Trask's principal sources are James S. Anderson (Fifth Wisconsin Infantry), who wrote letters to his family; Rosa Kellner, a hotel operator in her late teens, who kept a diary; and editors of the Democratic *Manitowoc Pilot* and the Republican *Manitowoc Tribune.* Anderson wrote about duty in Virginia, including the Peninsular campaign, Antietam, Rappahannock Station, and the Virginia campaign. He reveals that his support of the abolition of slavery increased, a feeling of jealousy that the Fifth Wisconsin was receiving insufficient credit compared to the other Manitowoc regiments, and family problems. The war front and the home front became as one when Anderson wrote about such issues as Manitowoc's lack of support for the widows and children of soldiers killed in the war. In Manitowoc the newspaper editors both reflected and inflamed civilian passions with their coverage of the draft, emancipation of the slaves, and local and national elections. The community also reacted to events unrelated to the conflict. Citizens briefly feared that the Sioux uprising of 1862 would spread to their region. Farmers endured drought and rain. The town prospered, but its social and economic structure fractured along economic and ethnic lines. Rosa recorded these events. She continued her support of the Union cause but worried about the health of her family and recorded personal feelings of inadequacy. By July 1864 Anderson, physically worn out and thoroughly tired of the war, returned home with his company. The community fanfare for the remaining fifteen members of his original unit was brief, and the men immediately set about reconstructing their civilian lives. Trask concludes with biographical information on the principal writers and a sketch of the town's postwar development.

576. **MASSACHUSETTS SOLDIERS.** "Letters from the Harvard Regiments: The Story of the 2nd and 20th Massachusetts Volunteer Infantry Regiments from 1861 through 1863 as Told by the Letters of Their Officers." By Anthony J. Milano. *Civil War: The Magazine of the Civil War Society* 13 (June 1988): 15–18, 20–27, 29–34, 36–39, 42, 44–45, 47–49, 51–54, 56–58, 60–73.
1861–1863. Letters. First Bull Run, Jackson's Shenandoah Valley campaign, Ball's Bluff, the Peninsular campaign, Antietam, Fredericksburg, Chancellorsville, and Gettysburg. The Harvard-educated officers that commanded these two regiments were appointed by Gov. John A. Andrew, who believed

that a liberal education and the inheritance of social traditions "are likely to produce in a man not only mental flexibility but also that sense of superiority which is invaluable to a commander" (p. 17). Milano adds that an air of gentlemanly superiority is a consistent theme expressed by these officers from Harvard. The author summarizes the organization of the regiments and quotes liberally from their writings to describe their reactions to the battles and the war in general. Milano concludes that these letters not only reflect the officers' socio-economic class consciousness and a desire to protect civilization as they knew it, but also the ideals inherent in the institution of Harvard College.

577. MASSACHUSETTS SOLDIERS. *Voices of the 55th: Letters from the 55th Massachusetts Volunteers, 1861–1865.* Edited and annotated by Noah Andre Trudeau. Dayton, Ohio: Morningside, 1996. 258 pp.

July 11, 1863–August 1, 1865. Letters. Fifty-fifth Massachusetts Colored Infantry. This correspondence is composed of personal letters to family and acquaintants and letters to the black press, primarily the *Weekly Anglo-African* (New York City) and the *Christian Recorder* (Philadelphia). Several memoirs are also included. The editor's introduction relates the evolution of the Fifty-fifth; the enlistment of recruits, who were overwhelmingly farmers from Ohio, Pennsylvania, and Virginia; its leadership by white officers; and duty at the Charleston harbor islands (primarily Morris and Folly Islands) and in Florida and Savannah. The unit was often broken into companies and brigaded with other black units. It served garrison and fatigue duty, on expeditions and demonstrations, and in the battle of Honey Hill. The general themes of these letters run the gamut of themes found in all soldiers' writings. Other topics are unique to the black soldiers as they express the goals they hoped to achieve by enlisting, comment on their contact with white soldiers of both the Union and the Confederacy, and reveal how they interpreted the federal government's unwillingness to pay black soldiers an amount equal to that of white soldiers. The appendixes include an account of Honey Hill written by Capt. Charles C. Soule in 1884, letters by regimental chaplain John R. Bowles, literal transcriptions of letters written by soldier John Posey, and an essay on the sources of information about the Fifty-fifth Massachusetts Infantry.

578. MASSACHUSETTS SOLDIERS (WORCESTER COUNTY). "Worcester County Soldiers in the Civil War." By Pamela J. Cummings. *Historical Journal of Massachusetts* 20 (Winter 1992): 32–52.

1861–1865. Memoirs and regimental histories. This work gleans the experiences of four men of the Fifteenth, Twenty-first, Twenty-fifth, and Thirty-sixth Massachusetts Infantries, all of which were raised in Worcester County. Following a socio-economic profile of the soldiers, Cummings summarizes their action in the Eastern Theater. (The Thirty-sixth served in the West.) The author scrutinizes such topics as competency of leaders, rations, quality of recruits, desire for home front support, attachment to comrades, reaction to combat, toll of military service on the men, and their welcome home.

579. NEW ENGLAND SOLDIERS AND CIVILIANS. *Yankee Correspondence: Civil War Letters Between New England Soldiers and the Home Front.* Edited by Nina Silber and Mary Beth Sievens. Charlottesville: University Press of Virginia, 1996. 169 pp.

1861–1865. Letters. The editors organized these letters into six chapters that reflect the most prominent themes of the Civil War correspondents. Chapter 1 focuses on the soldiers' military experiences. Chapter 2 examines the reasons soldiers and civilians believed the war was being fought. Chapter 3 reveals the soldiers' view of the South, Southern society, and the slaves, including the use of blacks as soldiers. Chapters 4 and 5 consider the impact of the war on the home front, including political, financial, and personal aspects. Chapter 6 is a lengthy collection of letters by a Vermont family, whose writings reflect various aspects of the war and suggest ways in which the war was changing the lives of New Englanders in general. In the twenty-four-page introduction the editors characterize the New Englanders who wrote these letters. As a group, they were not the fanatical abolitionists that tradition has made them out to be. In many ways they are shown to have been influenced by the changes that had spread throughout the North before the war. Those changes were creating the differences between the North and the South that would eventually lead to sectional conflict. But as the editors point out, New Englanders retained a significant degree of regional diversity. Each chapter is preceded by a brief foreword, and the writers are identified. The index illuminates additional themes and groups the writers by state. All of the letters are from manuscript sources.

580. NEW JERSEY SOLDIERS. *Upon the Tented Fields.* Edited by Bernard A. Olsen. Contributions by Thomas L. Waterman. Foreword by James M. McPherson. Red Bank, N.J.: Historic Projects, Inc. 1993. 336 pp.

July 31, 1862–June 10, 1865. Letters. This work contains the writings of six members of the Fourteenth New Jersey Infantry. The men were Sgt. Albert C. Harrison, Maj. Peter Vredenburgh Jr., Lt. William B. Ross, Lt. Marcus Stults, Pvt. Jacob R. Wolcott, and Pvt. Edward C. Jones. Only Harrison and Jones survived the war. Duty for the Fourteenth New Jersey included guarding railroad bridges on the B & O Railroad, duty along the Rappahannock River, the Virginia campaign, Sheridan's Shenandoah Valley campaign, the siege of Petersburg, the Appomattox campaign, and the Grand Review. The material is arranged chronologically into seven chapters, with introductions preceding each section. The work also contains numerous illustrations and a subject index.

581. NEW YORK SOLDIERS. *"I Will Try to Send You All the Particulars of the Fight": Maps and Letters from New York State's Civil War Newspapers, 1861–1863.* Compiled, edited, and annotated by David S. Moore. Albany: Friends of the New York State Newspaper Project, 1995. 134 pp.

1861–1863. This contains twenty-eight letters and fifty-three maps that appeared in twenty-seven New York state newspapers and in five out-of-state papers. The letters focus primarily on battles in the Eastern Theater—the Peninsular campaign, first Winchester, second Bull Run, Antietam, Fredericksburg, Chancellorsville, and Burnside's North Carolina expedition—and on Shiloh and Arkansas Post in the West. An introduction is provided to each chapter, and extensive footnotes explain individual entries. Biographical information on many of the writers is contained in an appendix. This work is the result of the New York State Newspaper Project, an attempt to inventory, catalog, and microfilm the state's newspapers.

582. PENNSYLVANIA SOLDIERS. *The Civil War Soldier's Own Stories: Letters, Poems, and Diaries.* By Harold Frederic. Kittanganning, Pa.: John T. Crawford Camp #43, 1991. 166 pp.

1861–1865. This compilation of writings by soldiers is intended to represent the 3,652 Civil War soldiers from Armstrong County, Pennsylvania. The diarists were Henry Young (Fourteenth Pennsylvania Cavalry), July 3, 1863–May 21, 1864; Robert Taylor (Thirty-eighth Pennsylvania Infantry), August 6, 1861–April 4, 1862; "An Unknown Soldier" (103rd Pennsylvania Infantry), March 28, 1862–September 20, 1863; and James F. Mackey (103rd Pennsylvania Infantry), January 1, 1864–March 14, 1865. Nine letters and eight memoirs are also included.

583. PENNSYLVANIA SOLDIERS. "The Pennsylvania Bucktails. (Part III) 'Dear Mother, Since Last I Wrote to You We Have Made the Fur Fly': Letters Home from the Bucktails." Edited by William J. Miller. *Civil War Regiments* 1, no. 3 (1991): 45–51.

July 6, 1862–July 19, 1863. Letters. Forty-second Pennsylvania Infantry (Thirteenth Reserves). These single letters from four original "Bucktails" relate different experiences at different periods: the capture and fate of some members at Mechanicsville; death and burial of a comrade at second Bull Run; camp life; and the high morale after Gettysburg. A newspaper article of June 19, 1861, is of interest because the editor says it verifies that at this early date the regiment's shooting accuracy was already achieving folk-hero stature.

584. PENNSYLVANIA SOLDIERS. *"This War Is an Awful Thing . . .": Civil War Letters of the National Guards, the 19th & 90th Pennsylvania Volunteers.* Collected and edited by James Durkin. Glenside, Pa.: J. Michael Santarelli Publishing, 1994. 283 pp.

1861–1864. Nineteenth Pennsylvania Infantry (three-month) and Ninetieth Pennsylvania Infantry. Durkin blends narrative with official records, correspondence, diaries, newspaper clippings, and reminiscences to present a regimental history. The men of the Nineteenth were encamped near Baltimore from April to August 1861. Many then became a part of the Ninetieth when it was organized in October 1861. The regiment saw duty at Fredericksburg until May 1862 before marching to Front Royal in an attempt to intercept Jackson. The Ninetieth suffered heavy casualties at second Bull Run, Fredericksburg, Chancellorsville, Gettysburg, Spotsylvania, The Wilderness, and Weldon Railroad. In November 1864 it was consolidated with the Eleventh Pennsylvania. The content of the documents covers personal concerns of the soldiers, disciplinary measures (including an execution for desertion), one officer's request for resignation and another's dispute over his failure to receive promotion, and numerous letters of condolence. The postwar lives of several soldiers are also recounted. Many of the documents were located in pension files at the National Archives and the State Archives of Pennsylvania.

585. REDMOND, WILLIAM, and ROWLAND REDMOND. "Two Ulster Businessmen's Views of the American Civil War." By Grenfell Morton. *Irish Sword* 16, no. 64 (1986): 229–32.

1861–1865. Letters. New York City. These two Irish businessmen were involved in cotton exports and linen imports. As they wrote back to Ireland, they conveyed a lack of immediate involvement in the war. Business matters and the economic impact of the war were their concerns. They did say that the North was acting hypocritically when it took the stance that it was fighting to free the slaves, since the free blacks in the North were despised. The men interpreted the Democratic political victories of 1862 as condemnation of Lincoln's presidency.

586. UNION SOLDIERS. *Letters Home: A Collection of Original Civil War Soldiers' Letters. Antietam-Chancellorsville-Gettysburg.* Gettysburg, Pa.: Alan Sessarego, 1988. 27 pp.

1862–1863. This book contains fifteen letters, fourteen of which are from different New York, New Hampshire, Pennsylvania, Massachusetts, and Ohio units. One letter is from an unidentified soldier of the Third South Carolina Infantry. The letters are about the battles of Antietam, Chancellorsville, and Gettysburg. Several of the writers were surgeons.

587. UNION SOLDIERS. *Mr. Tubbs' Civil War.* By Nat Brandt. Syracuse, N.Y.: Syracuse University Press, 1996. 250 pp.

1861–1865. Letters. Brandt has blended excerpts from a collection of 177 letters (written by seventeen soldiers to Charles Tubbs) with historical narrative to illustrate how Tubbs experienced the war vicariously. Tubbs, who was an ardent Unionist and abolitionist, elected to remain a student at Alfred University, Union College, and Michigan University. Brandt characterizes the writers as "semiliterate farm boys as well as college students or fellow budding students" (p. 210). The men wrote from all theaters of the war and served with Ohio, Pennsylvania, and New York units. They expressed the gamut of soldiers' experiences and concerns. Brandt concludes with brief sketches of their postwar lives. In his acknowledgments Brandt remarks that his wife constantly admonished him to "Remember, you're telling a story" (p. xiii).

588. UNION SOLDIERS. *The Vacant Chair: The Northern Soldier Leaves Home.* By Reid Mitchell. New York: Oxford University Press, 1993. 201 pp. 1861–1865. Mitchell demonstrates how the writings of Northern soldiers reveal the manner in which their images of home and family shaped their view of the war. Americans of the era thought and spoke in familial imagery. As they expressed their opinions about the political world, they often utilized the concept of the family unit. Thus, a threat to the solidarity of the Union might be described as a threat to the family. (Mitchell distinguishes between all Union soldiers and those whom he believes epitomized the culture of the North.) To explore the meaning of the domestic imagery found in the soldiers' writings, Mitchell consulted recent studies on gender, domesticity, and the family. For example, he drew on gender studies to answer the question of why Northern society felt that it was the civic duty of its young men to take up arms in defense of the nation. Gender literature explains that the good "Republican mother" of the North inculcated her sons with a sense of patriotism. By becoming citizen-soldiers the Civil War era "boys" were acting in a mature, responsible manner. Soldiers from the same geographic area often served together, and the camps became extensions of their communities. News of home front activities or how soldiers behaved flowed back and forth from home to camp. Since Northern society had placed domesticity at the center of its society, the woman was seen as the key to what was being defended. Available nurses became surrogate mothers or sisters to the soldiers. Officers who found themselves commanding their "boys" as father figures also had to assume such feminine roles as attending to the soldiers' cleanliness and diet. The central role of the woman within society had its dark side when it was applied to the South. In the minds of many Northern soldiers Southern women were at the heart of the crisis because they had encouraged their men in the events that led to a rupture in the United States political family. Southern women were perceived not simply as mothers, daughters, or wives of opposing soldiers; they were the enemies, or sometimes "she-devils." Therefore, Northern soldiers felt they were justified in destroying the homes and property of noncombatants. Mitchell concludes that the strength of the Union-family ideology was one important reason why the North was victorious. Also, by the middle of the war Northern soldiers had developed a strong allegiance to fellow soldiers, who became members of a substitute family. Mitchell concedes that Southern soldiers felt the same about their homes and families and that the same small-unit cohesion developed within the Confederate army. But by late 1864 the tide of the war, as well as the decimation of military units, had demoralized Southern soldiers. And fear for the safety of their families in the face of Union forces invading the Southern home front caused large numbers of soldiers to desert, effectively rendering the Confederacy incapable of winning the war.

C. The South
Items 589–596

589. ARMY OF TENNESSEE. *Soldiering in the Army of Tennessee: A Portrait of Life in a Confederate Army.* By Larry J. Daniel. Chapel Hill: University of North Carolina Press, 1991. 231 pp.

1861–1865. In his preface Daniel states: "My mission was to discover exactly who were the men of the Army of Tennessee" (p. xii). In pursuit of his goal he read some 350 letters and diaries, and even more memoirs, written by ordinary soldiers with ranks of captain or below. He sought to find out how well they were clothed, equipped, and fed, and how they performed in battle, as well as about "more substantive issues as religion and morale" (p. xii). Although Daniel draws frequent comparisons with the Army of Northern Virginia, his focus is always on the war in the West as related by the soldiers. Daniel describes the army's diverse origins and touches on its literacy level, apolitical nature, and ragged, poorly disciplined appearance. Daniel believes that the soldiers were reasonably well fed and supplied. The medical personal of the army performed an admirable job. Medical records indicate that as the war lengthened, the mortality rate from wounds sustained in battle dropped and disease remained constant. The major theme of Daniel's study is that the unity within the Army of Tennessee was created by the cohesion of the lower ranks and that certain "glues" bonded these ordinary soldiers. One such glue was the hardships they endured. He shows how the army benefited from the constant drilling, the long marches, and the two lengthy winter camps. In addition, a period of relative inactivity between January 1863 and April 1864 served to bring the men together. During this period competitive recreational activities, sham battles, and reviews were often staged. Religion and religious revivals further strengthened the bond. A different type of glue was the severe punishments administered by Gens. Braxton Bragg and Joseph Johnston. Daniel devotes considerable attention to the soldiers' acceptance and criticism of both generals, as well as John Bell Hood. He also addresses morale and the soldiers' belief in their fighting ability. Reasons for the soldiers' chronically poor level of morale ranged from their failure to win conclusive victories to a decline in Southern nationalism and the absence of generals who could inspire them in the way that Robert E. Lee inspired the Army of Northern Virginia. Nevertheless, Daniel found that the soldiers emphasized their partial successes at Shiloh, Perryville, and Stones River and their near total rout of federal forces at Chickamauga. The men continued to write favorably about their performances throughout the Atlanta campaign. When the Army of Tennessee prepared for Hood's Franklin-Nashville campaign, they were buoyed by anticipation of a return to their home state. At Franklin they initially mounted an assault that Daniel describes as "a model of a disciplined courageous attack." Two weeks later, however, in defeat at Nashville, the army was totally fragmented. Daniel ends his account abruptly. He concludes with several typical letters of condolence and briefly describes the state of the army when it surrendered at Goldsboro, North Carolina, on April 26, 1865.

590. CONFEDERACY. *The Illustrated Confederate Reader.* Selected and edited by Rod Gragg. New York: Harper & Row, 1989. 291 pp.

1861–1865. This work includes a selection of excerpts from contemporary writings carefully matched with photographs and reproductions. In the initial chapter, "Soldiers of the South," men and boys are contrasted with the elderly veterans of the final chapter, "The Thin Gray Line." In the chapters between, soldiers and civilians relate their feelings about such themes as camp life, prisons, home life, and Sherman's march. All sources are fully credited.

591. CONFEDERATE SOLDIERS. *Confederate Letters and Diaries, 1861–1865.* Compiled by Walbrook D. Swank. Shippensburg, Pa.: Burd Street Press, 1992. 197 pp.

1861–1865. The book contains thirteen sets of letters and two diaries. Thirteen of the men were from Virginia units, and all but two wrote of service in Virginia. One lengthy diary was written from Camp Chase Prison.

592. CONOLLY, THOMAS. *An Irishman in Dixie: Thomas Conolly's Diary of the Fall of the Confederacy.* Edited by Nelson D. Lankford. Columbia: University of South Carolina Press, 1988. 154 pp.

February 23–May 25, 1865. Diary. Member of Parliament (County Donegal, Ireland). Conolly's blockade-running venture to trade cargo for cotton was thwarted when his ship was damaged shortly after leaving England. However, Conolly continued the journey to visit the South, landing first at Nassau and then being transported to the North Carolina coast, south of Wilmington, where he landed on February 26. He proceeded to Richmond, arriving in the capital on March 8, 1865. On April 3 he left Richmond and went to Baltimore, Washington, Philadelphia, and New York before returning home. Conolly appears to have been oblivious to the crumbling Confederacy until April 2. On that day he noted that Petersburg was in Yankee hands, government officials in Richmond had fled to Danville, and the conditions in Richmond were chaotic. Somehow during his almost six-week stay in the Confederacy, Conolly managed to be hosted by a number of prominent parties, and he penned glowing impressions of most. At a dinner with Jefferson Davis, Conolly thought the president to be a remarkable, dignified man, but his comments about Varina Davis were less charitable. When he visited Robert E. Lee at Petersburg, Conolly was impressed with the general's physical presence as Lee pointed out the Confederate defenses of Richmond. He described Adm. Rafael Semmes at Drewry's Bluff as "looking as hard & determined as flint" and reported that Semmes "was sure the Confederacy could & would fight it out to a success!" (pp. 65–66). Writing in Washington on April 16, he briefly mentioned the "ferment" surrounding Lincoln's assassination. In Philadelphia on April 23 he noted the large crowd waiting to get a view of the president's body in the early morning hours. The entries written between April 15 and May 17 are a record of his social life, which included an unsuccessful courtship. The editor's notes detail this unusual visit and identify people Conolly mentioned. Segments of this work appeared in historical periodicals between 1987 and 1989.

593. GRENVILLE, RICHARD. *Letters from America, September 1860–January 1863.* Edited by David Powell. London: Janus Publishing Company, 1995. 132 pp.

September 30, 1860–January 5, 1863. Letters. Young Richard Grenville traveled from England to investigate business prospects in America for an unidentified trading firm in London. These letters are reports to a member of the firm. Grenville spent a brief time in New York City and Washington, D.C., but for most of this period he was in Richmond and other cities of the South. In his first letters Grenville told the company that a "volcano" was about to erupt in the United States. For the next two years he explained his perception of the cause of the conflict, reported on battles, and assessed opportunities for commerce. During 1861 Grenville traveled by railway to Chattanooga, Memphis, Jackson, New Orleans, Mobile, Atlanta, Charleston, and Richmond, reporting both physical access to the cities and the spirit of enterprise he found among the people. Grenville was aware that the geographic features he described and local loyalties he perceived affected both commerce and the military. For example, he predicted that trade between Columbus, Georgia, and Montgomery, Alabama, would be difficult because they were located in different states. He explained: "Each [state] guards its own independence from invasion without and especially from Richmond" (p. 45). By the end of 1861 Grenville thought that war was "non-existent," with the exception of first Bull Run. Most of his entries during 1862 were written from Richmond and are devoted to the battles. Grenville was sympathetic to the South, although he never analyzed its "Cause." When Lincoln issued the Emancipation Proclamation, Grenville was informed by his company's board that England and France were leaning toward neutrality. Grenville then suggested an alteration in the company's policies, advising it to discreetly engage in silent partnerships with blockade runners. And he framed a plan by which the company would continue to explore partnerships with both sides but would be protected from financial loss regardless of who emerged the victor. At the end of 1862 he was pleased that the Yuletide festivities allowed him the success of "improving my circle of acquaintances who will be helpful to the company" (p. 127). Like much of his correspondence, the letter included a lengthy report on the battle of Stones River.

594. WOMEN, ATLANTA. "'It Is What It Does to the Souls': Women's Views on the Civil War." By Camille Kunkle. *Atlanta History* 33 (Summer 1989): 56–70.
1864. This collection of letters, scrapbooks, and reminiscences held in the Atlanta Historical Society is presented as an overview of the manner in which Atlanta-area women experienced the war. In Louisa Rice's letters she expressed concern for her husband (Col. Zachariah Rice), and she once begged him to come home. A scrapbook contains newspaper clippings that chastise Atlanta society for its mirth in time of crisis. Several women related how the Yankee soldiers behaved on Georgia farms and at the burning of Atlanta. Other women described the roles of the women who worked at the hospitals. The collection also contains news of refugees in the city, families who were forcibly transported away from Atlanta by Sherman, women who were alone and had to relocate by themselves, and one family who remained in the city while it was burned. Other documents relate how, as soon as the Yankees left the city, Atlantans eagerly returned. One woman described what remained of her home and remarked on both the presence and absence of slaves. Kunkle concludes that the common thread running through this collection is the mixture of mundane everyday activities with the disruptive elements of war.

595. WOMEN, SOUTHERN. *The War the Women Lived: Female Voices from the Confederate South.* Edited by Walter Sullivan. Nashville, Tenn.: J. S. Sanders & Co., 1995. 319 pp.
1859–1865. The work contains thirty-one accounts excerpted from previously published accounts written by women from all regions of the South. It is divided into five sections, beginning with "Hope and Glory" and concluding with "Last Things."

596. WOMEN, SOUTHERN. "Altars of Sacrifice: Confederate Women and the Narratives of War." By Drew Gilpin Faust. *Journal of American History* 76 (March 1990): 1200–1228.
1861–1865. As Faust explores the influence of Southern women on the Confederate war effort, she demonstrates how personal diaries may be utilized as primary resources for social themes. At the beginning of the Civil War the Confederacy mobilized Southern women for the "cause" by using the rhetoric of female patriotism and sacrifice that was consistent with their antebellum identity. However, the author shows that as the war lengthened, "the focus of Confederate ideology on female self-abnegation and sacrifice as ends in themselves would alienate many women from that rendition of their interests, from the war, and in many cases, from the Confederacy itself" (p. 1201). Roles allotted to women from the beginning of the war included being defenders of the moral order, mourners of the dead, and contributors of materials needed on the home front and by the soldiers. As the war went on, however, more women objected to performing these duties, especially when such burdens as managing slaves, surviving with fewer commodities, and facing life without male guidance were added to their prescribed roles.

"Women thus began to regard their difficulties as a test of the moral as well as the bureaucratic and military effectiveness of the new nation and tied their patriotism to the competency of the state's performance in these matters of personal concern (p. 1223). By early 1865, when many women had "deserted the ranks" by refusing to continue to accept the deprivations, "Southern women undermined both objective and ideological foundations of the Confederacy" (p. 1228). In addition to utilizing women's personal narratives, the author documents her thesis with other writings by and about women of the Confederacy. In her *Mothers of Invention: Women of the Slaveholding South in the American Civil War* (Chapel Hill: University of North Carolina Press, 1996), Faust places the ideas expressed in this article in their broader context. Both this article and the monograph include exhaustive bibliographies on gender studies of this era.

INDEX

References are to entry numbers.

This index includes: (1) the soldiers, civilians, and foreign travelers (in italics) and the editors of these narratives; (2) the titles of books (in italics); (3) the troops of the states, as well as the Confederate and Union armies; (4) the battles (with dates), states, and places mentioned in the annotations; and (5) selected subjects.

Abbington, Va.—453

Abbott, Charles Frederick—1

Abbott, Henry Livermore—2

Abbott, John Tucker—1

Abbott, Peyton O.—480

Aberdeen, Miss.—50

Abernathy, Charles—466

Abernathy, Martha Stockard—466

Accidents, camp—*Union Military*: 49, 83, 125, 136, 199, 269, 272. *Confederate Military*: 334, 369, 398. *South Civilian*: 474

Adams Co., Ill.—179

Adams, Henry—545

Adams, Virginia M.—90

Adamson, Alberta R.—48

Addison-Darneille, Henrietta Stockton—467

Addison, Edward T.—205

Afton, N.Y.—252

Agnew, Samuel A.—468

Aides and staff officers—*Union Military*: 36, 52, 84, 106, 119, 129, 132, 162, 183, 208. *Confederate Military*: 330, 353, 366, 369, 375, 415, 424, 436, 446, 448

Aker, Washington—3

Akers, Monte—496

Alabama—*Union Military*: 6, 44, 83, 86, 123, 170, 193, 217–18, 267. *Confederate Military*: 341, 359, 369, 393, 399, 407, 459. *South Civilian*: 498, 510, 522. *Anthologies, Studies, and Foreign Travelers, South*: 593. *See also* specific places and battles.

Alabama, Streight's raid into (Apr. 11–May 3, 1863)—*South Civilian*: 498

ALABAMA TROOPS (CONFEDERATE)

Artillery, Light

Jeff Davis Battery: 449

Lumsden's Battery: 432

Infantry

Fourth Regiment: 341, 363

Eighth Regiment: 450

Ninth Regiment: 498

Tenth Regiment: 394

Twelfth Regiment: 348, 463

Twenty-third Regiment: 522

Twenty-fifth Regiment: 399

Thirty-fourth Regiment: 432

Fortieth Regiment: 460

Forty-fourth Regiment: 412

Forty-eighth Regiment: 359

Fifty-third Regiment: 407

ALABAMA TROOPS (UNION)

Cavalry

First Regiment: 193

Albertson, Joan W.—97

Alcohol. *See* Vices.

Aldie, Va. (June 17, 1863)—*Union Military*: 115, 136. *Confederate Military*: 383

Alexander, Edward Porter—312, 369

Alexander Neil . . . (Neil)—174

Alexandria, La.—132, 395, 430

Alexandria, Va.—12, 23, 105, 242, 252, 311

Alford Brothers. (Alford Family)—4

Alford Family—4

Alford, Franklin—4

Alford, James W.—4

Alford, Lafayette—4

Alford, Mary—4

Alford, Terry—298

Alford, Wayne—4

Alfordsville, Ind.—4

Allatoona, Ga. (Oct. 5, 1864)—*Union Military*: 5. *Confederate Military*: 336

Allatoona Hills, Ga.—*See also* Dallas, Ga.

Allen Family . . . (Allen Family)—313

INDEX

Bradford, Anna—534
Bradford, N.H.—195
Bradley, Kersey—27
Bradley, Marlin H.—27
Bragg, Braxton—353, 369, 409, 589
Bragg, William Harris—479
Brandt, Nat—587
Brandy Station, Va.—299, 383, 402
Brandy Station, Va. (June 9, 1863)—*Union Military*: 65, 115, 269. *Confederate Military*: 320, 325, 383, 402, 424, 436, 448, 455
Brashear City, La.—430
Brawner's Farm, battle of. *See* Gainesville, Va.
Bray, W. Joseph, Jr.—374
Brazos Santiago, Tex.—35, 173
Breckinridge, John C.—353
Brendel, Johnny—28
Brenner, James T.—13
Brent, Joseph L.—419
Brevard, Keziah Goodwyn Hopkins.—477
Brewster, Charles Harvey—29
Brice's Cross Roads, Miss. (June 10, 1864)— *Union Military*: 62, 83, 246. *Confederate Military*: 378. *South Civilian*: 468
Bridgeport, Ala.—117, 225
Briggs, Lucia J. R.—309
Brimfield, Ohio—13
Brinker, William J.—434
Brinkman, Harold D.—220
Bristoe campaign (Oct. 9–22, 1863) and battle of Bristoe Station—*Union Military*: 2, 12, 28–29, 110, 128, 194, 198, 239. *Confederate Military*: 379, 402, 436, 448
Britton's Lane, Miss. (Sept. 1, 1862)—*Union Military*: 21
Broadhead, Sarah M.—280
Brook, Dan R.—212
Brookes, Timothy R.—221
Broome, John Lloyd—30
Broomfield, William—31
Browder, George Richard—478
Brown, Charles G.—32
Brown, Frederick G.—188
Brown, John, raid on Harpers Ferry—219
Brown, Joseph E.—438, 479, 547
Brown, Murray L.—406
Brown, Robert Carson—32
Brownlow, William G.—339, 513

Brownsville, Tex.—35, 434, 494
Bruce, Frederick—416
Brush, Seba Bogart—480
Buck, Erastus—33
Buck, slave—340
Buckner, Simon Bolivar—317, 328
Buck's Book. (Buck)—33
Buffalo Mountain, W.Va. *See* Camp Alleghany, W.Va.
Bull Run, first (July 21, 1861)—*Union Military*: 50, 57, 64, 108, 112, 116, 254, 260. *North Civilian*: 298. *Confederate Military*: 312, 318, 321–22, 324, 339, 341, 345, 348–49, 356, 363, 367, 369, 394, 405, 423, 425, 437, 463. *South Civilian*: 482, 498, 506, 527, 534. *Anthologies, Studies, and Foreign Travelers, General*: 562–63. *Anthologies, Studies, and Foreign Travelers, North*: 576. *Anthologies, Studies, and Foreign Travelers, South*: 593
Bull Run, second, campaign (June–Sept. 1862) and battle (Aug. 29–30, 1862)—*Union Military*: 2, 12, 15, 28, 64, 85, 108, 115, 125–26, 129, 141, 146, 158, 172, 176, 187, 219, 231, 237, 242, 249, 253, 257, 260, 265, 271–72, 276. *Confederate Military*: 312, 315, 320, 323, 325, 327, 335, 341, 367, 374, 394, 411, 431, 437, 439, 448, 454–55. *Anthologies, Studies, and Foreign Travelers, North*: 581, 583–84
Bullock, Eliza, slave—483
Bull's Gap, Tenn. (Nov. 11–13, 1864)—*Confederate Military*: 453
Bumbera, Marlene C.—229
Bunkers, Suzanne L.—527
Bunten, Sirene—281
Burbank, Jerome—34
Burford, Elisha Spruille—329
Burgess, Lauren C.—252
Burgess, Tim—385
Burgwyn, Henry—330
Burgwyn, William H. S.—330
Burial of dead and retrieval of dead and wounded—*Union Military*: 4, 49, 82, 100, 124, 183, 251, 265, 268. *Confederate Military*: 317, 322, 368, 408, 417, 423, 460. *See also* Battle . . .
Burke Co., Ga.—537
Burkittsville, Md.—414

DATE DUE

NOV 0 4 '01			
DEC 15 01			
DEC 15 0			

HIGHSMITH #45115

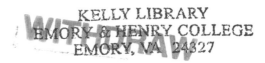